Democracy of Sound

Democracy of Sound

Music Piracy and the Remaking of American Copyright in the Twentieth Century

ALEX SAYF CUMMINGS

OXFORD
UNIVERSITY PRESS

OXFORD

UNIVERSITY PRESS

Oxford University Press is a department of the University of Oxford.
It furthers the University's objective of excellence in research, scholarship,
and education by publishing worldwide.

Oxford   New York
Auckland   Cape Town   Dar es Salaam   Hong Kong   Karachi
Kuala Lumpur   Madrid   Melbourne   Mexico City   Nairobi
New Delhi   Shanghai   Taipei   Toronto

With offices in
Argentina   Austria   Brazil   Chile   Czech Republic   France   Greece
Guatemala   Hungary   Italy   Japan   Poland   Portugal   Singapore
South Korea   Switzerland   Thailand   Turkey   Ukraine   Vietnam

Oxford is a registered trademark of Oxford University Press
in the UK and certain other countries.

Published in the United States of America by
Oxford University Press
198 Madison Avenue, New York, NY 10016

© Oxford University Press 2013

Library of Congress Cataloging-in-Publication Data
Cummings, Alex Sayf.
Democracy of sound : music piracy and the remaking of American copyright in the twentieth century /
Alex Sayf Cummings.
pages cm
Includes bibliographical references and index.
ISBN 978-0-19-985822-4
1. Copyright—Music—United States—History—20th century.   2. Piracy (Copyright)—United
States—History—20th century.   I. Title.
KF3035.C86 2013
346.7304'82—dc23
2012041759

1 3 5 7 9 8 6 4 2
Printed in the United States of America
on acid-free paper

For Sandy, Barbara, and Darrell

CONTENTS

ACKNOWLEDGMENTS

This project has come a long way since Joshua Wright, Antonio Del Toro, and I discussed the possibilities of file sharing and free media in the summer of 2004. For most of our lives, access to knowledge had been largely circumscribed by the ability to pay for it. I remembered how my mother, a single parent on a tight budget, had purchased volumes of an encyclopedia series at the grocery store when I was young, in the hope of providing me with a valuable resource; we only made it through the letter D, but I still spent hours thumbing through the volumes we had and learned a lot about Buddhism anyway. The idea that music, history, science, and so many other things of value and merit could be freely available to almost everyone all the time was a remarkable prospect. Wikipedia represented this new world as much as Napster, the music file-sharing network; to me, learning from a free encyclopedia did not seem so different from downloading free songs. This book is a product of its time, a moment in the early twenty-first century when all the structures of publishing, recording, and broadcasting were in flux. Its strengths belong to the many brilliant people who helped me write it; its shortcomings derive from the limits of my own historical vision.

Anyone who writes a book, especially a first one, probably feels like it took a cast of thousands to do so. This volume is no exception. First and foremost, Betsy Blackmar contributed to the doctoral thesis with her tirelessly inquisitive nature. She loved to give me "a hard time," as she put it, and she did so with a smile. Whatever depth or insight this work might possess owes in large part to her. My other mentor was Barbara Fields—a fierce critic, kindred spirit, and valued ally since I first came to New York from Charlotte. I could always turn to her as a fellow Southerner in the big city. Her impatience with pompous, unreflective jargon dissuaded me from the temptation to lean on fuzzy language, while her intellectual honesty and defiance of conventional wisdom will always be an inspiration. The dissertation also benefited from the perceptive input of Sarah

Phillips, who encouraged me through the first seminar paper that launched the project, as well as Brian Larkin, Andie Tucher, and Eric Foner. And none of it might have been written if not for the inspiring scholars I encountered at the University of North Carolina at Charlotte, including Julie Hicks, Sam Watson, Jeffrey Meyer, John Flower, Kathleen Donohue, and Cynthia Kierner.

No historian can succeed without the generosity and good will of numerous archivists, librarians, and other knowledgeable and helpful professionals. Throughout this project, I have turned to the incomparable Dan Morgenstern of the Institute of Jazz Studies in Newark, who regaled me with stories of his rich life experiences with the musicians, collectors, and other colorful characters who populate the history of music in the twentieth century. At Middle Tennessee State University's Center for Popular Music, I was privileged to receive invaluable assistance from Lucinda Cockrell, Martin Fisher, and Grover Baker, and Mary Lynn Cargill of Columbia University's Butler Library initiated me into the mysteries of congressional committee reports. The boundless enthusiasm of Bill Schurk led to the discovery of a treasure trove of bootlegs at the Music Library and Sound Recordings Archive of Bowling Green State University, while Susannah Cleveland and the rest of the staff have helped me time and time again.

I would also like to thank the many institutions that provided material support for my research. Columbia University's Department of History and Graduate School of Arts and Sciences gave me the opportunity to live in one of the world's great cities and enjoy access to the finest intellectual resources for five years, and a fellowship from the Consortium for Faculty Diversity allowed me to continue this work for two years as I finished the dissertation. I was fortunate to receive yet another year of support from the American Council of Learned Societies as a postdoctoral fellow, which freed me from the pressures of teaching as I made the most crucial revisions to the manuscript. Several sections of this book have previously appeared in print; I would like to thank the reviewers and editors for their insightful feedback as well as Oxford University Press and the University of Pennsylvania Press for granting permission to reprint them here. Portions of Chapters 1 and 5 appeared in the *Journal of American History* in a December 2010 essay entitled "From Monopoly to Intellectual Property: Music Piracy and the Remaking of American Copyright, 1909–1971," and part of Chapter 2 appeared as "Collectors, Bootleggers, and the Value of Jazz, 1930–1952" in Susan Strasser and David Suisman, eds., *Sound in the Age of Mechanical Reproduction* (Philadelphia: University of Pennsylvania Press, 2009).

Finally, a number of individuals have pushed this project from dissertation to book. Siva Vaidhyanathan, Charlie McGovern, and a third reviewer gave rich, suggestive, and enlightening comments on the manuscript, and my editor Susan

Ferber has been a terrific partner in the complex and challenging enterprise of publishing a first book. Elaine Rose kindly took time to discuss the life of her father Boris, a fabled yet little-understood figure, and I cannot stress enough how much I appreciate her sharing her stories and records with me. I would also like to extend my thanks to Bill Golden, Francis Pinckney, George Stephanopoulos, and others who enriched this book by sharing their personal experiences. My friends and fellow scholars have contributed enormously by reading the manuscript and offering insightful suggestions; most notably, Ryan Reft and Joel Suarez have been great friends who endured a series of periodic panics and freakouts with good cheer. I owe a debt of gratitude as well to the wonderful coworkers who have advised and guided me through the early stages of my career, particularly Tom Ellman at Vassar College and Rob Baker at Georgia State. Last but far from least are my family—my mother and stepfather, Sandy and Andy Shepherd, and my grandparents, Barbara and Darrell Cummings, who always encouraged learning and creativity from the earliest age and instilled the belief that a working-class kid could go anywhere and accomplish anything. I would also like to thank my father Taher, stepmother Crystal, and brother Jamaal for all their love and support. Saira Mazhar has been my dearest friend since long before this project began to take shape, and her love has sustained both me and the book as life took us from Karachi to Queens and beyond. I hope she some day gets that nictitating membrane she always wanted.

Democracy of Sound

Introduction

Shout out to the bootleggers who supply my shit
the fans online trying to find my shit
and to the niggas listening but won't buy my shit
and catch me in the street and wanna ride my dick
y'all niggas is the worst, see me like
"J. Cole homie, can you sign my burnt CD"
nigga please, an album ten dollars
you act like it's ten g's
this food for thought cost the same as 2 number three's
so at ease with that broke shit
we all tryna get a dollar boy, no shit

—J. Cole, "The Autograph" (2010)

Like many people, rapper J. Cole is not sure how he feels about music piracy. He praises the bootleggers who copy and sell his mixtapes on the street, but he is impatient with fans who copy his music without paying a dime. As of this writing, "The Autograph" had not been formally put on the market. It was unavailable for sale on iTunes, but one could download it as part of the *Friday Night Lights* "mixtape," a set of electronic files available for free on his website; hear it on college radio; and listen to it on YouTube. The people who distribute his music make it possible for fans to hear him, yet Cole is irked by fans who ask for his autograph on discs they copied themselves. Is it just a matter of disrespect?[1]

Cole is not the first person to have mixed feelings about piracy. Americans have struggled with the problem of unauthorized reproduction—called "piracy," "bootlegging," or "counterfeiting," among other terms, depending on the circumstances—ever since Thomas Edison etched the first sound waves onto tinfoil in his New Jersey lab. Sound recording opened up a variety of new questions about art, economics, and law. Would a wax cylinder or shellac disc be treated, in legal terms, the same way as a novel or photograph? For much of the last century, the answer was no. Who would own the rights to sound waves—the musicians, singers, or speakers who made the sounds? The producers and engineers who captured the sound and shaped it in the studio? The record label that paid everyone involved? And who was allowed to copy what, and under what circumstances?

Copyright interests are prone to paint copying as a cut-and-dried matter of morality. The Motion Picture Association of America runs an ad before movies showing how pirates take food out of the mouths of set painters and other working-class members of the film industry. Record labels say that listeners, through their wanton copying and file sharing, threaten to kill the goose that lays the golden eggs—the creative artist. It is not surprising that these arguments resonate with much of the public. Copying evokes cheating, plagiarism, and unoriginality. Many people, familiar with the ordinary injustices of everyday life, see piracy as just another example of someone getting rich off another person's work. The artist is a worker, "tryna get a dollar," like anyone else.[2]

Such moral convictions may help to explain the hard shift toward stronger copyright laws in America during the last forty years, but they do not account for the many ways in which people copy and use each other's work every day. American law has long recognized, first informally and later by statute, that a certain degree of copying, categorized as "fair use," is acceptable. A teacher can make copies of a poem to discuss in class. I can cite a verse from J. Cole in this book, just as a film critic can quote lines from a movie in a review. And, of course, copyright in the United States has never been an immortal right. The public domain makes freely available all works produced before a certain date, although the ever-expanding scope of property rights has begun to threaten the existence of such a commons of creativity from the past.

The ethics of copying have vexed people since the early days of the printing press. As printing technology spread throughout Europe in the sixteenth century, the possibility of rapidly manufacturing words and images prompted Europeans to develop what would become modern ideas of ownership and authorship. At first, readers did not necessarily link a particular combination of words to a particular author, and printers circulated texts that mutated and evolved through multiple rounds of copying. Soon, however, economics and the politics of censorship intervened. In England, the Crown developed the idea of copyright, granting only the Stationers' Company, a printers guild, the right to produce texts that were approved by the government. Given the religious and political conflicts then unfolding across Europe, a policy that controlled the proliferation of texts was a good bargain for both the government and the printers. Notably, though, the original copyright did not belong to the author but rather to the printer who published a text. Counterintuitive as it may be, this situation remains familiar to many creative people in today's world, who often do not own the rights to their work.[3]

When Americans began to consider how to run their new country in the 1780s, they looked to the legacy of English copyright for cues. The Constitution made it clear that the federal government had the right to regulate what we would now call "media." In the language of the eighteenth century, it was in the public interest for Congress to "promote the Progress of Science and useful Arts, by securing for limited Times to Authors and Inventors the exclusive Right to their respective Writings." The key elements of English law were there: copyright was not a permanent right, but one that would encourage authors to publish by offering the prospect of profit "for limited Times." The first federal copyright law provided only fourteen years of protection, and was limited to books, maps, and charts. Music was not specifically included in the law until 1831.[4]

Copyright, in short, has always been the creature of shifting political interests and cultural aspirations—always incomplete, always subject to change. The United States in the nineteenth century resisted the idea of recognizing the copyrights of other nations, being content to make the cultural fare of Europe cheaply available to its citizens. New media such as photography and sound recording had to be fitted into laws that were primarily written to address works produced by the printing press. As pirates copied sheet music and, later, records, businesses lobbied to have laws passed to protect their products from reproduction; typically, they then pushed for the new protections to be more stringently enforced. At the same time, different interests in the same "business"—for example, songwriters, record labels, radio stations, and jukebox operators—all had different opinions about how works such as songs and sound recordings should be regulated.[5]

Indeed, sound recording set off conflicts over culture and property that profoundly shaped the course of copyright law in the twentieth century. It introduced a kind of medium that could not be perceived with the naked eye. All previous copyrightable works could be seen, whether words on a page, musical notes, or the lines and colors of a photograph. Sound, however, was mechanized; the listener was separated from the content, which was mediated by the stylus and the Victrola horn. Sound also confounded ideas of ownership by making it possible for the same work, a piece of music or a spoken text, to be produced in multiple versions by multiple artists. A hundred players might perform a Joplin rag in a hundred ways, with different instruments, at different speeds, and in different styles. Was each a distinctive work? Americans wrestled with these questions for almost a century following the invention of recording.[6]

Piracy set all these conceptual problems into sharp relief. The early recording industry was perhaps as chaotic as the early days of printing in Europe. Composers clamored to earn income from the recordings made of their music, while competitors in the "talking machine" business copied each other's products. As recorded music grew into a mass medium in the early twentieth century, a system of major labels that marketed hits to national markets emerged, organized along much the same lines as corporations that manufactured cars or soap. But listeners and collectors experimented with ways of copying recordings, and tiny markets for bootlegs emerged by the 1930s. Americans toyed with different modes of experiencing music, apart from buying a record or listening to one on the radio; they collected, copied, and shared records; bootlegged live performances and radio broadcasts; and sold rare and ephemeral recordings in samizdat fashion.

This book asks how American society dealt with the prospect of uncontrolled copying in a century when culture industries rose to new prominence in the nation's economy. From the time Wynant Van Zandt Pearce Bradley bootlegged Italian arias to the leak of Bob Dylan's basement tapes, the United States emerged as an industrial world power. As piracy became more ubiquitous in the 1960s and 1970s, Americans began to discern the outlines of a new post-industrial economy, one geared toward producing the very expressions that pirates copied. Early on, copying was everyday business in a disorganized, developing record industry. In time, piracy moved to the fringes of the music business and later reemerged as a mortal threat to it, with the introduction of technologies such as the compact cassette (1963) and the online file-sharing network Napster (1999). The legal suppression of new forms of copying and sharing reflects changing trends in American political culture, revealing the shift from a hands-off cultural policy that emphasized free competition (copy and compete) to a more aggressive stance that protected capital investment in the name of economic growth.[7]

Capitalism has always made more with less, whether it is the labor and time necessary to make a shoe or the land needed to make a bushel of wheat. Culture is no different. Alongside the arc of industrial to post-industrial—from manufacturing, that is, to "information"—one can also trace a line from mass production to mass reproduction. Printing made it possible to turn music from an ephemeral experience, a performance, to a text that could be manufactured en masse. The innovations of Edison and Emil Berliner, who invented a technique for mass-producing disc records, did the same for sound. The industries built by the entrepreneurs who followed them sought to sell as many copies of a few records to as many people as possible, maximizing the capacity of a label's factories and sales force. Then, with growing access to media such as magnetic tape and the Internet, the record industry lost its near monopoly on the means of production, and bootlegging was no longer confined to a small number of collectors and underground labels. Piracy and home recording are new frontiers of production, harnessing labor and technology to make more music—more CDs, more MP3s, more performances circling the world—than ever before. Seen this way, the travails of the music industry in the twenty-first century look like a classic instance of the perennial capitalist problem of overproduction.[8]

Music posed some of the earliest and stiffest challenges to the nascent information economy for several reasons. Music is compact; for pirates in the 1890s, a piece of sheet music was easier to copy than a novel, and an audio file today is typically smaller than a movie file. Music is social, something that people want to share with each other and experience together. Courtship, for instance, frequently involves the mix CD, the concert, the quoting of lyrics in a love letter. One friend wants to tell another about a new and little-known artist, to share in the fruits of a good find. This social dimension of music emerged when Americans began to collect records in the 1930s, archiving and at times copying the legacy of recorded music up to that time; it was clear when listeners circulated copies of rock outtakes, Grateful Dead concerts, and hip-hop bootlegs later in the century. Such practices have, at times, pushed the music industry to adapt to consumer interests, although retaliation in the courts and Congress was a more common response.[9]

Journalists and many scholars have been keen to draw bright lines between different types of copying, distinguishing, for instance, a concert "bootleg" from a "counterfeit" of an officially released record.[10] To some extent, these distinctions have merit. Scale and intent matter; a person who tapes a copy of an LP for two friends is different from a Mafia-run factory that produces thousands of copies of the same recording. When classical aficionados traded recordings of operas that had never been officially released by a label, they were documenting moments in cultural history that might otherwise have been lost. The vocalists who appeared on such recordings might not have been happy about their work being recorded and distributed without their consent, but this bootlegging can be credited with serving a greater interest than profit alone.

This book treats all kinds of copying as points along a spectrum of unauthorized reproduction. British sociologist Lee Marshall has defined piracy as "the unauthorised copying of a published work," in part to emphasize that bootlegs, his chosen subject, are documents of performances that had never been officially published, such as concert recordings. For Marshall, bootlegs should be treated differently from purely commercial pirated or counterfeit works, since these records supplement rather than substitute for music that is already on the market. In other words, bootlegs do not hurt the record company's bottom line since the person who is interested in buying a live disc of Phish or Prince is almost always a fan who will buy their official releases as well.[11]

The difference between "piracy" and "counterfeiting" has been somewhat fuzzier. Many critics attempt to justify bootlegs to carve out a legal or ethical space for a certain degree of copying, but pirated works have less often benefited from such advocacy. Typically, a counterfeit is an unauthorized copy that attempts to pass itself off as the "real thing," mimicking the packaging and style of the original release, whereas a pirate recording may include previously published material but with a different cover, title, or track listing. According to this definition, a counterfeit would be an unlawful copy of the Beatles' *Revolver*, while a tape compilation called *Ten Golden Beatles Hits* would be a pirated work.[12]

These terms, while helpful to a degree, do not always fit real recordings very well. Pirate tapes and disks jumble together officially released material with live performances and studio outtakes, blurring the line between bootleg and pirate. An online "torrent" file that allows a user to download hundreds of files by one artist does not discriminate either. Indeed, the idea of a counterfeit recording matters little online. Moreover, the critical issue of intent—is the copying done for profit, for the love of the music, for the greater good?—is not always clear. Bootleg labels that reproduced old recordings of Blind Lemon Jefferson or Bix Beiderbecke in the 1950s might have meant to make a profit, but they were also making it possible for people to discover music that had been neglected by the major labels.[13]

For this reason, the words "bootleg" and "pirate" are used more or less interchangeably in this book. Whatever a copier's intent, he or she is always copying something produced by someone else without permission. This characteristic defines all pirate works—even the use of "samples" that grew out of hip-hop culture in the 1970s, when DJs learned to mix parts of different records together. A tape recording of a DJ set at a Bronx roller rink may contain parts of Kool and the Gang and James Brown; it is both a copy of those artists and a bootleg of the DJ who combined them. Piracy defies categorization just as easily as it confounds legal judgment.

This book begins in the late nineteenth century, when a new "talking machine" industry struggled to find its footing and legal regulations were practically nonexistent. Artists had to defend themselves against unauthorized use of their name and their recorded performances, while various companies experimented with different formats and paid composers nothing for the music they recorded. At this point, it was far from clear that sound recording would become a chiefly musical endeavor. Chapter 1 follows the evolution of piracy, the music industry, and legal thought about what constituted property and theft. The conclusion reached by Congress—that composers deserved to benefit from recordings of their work but that record companies did not enjoy a copyright for their recordings—set up a struggle over property rights that unfolds over the next five decades. Chapter 2 examines how collectors, listeners, and entrepreneurs took advantage of this legal gray zone to rerelease old and out-of-print recordings, beginning in the 1930s. These activities landed bootleggers in court, but the results were often indecisive. Chapter 3 traces the rise of magnetic recording as a new medium for sound, from its humble origins on wire in the 1880s to the eventual success of the high-fidelity market after World War II. Tape recording offered devotees of genres like opera new ways to copy and exchange classical music, a taste that appealed to a minority of well-heeled consumers, before the advent of the four-track, eight-track, and compact cassette in the 1960s opened up recording to a much broader—and younger—audience.

The second half of the book explores the impact of piracy as it mutated from the practice of a select few with esoteric tastes into a potentially mass market, triggering political action and legal reforms that define the contours of intellectual property law to this day. Chapter 4 follows the spread of piracy to pop music, particularly rock, as a young generation embraced both tape technology and radical rhetoric to position bootlegging as part of a general social ferment in the late 1960s. A moment of possibility opened between 1969 and 1971, when a large, creative, and unruly pirate market operated parallel to the mainstream music industry, and a copyright for recordings finally passed in Congress. Although the intentions of bootleggers were often less than noble, the alliance between bootlegging and counterculture produced a legacy that documented much of the music of the age on illicit records.

The flamboyance of the bootleggers, though, came at a price. States and then the federal government granted unprecedented protections to recordings, as composers, musicians, and labels united against the common foe of rampant piracy, a battle that unfolds in chapter 5. The Supreme Court offered its endorsement of the new property rights, which in many cases went well beyond anything previously passed and arguably impinged on the limitations of copyright set out in the Constitution. Chapters 6 and 7 bring the story into the 1970s and 1980s, as pirates in the United States adapted to a newly hostile legal climate, developing new networks of production and exchange. New genres such as jam music and hip-hop challenged ideas of ownership, and piracy reached epic proportions in the developing world.

The reaction was both predictable and paradoxical. "Intellectual property," a relatively novel term in the 1970s, became the subject of organized political pressure, as the Reagan and Clinton administrations embraced copyright as an issue in trade negotiations. Laws became more punitive, yet piracy remained nearly as pervasive as ever, even as new technologies (such as the compact disc) were introduced to stem the problem. People continued to tape, pirate, and exchange. The advent of widespread Internet access paved the way for the compressed audio file (most prominently, the MP3) in 1993 and a new era of unconstrained panic and lawlessness with the rapid rise of the file-sharing network Napster.

In the early twenty-first century the public continues to flout the demands of copyright interests to control how their products are produced and distributed, but new businesses have emerged that attempt to reconcile the yen for free culture with property rights. YouTube, for instance, permits users to circulate a recording of the same Jimi Hendrix concert that a bootlegger might have sold in the early 1970s—at least until a record company or other media conglomerate asks that the clip be removed. A great deal of music and video ends up available online anyway, allowing for a degree of unauthorized reproduction to occur within a for-profit context. Rights owners get to exercise a veto on their work being reproduced; fans get to share work that may not be available anywhere else, such as an old TV clip from the 1970s; and Google, the site's owner, makes money off both the music and the efforts of the fans who upload, remix, and mash up the material. The model is not without its critics, of course. Media conglomerate Viacom sued YouTube in 2007, for example, accusing the service of enabling flagrant and widespread copying of its television shows, movies, and music.[14]

YouTube may herald a new era in which companies like its parent Google replace record labels as the intermediaries who profit from artists' work. If so, it might be a case of "new boss, same as the old boss"—or even "worse than the old boss," as musician David Lowery warned in 2012.[15] Regardless, media like YouTube and Facebook domesticate an impulse to share and use music that Napster once harnessed, that bootleggers have catered to since the 1890s, and that copyright interests have fought almost as long. This communal element of culture—the part that says, "this is here for everyone," not for the artist, not for business, not for myself—is visible in the captions of videos on YouTube:

> "taliban song"—toby keith God bless our troops! do not own any of the material. made for the enjoyment of others.[16]
>
> Bonus track on the Whatever and Ever Amen album by Ben Folds Five. I like the feel of this song, so enjoy. (No copyright infringement intended, whatsoever)[17]

Toby Keith and Ben Folds Five recorded songs in a studio, which fans have now uploaded to YouTube with only a still image to accompany them. Essentially, the upload is a copy of the sound recording and nothing else. The sounds are distributed online and issue from potentially millions of computer speakers, but "no copyright infringement [is] intended, whatsoever." The contradiction between this desire and the rights of artists and businesses lies at the heart of this ongoing history.

PART ONE

THE BIRTH AND GROWTH OF PIRACY, 1877–1955

1

Music, Machines, and Monopoly

Music lends itself to reproduction. A musician composes a song by fumbling for the right chords, and then transcribes the sequence of sounds as notes and words on paper. The written composition is of little use unless someone brings it to life. The performance is then captured as a sound recording, which can be reproduced on a massive scale and replayed again and again. Other performers cover the song made famous by the original artist, making their own copies of the underlying musical script. Later on, musicians take fragments of the recorded performance and incorporate these samples into new electronic works. When I download the song from an online file sharing network, my computer makes a new copy of the recording in a folder for the music player iTunes, as well as a separate copy in the "shared" folder that provides access to the file for other searchers online. As a music publisher complained early in the twentieth century, "Cheap music is more easily copied than a book or any other work of literature."[1]

At each step, a new and different version of the original music is created, whether a performer's recording of a composition, a cover artist's reinterpretation of another recording, or the digital file extracted from a compact disc. The fact that one piece of music can be split into written symbols, mechanical sounds, and multiple interpretations has caused many headaches for those who have tried to figure out who owns the scripts and vibrations. Consumers, entrepreneurs, lawmakers, and musicians grappled with this conundrum, as the technological means of reproducing music grew increasingly numerous and complex over the course of the twentieth century. From the first mechanical reproductions of music in the 1870s to media as different as magnetic tape and the Internet, locating the author of a musical creation—or the owner of a musical commodity—has proven difficult.

What counts as music, and who should be able to control it? Is it the idea of a melody, the written composition, the live performance, or the inscription of a performance on vinyl, tape, or disc? Should the songwriter, performer, or record company have the exclusive right to control the production of a sound recording and benefit from selling copies of it? For much of the twentieth century, legal authorities could not answer these questions, and federal copyright law actually held that no one owned the recording itself once it was published. Under a system established by Congress in 1909, the songwriter (or the publisher who held the rights to a song) could choose to license the first mechanical use of a composition, but any subsequent renditions were beyond the copyright holder's control. The composer would receive a flat royalty for each copy made of a recording of the song, but that was all. And, until 1972, the producers of mechanical copies of music, such as long-playing (LP) vinyl records, piano rolls, or wax cylinders, could not copyright their products.

Throughout this period, Americans weighed musicians' and companies' interest in controlling the products they created against the public's interest in having uninhibited access to music. During the Progressive Era, Congress feared that the recording industry would be consumed by monopoly and favored protecting the public domain over strengthening property rights. Courts subsequently wrestled with the dilemma of how to respect the value that artists and entrepreneurs had invested in recordings, even though lawmakers had explicitly excluded any such consideration. As usual, attention to copyright surged upon the introduction of popular new forms of communication. As media such as the phonograph and radio became familiar to American society in the early twentieth century, judges and legislators had to grapple with the ways various technologies affected the rights of copyright owners. Many of the new gadgets, whether a paper piano roll or a shellac disc, involved the reproduction of sound, and mechanical reproductions provoked some of the most heated debates about the proper assignment of rights. The earliest cases sought to mark the line between the copyrightable music and the machine that conveyed it; once the Copyright Act of 1909 provided an ingenious way of drawing that line, courts faced new questions about whether or not record companies (and, in a related case, a news agency) had any right to prevent others from copying or otherwise exploiting their works.

The Machine That Talks, Sings, and Steals

One year before Edison first etched a sound pattern on tinfoil in his New Jersey lab, the playwright Griffin Hall penned a curious skit called *The Bogus Talking Machine, or the Puzzled Dutchman.* In this 1876 "Negro Farce," a sly professor named Stanley fools a circus owner named Martello into giving him $5,000 to build a machine that talked. Stanley gets Pete, a black boy, to sit inside a box and talk. The boy is reluctant at first, noticing that the box says COD. "You can't sell dis chile for any codfish," he says.[2] Stanley explains that he will pull one string for the boy to whistle and another for him to holler. Pete wonders why the professor's head "is like a poor man's pocket," but he complies. Both Martello and his servant, the Dutchman, are terrified by the talking box, the latter so much that he cries out for "lager bier und sour krout." Pete claims to be the devil, as if the machine were possessed by an evil spirit. "Oh! Blease, Mr. Debil, don't dake me," the Dutchman implores. "I vill gi you mine frow, mine beer, mine money, mine grout, and mine everytings."[3]

For Griffin Hall, a talking machine would be a machine that mimicked a human being, but the boy in his play merely imitated such a machine. The professor assumed that a machine that could reproduce the sound of human communication, and even interact intelligently with humans, would evoke wonder and fear in others. His talking machine was an agent of deception, a recurrent theme throughout discussions of sound reproduction.

In fact, the early history of the talking machine was full of imitators, copycats, and frauds who reproduced the recordings of others for sale on the disorderly market of the late nineteenth century. The disarray in the industry resulted in part from uncertainty about which recording format would prevail and what uses would be made of multiple new technologies. Would consumers buy a wax cylinder machine to make recordings in their homes and offices, as Thomas Edison predicted? Would they purchase records to listen to stories or music? Like the boy in the box, the sounds inscribed on early phonographs simply provided the aural content for a physical object, engraved on the surface of a wax cylinder only to be wiped away and replaced by the traces of other sounds. *What* the talking machine said mattered less than *that* it spoke and, perhaps, how well it spoke. Record manufacturers tended to emphasize the technical quality of their mechanical reproductions rather than the musical or literary performances contained in them. The bawdy stories, tinny songs, speeches, and jokes were often brazenly appropriated by competitors as the market for recorded music gradually took shape, and phonograph companies—largely consumed by patent battles involving the technology of recording itself—devoted little attention to asserting rights to the performances contained on their products.[4] A few firms did move to protect the value of the performances they recorded and sold in the first decade of the twentieth century; Emile Berliner, for instance, sued New York's Standard Talking Machine Company for violating his patents in 1898 and subsequently sought an injunction when several of the company's leaders went on to copy Victor recordings through the American Talking Machine Company in 1904.[5]

The Bogus Talking Machine is also a reminder that, in the earliest days of recording, the "talking machine" was just that—a vehicle for human speech. Edison initially conceived of his invention as a tool for capturing ordinary voices as much as singers or musicians; the original impetus for the phonograph had been his desire to record messages sent over the telephone.[6] The early avatars for sound recording were characters associated with speech. The most iconic, the little white dog named Nipper, has defined the Victor image up to the present day. Nipper also bequeathed to the world "His Master's Voice," a slogan that became synonymous with Victor—even though the phrase has been completely severed from its original context. The image was based on a painting by the brother of Victor pioneer Eldridge Johnson, in which Nipper listens to a wax cylinder recording of his owner's voice. The dog looks rapt and attentive, as if his master were standing right there. The cylinder, of course, could be recorded on and could indeed have contained a reminder made by the pet's owner. When Victor adopted the image of the dog, the cylinder was replaced with a disc phonograph, a medium that did not allow consumers to make their own recordings. Unless the dog belonged to a recording artist like Enrico Caruso, it was unlikely to feature the actual voice of his master.[7]

Soon after, the Ohio Talking Machine Company not only copied Victor's phonograph patents but also used a wry variation on the company's trademark image. The outfit at first placed a shaggy dog next to its phonograph, above the slogan "Familiar Voices." In 1904 the company's Talk-O-Phone brand swapped the dog for a parrot, an animal better known for talking than singing, and Ohio soon dropped the "Familiar Voices" slogan in favor of "Learning a Few New Ones."[8] Another pirate, Zon-O-Phone, used the slogan "On Speaking Terms," and pictured a child leaning into a phonograph much like the attentive Nipper.[9] Like "His Master's Voice," the slogan implied an interpersonal relationship with a machine that did what no other could—talk.

Americans of the turn of the century broadly associated sound recording with communication, rather than with music or entertainment alone. Promoters of cylinders and discs emphasized the accuracy of their devices in replicating human expression, and they pointed to the "original" quality of a recording as proof of its precision and truthfulness. Like the Victor player, the machines would capture the essence of a person; after all, the recording had to be excellent for Nipper to mistake it for his master. The Norcross Phonograph Company of New York did not trumpet the aesthetic quality of the performances on its recordings, but rather blared "GREAT VOLUME, PERFECT REPRODUCTION, AND FINE QUALITY OF TONE" across the top of its ads in 1897.[10] The comedian Russell Hunting also advertised his records as "loud, clear and distinct" the year before. The ad pointed out that the "Standard Humorous Talking Records" were distributed to "all parts of the English speaking world"—a crucial fact, since many of the recordings consisted of stories about the antics of two greenhorns, Hiram and Casey. (In one episode, Casey tries to auction "a pug dog, a pair of gentleman's pants and photograph picture of Napoleon Boneypart.") A spoken story is

Are You Interested
in Musical Records?

WHAT I DO

I GUARANTEE
ABSOLUTE
SATISFACTION

I handle High-class Original Records only

I personally test all Records before shipping

I guarantee all Records I handle

I advise my customers of the Newest, Latest and Best Records

I strive to please my patrons in every way

I ship goods promptly and exactly as ordered

"I do not substitute something that is Just as good"

SEND FOR CATALOGUE

ROGER HARDING

MANUFACTURER OF   Musical Records for the . . . . . .
Phonograph and Graphophone

NO. 18 E. 22d STREET, NEW YORK

Figure 1.1 Phonograph maker Roger Harding's guarantee of quality suggested that a copy was unacceptable even if it was "just as good," implying that other dealers were careless and maintained less exacting standards. *Source: Phonoscope* 1, no. 10 (August–September 1897): 3.

much less likely than music to be appreciated among people of different tongues around the world.[11]

Companies emphasized that their recordings were loud and clear because they were "original," as opposed to the inferior records that unscrupulous competitors made by copying the sounds inscribed on other firms' cylinders and discs. In 1897 John Monroe of Portland, Oregon, assured readers of *The Phonoscope: A Monthly Journal Devoted to Scientific and Amusement Inventions Appertaining to Sound & Sight* that his records were all "'original,' 'no duplicates,' made one at a time, every word guaranteed to be clear and distinct, and we are the only parties now making them."[12] Monroe specified "one at a time" because, at the time, wax cylinders could only be recorded individually; an artist would sing or speak into several engraving machines at once to make multiple "copies" of a performance, and the resulting record itself was difficult to copy. Russell Hunting, for instance, was paid a dollar per minute for his services in front of the cylinder's horn on at least one occasion.[13] J. W. Meyer of New York's Globe Phonograph also announced that his records were original in 1896. "I am making my own records, and can guarantee each one first-class in every respect, loud, and each word distinct," the singer said, "and also without that disagreeable noise found in duplicate records."[14]

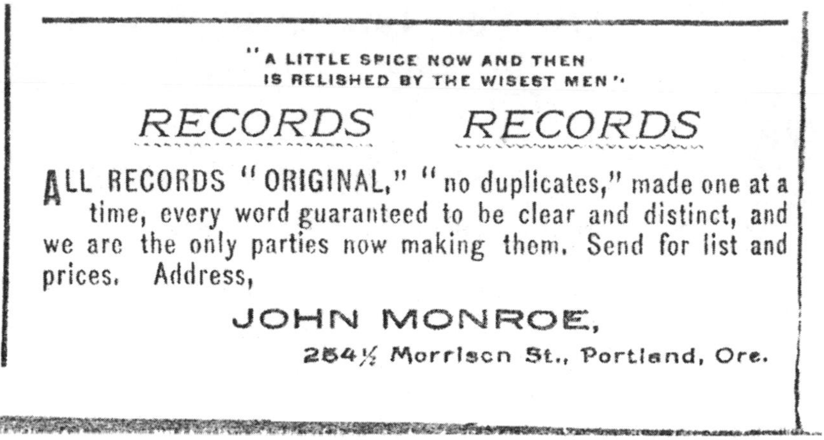

Figure 1.2 John Monroe assures readers of *The Phonoscope: A Monthly Journal Devoted to Scientific and Amusement Inventions Appertaining to Sound & Sight* that he personally makes his own records "one at a time," unlike other unscrupulous dealers who copy other people's records and pass off inferior copies as originals. *Source: Phonoscope* 1, no. 10 (October 1897): 2.

In the hurly burly of the early record industry, virtually nothing was sacred. Copyright laws did not address how the music on cylinders and discs ought to be regulated. Congress did pass a bill in 1897 to give composers the right to control performances of their work, so that music venues, for instance, had to remunerate songwriters. The new law, though, proved difficult to enforce and only applied to live human performances—the scratchy sounds that issued from wax cylinders in homes and public phonograph parlors did not count as public performances.[15] Thus, early entrepreneurs in sound recording were free to run riot with other people's work, recording performances of songs without paying composers, copying recordings by other companies and artists, and even sticking the names of well-known artists on recordings by unknowns.

Numerous artists took to the press to protest that their names and likenesses were being used to sell recordings they had not made. In one poignant example, the bandleader John B. Holding complained that a company was selling recordings under the name of his outfit, the Gilmore and Holding Band, even though they only recorded for the Columbia Phonograph Company. "The authority to use the name of Gilmore and his men for phonograph record-making work was granted to me by Mr. Gilmore some time before his death," Holding wrote in 1897. "The Band to-day is composed of the same musicians who worked so long under the direction of this famous master. Is there no redress for such a fraud?"[16]

Holding was not the only artist decrying the unauthorized use of his identity. Hunting also highlighted the veracity of his records because "certain unprincipled

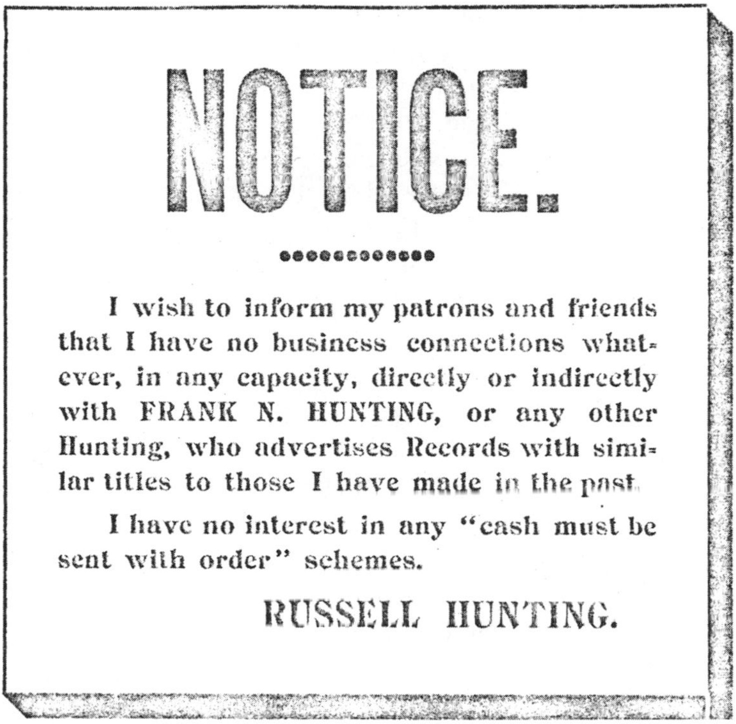

NOTICE.

●●●●●●●●●●●

I wish to inform my patrons and friends
that I have no business connections whatever, in any capacity, directly or indirectly
with FRANK N. HUNTING, or any other
Hunting, who advertises Records with similar titles to those I have made in the past.

I have no interest in any "cash must be
sent with order" schemes.

RUSSELL HUNTING.

Figure 1.3 Comedian, recording artist, and entrepreneur Russell Hunting advertises in the first issue of *The Phonoscope*, decrying imitators who tried to dupe consumers into buying recordings not actually made by Hunting. *Source: Phonoscope* 1, no. 1 (November 1896): 17.

individuals and corporations are duplicating my work, thereby deceiving the public by furnishing a record about one-third as loud as the original."[17] Hunting's emphasis on volume strikes the contemporary reader as odd. He complained that piracy was bad, not because his competitors took advantage of the imaginative element of his story or the skill that went into performing and recording it, but because the unauthorized copy failed to be as loud as the original, damaging the reputation of the Casey records and defrauding the consumer. For Hunting, the technical quality of the device mattered more than its creative content.

Russell Hunting had reason to be concerned about unwarranted duplication. At one point, a man going by the name of Frank N. Hunting advertised and sold recordings of his monologues, implying that the two were related. Like Holding and others, Russell Hunting turned to the press to warn the public about the knockoffs.[18] In another incident, Russell Hunting had agreed to record his popular storytelling routine, "Cohen at the Telephone," for the Leeds and Caitlin recording company in the 1890s. He signed on to record "Cohen" ten times, at a rate of $5 for each performance. He sang into four different phonograph horns, which would inscribe his sounds on four different cylinders. However, in the middle of his fourth round, Hunting noticed that an office boy was carrying twenty-five cylinders of his performance through the studio.[19] He suspected that Leeds and Caitlin were making additional copies of his performance without paying him, apparently by producing inferior second-generation copies from the cylinders he originally recorded. When he threatened to out the company's misdeeds to the press, Leeds relented and paid him for the additional copies.[20] Thus, although a first-generation recording might be a "copy" of a live performance, it was still more original than the copy of the copy, which Hunting considered to be an inferior imitation. The purported purpose of the talking machine might have been to imitate real people, but men like Russell Hunting sought to distinguish themselves from those who copied the imitators. "A poor article is never imitated," Hunting asserted. "GOOD ONES ALWAYS ARE. Imitation is the highest flattery."[21]

The Push for Reform

R. R. Bowker wrote like a man who had fought many battles and nursed more than a few wounds in the process. As the journalist and editor looked back in 1912 on a life of fighting for the enlargement of copyright, Bowker noted "a recurring sense of the losses which the copyright cause has suffered during the long campaign for copyright reform."[22] He saw his mission as the unenviable one of pushing an obstinate America down the path of world progress. The nation, he felt, must catch up with European powers that had already expanded copyright laws, extending the term of protection to the life of the author plus fifty years. Although the 1909 reforms he earnestly advocated in Congress did improve the terms for rights holders, Bowker still dreamed of the day when America could "enter on even terms the family of nations and become part of the United States of the world."[23]

Congress had been considering a major revision of copyright law for years, but none of the pamphleteers and boosters were able to push lawmakers to action as effectively as the player piano and the phonograph did. The player piano today may seem like a quaint artifact of a remote American past, yet the piano and the paper rolls that conveyed music to its mechanical teeth forced American artists, jurists, and politicians to rethink the lines between idea, music, and machine. To a greater extent than even the phonograph, the popularity of which would soon consign the piano roll to antique stores and museums, the arguments over this medium defined the way music was recorded and sold in the United States for much of the twentieth century.

Hearings for a new copyright act had begun in 1905, but before any legislation was passed, two court cases pushed Congress toward the speedy resolution of the problems posed by sound recording. What was most pressing about these decisions was the potential conflict between them. In *White-Smith v. Apollo* (1908), the US Supreme Court held that the "copying" of music in piano roll form was legitimate because the roll was part of a machine and, thus, not copyrightable; whereas in *Fonotipia v. Bradley* (1909), the Circuit Court for the Eastern District of New York ruled that the unauthorized reproduction of phonograph records amounted to deceptive and unfair conduct. The decisions laid out separate lines of reasoning that would define the complicated legal evolution of recorded sound for years to come.

The debate over copyright and sound recording can be said to have begun on the plantation—or, at least, in some fantasy of the South that germinated in the creative subconscious of late nineteenth-century Americans. On the cover of the sheet music for Adam Geibel's 1897 hit "Kentucky Babe," a stereotypical cartoon of an impish African American spies out from below a banner that reads "A Plantation Lullaby." To the right are the labels "40 cents" and "Copyright for all countries." In the middle is a picture of a daydreaming young man, identified as "Harry Clinton Sawyer, *Chanteur Excentrique*." Musical compositions had been protected under federal copyright law since 1831, and Geibel sold the rights to produce sheet music of his song to the White-Smith Music Publishing Company. Little did Geibel or White-Smith suspect that the right to present this music to the public would also be taken up by another company, Apollo, which created perforated paper rolls for automatic pianos.[24]

White-Smith believed that a piano roll that tamped out the melody of "Kentucky Babe" was as much their property as the sheet music that represented it in treble clefs and quarter notes. If another company could sell their song as a roll without paying them a cent, White-Smith might suffer diminished sales of the original written music. What was the difference between the holes punched in paper that cause a piano to play a particular melody and the musical notation representing a song? The music publisher's attorney, Livingston Gifford, argued that mechanical reproductions were covered under the Constitution's protection of an author's "writings," which originally referred to books, maps, and charts but had been extended to include photographs and paintings. "'Musical composition,' the term of the statute under which this case comes," he proposed, "is broad enough to include perforated music."[25]

The Apollo Company, however, insisted that copyright could not apply to a piano roll. The perforated paper was part of a machine, which was only subject to patent. "Things intended for mechanical function—for use in themselves—will not infringe copyright," Apollo's lawyers Charles Burton and John O'Connell told the Supreme Court, "and are not copyrightable merely because of incidentally being able to perform some part of the function of things copy-rightable." They also insisted that the judges stick to the wording of the current copyright statute, which did not address any mechanical reproductions of music. Their argument had some grounding in international law. Since the making of music boxes and musical clocks was an important industry for Switzerland, the Berne Convention of 1886 had exempted mechanical devices from copyright law. Popular composer Victor Herbert, however, told the *New York Times* that a music box was in no way the same as a player piano roll. "No possible harm to the composer could be foreseen," Herbert charged, "because the reproducing device [the music box] was a permanent, unchangeable part of the instrument and the selections reproduced by the same were limited to but few short pieces."[26]

During the oral arguments, the courtroom was full of gadgets; music boxes, wax cylinders, and an easel draped with perforated paper were on display.[27] On the cylinder phonograph, a metal stylus etched the pattern of vibrating sound waves; the stylus could retrace the grooves to recreate the sound, and users could shave the pattern off to record a new sound in the wax.[28] Although the flat disc phonograph invented by Emile Berliner in 1888 lacked this re-recording capability, the hard-rubber discs produced louder sound than cylinders, which often required users to listen through rubber tubes and earplugs.[29] Curiously, there is no evidence that disc recordings were present in the courtroom during the trial. In 1908, the cylinder was still at the height of its popularity.[30] The plaintiffs wanted to illustrate to the judges the array of old and new recording technologies. They hoped that a demonstration of the player piano versions of "Little Cotton Dolly" and "Kentucky Babe" would persuade the judges that the sound generated was sufficiently similar to White-Smith's original written compositions to constitute copyright infringement. "Chief Justice [Melville] Fuller, with a twinkle in his eye, inquired whether or not it was proper that Justice [John] Harlan, who is from Kentucky and is a vigorous youngster of some seventy-four years, should sit in the case," the *Washington Post* reported. "None of the justices laughed louder than Justice Harlan."[31]

The experiment may have amused the Court, but it did not accomplish what White-Smith intended. The justices looked at the various objects before them and concluded that they were fundamentally different from the visual materials covered by copyright. Writing for a unanimous Court, Justice William Day defined a copy as "that which comes so near to the original as to give to every person seeing it the idea created by the original." Neither the grooves on a wax cylinder nor the holes in a piano roll were intelligible to the human eye, unlike a score, a painting, a photograph, or a novel. They conveyed no meaning, in Day's words, and thus could not receive copyright protection. Like a computer disk or video game cartridge, the piano roll contained and communicated information in a way no one could understand without the help of a machine, and the Court believed copyright was limited to expressions that were visually accessible.[32]

Though he concurred in the decision, Justice Oliver Wendell Holmes Jr. still felt uneasy with the Court's interpretation of the statute. For him, copyright applied to any "new collocation of visible or audible points of lines, colors, sounds, or words." Any machine that recreated such an assemblage of sound made a copy of it, and if the current law did not permit this expansive view, then he believed Congress ought to change it. Indeed, the *Washington Post* reported that members of Congress followed the case closely.[33] Copyright reform hearings then being held had commenced three years earlier, but the Patents Committee held off drafting a fresh proposal for copyright reform until the Supreme Court issued its decision. In a way, the Court threw down a gauntlet that pushed Congress to bring the reform process, frequently a long and contentious one, to a close. President Theodore Roosevelt had called for a comprehensive revision of copyright law in 1905, citing the "many articles which, under modern reproductive processes, are entitled to protection." However, Congress failed to resolve the differences between various copyright interests, only passing the Copyright Act of 1909 after the Supreme Court handed down its provocative decision.[34]

Legal scholars have subsequently described the *White Smith* decision that music must be visually perceptible to be copyrighted as "incredible" and "truly shocking," but the Court felt obligated to rule only on the existing statute, which made no mention of mechanical renditions of music. In fact, leading law journals at the time viewed the ruling as logical and straightforward.[35] Perhaps recognizing the shortcomings of the existing law in regard to new technology, the Court concluded that "considerations of the hardships of those whose published productions are not protected by the copyright properly address themselves to Congress and not to the courts."[36] The songwriters and their business partners had been pressing their case since 1905, and the *White-Smith* case lent new urgency to their quest to expand the scope of musical copyright.

Copyright Reform in the Progressive Era

In 1905, Congress went where the copyright holders were. Lawmakers left Washington in March with five copyright bills unresolved, and the Senate Committee on Patents arranged a conference in New York the following May to hear from a variety of interested parties: academics, artists, song publishers, and newspapermen, each representing some part of the city's diverse media. "It is generally admitted by those most directly concerned that the copyright laws of the United States need revision," the Librarian of Congress, Herbert Putnam, observed in April 1905. Putnam decided to hold the meeting where those "most directly concerned" could easily offer their views on reforming copyright.[37]

Finding receptive ears at these meetings, representatives from publishing, music, and the visual arts pressed for the idea of divisible copyrights. For example, dramatists wanted separate "show-rights" and "stage-rights" for their works. Most speakers advocated greater punitive damages for infringement and the extension of copyright for "as long a period as possible."[38] Preferably, copyright would be defined separately for each category of works. Brander Matthews, a Columbia University literature professor, suggested that newspapermen might need a shorter copyright than the author's-life-plus-fifty-year term that his group, the National Academy of Arts and Letters (NAAL), sought. "The first thing to do is to let each one of the particular specific callings state what it wants," he said.[39] A musician, after all, might want rights that individually address printing, performance, and recording of his work. "I know that in France you cannot play a tune on a hand organ without the permission of the holder of the musical copyright," Matthews said, while not explicitly advocating the same law in America.[40]

Music publishers bemoaned the increase in illicit copying that accompanied the decreasing cost of printing. The development of photolithography in the nineteenth century greatly enhanced the efforts of sheet-music copiers. New technology permitted pirates to create nearly identical copies of sheet music without the sloppy mistakes that had plagued earlier imitations.[41] At the New York conference, George W. Furniss of Music Publishers' Association described the process:

> A person with ten or fifteen dollars in his pocket can go down the street and have a popular composition photographed and put into plates and placed on the market in a very short time, and it will cost several hundred dollars to capture a few pirated copies, with no chance of getting any relief from the individuals in that line of business.[42]

In one such case, a competitor sold hymns owned by the Oliver Ditson Company under different names, and Furniss asked Congress to allow copyright owners a greater window of time in which to investigate such pirates before they had to file suit. "It took us a long time to find them," he added, "because we were not all churchgoers ourselves." Even when a piece was an outright copy, the excellent quality of reproduction could keep investigators from decisively identifying the song as a knockoff.[43]

In these early hearings, the publishers were concerned with tweaking procedural issues in the copyright law, such as the period of coverage or the time allowed to take legal action against infringers. They did not press for a fundamental change in the scope of copyright. Although the Librarian of Congress mentioned the rising use of technology, the music publishers did not dwell on the question of sound recording or mechanical reproduction. "There is a suit on now that has already cost twenty thousand dollars against the mechanical instrument men, who have taken our tools without any consideration at all," Furniss remarked. "We believe, however, that we shall succeed in that. We believe that the present law will be sufficient to protect us."[44] If anything, in 1905 they were more perturbed by the ease of copying sheet music that cheaper printing technology had allowed.

The copyright forces found a less congenial atmosphere at hearings in Washington the following year. By 1906, the music industry worried about mechanical reproduction more than before. Confusion surrounded the status of sound recordings in the existing law, and few were sure of the status of written music in the new legislation. Representative Frank Currier (R-NH), chair of the House Committee on Patents, quizzed composer Victor Herbert about whether the talking machine companies enjoyed protection for the records they make. "I think they do," Herbert averred. If one company started copying another's records, he said, "they would go for them," but Currier was not convinced. The two went on for several minutes, Herbert saying the piano roll and phonograph companies had legal protection and the congressman saying he was pretty sure they did not. In any event, Herbert said, sheet music was definitely not shielded from unauthorized reproduction. "Since the courts have held that the perforated roll is not an imitation of the sheet music," he lamented, alluding to the *White-Smith* case, "we have absolutely no ground to stand on."[45]

Meanwhile, the talking machine companies seized on the conceptual muddle of copyright law to push their own interpretation of property rights. If the music publishers, who represented most composers, were going to get rights to mechanical versions of their music, then the makers of piano rolls and phonographs should receive a copyright for their unique reproductions. Horace Pettit, speaking for the Victor company, suggested that Congress insert the term "talking machines" into the list of categories of goods covered by copyright. The proposed law made no mention of mechanical reproductions as a distinct type of copyrightable expression, even though the drafters were otherwise specific in listing books, photographs, and dramatic works as eligible. According to Pettit, the phonograph recording of a specific performance by a great singer was a unique artistic work worthy of the protection of the federal government. "The particular characteristic utterances of a singer, or recitationist, or of an actor, or of an orator, or the particular instrumentation of a pianist, or leader of an orchestra," he said, "independent of the composition itself... should be equally entitled to protection, as a photograph or reproduction of a work of art."[46]

The committee offered ready, if not fierce, questioning. If a scholar gives a lecture in one place and Victor records it, Rep. Robert Bonynge (R-CO) asked, would Victor then own the lecture and be able to prevent the man from giving it again, or, perhaps, making another recording of it? Pettit insisted that the copyright for the abstract content would remain separate from the distinctive material expression of it—that is, the words or ideas of the lecture, as opposed to the actual vibrations engraved on a cylinder or disc—but this notion was difficult for many to understand in 1906. The words of a story and its particular appearance as a printed novel itself could not be severed in American law, which had always protected the tangible expression of an idea and not the idea itself. Sheet music and the phonograph presented a situation in which the same germ of creativity was represented in two distinct ways.[47]

Pettit struggled to analogize the phonograph—"a writing upon a record tablet...not to be read visually, but audibly to be read through the medium of a vibrating pencil"—to traditional "writings" like books or photographs.[48] His challenge was to portray the phonograph as similar to the kinds of works already protected by copyright, yet sufficiently different from a written composition to merit a separate copyright. "It is a picture of the voice, as perfectly as a photograph is a picture of a man, or of a thing," he said, "and all the personality and all the characteristics of speech of the man uttering it are there recorded."[49] Did he mean to suggest that the picture was exactly the same as what it represented? Was the "picture of the voice" identical to the written words and tones articulated by the voice, or a distinctive work in its own right?

In this regard, what Congressman Bonynge first thought of the content of the recording—a lecture—is key. Thomas Edison initially imagined the phonograph as an office dictation device, with domestic applications such as recording a baby's first words or the voice of a grandparent for posterity. He did not anticipate that the medium would be dominated by the sale of prerecorded material, whether musical or literary in nature.[50] In this still-early phase of sound recording, the devices were known as talking machines, not "singing machines," and the notion that one performance of a lecture would be so different from another as to be exclusively used by one company did not seem self-evident. Like Pettit, Bonynge grappled for the right words: "Do you mean that if the lecturer delivers the lecture to one of the talking machines that you should take a copyright upon that disk, or whatever it is, that record, I suppose is what you call it?"[51] What set one version of the lecture apart from the other? If the talking machine company owned the copyright for a recording of those words, how could the lecturer be free to make another record of the text for another company?

Whatever the artistic merits of the individual recording, the talking machine companies were quick to point out its financial significance. Even if a singer's performance was not recognized as a separate work of art, the company paid him, and him specifically, a tidy sum to record it. "We might pay Mr. Herbert or Mr. Sousa or Mr. Caruso, or any of the opera singers, a thousand dollars for making a record," Pettit said.[52] As the bandleader and composer John Philip Sousa, who was no fan of the talking machines, noted, "They [the talking machine companies] get much more out of the human voice.... They pay Caruso $3,000 to make a record in their machines, because they get the human voice. And they pay a cornet player $4 to blow one of his blasts into it."[53]

The public did not want just any human voice, though. They would pay good money to hear world-famous tenor Enrico Caruso sing an aria, and, with the rise of jazz, Victor might soon offer more than $4 for a particular cornet player's "blast." The Congressional hearings came at a time when phonograph companies began to experiment heavily with advertising, cultivating the celebrity of recording artists like never before. The images of stars like Caruso, Emma Calvé, and Pol-Henri Plançon gave the phonograph a mystique of highbrow sophistication that Victor was willing to spend large sums to create.[54] Pettit suggested that the talking machine companies should receive copyright protection for their recordings because it took a sizable investment to create the product the public most wanted. Why should another company be able to exploit the commercial

ATTENTION!

THE EXCELSIOR PHONOGRAPH CO.

Having secured the plant of The Roger Harding Phonograph Company and enlarged it to three times its former capacity beg to inform the users of Phonographs and Graphophones that they are now prepared to furnish

GUARANTEED ORIGINAL RECORDS
of the Highest Standard of Excellence

Superior Master Records by Harding, Porter, Hunting, Quinn, Gaskin, Johnson, Ossman, banjo, Chambers, cornet, Schweinfest, piccolo, Tuson, clarionet, Vocal Quartettes, Trios, Duetts, Talking Records, etc., etc.

WE HANDLE NO DUPLICATES

ANY SPECIAL RECORDS MADE
TO ORDER AT SHORT NOTICE

LIBERAL DISCOUNT
ON LARGE ORDERS

Excelsior Phonograph Company
NO. 18 E. 22d STREET, NEW YORK CITY

Figure 1.4 Like so many of its competitors, the Excelsior Phonograph Company wanted consumers to know that each of its records was original and individually "made to order," offering the distinctive performances of particular performers as well as more generic fare, such as "piccolo," "banjo," or "Vocal Quartettes." *Source: Phonoscope* 1, no. 16 (November–December 1897): 16.

advantage that Victor had created by hiring Caruso? "It is perfectly possible, within the known arts, for that record, after we have made it, to be reproduced by a mere copperplating process by somebody else and copied," he said, "so that we would pay the thousand dollars or so and have no protection against the party manufacturing a duplicate of it." In other words, money talks. Even Sousa agreed on the general point when Representative William Campbell (R-OH) asked if he was seeking greater incentives to write music. "Oh, yes," the bandleader said. "I can compose better if I get a thousand dollars than I can for six hundred." The congressmen guffawed at Sousa's frankness. "That is the real reason," Campbell concluded.[55]

The exchange did not merely reflect Sousa's pecuniary instincts. Rather, American copyright had always centered on commercial incentives. Lawmakers traditionally premised copyright on the principle of giving just enough protection to encourage artists to bring their creative works to the market. The Constitution aimed "to promote the Progress of Science and useful Arts, by securing for limited Times to Authors and Inventors the exclusive Right to their respective Writings and Discoveries."[56] A composer's song did not belong to its creator forever. Rather, legislators aimed to provide a window of time in which a creator could reap sufficient benefit from the work to be motivated to create it in the first place. When the Connecticut Assembly granted the first copyright during the Revolutionary War, the protection lasted only five years.[57] Congress did not even include music in copyright law until 1831, a limitation that reflects the law's modest ambitions.[58]

The congressmen who wrote the Copyright Act of 1909 continued to be skeptical of efforts to make copyright a more permanent property right, emphasizing instead the importance of preserving the public's access to creative work. When R. R. Bowker and his allies in the professional associations pushed hard for a copyright term of the author's life plus fifty years, Congress did not listen. As Congressman William Sulzer (D-NY) quipped, Russia provides such a term for copyright because there the artist "does not get to live very long."[59] Legislators decided to keep a term of twenty-eight years, after which an author could renew for another twenty-eight years. If no one expressed interest in renewal, then the work would revert to the public domain, and anyone could make use of it.

If the object of American copyright had been to give artists a reason to invest their labor in creative work, Pettit and other lobbyists focused instead on the financial incentives of big business. Sound recording raised the question of how copyright should work when the creator in question is not a solitary novelist or songwriter, but a capital-intensive corporation using costly technology and marshalling the efforts of many contributors to make a final product. The earlier hearings in 1905 had posed the question from a different angle, when lawmakers discussed the status of composite works like encyclopedias. The committee groped for a term that could describe the legitimate owner of the copyright for such a product. The term "proprietor" had been used in the law, but the Register of Copyrights, Thorvald Solberg, observed that the courts had defined a "proprietor" as an "assignee of the author," not as a corporate author per se.[60] One committee member noted that many scientific works were being written collectively, and another raised the example of forewords written by several professors for a series of books. "The promoter, the projector, the man who has gotten it up is Professor Gayley," Brander Matthews of the NAAL observed, "but the person who is supplying the money is another; there is a double case—can the editor take out the copyright or is the publisher to do it?"[61] Matthews hit closest to the target, opening the question of whether a company that manages the allocation of labor and capital, creating nothing itself, ought to be the holder of a copyright.

In 1909 as in 1905, Congress dodged the issue. Sound recording was a fresh and unfamiliar medium, and the politicians chose not to prolong an already complicated process of copyright revision, which affected so many interest groups. It appeared altogether too difficult to assign some kind of copyright to specific renditions of music represented on rolls of paper or in phonograph grooves, since the appropriate "author" was so hard to identify.

One author was already on hand — the composer — and the Copyright Act protected a composer's right to benefit from reproductions of a musical work while allowing the talking machine companies a degree of latitude to reproduce a performance of that work. The phonograph and piano roll firms did not obtain copyright protection for their products, but they did receive a unique license (literally) to exploit the work of songwriters. The compulsory license system treated music differently from any other category of copyrighted material; it allowed companies to record and manufacture versions of the original article by paying a flat rate per copy produced. Under the system, when George Gershwin wrote "When You Want 'Em, You Can't Get 'Em (When You've Got 'Em, You Don't Want 'Em)" in 1916, he was able to choose how the song was first recorded. After the initial recording was released, though, any other company could hire Frank Sinatra or Billie Holiday to record renditions of the song, as long as it paid two cents per copy to Gershwin (or his publishing company).[62]

Congress also favored limiting copyright on the basis of property rights, however counterintuitive that notion may sound to twenty-first century ears. Copyright was not just an author's property; it was also a kind of monopoly. For twenty-eight years, at least, the copyright holder had absolute control over how a book, photograph, or play would be reproduced. However, this power could be pernicious if it limited the way a consumer made use of property once purchased. For instance, at the 1906 hearings, music publishers had sought to bar the renting and sharing of sheet music on the grounds that the copyright owner retained the right of performance. They suggested that only the purchaser of a song received the right to perform the song, as a sort of license. If a church choir wanted to perform a cantata, it would have to buy one copy of the music for each of its singers. When Congressman John C. Chaney (R-IN) asked if the publishers' position was that "the property itself does not carry the right to use it," an industry representative agreed enthusiastically.[63] However, Representative John Gill, Jr. (D-MD) insisted that the purchaser of music acquired "a property right which he can use as he pleases."[64] Gill compared the composer to a patentee, who can control the reproduction of his product but not its use. If a man buys a tractor, he can freely loan it to his neighbor without seeking the tractor company's permission. In Gill's view, limiting the way the same man could use a song he purchased would be an unwarranted invasion of his property rights.

Congress also had other more specific anxieties about monopoly on its mind. Aeolian, a piano roll company, had bankrolled White-Smith's case against Apollo, hoping to test the judicial waters before making too great an investment in machinery, inventory, and contracts for rights to music. The manufacturer struck a deal with numerous publishers granting it exclusive permission to record the publishers' songs if the composers prevailed in the case.[65] The Supreme Court, of course, ruled against the copyright holders. However, if Congress allowed composers and publishers to negotiate exclusive licenses with mechanical reproducers, then Aeolian would have had a shot at cornering the industry.

The company's scheme discomfited congressional observers, who feared "an absolute unqualified monopoly" would fall into Aeolian's hands.[66] The copyright reform bill evolved during the presidency of Theodore Roosevelt, when politicians embraced the cause of battling trusts of all kinds; music seemed no different than oil or ice in this regard.[67] Indeed, the notorious Keith organization was busy consolidating control over the nation's vaudeville industry, and the talking machine business looked ripe for a takeover.[68] Smaller piano roll firms worried that a monopoly would form, and some composers blasted the Aeolian scheme as dirty dealing by the "phonograph trust."[69] The compulsory license provided a clever resolution of these concerns, as it gave the composer a degree of control over his composition and a source of revenue, while also preventing a recording company from controlling how any particular song was recorded.

When Congress considered copyright reform in the Progressive Era, the balance of power still teetered between those who wanted to strengthen the rights of copyright owners and those who sought to defend free access to the arts. The new copyright reform, with its compromise between composers and recording companies, won unanimous approval from the House and Senate Committees on Patent, and the bill sailed through both chambers, winning final approval in the Senate on March 3, 1909.[70] The legislation was the result of long, careful negotiation and had the support of Republicans and Democrats. Shortly before passage, Senator Albert Kittredge (R-SD) assured his colleagues, "This subject has been before the Patent Committee for four or five years, and the committee has expended a great amount of time and has worked hard in order to secure an agreement."[71]

If anything, the political leaders of 1909 chose to err on the side of caution. When the committee proposed letting churches and schools perform copyrighted music without seeking permission, the publishers' lawyer, A. R. Serven, commented that "enforced charity, whether by statute or by violence, is vicious and ought never to be resorted to." The committee chairman retorted, "[Copyright] is, by the way, direct charity, because ... your rights are purely statutory."[72] In other words, copyright was a privilege granted by the government, not a moral right possessed by creators. Many of the testifiers disagreed, viewing the creative artist or rights owner as the greatest priority for the law. As the painter John LaFarge told Congress, "The originator of a thing should not be put to proving his case against the outside world, but the outside world should prove their case against him."[73] At the very outset of the revision, Librarian of Congress Herbert Putnam observed, "The district attorney has remarked that our statutory laws ought to be in two parts, the first, of laws to be followed, and the second of 'moral yearnings.' In our proposals for copyright we had, I think, better leave the moral yearnings to a later generation or at least a later session of Congress."[74] The quip came true. Later generations and later Congresses would expand the scope of copyright to suit greater moral aims, but, in the meantime, the "copyright forces" got less than they asked for.

Pirate Arias, Bootleg News, and Other Problems from Europe

While the ink was fresh on the new copyright act, the Eastern District Court of New York handed down one of the first decisions on a clear case of piracy. The case involved a colorful and mysterious character who arguably pioneered piracy and the legal hijinks associated with it: Wynant Van Zant Pearce Bradley. This entrepreneur, whose name soon became familiar to court observers, started out pirating records for Zon-O-Phone. In 1902, he trademarked the terms "Talk-O-Phone" and "Monogram," and ventured out from his native Brooklyn to enlist investor Albert Irish's help in starting the Ohio Talking Machine Company. Ohio brought out a line of phonographs that closely imitated the Victor company's machines. The various models bore the names of (Victor) Herbert, (John Phillip) Sousa and other noted composers, apparently without permission.

Even the logo for "Monogram" discs used bold-faced letters for "gram," likely hoping to link itself to Victor's "gramophone" in the consumer's minds. Victor soon filed suit against the company for patent infringement; Albert Irish went bankrupt; and Bradley took to inveighing against the "Victor interests" in the pages of *Talking Machine World*. By the time Victor won the patent case, Bradley was in hot water again for a disc-pirating operation, Continental Records.[75] The Italian label Fonotipia Records sued Bradley for copying arias that it had licensed Columbia Records to produce and sell in the United States. Columbia and Victor joined the suit as plaintiffs, alleging that Bradley also imitated their products, and the Circuit Court of the Eastern District of New York heard the case in 1909.

Continental was a wisp of an organization. Bradley claimed only to be its salesman, but the court could not dig up any other name in connection with the company. Continental stated its base as New Baltimore, New York, though no office or plant could be found there. When Columbia's agents purchased some records from Continental, the receipt showed the address of a storage company. Music historians Allan Sutton and Kurt Nauck believe Continental made new masters from commercially available discs, shipped the new molds to "an undisclosed foreign location," and then exported them back into the United States.[76] That the court could find no office or plant for the company suggests that this export-import scheme may have been true. However, Bradley could just as easily have pressed the records at a secret factory or shop in the United States. He might have told the court that the goods were imported in the hope that the product's ostensibly "foreign" status would deflect copyright concerns. The arias Continental copied were originally recorded in Italy, and a consumer might expect them to be foreign in any case.

Justice Thomas Chatfield observed that Columbia's "originals" themselves were copies, in a sense. Using the disc method pioneered by Emile Berliner in 1888, the sound waves of a performance were etched onto a flat disc called the "master" record.[77] From this first matrix, Chatfield observed, "numberless reproductions, substantially duplicates even in minute details of the original record" were made.[78] Earlier wax cylinder recording required the singer to perform a song over and over again; the cylinders were engraved in small batches, with recorders arrayed around the performer to capture the sounds simultaneously. True mass production was not possible until Berliner invented a master disc from which any number of other discs could be pressed. In a sense, the cylinder recordings were more "original" than the discs sold by Columbia, because the latter were copied en masse from the initial master record. Nonetheless, the court distinguished between Columbia's "duplicate originals," which were mass-produced from an original recording of the performance, and Bradley's copies. "The defendant's records are not duplicates," the judge reasoned, "even in the sense that they are removed from the original singing by but one reproduction from a matrix.... The Continental Record Company makes its records from commercial discs of the complainants and must produce a second matrix before the copies can be pressed or stamped."[79] The pirated records were a further step removed from the real thing.

Justice Chatfield noted that Bradley had not exactly imitated the distinctive red label of Victor's records, which the company used to distinguish its high-end line of classical music. In fact, the Bradley records did not look much like the originals from which they were copied, meaning that the pirate could not be accused of "palming off" his copies as if they were the originals.[80] Continental's advertising made it clear that the records were duplicates, containing the same sounds but not identical to the originals as material objects. The judge noted, though, that Continental's claim of equal sound quality was "a question of fact...in which the public is interested."[81] If consumers believed that Continental records were just as good as Victor records, and then discovered that Continental played poorly, they might be reluctant to buy either one in the future. The court found that Continental made its records of less durable material, which was prone to "scratching and irritating sounds."[82]

In a sense, Bradley's knockoffs resembled the cheap generic versions of contemporary name-brand products, such as cereals or toaster pastries. In the *Fonotipia* case, however, the court ruled that generic editions of musical recordings could not be sold alongside the original, name-brand product. The performer's right to his or her creative work did not figure much in the decision—as the judge noted, the musicians had worked under contract for Fonotipia and were not involved in the lawsuit. Instead, Bradley was faulted for his false claim of equal sound quality and for taking advantage of Victor's reputation.[83]

Both the talking machine ads and Bradley's legal strategy suggest that distinctions between original and copied records had been commonplace in the market until the *Fonotipia* decision. Russell Hunting and other early recording artists were well aware that unauthorized copies of their recordings circulated on the market. Listeners did not necessarily identify one recorded performance as the exclusive product of one record company, and Bradley sought to exploit this uncertainty for all it was worth. The Supreme Court's *White-Smith* decision held that anyone could produce piano rolls of songs, since this use was merely a mechanical application and not a copyrightable expression in itself, but just a year later the *Fonotipia* ruling declared that disc recordings could be regulated by law, through principles of fairness, consumer protection, and the public interest. "The reproduction of songs by famous singers and artists is both educational and beneficial to the people as a whole," Chatfield wrote, "and the court cannot but take notice of the fact that music has an educational side, and appeals to substantially everyone, even though they be unconscious of the result."[84] The judge associated a recording with the performer, whom record companies paid to record and cultivated as popular sensations. If the court had ruled otherwise, men like Bradley could have undermined the link between a star performer and the company that had contracted his services, and recorded sound might have served as fodder for any company to exploit.

It is important to note that *Fonotipia* did not create a new property right. The phonograph recordings were not eligible for copyright, as *White-Smith* made clear, and the new Copyright Act itself did nothing to change their legal status. As the *Harvard Law Review* observed, the case involved "nothing more than the reproduction of an unpatented and uncopyrighted article."[85] The district court's ruling against Bradley centered on the notion of unfair competition, holding that he had not violated copyright but, rather, had exploited his competitor's investment in the recordings. The court observed that the Victor Company had built an expensive plant in Camden, New Jersey, and spent a great deal of money on advertising its product. "It may be argued that the imitation would go out of the market and be removed from interference with the original if the product proved unsatisfactory," Justice Thomas Chatfield said in the ruling, "but it would seem that business reputation and excellence of product are entitled to some protection from imitations which discourage further use."[86] If nothing else, the capital investment in both production and promotion should be immune to unauthorized use. The company's reputation was a possession of sorts; advertising could create a value in the good that the court was bound to protect.

Fonotipia covered ground that was revisited in 1918 by a better-known ruling, *International News Service v. Associated Press*, which recognized a quasi-property right in "hot news." The International News Service (INS) had paid employees of the Associated Press (AP) to reveal the latest information telegraphed from the war in Europe, which was then published in INS's newspapers at the same time as AP's.[87] The Court condemned INS for "taking material that has been acquired by complainant as the result of organization and the expenditure of labor, skill, and money, and which is salable by complainant for money, and that defendant in appropriating it and selling it as its own is endeavoring to reap where it has not sown."[88] The fact that Archduke Franz Ferdinand had been shot, triggering the outbreak of World War I, was not in itself AP property, but its significance to the public was owned by the organization that did what it took to collect the information. Its newsworthiness was value that the company created, capital transmuted into history.

Copyright law had always protected the specific expression of an idea, but never facts. As a later court observed, "The case presented particular difficulty because of the great public interest in the freest dissemination of the news."[89] However, in *INS* the Supreme Court found that news organizations could enjoy a limited right to own information itself, turning to a similar argument of unfairness that underlay the *Fonotipia* ruling. Limiting the circulation of important news might be bad for the public, the judge reasoned, but not having the news at all because the AP's profit motive was diminished was worse. "Stripped of all disguises, the process amounts to an unauthorized interference with the normal operation of complainant's legitimate business precisely at the point where the profit is to be reaped," wrote Justice Mahlon Pitney for the five-to-three majority.[90]

The "hot news" doctrine offered a limited right that, in some ways, resembles the compulsory license. The music publishing system created by the 1909 Copyright Act empowers the composer of a piece of music to authorize the first recording of the composition; afterwards, anyone is free to record his own version, paying a flat royalty for each copy that is produced. The *INS* decision allowed news organizations to take advantage of their reportage before anyone else did, much as composers could choose when and if their music would be recorded. Whoever went to the trouble of obtaining the scoop was entitled to benefit from circulating the information for some amount of time, at least so long as the news is "hot." Both the compulsory license and the *INS* ruling respect the right of an individual (or, more likely, a firm) to benefit from investing labor and capital into the production of an intangible good, which is then presented as a material thing, like a piano roll or a newspaper.

Corporations had secured ground for their ownership of news and sound recordings, or at least for some of their qualities. At a time when companies were building large, complex organizations to report wartime news or to manufacture and distribute recordings around the world, these decisions opened a path for businesses to own information outside of copyright law. More important, these decisions meant corporations could own something more abstract: the "hotness" of news, or the bankability of a star performer. Struggles over sound recording and copyright broke out at precisely the moment when nascent media giants like Victor were staking out territory in the public sphere through advertising. Victor, in particular, became known as one of the most aggressive pioneers in the use of modern advertising.[91] The reputation of its highbrow Red Seal line of records or its stable of opera stars was expensive to create yet cheap for others to exploit, just like the value of news gathered by the AP in Europe. The legal successes of these companies anticipated later high-stakes conflicts between those who made everything from records and phonebooks to lampshades and video games, and others who would copy them.[92]

Such steps remained tentative in the early twentieth century, though. Copyright was still constrained by doubts about monopoly and the uncertainty that surrounded evolving technological and cultural forms. Decisions like *INS* reflected a Progressive Era predilection for limiting the control of information. In his dissent, Justice Louis Brandeis voiced these concerns. "The creation or recognition by courts of a new private right may work serious injury to the general public," he wrote, "unless the boundaries of the right are definitely established and wisely guarded."[93]

The coming decades would provide numerous opportunities for songwriters, musicians, entrepreneurs, and listeners to argue about how best to bound and guard those rights. How much should a company's investment be protected? How far could courts extend the ownership of expression before straying into Congress's territory? Although the *Fonotipia* ruling condemned copiers who put out an inferior product, shady dealers continued to furnish secondhand records in the shadows. The rise of a collecting culture among music fans led to the copying and exchange of records that were out-of-print or otherwise unavailable, and the emergence of radio as a medium threatened the revenue of music publishers and record companies even as it furnished the public with a new source of "free" sound.

2

Collectors, Con Men, and the Struggle for Property Rights

The boundaries between legitimate and illegitimate, real and fake, original and copied continued to be fuzzy at times. Congressional reform had denied record companies copyright protection for their products, yet the *Fonotipia* decision seemed to condemn unauthorized copying of recordings. Into this legal confusion a whole host of characters made their moves—industry wheeler-dealers, record collectors, radio stations, musicians' unions, bootleggers, even the Mafia—all with their own ideas about how sound recordings ought to be produced and exchanged. Collectors believed the public had a legitimate interest in keeping recorded music in circulation, and bootleggers stood ready to supply the demand if the major labels failed to do so. Meanwhile, radio posed a new set of challenges; unions believed that musicians should own the rights to the recordings they produced, or at least benefit from royalties when the records were played on the radio. Record companies could not decide whether broadcasters unlawfully reproduced their products or helped promote them, as some stations sold bootleg disks of the performances they aired.[1] The legal status of recorded sound remained in flux.

The career of Eli Oberstein reveals how some in the music business played fast and loose with recorded sound in the mid-twentieth century. Oberstein had been a colorful producer and executive at RCA Victor in the 1930s, helping to launch the recording careers of Artie Shaw and Glenn Miller.[2] Upon his abrupt departure in 1939, Oberstein started his own company, the US Record Corporation, which sold cheap recordings under the Varsity label. Oberstein's ambition to bring numerous artists along from RCA Victor faltered, but he still managed to get records on the shelves by reissuing old recordings from labels such as Crown, Gennett, and Paramount, seemingly by copying from commercial recordings rather than the original masters.[3]

Scholars disagree over whether Oberstein obtained the proper legal permissions to sell the records, but the murky origin of many such bargain-bin discs only exemplifies the career of an entrepreneur known for working along the edges of the law. Howls of "bootlegging" arose when Oberstein mysteriously managed to keep churning out records during a major strike by the American Federation of Musicians (AFM) in 1942, though the records were credited to unknowns like Johnny Jones. "It's very simple," Oberstein said, "I pick up any tune I like, and the records just come in."[4] Oberstein claimed that he dodged the restrictions of the strike by recording in Mexico, although many suspected that he was, in fact, recording in New York hotel rooms with amateur musicians and willing strikebreakers. In this context, "bootlegging" meant defying the strike by making new recordings, rather than copying other people's records.[5]

Oberstein's tactics continued to stir controversy in the industry until his death in 1960. In some cases, Oberstein relabeled a recording with the name of a made-up artist, attributing a blues tune to "Sally Sad" or "Big Richard." Although the names can be dismissed as inane, the tactic reveals a certain sense of humor.[6] Between 1940 and 1942, Oberstein's Top Hat label released a series of "party records," which featured mild sexual innuendo and sometimes carried a label stating that they were meant only for home use, as at a party.[7] ("We have now reached the double-entendre era," Oberstein wryly told *Time* in 1940.)[8] The flip side of these risqué records often featured a copy of a performance recorded for one of Oberstein's earlier record label ventures, although the performance was attributed to a pseudonym.[9] His record of "She Tried It Last Night" features no performer's name at all.[10] Oberstein later aroused the ire of opera singer Regina Resnik, when in 1954 he recorded and sold copies of her radio performance of Wagner's *Ring* cycle under a different name. He also sparked controversy in 1959 when a German court prohibited distribution of a record, *Songs and Speeches of Nazi Germany*, which Oberstein had supposedly released—an accusation he bitterly denied until his death the following year.[11]

Unlike Wynant Van Zant Pearce Bradley, Oberstein did not seek to exploit the popularity of another company by counterfeiting its recordings or repackaging them. The use of a pseudonym like "Sally Sad" suggests that, in the obscurity of the bargain bin, music might be an anonymous product and not the distinctive work of an esteemed and promoted artist. Indeed, Oberstein's copying and reissuing recalled the techniques of music publishing pirates earlier in the twentieth century, who would reproduce hymns and other tunes but make up different names for them to avoid notice. The cases of Bradley and Oberstein show how muddled ideas about ownership and authorship remained well into the twentieth century. An inferior knock-off of an Italian aria or a disguised blues number suggested that recorded sounds might not be tied tightly to any particular company or performer. Sound could be a sort of anonymous fodder for entertainment, like the motion picture reels that pioneering studios once sold by the foot; such films lacked credits because the companies worried that actors could gain greater bargaining power if their identities were known and they became popular with the public.[12]

However, like movies, musical recordings became vehicles for star performers and their perceived talents in the early twentieth century. A recording was not merely a "mechanical reproduction" of a song, like the holes punched into a paper piano roll. Listeners attributed a distinctive quality to a particular artist's performance of a song—a value that could be appropriated, rightly or wrongly, through copying. A pirate record with a mistaken title and no artist attribution made little sense if the public sought familiar songs by well-known performers. The status of recordings as valuable artistic works solidified as listeners began to curate the growing body of recorded music in the 1920s and 1930s; in the process, they laid the groundwork for a new bootleg market, as well as the subsequent legal backlash that permitted record companies to begin asserting rights of ownership to their recordings.

Despite numerous attempts, the recording industry did not secure federal copyright protection for its products until 1971. Recordings were technically uncopyrightable for decades, and various pirates seized on the apparent loophole in federal law to copy works without seeking permission. Beginning in the 1930s, some bootleggers reproduced out-of-print works that had been abandoned by the major record labels without incurring any legal reaction. However, disputes over the legitimate use of recordings did arise throughout this period, producing a variety of contradictory legal opinions. In particular, two decisions by courts in New York—*RCA v. Whiteman* (1940) and *Metropolitan Opera v. Wagner-Nichols* (1950)—epitomized the contrary claims of ownership and creativity that drove this long-running debate. Although the courts split on the question of whether they could constrain piracy in the absence of federal copyright, leaving the status of sound uncertain, the outlines of a new justification for property rights began to take shape. When a court determined that the Metropolitan Opera had a right to reap the value of its popularity and reputation, it created a rationale of ownership that would powerfully reshape copyright in the 1960s and 1970s.

The Emergence of Collecting Culture

In the late 1920s a new breed of listener entered the scene of American popular culture—the jazz record collector, who appreciated jazz as an art form and sought to hoard the artifacts of its early evolution. Many of the recordings these fans collected had been produced in low numbers by small or unstable companies. The records they loved best had been targeted largely at African American consumers, who played the discs until they were nearly rubbed raw. "Your sole consolation was that early jazz was like folk music, a people's music," collector

Charles Edward Smith reflected years later, "and the grooves were sometimes all but gone, only because people who had loved it had listened to the records again and again."[13]

In any case, the early recordings of jazz were fragile and few in number. Major companies like RCA Victor and Columbia did not see much to be gained by keeping obscure records in print. "The large mass-distribution organizations can handle, to their own satisfaction, only those large-selling items which have mass appeal," collector Wilder Hobson observed in 1951, when the movement for collecting and preservation that he and his colleagues had started years before was bringing music copying to a head as a legal issue. "The pirate may be ethical or unethical, as you choose, but he is frequently engaged in offering time-tested, out-of-print works of art which the big recording interests have not felt it worth-while to issue."[14]

Devotees like Hobson had discovered how scarce the relics of Bix Beiderbecke and other collector favorites really were, and they duplicated these records for their friends. Then, in the late 1930s, collectors began the Hot Record Society to reissue classic recordings as an indifferent music industry looked the other way, establishing a precedent for record copiers who catered to jazz enthusiasts after World War II. In the process, the spirit of collecting collided with the dubious ethics of copying. Collectors gathered up things that were valuable because they were rare, whereas copiers made rare goods less so. Although bootlegging may seem to contradict collecting, in this sense, the two practices often coincided, meeting on one side of the law and then the other.

Record collectors and copiers reinterpreted the economic, legal, and social meaning of sound, offering their own answer to the question of how to deal with the accumulating backlog of recorded music. Working with wax and vinyl, they prefigured consumers who copied, compiled, and shared recordings through such media as magnetic tape and computer networks later in the twentieth century. Bootleggers highlighted the potential for recorded sound to have long-term commercial value at a time when the music industry still treated recordings as products of the moment, aimed at contemporary markets and abandoned as consumer tastes shifted.[15]

Collectors insisted that performances of the past ought to remain available, and if large companies could not make a profit by keeping such recordings in circulation, individual fans and entrepreneurs would copy and distribute the music themselves. By buying, selling, and copying the out-of-print discs of yesteryear, collectors showed that recordings did have an enduring value that the original producers—artists and record companies—would have an incentive to protect. In the process, bootleggers tested the limits of how listeners could legitimately use the products of modern culture industries, while provoking a reconsideration of the meaning of recorded sound as both art and property.

Intellectuals began to reevaluate jazz during the 1930s, at a moment when the public was embracing swing as popular music. Primarily white readers and writers developed a critical discourse about jazz in magazines such as *Down Beat*, and some on the Left embraced it as a people's music opposed to the values of fascism.[16] In 1934, France's Hugues Panassié broke ground on theorizing an aesthetics of jazz, and his countryman Charles Delaunay soon inaugurated the project of cataloguing jazz recordings. Americans took note and began publishing "the little jazz reviews," according to folklorist Alan Lomax, who remembered "frightfully serious and sophisticated jazz critics" descending on Jelly Roll Morton at the Jungle Inn, a club in Washington, DC. Morton saw his early innovations like "The Pearls" and "Wolverine Blues" played on the jukebox.[17] Jazz magazines sprouted up in the late 1930s in response to the growing public interest in swing music.

The new craze prompted the emergence of a breed of connoisseurs who preferred small group improvisation and badmouthed the tastes of the mainstream.[18] Some critics believed that popular swing was compromised by commercialism and that earlier and less popular forms of jazz were more authentic or artistic. Some perceived jazz as an earthy "folk" genre, while others envisioned it as a high art that could compete with European classical music.[19] Whatever their vision, such jazz aficionados in the 1930s and 1940s disdained swing as artless pop music; their journals resemble the tiny, self-published zines of the late twentieth century, which frequently favored independent or avant garde subcultures.[20] These small jazz journals cultivated a market for rarities, with the value of a recording determined by the number of copies that had come into the hands of collectors.

Affluent white collectors described searching for the scattered remnants of early jazz as if they were anthropologists doing exotic field research. Often enough, the field consisted of the homes and neighborhoods of black Americans, who made up much of the initial audience for the music. "Many of the collectors' items were originally issued purely for Negro consumption," collector Steve Smith wrote in 1939, "and consequently were sold only in sections of the country which had a demand for them." White men canvassed black neighborhoods in Philadelphia, Chicago, and Kansas City, often going door to door. One collector in New York abandoned this method and just left his card "with all the janitors in Harlem," who would contact him when they came across an item of interest.[21]

Collector Dick Rieber described one such excursion in an early jazz fanzine. His article "First Thrills in Beulah Land" described a Philadelphia neighborhood that proved to be a "collector's Eden" because the residents were willing to part with their records for much less than their potential value. The local children followed Rieber through the streets and directed him to homes where records could be found.[22] The Beulah of his title could not understand what he wanted with all the old records. Her collection included sermons, washboard bands, blues, jazz, and much more. Rieber paid $5 for sixty of her records, even though he knew one of the discs to be worth $2 by itself. "Beulah, though she didn't know it, was giving me one of my biggest collecting thrills," he wrote. Rieber did not clarify whether it was the joy of discovering unexpected treasures or the thrill of buying someone's possessions for drastically less than they were worth that excited him so much. In any case, the story is a familiar one. He managed to buy up records from several of Beulah's visitors, too, who had heard that a white man was looking for the blues. ("And old blues at that!" he added.) He even claimed to find Bessie Smith's sister living nearby, but she would part with none of her records.[23]

Observing the jazz scene in 1939, music writer Steve Smith gently mocked the devotees of genuine, original recordings with their "little black books" full of recording dates and master numbers. "I sometimes wonder when there is time for listening to the music," he wrote.[24] If two such collectors were sitting in a club, he said, they would be so wrapped up in competitively comparing notes that they would pay little attention to the music performed around them. Smith credited collectors with contributing to the storehouse of knowledge about the music, but he saw little point in memorizing data or keeping a record just because Louis Armstrong was known to have been in the room when it was made. Similarly, some fans frantically pursued any little trace of their single favorite musician. "These fanatics are the loneliest people in the world," Smith wrote, "shunned by other collectors who regard them as not fit to talk to." Rather than having a genuine love of the music, whoever might be playing it, they only paid attention when their idol began plucking, tapping, or blowing away. Worst of all, Smith thought, were the collectors who only got into the game because they heard that old jazz records were increasing in value. They hoped to catch a windfall and did not care for the music much at all. At least the fanatic and the know-it-all listened to jazz.[25]

Some fans focused on history and authenticity, and would only accept original recordings. A diehard follower of a particular performer such as Bix Beiderbecke, on the other hand, might settle for any reproduction of an unheard recording, no matter what it looked like. For his part, Smith defined mainstream collectors in contrast to both these kinds of men of narrower motivations. "The majority of hot collectors are quite normal human beings who do not go to extremes," he wrote. "They look mainly for the classics of hot, for the thrill of possession and enjoyment. They, too, keep up the search for rare records, but solely in the hope of finding something satisfying to the ear, as well as something they consider to be of historical significance."[26] Here, Smith identified a mix of reasons behind the movement: aesthetic appreciation, historical preservation, and the fetish of possession all drove him and his fellows to collect.

Although some collectors did insist on having the original disc, the small-scale copying of records in the 1930s suggests that others would accept a copy.[27] "There are those who will have nothing but the original label," Smith observed, "and who will turn down a clean copy of a record in preference to [the original] in bad condition because the latter has what is known to be an earlier label." However, fans who cherished a record not only for its historical character but also for the sound it contained would settle for unofficial copies of rare works. "One often had acetates made from discs owned by a fellow collector," according to Charles Edward Smith. "These were called 'dubs' and were brought out on display apologetically, like fish bought in the market instead of caught properly with rod and reel."[28] The word "dub" originated in the late 1920s, meaning to "double" an object. The term connotes a practice of making individual copies, doubling an item one copy at a time, rather than mass producing it in large batches.[29] The verb was fittingly used by those pragmatic collectors who made copies of rare records for each other. Speaking of the music of Sidney Bechet, George Hoefer wrote, "The original record is so rare that it is almost impossible to even find a copy from which to dub an acetate."[30] The collector, critic, and producer John Hammond once had to seek out the Chicago musician Meade Lux Lewis in person because he could not find a Lewis record of good enough quality to copy.[31]

Although the phonograph disc surpassed the recordable wax cylinder in popularity by the 1910s, it was technically possible, albeit difficult, for consumers to make their own disc recordings.[32] Record-copying technologies appeared on the consumer market as a response to the economic woes of the Depression.[33] RCA confronted the calamitous drop in music sales during the early 1930s by marketing record players that could connect to a separate disc recorder. Presumably, consumers would make their own recordings if they could no longer afford to buy records. "The new recorder utilized a small, pre-grooved, 6-inch disc made from a piece of cardboard with celluloid plastic laminated to each side," writes historian David Morton. "Later, solid plastic blanks were sold in 10- and 12-inch sizes. The recording attachment used an electromagnetically driven stylus to emboss the recording into the pre-grooved disc."[34] After World War II, the cumbersome and delicate operation of a disc recorder, available to those with the money and inclination to record and copy music, would give way to the more flexible, user-friendly medium of magnetic tape, particularly with the rise of the high-fidelity home-recording market in the 1950s. "Disc home recording requires a great deal more skill than magnetic home recording, and if a mistake is made in the process of recording, the record is lost," the engineer Semi J. Begun argued in the 1940s.[35]

Manufacturers improved disc-recording sets and lowered prices slightly throughout the 1930s, but in an era of economic distress consumers were

Figure 2.1 The music from an African American musician's horn becomes a disc and is passed from the record company to consumers, collectors, and bootleggers in this visual representation of bootlegging from *Record Changer*'s January 1952 issue. *Source*: Courtesy of the Brad McCuen Collection, Center for Popular Music, Middle Tennessee State University. Reprinted by permission of Richard Hadlock.

unlikely to exchange their old record players for newer models with fancy new accessories. Indeed, people were hardly buying records, opting instead to listen to the radio for free. Remco's Babytone recorder, introduced in 1936, cost $125, and Universal Microphone offered models ranging from $92 to $375 soon after.[36] Begun noted that a few companies offered radios with built-in disc recorders in 1940, but to little avail. A few well-heeled music aficionados like Hammond, a Vanderbilt heir turned activist and jazz impresario, could afford a disc-cutting machine to reproduce records and share them with friends, but home-recording technology failed to take off in a big way until after World War II, with the emergence of reel-to-reel magnetic recording and the high-fidelity market.

While dubs were a necessary evil for collectors, groups of jazz enthusiasts began launching their own programs to distribute copies of classic recordings soon after collecting emerged as a hobby. England's Brunswick label copied some "classic swing" records in the early 1930s, and Panassié led the reissue charge in France with his magazine *Jazz Hot*. Milt Gabler had pioneered the concept in the United States through his Commodore Music Shop on New York City's 42nd Street. Beginning in 1934, Gabler sought licenses from record labels to produce small batches of jazz records that were no longer in print. The Commodore Music Shop became a hot spot for jazz enthusiasts in New York, and soon some of the "hipoise" who hung around the store, which moved to a bigger space on 52nd Street in 1938, launched the Hot Record Society (HRS).[37]

"The reissue adherents made like Don Quixote on a hot kick," Charles Edward Smith recalled. They took on the task of reintroducing recordings that the major labels had let lapse into obscurity years before, a job they considered noble and, perhaps, quixotic. When Panassié visited the United States for the first time in 1938, he joined with Steve Smith, Russell, and others to start the Hot Record Society, which distributed copies of old tunes to its members and irregularly issued its own journal, the *H.R.S. Society Rag*.[38] The New York–based HRS got permission from record companies to copy their old records, he explained, because "(1) no one had discovered any loopholes in the copyright situation, and (2) pressings often had to be done through record companies, subsidiaries or firms in some way associated with them."[39]

Permission did not mean cooperation, though. The labels condoned the activities of HRS with indifference; the only evidence of their tacit support is the fact that the Society never suffered any legal retaliation, unlike later bootleggers who also made copies of out-of-print recordings available to the public. HRS had to seek out the best copies of records, since firms such as Decca and Columbia would not let them use their masters. Society members tracked down the original musicians and urged them to share their knowledge about the recording sessions, suggesting that the buzz around a rediscovered classic might raise their profile in the music world. That said, "a hot chorus blown through a bust-up horn in 1924, whatever its merit, didn't bring home the bacon a decade later," Smith admitted, but many old hands were willing to contribute anyway. In 1941 Columbia told HRS it could reproduce the *Red Onion Jazz Babies* record by Clarence Williams. HRS made new masters of the record, and Williams joined in to provide the historical context for the recording. However, Columbia withdrew its consent shortly before the record's release date. In fact, the whole program ended soon after, as the three major labels decided to try producing their own reissues in the early 1940s, and then the outbreak of a new world war put everything on hold.[40]

In its time, the *Rag* strove to be "strictly for, by and about collectors," and featured in-depth articles on its members, such as Hammond, "Dean of the Swing Critics," and Wilder Hobson.[41] The portraits show that the Hot Record Society crowd hailed from prestigious schools and thought of itself as an elite of music lovers. William Russell had studied classical violin in Chicago and taught music before becoming obsessed with hot music.[42] He was also an accomplished avant garde composer, whose work influenced John Cage. Of Hobson, Frank Norris observed that "he had the most inclusive collection of jazz records"—in 1929, before the collecting craze got into full swing—though it was hard to say whose collection was best since "a lot of jazz philatelists have muscled into the tribe."[43]

Writers in the *Rag* scorned mainstream critics, sometimes contrasting their own views with the ignorant pronouncements of other music reviewers.[44] At the same time, they disdained pedantic terminology and impenetrable jargon in the discussion of music, lending a populist air to an otherwise elitist enterprise. The Society's first bulletin proclaimed its pursuit of a middle path between snobbery and populism: "We will choose to reprint discs that are distinguished both by greatness of performance and by rarity, leaving the corn to the hillbillies and the more accessible hot records to the assiduousness of individual collectors."[45]

This statement rings with the self-assurance that characterized the collectors' division of jazz music between good and bad, legitimate and illegitimate. The white critics and collectors of the Hot Record Society sought to perpetuate recordings that they considered to be worthwhile, and they could use their status and resources to impose particular standards of value on the work of some African American musicians. In this sense, HRS served as a cultural gatekeeper as much as the record company that neglected to keep a certain recording in print. What the Society chose to copy and distribute would continue to be available, while music that did not meet their standards would succeed or founder according to the fortunes of the marketplace. Hammond praised both the little-known performers of blues, gospel, and jazz and bigger stars, such as Benny Goodman and Billie Holiday, with whom he had commercial interests as a producer.[46]

The Problem with Pop

Copying records in relative obscurity, collectors and small bootleg labels could carry on without bothering anyone too much. But what happened when people copied and distributed popular music? The rise of radio in the 1920s sparked a number of disputes over how recorded music could be legitimately reproduced. Radio was, after all, another way of replicating sound, just like a piano roll or a home disc engraver. When Americans experimented with the medium as a means for broadcasting, no one was certain what kind of programming would dominate—the reading of news, the playing of phonograph records, the live performance of music, or something else. Some businesses even set up stations for the sole purpose of advertising their own products and services.[47] Meanwhile, record companies, musicians, and songwriters could not decide whether the new radio stations would benefit them as a means of promoting their goods and services, or merely profit from the use of their works. As record sales plummeted during the Great Depression and competition with free music on the radio increased, the question became especially acute.

Music publishers were the quickest to take action, ever mindful of those who would exploit their written music for free. Victor Herbert joined with other artists to form the American Society of Composers, Authors, and Publishers (ASCAP) in 1914, aiming to regulate the use of musical compositions in places like stores and restaurants. In the 1917 case *Herbert v. Shanley,* the Supreme Court ruled that composers were entitled to remuneration from commercial establishments that played recordings of their compositions to entertain and entreat customers. The precedent permitted ASCAP to demand that any station airing songs written by its members had to pay for licenses, just like commercial establishments such as stores or restaurants where music was played.[48]

Some smaller stations ignored the demands, but most eventually acquiesced. The majority of airtime in the early days of broadcasting was given over to live performers rather than recordings, an arrangement that pleased many parties; before the invention of electrical recording improved the sound quality of pho-nographs in the late 1920s, records sounded significantly worse on the air than live performances. Concerts provided a more abundant, fluid supply of music than discs, which typically contained, at most, four minutes of music on each side, could offer. Stations and hotels collaborated to turn performances into major events, drawing listeners both at home and in person.[49] And, finally, per-forming live on the air provided musicians a potentially lucrative opportunity to play regularly and gain an audience. For many performers in the 1920s and 1930s, phonograph sales and radio performance were two separate streams of income.[50]

It remained for a 1940 ruling to address the unclear status of sound recordings on the air. Common law had long provided creators with a de facto copyright for their unpublished works that protected them from appropriation prior to their release to the public. Only published works could be formally registered for fed-eral copyright protection. The definition of "publication," though, was unclear. Recording a performance and pressing it as a record for sale to the public would seem to constitute publication, just as much as printing and selling a novel in the marketplace. But was a radio broadcast of a performance a publication of it? Did the artist forgo his "common law copyright"—his right of ownership for works that had not yet been distributed to the public—when a disc was pressed or a performance was broadcast? These questions emerged with the large-scale dissemination of sound through the new medium of radio, and neither the juris-prudence of music nor the legal negotiations of the songwriters through ASCAP addressed the curious status of sound.[51]

The bandleader Paul Whiteman won riches and fame by domesticating jazz for white audiences, and his opposition to having his records played on the air raised important questions about who owned recorded sound and how it could be reproduced. Some record manufacturers had for years marked discs with labels like "Not licensed for Radio Broadcast" or "Licensed…only for Non-Commercial Use on Phonographs in Homes."[52] They believed that the consumer who purchased a product with these provisos attached was bound by a license to use the record accordingly. Like record piracy, though, radio could make a recorded performance available to the public without the per-mission of the original artist or production company. Around 1937, WBO Broadcasting purchased several RCA recordings of Whiteman's orchestra, and subsequently aired them on the New York station WNEW, despite the fact that the record's label declared, "Only For Non-Commercial Use on Phonographs in Homes. Mr. & Original Purchaser Have Agreed This Record Shall Not Be

Resold Or Used For Any Other Purpose."[53] Whiteman had recorded for RCA under several contracts; for some of the recordings, the bandleader had signed all his rights over to the record company, but a later contract stipulated that he reserved the right to determine whether his performances would be broadcast.[54] RCA and Whiteman sued WBO in 1939, alleging that by reproducing the works on the radio without permission, the broadcaster had violated their property rights in the recordings.

Did either a record company or a performer have any right to control how others used a sound recording in the absence of federal copyright protection for such a work? The District Court for the Southern District of New York ruled in 1939 that even though Whiteman had signed over whatever rights he might have to the recording company, he and RCA were still entitled to enjoin the broadcasts on the grounds of unfair competition. "It is evident," Justice Vincent Leibell stated, "that the complainant and the broadcasting stations using complainant's records are competitors in the business of public entertainment."[55] In other words, the radio broadcast of the record competed with RCA's sale of the disc as well as Whiteman's efforts as a recording artist and live performer.

Everyone had a reason to dispute the decision. WBO Broadcasting did not believe that it was unfairly competing with either the record company or Whiteman by broadcasting the records. The ruling undermined RCA's claim of ownership of the recording, because the court concluded that the record label had not made any creative contribution to the work. "The well-known manufacturers of phonograph records use the same apparatus and methods," Leibell wrote. "The average person could not tell by listening to the finished record which company made the record or which musical director supervised its recording or who manipulated the dials, arranged the microphones or handled the other mechanical devices used in getting the physical recording."[56] And Whiteman was not satisfied, because the court decided that he did not own his performance— even if the radio station's use of the record amounted to unfair competition with his own products and services.[57] In other words, the district court ruling held that the broadcaster was freeloading on Whiteman and RCA's work, without recognizing any property right for the producers of the recording.

All the plaintiffs and defendants appealed to the US Court of Appeals for the Second Circuit, where Justice Learned Hand rejected the ideas of unfair competition *and* property rights in recorded sound. If the record was, in the constitutional sense, a "writing" that could be protected by copyright, but Congress had consciously chosen *not* to include it in the law, Hand did not believe it was his place to create a new right of ownership.[58] Hand observed that cases like *Whiteman* tended to inch the scope of property rights outward, and he drew near to the term "intellectual property" long before it became commonplace: "This right has at times been stated as though it extended to all productions demanding 'intellectual' effort."[59] All workers who were involved in the making of a record had a stake in the case, Hand said; yet he cast doubt on the notion, which would become more accepted in later years, that the technical production of the recording itself deserved protection by the state. "For the purposes of this case we shall assume that it covers the performances of an orchestra conductor," Hand wrote, "and—what is far more doubtful— the skill and art by which a phonographic record maker makes possible the proper recording of those performances upon a disc."[60] Both the conductor and the technician on a phonograph recording contributed in some way to the creation of a distinctive work:

> It is only in comparatively recent times that a virtuoso, conductor, actor, lecturer, or preacher could have any interest in the reproduction of his performance. Until the phonographic record made possible the preservation and reproduction of sound, all audible renditions were of necessity fugitive and transitory; once uttered they died; the nearest approach to their reproduction was mimicry. Of late, however, the power to reproduce the exact quality and sequence of sounds had become possible, and the right to do so, exceedingly valuable; people easily distinguish, or think they distinguish, the rendition of the same score or the same text by their favorites, and they will pay large sums to hear them.[61]

As Hand recognized, the recording of a performance was an invention apart from the composition upon which it was based. There were things about a particular performance that listeners loved and would pay good money to hear. But lacking the guidance of Congress, he asked, how could the court parse the qualities that a record producer, a singer, or a session musician gave to a recording? The judgment was too subjective and political for a court to make.

RCA based its argument partly on the *INS* precedent, but the court did not agree that playing the records on the radio was the same as one news organization copying the "hot" stories that another went to the trouble of collecting. Indeed, Hand refused to turn that ruling into a general rule, insisting that it only applied to the specific situation of publishing news in a national market. "That much discussed decision really held no more than that a western newspaper might not take advantage of the fact that it was published some hours later than papers in the east, to copy the news which the plaintiff had collected at its own expense," Hand wrote. "In spite of some general language it must be confined to that situation; certainly it cannot be used as a cover to prevent competitors from ever appropriating the results of the industry, skill, and expense of others."[62] Ideas, he argued, were the basis of all creative effort and their use could not be overly restricted because one person complains that his products were used in an unintended way. In any case, the court ruled that extending protection was always a matter of "more or less," which was best measured by Congress—and the courts should err on the side of less restriction, rather than more, in cases that Congress had not addressed.

Justice Hand had earned a reputation as a partisan of free speech and was suspicious of monopolies, which is how he described copyright in the *Whiteman* case. "Copyright in any form, whether statutory or at common-law, is a monopoly," Hand wrote. "It consists only in the power to prevent others from reproducing the copyrighted work. W.B.O. Broadcasting Corporation has never invaded any such right of Whiteman; they have never copied his performances at all; they have merely used those copies which he and the RCA Manufacturing Company, Inc., made and distributed."[63] In a popular speech he delivered at a Central Park rally in 1944, Hand suggested that "liberty is the spirit that is not too sure that it is right," and copyright is one such issue where he was reluctant to afford too much certainty to the claims of those who produce and own intellectual works.[64]

Other courts, however, continued to encounter difficulty in marking out exactly the "more or less" of state protection. Some affirmed Hand's skepticism about rights to intellectual property while others aimed to protect creators from "offensive" business practices. In the latter group, *Metropolitan Opera v. Wagner-Nichols* (1950) broke with *Whiteman* by ruling that courts should prohibit commercial behavior that seemed plainly unfair to prevailing sensibilities.[65] The New York Supreme Court appealed to a "broader principle that property rights of commercial value are to be and will be protected from any form of commercial immorality."[66]

Again, broadcasting provided the occasion for a dispute. The defendants' bad behavior consisted of recording and selling copies of radio broadcasts by the Metropolitan Opera, when that organization had already signed a contract with Columbia Records to market recordings of the Met's music. American Broadcasting joined Columbia and Metropolitan as a plaintiff in the case because the Opera had also signed an exclusive agreement with the broadcaster to transmit the performances over radio. The Met argued that Wagner-Nichols had reduced both the value of its contracts and its ability to secure similar agreements in the future; in this case, the contract issue carried a greater weight than in *Whiteman*. In the earlier case, Judge Hand ruled that although the records carried a label forbidding any use other than home listening, this restriction did not bind the purchaser to abide by it. Wagner-Nichols, however, had interfered in the contractual arrangements between the Met and those who distributed its works, and these agreements had a clear monetary value to the Opera. The defendants also took advantage of the Metropolitan Opera's sixty years of "extremely expensive" investment in developing a musical outfit with an unparalleled reputation.[67]

For the New York Supreme Court, these injuries outweighed claims by the defendant that their conduct did not meet the traditional definition of unfair competition. Defense lawyers argued that Wagner-Nichols did not "palm off" their products, since Wagner-Nichols did not try to deceive the public into believing that their records were identical to any released by Metropolitan or Columbia. Indeed, the particular performances sold by the defendants were not the same ones Columbia recorded and released. Moreover, the defendants pointed out that they did not infringe on any federally recognized property right, since the Met did not claim any rights to the compositions performed and Congress had not extended copyright to performances or recordings of them.[68]

The court found these arguments unpersuasive. The fact that Columbia did sell recordings of the Opera meant that people still might mistake Wagner-Nichols's discs for the products Columbia had legitimately produced. More important, the court considered the activity wrong even if the charge of palming-off was unclear. "With the passage of those simple and halcyon days when the chief business malpractice was 'palming off' and with the development of more complex business relationships and, unfortunately, malpractices, many courts, including the courts of this State, extended the doctrine of unfair competition beyond the cases of 'palming off,'" Justice Greenberg concluded. Even without deceiving the public, a business could unfairly exploit the "commercial advantage" that rightfully belonged to someone else.[69]

Greenberg's argument goes to the root of unfair competition, as well as to the role the doctrine would play in the recording industry. As a matter of common law, the idea of unfair competition grew out of trademark disputes in the nineteenth century, in which one business would sue another for using its name, thus exploiting the "good will" that consumers already felt toward the more established company.[70] For example, imagine that Smitty's Breadsticks had shown the public over fifteen years that it sells quality breadsticks with a smile, and also spent money on ads to familiarize people with its good name. Another merchant that uses the name Smitty's to sell breadsticks would unfairly benefit from the positive feelings that the original Smitty had earned (or acquired, through advertising) for his own business. A pirate could impinge upon and even adversely affect the reputation that a recording artist had developed over time, whether or not the pirate explicitly tried to "palm off" its product as identical to any item released by the artist. In this sense, rulings on piracy protected the right of an artist or company to benefit from the good will they had generated among the public—and this notion of good will could easily apply to the popularity enjoyed by a heavily promoted recording artist, in the sense that the pirate would unfairly exploit the time and energy invested in making a recording popular.[71]

Like *INS* and *Fonotipia*, the *Metropolitan* case dealt with the difficulties of regulating the production of cultural goods—whether a newspaper or an opera recording—as industries grew increasingly complex. The dispute in *Metropolitan* entangled musicians, lawyers, radio stations, and record labels in a web of contracts that held value for all involved, as the products and services some offered potentially conflicted with those of others. The question was not so simple as a composer or novelist creating a work and publishing it. Various phases of performing, broadcasting, recording, and retailing were involved in the business of classical music. "The courts have thus recognized that in the complex pattern of modern business relationships, persons in theoretically noncompetitive fields may, by unethical business practices, inflict as severe and reprehensible injuries upon others as can direct competitors," the ruling said.[72] In this complicated case, the finer details of palming off and property rights did not matter where business practices had a distinct whiff of unfairness. The New York Supreme Court's ruling in *Metropolitan* is reminiscent of Justice Potter Stewart's oft-quoted comment on pornography: it may be hard to define what unfair competition is, but a court will know it when it sees it.[73]

The Surge of Bootlegging after World War II

"Now there is a babel of labels," Frederic Ramsey Jr. wrote in the popular periodical *Saturday Review* in 1950. A wave of new entrepreneurs had succeeded Ramsey and his friends in the Hot Record Society, catering to collectors by reissuing the scarce recordings of early jazz. Labels such as Biltmore, Jazz-time, and Jay were based in post-office boxes. A former baker in the Bronx had started turning out copies of jazz classics through a variety of labels, such as Anchor, Blue Ace, and Wax, in order to confuse any labels or lawyers who came sniffing down his trail. So many labels had popped up to meet demand for the old records that some were copying the products of other pirates. Their evasive tactics indicate that, unlike Hot Record Society, these businesses did not operate with the sanction of the record companies that owned the original masters. Still, Ramsey argued that the bootleggers prospered under a policy of benign neglect. One New York pirate showed him a letter from the Copyright Office which stated that recordings were not protected by law. "That means that anyone can dub a recording and sell pressings," the man insisted. In any case, Ramsey felt that the majors were not paying attention. Why, he asked, did the mainstream music industry let bootleggers have the reissue market? "Ah, it wasn't worth the trouble to put out that moldy stuff," one executive told him. "It never sold anyway."[74]

When sales of the moldy oldies got too high, though, the major labels saw an interest in testing their rights in court. "Guys were afraid of the big companies,

Figure 2.2 A collection of recordings by Benny Goodman repackaged in LP form and released by the Jolly Roger label, circa 1950. *Source*: Courtesy of Music Library and Sound Recordings Archive, Bowling Green State University.

and the big companies were afraid of each other," one pirate explained. "But now, they're getting bolder. They found out there's sort of a feeling with big record company brass that it's O.K. for a little fellow to dub and sell if his sales just don't get too good"—a ceiling of about 1,000 records, in his estimation.[75] Sales did indeed look good in 1950. The successful rollout of the vinyl LP record by Columbia two years earlier offered listeners a more durable medium with a longer potential running time than traditional 78 RPM (revolutions per minute) records, but it also meant that many recordings would not be rereleased in the new format.[76] Pirates stood ready to fill any gap that resulted. The bootleg boom received more sympathetic coverage in the *Saturday Review* than in the jazz journal *Down Beat*, which condemned the copiers as "dirty thieves." Fellow Hot Record Society alum Wilder Hobson followed up on Ramsey's piece a year later, observing that "the recording seas are now full of piracy."[77] By then, the three main companies—Columbia, Decca, and RCA Victor—had begun their own series of reissues to co-opt the collectors' market.[78]

Interest in the origins of jazz had attained new heights by the early 1950s. Alan Lomax's effort to document folk, blues, and jazz had led to the 1950 publication of the oral history *Mister Jelly Roll*, in which Morton recounted the heterogeneous array of musicians and styles that had developed in fin de siècle New Orleans. (The memoir was also Jelly Roll's bid for a starring role in the origin story.) Working at the Library of Congress, Lomax had tried to prevent the work of Morton and his contemporaries from vanishing, and others assisted in this task by illicitly copying the recordings. "I am informed that every known commercial record cut can be purchased—if not on original labels, at least as unauthorized reissues," Lomax wrote. "Jazz, even in its antiquarian phase, operates

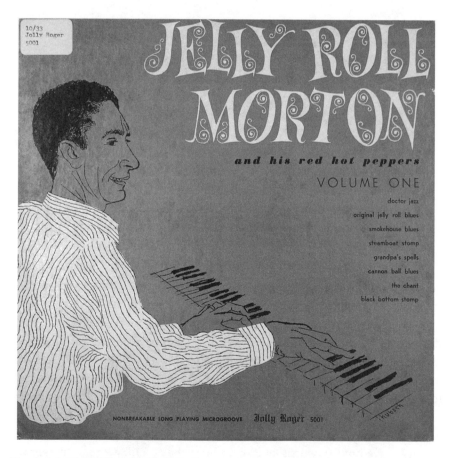

Figure 2.3 This collection of Jelly Roll Morton recordings captures the spare visual flair of many Pax and Jolly Roger recordings, though, unlike Pax records, this Jolly Roger LP featured no liner notes on the back of the jacket. *Source*: Courtesy of Music Library and Sound Recordings Archive, Bowling Green State University.

a bit beyond the pale."[79] The popularity of *Mister Jelly Roll*, which influenced the later oral histories of Studs Terkel and Theodore Rosengarten, attests to the surging interest in "antiquarian" jazz at this time.

After World War II, illicit bootleggers jumped into the niche for out-of-print music that the likes of Milt Gabler and the Hot Record Society had opened up. As Ramsey observed, listeners had "for the past fifteen years...been thirsting to hear certain rare records by the great maestros of jazz." During the war, when supplies of shellac were limited, the music industry could not afford to waste resources on marginal, niche records, making the prospects for historically significant reissues dim. Even when the limitations of war ceased, major labels chose only to resurrect a handful of older recordings as "prestige items," failing to satisfy the demands of collectors and antiquarians. "It is assumed that such items will both pay their own way and have promotional value for the entire list," Charles Edward Smith observed in 1952. "The suggestion that the major record companies accept a position of custodianship for recorded hot jazz performances must be regarded as unrealistic. Unless it were presented as something more than a gratuitous notion, it would quite likely meet with tolerant smiles from those who stand to profit more from the exploitation of a current crooner than the rediscovery of a Bessie Smith."[80] As a result, bootleggers stepped in to meet a demand that had once been met by licensed reproducers like Hot Record Society.

As bootlegging spread in the late 1940s, a court case tested the limits of property rights for recorded sound, resulting in a decision that left the door open to piracy. A ruling by the US District Court for Northern Illinois, *Shapiro, Bernstein v. Miracle Records* (1950) dealt with the ownership of a particular interpretation of a musical idea, as embodied in a record.[81] While working as a groundskeeper at Chicago's White Sox stadium, pianist Jimmy Yancey helped develop boogie woogie, a genre of jazz that focused more fully on the piano than did any other form. He taught the style to Meade Lux Lewis, who wrote and recorded the tune "Yancey Special" in his fellow pianist's honor. When Lewis later sued another company for allegedly copying "Yancey Special," Yancey himself came forward and insisted that the composition did not originate with Lewis anyway, thus rendering his infringement claim meaningless. Justice Michael Igoe, in turn, ruled that all these claims were irrelevant, since the similarity between the compositions was simply too basic to warrant copyright protection. The only thing the recordings have in common, he wrote, is "a mechanical application of a simple harmonious chord."[82]

In other words, the distinctive rhythm of "Yancey Special" was not a copyrightable expression. "The purpose of copyright law is to protect creation," Justice Igoe wrote, "not mechanical skill," which is all the innovations of boogie woogie amounted to in the eyes of the court.[83] If anything, what was copied was not a song, but a new genre or style of performance. Justice Learned Hand had ruled similarly in 1940, when his decision in the case *RCA v. Whiteman* held that the US Copyright Act did not allow for individual recorded performances to be owned. Although Hand had conceded that a recording might contain some elements of genuine creativity, the law simply did not provide copyright for various interpretations of the same composition. In Igoe's view, Yancey and Lewis were merely arguing over different ways of playing a tune, not a copyrightable expression.[84]

As Bill Russell observed in one of the earliest studies of the new genre, many critics alleged that "the Boogie Woogie has no melody." Yet melody was the solid core of written music, as traditionally protected by copyright. If the *Miracle* opinion held, there would be nothing copyrightable about the frenetic improvisation that made up a recording by boogie artists Pine Top Smith or Cripple Clarence Lofton. The rapid-fire piano pieces danced around a theme, consisting "of simple and logical yet satisfying patterns of notes in a limited range, usually proceeding conjunctly," in Russell's words. "Often in the more elaborate melodic texture there is incessant arabesque and figuration based on the essential notes of the melody."[85] Igoe's ruling would seem to rule out protection not just for "Yancey Special" and its imitators but also for a whole species of jazz whose originality derived from nimble involutions of a tune that sounded only like "mechanical skill" to the judge's ears. US copyright only protected written compositions, and neither Lewis nor Yancey could claim to own the unique style that characterized their recordings. The decision showed how existing copyright law failed to address elements of distinctiveness and value that could be found only in a recorded performance, such as the improvisation that distinguished Yancey's

Figure 2.4 The December 1951 issue of *Record Changer* lampoons RCA Victor's unwitting involvement in bootlegging by showing the iconic dog Nipper walking the plank. *Source*: Courtesy of the Brad McCuen Collection, Center for Popular Music, Middle Tennessee State University. Reprinted by permission of Richard Hadlock.

work. The Yancey case also prompted a wave of anxiety in the recording industry about whether their products would be copied by other firms. Since the decision came from a district court in Chicago, *Variety* suggested that it spawned a bootlegging boom in the Midwest.[86]

Fears of a fresh wave of bootlegging were realized in 1951 when a major label was caught pirating its own records. "RCA *Victor*, sworn enemy of disc piracy, is currently engaged in pressing illicit *Victor* and *Columbia* LPs for one of the most blatant of the bootleggers!" howled the *Record Changer*, a jazz collectors' magazine, on the cover of its November 1951 issue. RCA ran a custom pressing service that manufactured small batches of records for labels that were too small to have their own facilities. One such outfit was Jolly Roger, which had contracted with RCA during the summer of 1951 to press hundreds of records at a cost of 65 cents a piece.[87] "Without exception, this material consisted of master acetates made from old *Victor* and *Columbia* sides strung together to form long-playing records," *Record Changer* observed.[88] Jolly Roger compiled unique LPs of recordings that the likes of Sidney Bechet and Jelly Roll Morton had made for Victor, as well as some tunes from the Columbia catalog. The outfit also had RCA press records of Louis Armstrong, who remained, unlike Morton and Bechet, one of the biggest stars of contemporary jazz. Anyone in the industry should have realized that he would not be recording for such an obscure label, *Record Changer* argued.[89]

The situation was particularly embarrassing because the record companies had just started making noise about piracy or "disk-legging." *Variety* reported that the Harry Fox Agency, representative of song publishers, had begun investigating bootleggers at the behest of the labels in August 1951. The entertainment industry rag reported that the records were being wholesaled in batches of 500 at 30 cents a piece.[90] The number of records accords with the accounts of other pirates, who spoke of a range of up to 1,000 copies. RCA had actually become one of the loudest critics of piracy in the months prior to the Jolly Roger revelation. The company announced in September that it would begin retaliating against pirates. "Up until recently, the bootleggers had more or less confined themselves to the jazz field, where they sold dubs of the out-of-print Victor collector items," *Variety* said. "In recent months, however, several bootleg firms have been distributing straight copies of current Victor hits under a variety of labels."[91] Little did the company's leaders realize that their own employees were helping the bootleggers raid the Victor catalog, using their own facilities. As the *Record Changer* deadpanned, "One high RCA spokesman had heatedly informed us that they would 'seek injunctions and damages, prosecute, throw into jail and put out of business' not only the operators of bootleg labels but also those processing and pressing plants that serve them (apparently considering the latter as guilty as the former)."[92]

The bootleggers' chutzpah had pushed their activities into the open. Dante Bollettino, a young jazz enthusiast, had run Jolly Roger's parent company, Paradox Industries, for three years prior to his run-in with the law in 1951. Prior to Jolly Roger, his Pax label had released elegant reissues of musicians such as Cripple Clarence Lofton, the Chicago boogie woogie pioneer who influenced the likes of Meade Lux Lewis and Jimmy Yancey.[93] The back covers of Pax records featured detailed liner notes by Bollettino and jazz writers such as George Hoefer, which described the historical significance of the music and, in many cases, told of when and where the performances were recorded.[94] The label, based in Union City, New Jersey, promised "Records for the connoisseur," compiling anthologies like *New Orleans Stylings* and *Americans Abroad: Jazztime in Paris*, which culled the best of lesser-known artists.[95]

Jolly Roger, in contrast, dared to go further. There was the swagger of the name, and the fact that Bollettino had marched right into enemy territory to have his records made. "They [RCA] apparently did not react at all when confronted with a label that every schoolboy would know meant, by definition, 'a pirate flag,'" marveled the editors of the *Record Changer*. "Record bootlegging is just as often referred to as record piracy...catch on, Victor?"[96] The label also reproduced fare that was not quite as obscure as Pax's. A Jolly Roger catalog from the early 1950s lists one Frank Sinatra, two Bessie Smiths, and seven different Louis Armstrong records.[97] While some of the performances were out-of-print, names like Armstrong and Sinatra were bound to raise some eyebrows eventually. Jolly Roger records featured the same style of starkly colorful and iconic covers as Pax records had, but they lacked the liner notes and other identifying features. Their back covers were blank.[98] Perhaps Bollettino realized that the Jolly Roger venture might elicit more attention and wanted to minimize his own mark on the records.

In any case, he had gone too far. Armstrong and Columbia sued Paradox in February 1952, and the story made headlines in *Business Week* and *Newsweek*. Seeking an injunction, the plaintiffs cited the *Metropolitan* decision of two years prior.[99] "This marked the record industry's first major reaction to the bootlegging problem," *Business Week* noted.[100] Facing the legal might of the music business, Bollettino decided to settle out of court. "My lawyer insisted that we had a good case and could win, but I knew the record companies would feel they couldn't afford to lose and would throw in everything they had," he reflected in 1970, sitting in a fabric shop he had opened in Greenwich Village. "I was only twenty-three and didn't have the money for a long expensive court case...But afterwards the big companies began to reissue more jazz records, so maybe I accomplished something after all."[101] For Bollettino, the bigger goal was to ensure that at least some of the music he copied would continue to be available to the public.

Perhaps Bollettino and his fellow pirates simply drew too much attention. They proved the viability of a market that the big record labels had left fallow and, in fact, relinquished to collectors for years. "Disk bootleggers, who have been coining considerable profit from their operation of selling dubs of cut-out jazz sides, are being rapidly squeezed out of business," *Variety* declared, as the major labels started their own reissue programs.[102] However, Bollettino shot back at the industry. "Columbia and the 'majors' have failed to make or keep jazz records available to the public," he told the press. "Their few reissue programs have started out with a big hullabaloo and fizzled out simply because it is not profitable to try to sell a few thousand copies of a record...Only a small firm with low overhead can profitably reissue such records."[103]

Though torn, the jazz writers echoed this criticism of the major labels, saying that the companies had failed to honor their responsibilities as custodians of culture. Some of the majors had tried reissues, but "usually it only served to emphasize the gap between 'their' standards and 'ours,'" the editors of *Record Changer* opined. "There is much more to jazz than Armstrong and Goodman and a scattering of sides by a few other people, although obviously you can come closer to breaking even or showing a profit with those names."[104] An obscure Bix Beiderbecke record was not worth the time and money of a promotional machine that was accustomed to manufacturing records en masse and hyping them nationwide. Regardless, *Record Changer*'s publisher Bill Grauer, the jazz writer John Hammond, and the bootlegger Sam Meltzer all claimed to have been rebuffed when they sought to reissue old recordings legally by obtaining licenses from the major labels. In doing so, these critics maintained, the companies denied the public a portion of its heritage. "It involves a moral and artistic burden that they automatically took on when they first decided to make their money in part by the commercial recording and distribution of material that 'belongs' (by virtue of its cultural significance) to the people as a whole," a *Record Changer* editorial argued.[105] Elsewhere, the editors wrote, "We are not so naïve as to believe that all, or even many, bootleggers are motivated solely, or even partly, by noble impulses." Still, their activities served the public when scarce music was preserved and perpetuated.[106]

Numerous bootleggers scrambled to get out of the business after the public demise of Jolly Roger, but piracy persisted. In some instances organized crime sought to take advantage of the ephemeral popularity of a hit single by dumping its own copies of 45s on the market. In 1960 Robert Arkin of the Bronx and Milton Richman of Queens were charged with copying Cameo singles of rock and roller Bobby Rydell's "Ding-A-ling" and "Wild One." Operating out of Fort Lee, New Jersey, their Bonus Platta-Pak company worked with an accomplice in Hollywood named Brad Atwood.[107] In October seven men were arrested in Los Angeles, including Atwood. "More than half the shelf stock in [Los Angeles]

'Bootleg' Recordings

Figure 2.5 Balt Yanez of the Los Angeles District Attorney's Office examines boxes of bootleg records confiscated in an elaborate sting against a pirate network that linked North Hollywood to Bergen County, New Jersey. *Source:* "Fake Record Ring Broken; 7 Men Held," *Los Angeles Times*, October 3, 1960, 2–3. Reprinted by permission of *Los Angeles Times*.

county of one particular recording were bogus reproductions," the *Los Angeles Times* reported. "Undercover agents wormed their way into the ring and were actually helping load records purchased by two other agents of the district attorney when yesterday's raids were made. [District Attorney] McKesson said the bootleggers were making their reproductions using facilities of legitimate record manufacturing firms at night and on weekends."[108]

More persistent were the small entrepreneurs who copied records that the major labels had no interest in reissuing. In the 1960s, many bootlegs entered the United States from abroad. Pirate Records of Sweden made available the likes of Barbecue Bob and Blind Lemon Jefferson, blues singers of the 1920s and 1930s. The label pressed records in batches of 100 and requested correspondence in English or French.[109] Swaggie, based in Melbourne, Australia, reprinted records from as far back as 1917, including well-known performers like Sidney Bechet and lesser-known acts from the 1920s, such as Tampa Red's Hokum Jug Band. The Swaggie catalog plainly listed which labels had originally released the material, and label head Nevill L. Sherburn wherever possible pursued licensing agreements with artists and record companies to reissue their work.[110] In 1966, the manager of Fats Waller's estate even asked Steve Sholes at RCA Victor if the label would work with Swaggie in releasing some lost recordings Waller had made while working for Victor:

> Can something be arranged for Swaggie on the V Discs made by Fats on that memorable session, when Old Granddad flowed fluently…as Fats would remark…and all concerned had a ball…. "Eat, drink and be merry, for tomorrow we die." That was Fats' motto thruout his short lifetime and that date on September 23, 1943…turned out to be "fini" at Victor. I sincerely hope that something can be arranged [to] get these records on the market, for they contain numbers from the musical "Early to Bed"…Fats' Broadway musical which was never recorded because of the musicians strike [111]

Ed Kirkeby's request did not find a sympathetic ear. The letter ended up in the files of RCA's Brad McCuen, who since 1964 had investigated labels such as Folkways for allegedly reissuing Victor's old blues, folk, and jazz records.[112] During his research, McCuen learned of the Jolly Roger incident and the surge of piracy in the early 1950s. Writing to Sholes, he compared the new wave of copiers to the Blue Aces and Jazz Panoramas of old. "There are now at least a dozen labels openly offering for sale our masters without permission," McCuen wrote. "Included are the labels Palm Club, Swaggie, OFC, Historic Jazz, Limited Editions, Pirate (Sweden), etc. I feel we should discuss making a stand against these illegal labels if for no other reason than to protect our Vintage futures."[113] McCuen's goal was to protect his employers' long-term corporate interest in securing exclusive control of their recordings, even if the company did not necessarily intend to produce and sell them. The prevalence of firms like Swaggie indicated that the desire for old records had not

Table 2.1 **RCA's List of Suspected Pirate Labels in the Mid-1960s**

Name	*Details*
1. Swaggie Records	Box 125, South Yarra, Melbourne Australia. Probable owner: Nevill L. Sherburn
2. RFW Records	Box 746, San Fernando, California 91340. Fats Waller
3. Palm Club Records	V-Discs, E.T.S
4. Testament Records	Library of Congress
5. RBF Records	Subsidiary of Folkways Records
6. Historical Jazz	Box 4204, Bergen Station, Jersey City, New Jersey 07304
7. Roy Morser	Box 225, Gracie Station, NYC 10028. Duplicators.
8. Pirate Records	Box 11063, Stockholm, 11, Sweden
9. Old Timey Records	Box 5073, Berkeley, California. Subsidiary of Arhoolie Records. Owner: Chris Strachwitz. Specialized in country & western
10. Blues Classics Records	Blues and jug bands
11. Origin Records	Blues
12. County Records	Country & western
13. Max Abrams	1108 Celis Street, San Fernando, California. Duplicator
14. OFC Records	Probably European import
15. Folkways Records	165 W. 46 Street, NY, NY 10036. Owner: Moe Asch. Jazz and folk.
16. Melodeon Records	Spottswood Music Company, 3323 14 Street N.E. Washington, DC, 20017. Owner: Richard Spottswood
17. FDC Records	Probably of European origin. Jazz
18. Jazz Panorama	
19. Jazz Society Records	Sold through John Norris, Box 87, Toronto 6, Ontario, Canada.

Source: "Labels," Brad McCuen Collection—Piracy 1969, 97-023, box 18, folder 9, MTSU-CPM.

slackened, as entrepreneurs moved to fulfill the demand formerly met by the likes of Hot Record Society and Jolly Roger.

The ultimate question remained: who should be the stewards of the ever-growing legacy of recorded music? Should the companies that originally recorded and marketed the music decide whether it would remain available to the public, beyond the worn-out relics hoarded by collectors? Should music lovers be able to keep copies of old recordings in circulation despite the industry's disinterest or active opposition? Given the up-front costs involved in recording, advertising, and distributing an original recording, large firms such as RCA Victor could maximize their profits by selling large numbers of a few popular releases, rather than offering the public a wide range of records that each sold fewer copies.[114] A reissue of an obscure Sidney Bechet side, catering to perhaps a few hundred avid collectors, seemed a waste of RCA's sales staff and productive capacity.

Since the means of production—record-pressing plants—remained concentrated in the hands of a few major labels in the 1950s, those firms could exercise a wide degree of discretion about what music was available to the public. The American music industry of the 1940s and early 1950s was highly consolidated in a few firms, who sought to vertically integrate production and to deter competitors from entering the market.[115] And as legal scholar James Boyle has stressed, the vast majority of works go out of print in a few years. In many cases the actual owner of the work is difficult to determine (so-called "orphan works"), and even when the owners can be identified, they hold the power to decide whether to reproduce it or license the rights. Given these conditions, collectors and bootleggers alike feared that countless items of recorded music would become scarce and inaccessible as they receded into the past.[116]

The Jolly Roger case shows that entrepreneurs who wanted to market recordings to smaller, niche markets had to turn to the custom-pressing services of companies like RCA to have their records made, drawing on the infrastructure of the major labels to copy records that those firms no longer had an interest in selling. The persistence of outfits such as Swaggie and Pirate Records suggests that the mainstream industry's efforts to satisfy the demand for such music, once they recognized it, with reissue programs failed to provide the full range of out-of-print recordings desired by fans and collectors. Confusion about the ownership of recorded music left unclear who should decide whether a record would remain in circulation, and the Jolly Roger flap marked the beginning of the industry's effort to protect a newly understood value in recorded sound from the encroachment of unauthorized reproduction—a campaign that would bear fruit with the provision of copyright for sound recordings in 1971. Until then, the labels sought to deter anyone from copying the records that they no longer wanted to sell, with the aim of keeping such music unavailable until the established firms saw fit to reissue it.

This struggle only occurred because bootlegging showed the labels that their back catalog might be worth something—that recorded music retained meaning and significance in which the public had an interest long after it stopped being worthwhile for companies to keep in circulation. Collectors insisted that there was something uniquely valuable about each record, each variation, which copyright law had treated as incidental to the essence of the work. It was collecting that led to bootlegging, and bootlegging that led to legal suppression and, eventually, to an expansion of copyright restrictions that would make collecting more difficult. The primacy of performance and interpretation in jazz helped prompt this reconsideration of copyright. Some elements of creativity could not be captured in musical notation—the characteristic playing of an instrument with its own timbre, for instance—although American copyright law did not recognize them until the early 1970s. The wave of successful anti-bootlegging litigation in the 1950s followed a spike in the popularity of jazz bootlegs that jolted the record companies into action. But the industry's victory over Jolly Roger was short-lived. In the 1950s and 1960s, new media such as magnetic tape made recording cheaper and easier than before, and lovers of opera and other less-than-profitable genres argued that their copying served a wholesome purpose by capturing and preserving music that would otherwise sink in the commercial marketplace. And in the late 1960s, not long after McCuen hunted the copiers of folk and jazz, bootleggers turned to rock and roll, provoking a bigger legal battle than seen in the skirmishes of the 1950s.

3

Piracy and the Rise of New Media

The corrupt police captain Hank Quinlan sat in the parlor of his old flame Tanya, after a drunken bender took him south of the Rio Grande. Bleary-eyed and exhausted, Quinlan was comforted by the tinny sound of an antique player piano. "The customers go for it," Tanya said. "It's so old, it's new." Outside, the Mexican official Miguel Vargas waited with a tape recorder, hoping to capture evidence of Quinlan's dishonesty that could clear the good name of Vargas's wife, who had been framed for murder. Throughout the climactic scenes of Orson Welles's 1958 film *Touch of Evil*, Vargas lurks in the shadows, following close behind the police chief and his erstwhile sidekick Menzies, who wears a wire. Meanwhile, the staccato ragtime of the player piano plods along in the background.[1]

The juxtaposition of an old medium—one of the earliest ways of mechanizing music—and the new technology of the magnetic tape recorder paralleled the difference between Vargas and Quinlan. The former was a young, progressive law enforcement official, while the latter was a bloated, racist "good old boy" who ruled the American side of the border as his own personal fiefdom. In due time, the old guard was done in by the cleverness and diligence of the new. *Touch of Evil* reflects the emergence of new media in the 1950s, a decade when the use of magnetic recording spread beyond the military and industry and into the consumer marketplace in the United States. The transformation of this long-dormant technology into a medium that was accessible to large numbers of people challenged property rights by enabling new ways of using sound that had not been known to the jazz copiers of the 1930s and 1940s.

In conjunction with radio and television, magnetic recording provided a practical way for enthusiasts to capture music free of charge. Jazz writer John Corbett fondly recalled the era of the 1940s, when enthusiasts had been forced to find other ways to document and exchange the sounds they heard all around them. "There was a cruder, and in some ways more beautiful technological precursor: the acetate," Corbett says. The acetate was a flimsy, temporary disc recording, often used in studios to make demos and by radio stations to record and play commercials, which typically had a short shelf life in any case. In a time when "canned" (i.e., prerecorded music) was disdained on the air, live performances filled the radio waves. These unique arrangements and interpretations vanished into nothing as soon as they appeared, unless one owned a costly and delicate disc cutter.[2]

The acetate was beautiful because it was ephemeral—radio stations and studios used the discs for a brief time and threw them away. Even if preserved, the record deteriorated after so many listens. Before magnetic tape became common in recording studios, the acetate disc provided a temporary document of a session without committing to the costlier process of making a permanent master

Figure 3.1 "Never Available Heretofore!" Boris Rose declares on the top of this release from Jung Cat Records, one of the many labels Rose used to publish collections of broadcast recordings by Bud Powell, Miles Davis, and many other artists. No copyright notice, date, or address appears on the record, but the fine print exhibits typical Rosean humor: "A good musical record from Duck Run, Ohio." *Source:* Reprinted by permission of Elaine Rose.

recording.[3] Erasable and far less delicate, magnetic tape would soon supplant discs as the medium for basic studio recording, even though the sounds were subsequently transferred onto a vinyl LP, a new format in the late 1940s, for use by the general public.

Boris Rose, a compulsive collector and sound engineer from the Bronx, bridged the age of the Hot Record Society, the disc cutter, and the acetate and that of newer media such as LPs and cassettes. Rose recorded performances from the radio, making homemade acetates and LPs available to fans of jazz, classical, country, and countless other genres for decades. Each featured a unique cover, designed and Xeroxed by Rose himself. "We should thank goodness that someone was documenting these broadcasts," Corbett writes, "or they might have been lost forever."[4]

Rose's vast catalog contained virtually every genre of music from every contemporary outlet—concerts, radio, records, television so much that one pictures him sitting by the radio all day, every day, with his finger near the little red button on a reel-to-reel tape recorder. Subsisting on the rental income from a property he owned at Second Avenue and Tenth Street in Manhattan, Rose provided records on demand and at cost to anyone who found out about him; he was also an archivist, tirelessly documenting the past and present.[5] Although he mostly worked alone and hid behind dozens of pseudonyms, he was not, in fact, alone. Many others joined him in copying music in the 1950s and 1960s, as wartime uses revived the old technology of magnetic recording and consumer spending sped the development of the electronics industry.

The Long Rise of Magnetic Recording

For a new technology to gain popular acceptance, there first must be some organized interest that will invest enough capital to put the idea into practice and market it to consumers. Whether a corporation, government, university or some other combination of forces champions an idea, someone must pool resources and put them into action. It is never enough for one person to have a foggy notion of what a new invention might do and how it might work. The past is full of the forgotten names of men and women who had conceived of devices like the telegraph or telephone, but who never told anyone, or lacked the technical skills to develop the idea, or simply could not find a sympathetic ear to hear them out.[6]

Historians of technology call the development of an initial thought into a workable concept "ideation."[7] One might imagine that sound patterns could be etched on a surface and then replayed by tracing over the pattern, but before someone with technical ingenuity demonstrates how the sound could actually be recorded on wax or tinfoil, the idea comes to naught. In fact, French inventor Édouard-Léon Scott de Martinville developed a technique for engraving sound vibrations on paper in 1857, yet these "recordings" were only played back when researchers devised a way to translate the etchings into sound in 2008.[8]

Often ideation is also inadequate. Historian Brian Winston emphasizes the importance of a "supervening necessity," a social need that could be fulfilled through a technology that motivates those with influence, talent, or wealth to help perfect a design and bring a new device to the public.[9] The case of Oberlin Smith reveals how ideation itself is not enough for new technologies to succeed. An engineer in New Jersey, Smith first set out the ideas for magnetic recording in an 1888 article for *The Electrical World* magazine. Smith suggested that an electric current, when piped through a telephone circuit, would alter the magnetic arrangement of iron filings on a cotton thread. The thread would retain the pattern of the current, which could reproduce the sound when retraced.[10] However, Smith admitted that he lacked the time and the resources, such as a real laboratory, to test out his conjectures. Instead, he donated the ideas to the public, "hoping that some of the numerous experimenters now working in this field may find a germ of good from which something useful may grow."[11] He expected to get credit if someone else worked out the details, and concluded that knowledge would be advanced even if his ideas were conclusively disproven.

Subsequently, Valdemar Poulsen, an electrical engineering student at the University of Copenhagen, proposed his own model for magnetically recording on wire as a class project in 1893.[12] Only sixteen years had passed since Edison's laboratories pioneered sound recording on tinfoil, and the recording industry was still in its infancy. Magnetic wire could have become an important medium for sound. However, Poulsen's American Telegraphone Company ran through its capital before developing a marketable product, while the emerging major players of the record industry, such as Victor and Columbia, were already tied up in patent wars over cylinders and disks. Historian William Lafferty suspects that the telephone and phonograph industries may have colluded to snuff out Poulsen's new medium. The wire had its own shortcomings as well, since the device was prone to tangling and the sound it produced was too faint in the days before amplification.[13]

With the development of radio and the sound film in the 1920s, magnetic recording once again appeared as an alternative to other sound technologies. Poulsen's patents lapsed and advances in amplification made it possible for innovators to use magnetic wire in a variety of ways. The German engineer Curt Stille, for instance, pioneered uses of wire for railroads, the telephone industry, and office dictation.[14] Unfortunately for Stille, the ballooning inflation of 1920s Germany made it less expensive to hire stenographers than to invest in new technology. He joined with Ludwig Blattner in 1928 to develop the Blattnerphone, a magnetic tape machine that could provide the soundtrack for film screenings, but the big firms of the German film industry muscled the pair out of the business.[15] Prefiguring the breakthrough of magnetic recording in the United States, the Blattnerphone did enjoy a second life in the hands of the British Broadcasting Corporation. The BBC recognized the value of a medium that was reusable and durable, since the same tape could be used over and over to rebroadcast a previously aired program, record rehearsals, and capture important speeches for later replay.[16]

As in 1920s Germany, the resistance of established interests in the United States stymied innovation in magnetic recording. Numerous firms had approached AT&T, the telephone monopoly, with ideas for answering machines and similar recording devices that would attach to the existing phone system. The company rebuffed all such offers, but by 1930 was instructing researchers at Bell Labs to study inventions such as the Blattnerphone and Stille's Dailygraph wire recorder. Led by Clarence Hickman, engineers did indeed devise practical means of recording and playing back sound over the telephone lines, but, as Mark Clark has shown, the corporate leaders of AT&T made sure that magnetic recorders were used only within the organization. According to Clark, the company believed that people's fear that conversations could be recorded would lead them to use the phone system less, undermining AT&T president Theodore Vail's vision of "universal service."[17] In the 1928 decision *Olmstead v. United States*, the Supreme Court had ruled that federal investigators could collect evidence on (alcohol) bootleggers through wiretapping, which stoked public anxieties that anyone could be listening in on their calls.[18] Meanwhile, AT&T executives guessed that one-third of all phone conversations concerned illegal or immoral topics.[19]

One wonders what the executives were talking about on the phone, given their suspicious view of other telephone users. AT&T itself had an image problem in the 1930s and did not want to risk adding any more sinister tones to its perception by the public.[20] Since radio broadcasting in the United States was dominated by live performance, and AT&T viewed magnetic recording as a threat to its central control of the phone system, there was little prospect that the working models of magnetic recording would be widely adopted. Its introduction as a phonograph medium was also unlikely, because the Depression reduced demand for disc records, and listeners had turned to free entertainment on the radio.[21]

German companies pursued magnetic recording in the 1930s at the same time AT&T was withholding it. As the engineer Semi J. Begun observed, the Nazis were keen to buy up all the recording equipment they could, which the Gestapo could put to its own nefarious uses.[22] Begun himself had fled Germany in the 1930s, and subsequently worked on military contracts for recording equipment through the Brush Development Company. What had been for the BBC an easy way to reuse previously aired programs became for the Nazis a tool for repeating political messages over and over again on the airwaves.[23] However, the historian Hillel Schwartz likens the use of magnetic recording by Hitler's totalitarian regime to the simultaneous embrace of new means of photochemical copying by Franklin Roosevelt's New Deal and Britain's Conservative governments; in each case, states relied on new technologies to transmit and manage the vast amount of information generated by the expanding scope of government activity in the 1930s.[24]

In this sense, AT&T's use of magnetic recording as an office tool internally is as significant as its suppression of the technology as a consumer good. Already, the way was being paved for wider use, given the right social and political impetus: the medium would soon be used by offices, factories, snooping governments, and eventually by consumers after World War II.[25] In 1953, the *Los Angeles Times* described a number of applications that were popping up in the workplace, such as "a new superelectronic machine using magnetic tapes … designed to cut sharp corners in solving complicated problems" and "a phonoaudograph that ties one recording machine in with a number of phones." Businessmen began to use sound recording for dictation and other conveniences, as originally envisioned by Edison.[26]

World War II sped up the development process in two ways. First, the avalanche of wartime spending fell on companies exploring sound recording as much as it did on aerospace, computing, and other fields. Begun believed that progress in magnetic recording went further and faster during the war years than in all the time before. Magnetic wire was compact and resistant to heat and vibration, qualities that proved useful on the battlefield, as did the possibility of re-recording on the same medium multiple times. "Hardly any attention on the part of the operator is required during the recording process," Begun noted, which meant that soldiers and pilots with little technical training could use the tool without being distracted from other tasks. One such device, mass-produced by General Electric and the Armour Research Company for the Army and Navy, could record sixty-six minutes on a spool the size of a doughnut. "Instead of the customary pad and pencil now used by pilots in making note of what they see on scouting trips, they can dictate into a small microphone just as the busy office executive now uses a dictaphone," scientist R. H. Opperman reported in 1944, noting that the wire was highly durable and held up over thousands of uses.[27]

The war's other major contribution came at the end, when Americans learned that German recording technology had progressed further than previously understood. The US military discovered the Magnetophon, a reel-to-reel tape recorder developed by German engineers in the 1930s, toward the end of the war, and Americans were soon experimenting with the device back home. The technology rose to prominence by capturing the attention of Bing Crosby, who was eager to record his East Coast radio performances on magnetic tape and rebroadcast them later the same evening on the West Coast. Weary of performing twice every night, the singer left radio in 1944, after NBC refused to let him prerecord his show. In 1946, ABC got Crosby to return with the promise of recording on acetate discs, but the sound quality was too poor. When Crosby learned of the Magnetophon in 1947, he assembled a team of engineers to work on improving the technology; when their efforts fell short, he ponied up crucial funds to the Ampex Corporation, which allowed the company to expand its operation and produce a viable tape recorder by 1948. Crosby was the biggest star on the roster of record label Decca, which soon began using Ampex tape for its master recordings.[28]

Even before broadcasters adopted magnetic recording, the technology had made limited inroads with the listening public. The Brush Development Company had debuted its Soundmirror, a reel-to-reel recorder that used steel tape, at the World's Fair in 1939. By the next year, professors at Hunter College in New York City were using the device to help students correct speech impediments.[29] After the war, Brush marketed the Soundmirror to consumers as a way to capture "your favorite radio programs, records, children's voices, two-way telephone conversations." In 1947, the New York department store Schirmer's guaranteed that its "radio-television service department can show you better than anyone else how to operate Soundmirror in your home...how to hook it up to your own radio or phonograph...and how to install such accessories as the Telechron clock which enables you to record your favorite program while you are away from home."[30] A year later, Magnetic Recorders Company, a retailer in Los Angeles, urged consumers to "keep forever great moments of radio [and] record your own parties, speeches, conferences," using a Soundmirror with a built-in radio.[31]

Why did consumers begin showing interest in home recording in the 1940s? Recordable media were common in the early days of the music industry. The first phonograph was the wax cylinder, which could be recorded on, yet the cylinder rapidly lost ground to disc recording. (Two cylinders were sold for every one disc in 1909, but by 1914 the ratio had flipped to one cylinder for every nine discs.)[32] Henceforth, only a select few listeners had access to technology that could inscribe sound, which remained largely confined to the studios and pressing plants of record companies. Why, then, were people not interested in home recording in the early twentieth century? David Morton, a historian of sound recording, thinks the answer is simple: "Americans disliked standing before the recording machine and hated the sounds of their own recorded voices even more."[33] Of course, other factors likely contributed to the dominance of playback-only records as well. Emile Berliner's flat disc was more durable, clearer, and perhaps more convenient to store. The disc was also a permanent record—once recorded on, whether in a home or studio, it could not be erased and reused, unlike the later forms of magnetic tape and wire. For an amateur using a disk engraver, making a permanent record of false starts and flubs could be unappealing.

Cultural and economic conditions were also more auspicious in the 1950s than in the 1890s or 1930s, when manufacturers had previously introduced amateur recording systems with little success. The availability of radio and television provided fodder for home recording, beyond dictation at the office or performance in the home, as the Soundmirror's marketing suggests. In the 1890s and 1900s, people could document their own performances, and some even invited friends to bring their instruments over so each could make her own recording. At the time, the only other option would have been to lug the fragile equipment into a concert hall.[34] Companies such as RCA struggled to market home disk-recording machines in the 1930s. The difficult operation of such machines appealed to a small group of music enthusiasts and collectors, such as the members of the Hot Record Society, but for most Americans years of personal experience ingrained an understanding of discs as containers of prerecorded sounds. In his study of the early development of sound recording, Jonathan Sterne argues that the shift from wax cylinders to discs resulted from changes in middle-class leisure and family life. In the Victorian era of the late nineteenth century, the cylinder provided a way for families to entertain guests, listening to home recordings in much the same way a family might share a photo album or home movie with friends. The phonograph industry focused on selling prerecorded sounds rather than home recording equipment in part, Sterne suggests, because consumers took greater interest in a broader consumer culture outside the home, which radio and recorded music on discs symbolized.[35]

The rise of magnetic tape as a consumer good in the 1950s suggests that the habits of family life alone cannot explain the success or failure of home recording. Certainly, the domestic, suburban turn of American life after World War II may have contributed to a renewed interest in the shared experience of recording that Sterne describes in the Victorian Era. However, certain technical features of magnetic recording made it more appealing than the wax cylinder, which reached its peak of popularity years before the advent of electric recording in the 1920s improved the fidelity and amplification of recorded sound. Magnetic tape's greater potential for durability, flexibility, and quality stimulated the adoption of a "high fidelity" hobby by middle-class consumers in the postwar era, when prosperity enhanced the prospects for a new method of home recording to gain popularity.

Piracy and the Hi-Fi Mind

In the 1950s and 1960s, many guides to the technology of magnetic recording were published in the United States and Europe. Some explained the science for people who wanted to build their own equipment, while others focused on the uses to which tape recorders could be put.[36] "Tape recording is fun!" promised one guidebook. The technology could be used for taping sound from radio and television, making original recordings, and backing up fragile disc records.[37] The author also recommended making an "up-to-date reel of the latest hits" by collecting musical selections on tape for a party—one of the earliest examples of "mixing," the practice of arranging songs in an original sequence, which would become popular with the cassette and, later, the compact disc.[38]

Tape users could also convert their recordings into disc form. Since tape recording was still a relatively new technology, one could not expect that others would have compatible equipment to play a tape recording. Exchanging a record with friends often required putting the sounds on the widely accepted format of a phonograph disc. "The outstanding advantages of a disc recording is that it is permanent and it can be played back on any phonograph," the Rek-O-Kut company told consumers. "Because of this, most tape recordings ultimately end up on discs."[39] However, the Rek-O-Kut disc recorder carried a price tag of $459.95 in 1955—beyond the means of all but the most affluent hobbyist, although perhaps affordable for a small company or club. If buying a recorder was out of the question, record companies and professional studios offered "transcription services," which would press discs from tape recordings. (Dante Bollettino had used the custom-pressing division of RCA to make his jazz bootlegs in the early 1950s.) "If you can dispose among your friends and relatives and associates, of from fifty to a hundred copies of a standard-type LP record that may be of as fine a quality as anything on the market, yet at a price not more, but considerably less than the usual retail price—then you're 'in business,'" choral director Edward Tatnall Canby observed. He recommended taping glee clubs, church concerts, and speeches at special gatherings—any activity that involved a large number of people, who could be counted on to buy enough records to make the pressing practical.[40]

For Canby, making records was a way of being involved with music for those who could not play an instrument professionally or even sing in the choir. Musicians, music teachers, and musicologists often mocked the collector for being a passive recipient of sound, he said: "We can be active, too, on the technical side and plenty of us are 'doing,' most actively, in the building of better and better high fidelity outfits."[41] Home recording lent an active, almost artisanal aspect to collecting. For middle-class men in the 1950s, the appeal of an expensive hobby that could reaffirm the masculine virtue of practical expertise was significant. Tinkering with all manner of sound equipment to squeeze out the most precise and perfect Debussy could allow a man to feel both sophisticated and skillful. As Canby said, "The increment of pleased pride and heightened morale is incalculable."[42]

High-fidelity hobbyists saw recordings as documents of reality, and it was the job of men and their machines to make that reflection as accurate as possible.[43] Reviews in periodicals such as *High Fidelity* (founded 1950) and *Stereo Review* (1958) emphasized the clarity and balance of a recording and the quality of both the performance and the sound engineering in technical terms.[44] To be beautiful was to be "lifelike," and without distortion.[45] The Dutch, an ad for Philips humbly suggested, made such good sound equipment because they were obsessed with order and detail, as shown by their "meticulous rows of tulips." Their Norelco sound equipment could convey the "full tone wealth" of the music, with "all the glow, all the color the composer intended."[46] Even a snack food could be subject to this mentality of exactness. "Rye-Krisp is the only cracker with the high-fidelity crunch," a television commercial boasted in 1955. "When you break a Rye-Krisp in two, you hear all the highs and lows that you do not hear with any other crackers. Rye-Krisp gives you the full fidelity of eating enjoyment."[47]

Although *High Fidelity* magazine did devote some of its pages to jazz, the hobbyist literature focused overwhelmingly on classical European music. This genre seemed a natural fit for a discourse based on the refinement of presentation as much as that of performance. Moreover, its cultural cachet contributed to the self-image of consumers of both the music and the equipment, which were marketed to the "connoisseur" and "the man of discernment"—a man frequently presented in dressy clothes, his home always decorated with spare, modernist flair. A wine glass was often present.[48] "No home pretending to any degree of artistic cultivation is complete today without those precious discs containing in such small space so much of the world's priceless heritage of beauty," one guide to high fidelity asserted, recalling earlier claims that the phonograph would democratize access to the finest sounds of high civilization.[49] As Roy F. Allison reminded his readers, a great deal of technical knowledge separated the "layman" from the "high fidelity initiate."[50]

As with the jazz collectors of the 1930s and 1940s, the hi-fi world was by and large a boys' club. Writers on hi-fi discussed music in terms of "battles" and "tournaments" between different symphonies and even models of instruments, while further improvement in the fidelity of recording to real sound was described as a sort of triumph.[51] Men also wrote frequently of their wives' frustration with the noise, clutter, and unsightliness the hi-fi hobby generated, not to mention their husbands' obsession with it. As Dana Andrews admitted, his neighbors were none too pleased by the crystal-clear sound of Bartok blaring in the middle of the night, and his wife did not appreciate that massive amounts of sound equipment had taken over their home. "If I find her on a picket line along with the neighbors," he wrote, "I'll probably have to blame it on the irony of her bedroom being directly over the den, which houses an imposing battery of speakers."[52]

Andrews was not unique in his penchant for such "imposing" consumer goods. Indeed, this domestic struggle reflected the differing aspirations of men and women to acquire and flaunt the trappings of abundance. "The family home would be the place where a man could display his success through the accumulation of consumer goods," historian Elaine Tyler May has written. "Women, in turn, would reap the rewards for domesticity by surrounding themselves with commodities."[53] Like homesteaders who brought all their pots and pans and furniture out to be photographed in front of sod houses, suburbanites aspired to create a tableau of their material achievements in the home. Male readers of *High Fidelity* might like to show off their financial and technical prowess by owning an "imposing battery of speakers," but this commodity might not suit the vision of the home held by their wives. Electronics companies geared their ads to men's desire for respectability and masculine mastery, while the postwar boom and the ideology of consumerism provided the necessary conditions for gadgets like reel-to-reel tape recorders and disc cutters to flourish in the market, setting up new possibilities for copying sound.

Rarely did the topic of copyright or piracy arise in the early literature on home recording. When it did, the author offered a cursory warning about some recorded material being subject to copyright, before moving on to other aspects of the technology. ("Look out for copyright and union restrictions," Canby suggested.)[54] Joel Tall addressed legal issues in *Techniques of Magnetic Recording*, but only the potential for wiretapping and similar unethical acts. These books nearly always suggested recording music from the radio or television, but it was only one of many applications, along with speech correction, language learning, slide-show commentaries, leaving messages and so on. The copying and use of broadcast music seemed innocuous enough, useful for a teen's dance party if nothing else. Many of the compositions classical music buffs recorded had long been in the public domain, and federal law did not yet recognize any separate ownership of a recorded performance itself. However, the 1950 *Metropolitan* case maintained that selling records of a symphony's performance could amount to unfair competition, even if the compositions were not under copyright.

Perhaps the boosters of magnetic recording, a consumer technology still in its infancy, were reluctant to play up its potentially illegal uses. However, the increasing popularity of the medium made this prospect unavoidable. The amount of prerecorded material available on tape had been limited, and not everyone was going to practice a speech or record his own violin recital. Many hobbyists used the idle capacity of their tape recorders to copy material from radio, television, and concert performances.

A poignant symbol of this yen to document everything was Joe Gould, hobo and Harvard-educated fixture in Greenwich Village from the 1920s to the 1950s. New Yorkers remembered Gould wandering the streets of Manhattan, continually scribbling everything he heard in the city.[55] He promised to compile the notes into a massive volume called *The Oral History of the World*, arguing that such a chronicle would offer a far greater truth than the work of any historian. Reflecting on Gould's work in 1970, James Goodfriend argued that a great social history could be extracted from that manuscript, if anyone would take the time to sort through it. "The same problem will face another committee," Goodfriend said, "the one finally appointed to decide what to do with the huge archive of unauthorized recorded music—tapings of broadcasts, concerts, operatic performances, salon recitals, and commercial records of which the original masters have been lost."[56]

Like Joe Gould, the people who captured this music over the years were recording their times—making "An Aural History of the (Musical) World in the Twentieth Century."[57] Recordings captured evidence of reality, and every additional record provided additional information about the human experience. Thus, it made sense to document a particular performance of the Metropolitan Opera in concert or of Duke Ellington on the radio. Whereas disc recording had always been a delicate and difficult operation, tape recording opened the possibility, if in the imagination only, that everything could be recorded all the time.[58] Like Boris Rose, an amateur technologist could tape a vast number of radio broadcasts, providing raw material for a future historian who wants to know what was going on at the time.

Like the Hot Record Society, the hi-fi copiers also worried about important recordings slipping into obscurity. "Does a record company have the 'right' to withdraw (and therefore make unavailable) a recorded performance because its sales were not up to whatever standards the company might want to apply?" Goodfriend asked. Major record companies could not afford to provide audiences with every recording they desired, nor could they keep everything in print. A record had to be produced in large enough numbers to justify the effort of the sales staff to promote it to the public. "Hits," after all, rarely happen on their own; the music industry had long indulged in practices of plugging and payola, paying vaudeville artists to popularize new written compositions or bribing radio stations to give new records airplay.[59] Even with the added boost of advertising and organized bribery, men in the music business insisted that only one recording turns a profit for every nine that fail to break even. (This claim appears throughout the literature.)[60] If the firm added marginal or "historic" recordings to its already risky business model, the failure rate would be worse than

90 percent—at least for centralized, mass-production enterprises like Decca or Columbia Records in the mid-twentieth century.[61] Meanwhile, a "huge archive" of recorded music had accumulated for which only small demand existed, making the music impractical to produce for the companies that originally recorded and sold it.[62]

Goodfriend suggested that the government step in to help. Pirates might freeload off the efforts of artists and record companies, but they still put out recordings that no one else would make available. This need could be met by the government, which would collect all recordings that had been out of print for ten years or more and appoint a committee to determine what to keep. Citizens could then order the recordings in tape form for their own personal use, and educational institutions could draw from the immense catalog too. The recordings should cost twice the going rate for the typical album in the present day, he said, in order not to inflict unfair competition on the record companies. In other words, the government should not become music pirate number one.[63]

This proposal for public access to musical history may not have been radical, but it was rooted in exactly the same notion of cultural preservation that motivated the Hot Record Society and the jazz journalists of the *Record Changer*, who could not bring themselves to condemn bootlegging outright. "A musical performance...is something more than an item of commerce," Goodfriend wrote. "It is that, but it is something more too: it is an artistic document, and the public has an interest in its preservation, and perhaps in its availability as well."[64] He presupposed that a group of wise men could determine what is worth preserving, but this attitude was in keeping with the general cast of mind of both jazz and classical aficionados. "The current theory on such matters is to keep everything," Goodfriend said, touching on the collectors' instinct to document and hoard any piece of information, but he believed someone would have to separate the essential from the extraneous.[65]

The idea of a mail-order government music library went nowhere, of course, but many Americans had been working on a kind of decentralized version for years. The bootlegging of classical music performances was, after all, the stimulus for Goodfriend's proposal. Beginning in 1901, Lionel Mapleson, called the "Father of Bootlegging," produced some of the earliest live recordings at New York's Metropolitan Opera House, capturing two or three minutes of music at a time. Mapleson had to place his wax cylinder phonograph on the catwalk after audience members complained that the horn blocked their view of the stage.[66] The cylinders were the sole remaining documents of several artists who never recorded commercially. The New York Public Library and the Library of Congress made them available for study in the early 1940s, and librarian Phillip L. Miller offered copies of the records at $1.75 a piece.[67]

Pirates were often the first to issue recordings of many classical pieces. Recording, for instance, Richard Wagner's *Ring* cycle was such an epic undertaking that no major label had attempted it. Such a project was nearly impossible before the commercial introduction of the LP in 1948. Before then, each side of a disc contained only a few minutes of music, meaning that operas and symphonies were prohibitively expensive and cumbersome to produce. When they were attempted, these symphonies consisted of a string of abrupt fragments of the greater whole; the recordings were sold as a set of individual discs, which is why the term "album" was coined.[68] The greater capacity of the LP format and tape recording made the production of long classical works much cheaper and easier.

Eli Oberstein's Record Corporation of America (which cleverly bore the same initials as his ex-employer, the giant Radio Corporation of America, or RCA) entered the fray in 1954 with the first full recording of Wagner's *Ring des Nibelungen*. Issued on the Allegro label, it consisted of eighteen discs and claimed to have been recorded at the Dresden Opera House. The attribution was a clever ruse, since few in America had access to the concert halls of East Germany and other communist nations in the early 1950s. No one knew the names of any of the listed soloists, until soprano Regina Resnik realized it was her own voice on the recording. The concert had actually occurred at the Bayreuth Festival in West Germany, and after the Festival's lawyers pressed Oberstein's Record Corporation of America about the matter, the set was removed from the market.[69]

Similar antics occurred throughout the 1950s and 1960s. In 1951, at almost the same time that the more famous RCA got in trouble for printing bootleg copies of its own jazz records for Dante Bollettino, the public learned that the company had also manufactured unauthorized recordings of Verdi's *A Masked Ball* for an outfit called Classic Editions. The record jacket of *A Masked Ball* claimed that it had been recorded in Italy. However, Irving Kolodin of the *Saturday Review* revealed that the concert had been taped from a radio performance by the Metropolitan Opera in 1947. To make matters worse, RCA had exclusive contracts with two of the performers on the record.[70] (Of course, the company *was* technically manufacturing records by its own artists.) In 1965, the Period label issued sets of Mozart's *Entführung aus dem Serail* and two Verdi operas. The recordings had supposedly been made at the Patagonia Festival, where Ralph de Cross was said to conduct soloists like Claudia Terrasini and Magda Walbrunn. Again, the intrepid *Saturday Review*, which had defended jazz bootleggers in earlier years, accused Period of copying the concerts from European radio broadcasts and, in the case of Verdi's *La Traviata*, from a recording on the Deutsche Grammophon label. However, no one was sued. Indeed, Livingstone commented, "The whole thing was so funny that nobody did anything about it."[71]

These cases of deception raise serious questions about how and why people bootlegged music. Classical music buffs, who made up a large part of the audience for high-quality sound equipment, were both perfectionists and collectors. They wanted to document everything, including performances that established manufacturers were either unwilling or unable to provide. If this is true, then what is the value of a recording that is misrepresented as a performance by a made-up person in a made-up place? Shadowy firms like Allegro and Period tried to cover their tracks by using the techniques of disguise that had served pirates of sheet music and sound recordings for years, making up plausible names for unauthorized products. What collector wants to add a vintage Claudia Terrasini to his library if Terrasini never existed? One answer is that the first-ever full recording of Wagner's *Ring* was worth having, regardless of its provenance. Another is that a classical music listener in the know may have been able to spot a fake and make an educated guess about which performance it actually contained. These operas were not performed every day, and the people at *Saturday Review* had little trouble figuring out what was what.

To understand the rise of classical bootlegging in the 1950s requires understanding why people felt the need to record. Some copycats held to the documentary ethos of recording and looked at their work as a kind of craft. Like the high-fidelity hobbyists who used many of the same products, these bootleggers aimed to capture an experience in the clearest way, though they may have emphasized the music itself more than some of the technology-obsessed audiophiles did. One opera pirate said that he and his partner bootlegged "as a labor of love. We work slowly and produce few albums. Quality is what we strive for, and it's often hard to achieve with some of these old tapes. We do what we can to correct fluctuations of pitch and drops in volume, but we never doctor a sour note if the singer sang it that way. We want to document what really happened."[72] A man who went by the name Roland Ernest released numerous bootlegs of performances at Carnegie Hall, including what Clinton Heylin called "the most famous opera bootleg of them all," the breakthrough 1965 performance of Spanish soprano Monserrat Cabellé in *Lucrezia Borgia*. RCA claimed that Ernest sold 30,000 copies of the performance, which he denied. Some of his releases were so esoteric they sold fewer than 100 copies apiece, and Ernest had to drive a cab to support his activities.[73]

Akin to the pirates of contemporary opera were the "private labels," which specialized in out-of-print and nearly extinct recordings dating back to the earliest years of the music industry. Some items were recorded from cylinders and deteriorated discs that had nearly stopped functioning. Borrowing from collectors, privateers used acetate air checks—temporary discs produced by radio networks—to make new copies of music from the 1930s and 1940s. These labels often sold their goods through mail-order catalogs that were distributed

Figure 3.2 This detail from a Boris Rose catalog features mostly live recordings of jazz performers, released on "labels" such as Beppo and Big Molly. *Source:* Reprinted by permission of Elaine Rose.

to members of a small circle, and they managed to keep such a low profile that record companies rarely took legal action against them.[74]

Boris Rose, for example, offered everything from antique ragtime to comedy records, as well as movie soundtracks, broadcasts of Charlie Parker and Cannonball Adderley, and nostalgia items from the heyday of radio.[75] In this fashion, Rose invented a different label for almost every record he released, starting such companies as Bamboo Industries—Records for Most Jazz Ears, Jung Cat Records, Kasha King, and Lee Bee Discs. He signed the liner notes with pseudonyms like "Kentwood P. Axtor" and "Astyanax Schwartz." Some of his records, preserved at the Institute of Jazz Studies in Newark, New Jersey, featured homemade Xeroxed covers, while others possessed plain white sleeves much like the *Great White Wonder* bootleg of Bob Dylan that would draw so much attention in 1969. In effect, obscure operators like Rose maintained their own private versions of the government archive that Goodfriend had proposed. Rose was able to maintain such a vast catalog because he only copied discs on demand, when someone sent him a nominal sum ($1.50 or $2.00) to cover the cost of production.[76]

"I'm sure he did make money at times because he reinvested it in the music," Rose's daughter Elaine recalls. "He never let money really sit in the bank." She credits his experience of poverty during the Depression for his compulsive desire to collect—stockpile might be a better word—almost anything, from records to

Figure 3.3 A CD compilation of recordings by professional farter Joseph Pujol, also known as Le Pétomane, reveals Boris Rose's wide ranging taste as well as his penchant for rescuing music from obscurity. On the back of the sleeve, the *London Taxi News* is quoted as asking, "How could anyone seriously dislike an artiste who could blow out a candle from a distance of a foot, or the generation who applauded him?" *Source:* Reprinted by permission of Elaine Rose.

exercise bikes to stuffed animals. Rose also possessed the same zeal for documentation that gripped Gould, Goodfriend, and others. With the advent of the video home system (VHS) tape in the 1970s, he filled countless boxes with recordings of television programs. "Because so many people *don't* save anything, in that era my father was like 'well, we have to save this—it's going to be good for history,'" Elaine says. "He was always into preserving things for knowledge. And he was right in that sense. He was afraid that no one would be saving this."[77]

Although Rose and other privateers mostly evaded litigation, the legal status of sound recordings remained in flux throughout the 1950s and into the early 1960s. The 1955 decision in *Capitol Records v. Mercury* forced the Second Circuit

Appeals court to revisit the questions raised earlier by *RCA v. Whiteman* (1940) and *Metropolitan v. Wagner-Nichols* (1950).[78] The convoluted case involved recordings by the German company Telefunken, which had licensed Mercury to sell certain records in Czechoslovakia but gave Capitol the rights to sell in the United States. Capitol wanted to prevent Mercury from issuing the records stateside, while Mercury insisted it was free to sell the records; the recordings were not copyrightable under federal law, and Capitol had given away any possible common law copyright when the works were pressed and sold to the public. (Creators could retain a common law copyright for various kinds of work as long as they were unpublished.) The compositions involved were in the public domain, meaning the question was whether Capitol retained any kind of property right in the recordings themselves.[79]

The court struggled with the implications for copyright law, but still came down on the side of Capitol. In his opinion, Judge Edward Dimock determined that sound recordings were not copyrightable, pointing out that congressional committee reports from the Copyright Act of 1909 showed that Congress did not intend "to extend the right of copyright to the mechanical reproductions themselves."[80] He also observed that *Whiteman* reinforced this principle, but in the next breath said that the 1940 precedent was not, in fact, the law of New York. He instead raised *Metropolitan* as an example, and held that copying and selling someone else's performances without permission was illegal. Why? Because permitting that behavior "could not have been the intention of the New York courts."[81] Curiously, the Second Circuit Appeals Court concluded that manufacturing and selling records to the public did not constitute "publication," allowing Capitol to hold a common law copyright for the works even though Congress and previous courts had chosen not to protect sound recordings.[82]

In 1955, it may have seemed that American law had decisively swerved toward granting protection to works that were not technically covered by federal copyright law, but Americans continued to struggle over how much and what kinds of copying were fair. Two Supreme Court rulings in 1964 threw the whole debate into doubt by endorsing the notion that people were free to exploit any works that were eligible neither for copyright nor patent. The cases, *Sears, Roebuck & Co. v. Stiffel* and *Compco Corp. v. Day-Brite Lighting*, both dealt with lighting fixtures.[83] Although few would see a direct relationship between a lamp and a sound recording, these decisions directly bore upon how works outside the scope of copyright law ought to be regulated. Lighting designs did not pass the test of originality to qualify for patent, nor did they fall into any of the categories defined in the copyright act, which dealt with books, pictures, musical compositions, and other creative works. Thus, the distinctive grooves on a lighting fixture were no more protected by federal law than the grooves on a particular recording of the song "Hound Dog." The Supreme Court concluded in both *Sears* and *Compco* that state rulings in favor of a plaintiff who complained that a competitor copied its fixture design strayed too far into federal territory. If Congress chose not to protect a certain kind of creative object, the court concluded, then lawmakers probably meant to leave it open to free use.

In other words, copyright law by any other name was still the province of federal power. The reasoning derived from a belief in the supremacy of national authority, as well as a bent for leaving as many ideas and expressions in the public domain as possible. The liberal Supreme Court of Earl Warren belonged to an American tradition that distrusted monopolies, as did Learned Hand and Progressive lawmakers in earlier years. Inventing new rights for any kind of creativity, whether the design of a lamp or a musical performance, could be anticompetitive, limiting how others could express themselves and compete in the marketplace.[84] As with the unnamed but numerous freedoms covered by the Ninth Amendment to the Constitution, citizens enjoyed a "federal right to copy" all things not specifically limited.[85] The justices of the Supreme Court affirmed this right just as the Beatles were first invading America and changes in the technology of magnetic recording were about to unleash copying on a much wider scale.

Jets, Cars, and Cassettes

In the 1950s, magnetic tape was a high-dollar hobby and a collector's craft, as well as a technology that served practical ends in business and industry. In the 1960s it became a vehicle of popular amusement, carried into rock concerts in jean pockets and humming from a Thunderbird dashboard. The high-fidelity enthusiasts were the early adopters of the technology, and their willingness to spend large sums on a prestigious diversion enabled corporations to cultivate magnetic recording as a consumer good, albeit an upmarket one. The medium followed the path of television, which started out as an expensive and bulky product and became ever smaller and cheaper as it evolved.

The invention of a workable transistor in 1947 dovetailed with simultaneous leaps in the development of television and sound recording after World War II. The device was yet another spin-off from wartime research, derived from studies of the conductive properties of silicon and germanium at Bell Telephone Laboratories. Bell scientists discovered that a combination of germanium, plastic, and gold foil could greatly augment an electric current.[86] Engineers replaced large vacuum tubes with tiny transistors that amplified currents enough to power complex electronic devices, allowing the behemoth models of early television sets to shrink and radios to fit into a pocket. Manufacturers could also produce the components in large quantities and achieve immense economies of scale, reducing the cost of electronic goods. Masaru Ibuka, a founder of the Japanese electronics giant Sony, paid $25,000 for permission to use the transistor when he learned during a visit to the United States in 1952 that Bell was licensing the patent. Three years later, Sony unveiled one of the first low-price "pocket radios," though the company had to make shirts with extra-large pockets for its salesmen to wear when pushing the product.[87]

As Dana Andrews noted, a massive battery of speakers, tape heads, and turntables could overpower the living room of any hi-fi fetishist with money to burn. The pocket radio held out a prospect of cheapness and smallness that could help the consumer who had less space or money make use of magnetic tape technology. In the late 1950s, several companies tried shrinking the tape reel and putting it into a plastic box. RCA Victor developed a four-track tape cartridge in 1958, with little success.[88] In a similar effort to make recorded music more mobile, Chrysler had tried in 1956 and 1960 to install a disc record player under the dashboard of its cars. Understandably, few buyers chose the option, which could be cumbersome and even dangerous to operate on the road. Later innovators sought ways to make tape cartridges easy for a motorist to insert and remove from a player while driving.[89]

It was an eccentric car salesman who first initiated the fusion of cars and magnetic tape. Based first in Chicago and later in Glendale, California, Earl "Madman" Muntz managed to make a fortune selling cars during the Depression and the postwar recession by squeezing prices and promoting sales through wild antics. For example, Muntz would advertise a "special of the day"—a car that had to be sold immediately or he would smash it to bits on camera by nighttime. "Muntz is generally credited with starting the 'this guy's insane, come take advantage of his crazy prices' school of salesmanship," the tape collector Abigail Lavine says.[90] He got into the TV business right after World War II, searching for an angle that would allow him to compete with RCA, Zenith, and the other big companies. He constructed a barebones TV set that would sell cheaply in urban areas; the contraption would not pick up a signal from very far away, but Muntz figured that consumers in big cities like New York and Los Angeles would settle for the cheapest TV possible if the broadcasting antenna were nearby. His design philosophy came to be known as "Muntzing," which meant hacking away any components that were not absolutely necessary for the device to function.[91] Bill Golden, an engineer, recalled that the company's $99 TV was known in the industry as the "gutless wonder" in the 1950s because it had so few parts.[92]

While still in high school, Golden installed four-track players in cars in his west Texas hometown for several years before moving to California to work with Muntz. He had gotten his own four-track player from a local wholesaler in 1964, and, seeing an opportunity, asked for three thousand dollars' worth of tapes and players on consignment. Soon his driveway was full of cars every Saturday, while he and a friend installed players and sold tapes from a rack in the trunk of his car. "Everybody wanted one, you know, it was a 'thing' then," Golden recalled in 2007. "I guess it was kind of like iPods are now.... For a teenager at that time, [the car] was really a domain, and because of that it was a product that people would spend money on and put in their cars."[93] The two young men were making money hand over fist, and by 1967, Muntz had noticed that the four-track trade was unusually brisk for a Texas town of 50,000 people. Golden was then a senior in high school, and Muntz offered to bring him out to Van Nuys to work in his company when he graduated. Although Golden spent his first month on the assembly line, he said, "they moved me to Engineering when they found out I knew something about the product."[94]

Muntz needed a young man with a knack for electronics to help improve the four-track cartridge, which faced heavy competition from other formats by 1967. A chance meeting in early 1963 brought the Madman in touch with another tinkerer who contributed to the development of magnetic recording as a mass medium. Muntz's son loaned a Lincoln Continental to Shanda Lear, the teenage daughter of Bill Lear, the aviation pioneer, so she could pick her father up at the Santa Monica Airport. Noticing the four-track tape on the Lincoln's dashboard, Shanda saw an opportunity for her father, who had experimented with wire recording and car radios early in his career. Her business sense was correct; Bill Lear went straight to Muntz's house and worked out a deal to distribute the Stereo Pak four-track tape in the Midwest.[95]

Lear and Muntz were two of a kind. Both were entrepreneurs and inventors who enjoyed a challenge, refused to take no for an answer, and had worked their way up from the bottom with flinty determination. Both also saddled their daughters with eccentric names—Shanda Lear and Tee Vee "Tina" Muntz. (Both women aspired to be singers.) Lear had a reputation for cutting staff as much as Muntz liked to hack away superfluous parts from a prototype, and they both had a penchant for imprinting their personal marks on everything they touched.[96] Muntz went for white clothes, white décor, and a white Lincoln Continental, at least when he was not wearing red tights and a Napoleon hat to sell cars. Golden never forgot the white pool table he saw at the Muntz mansion. As their business partnership turned into a war of formats, the men showed what can happen when two ambitious and inventive control freaks collide.

Lear and his engineer Sam Auld first aimed to tweak the four-track model, dismantling and reconstructing the cartridge over numerous long nights, before deciding to start over from scratch. Lear considered recording eight tracks of sound on a single band of tape, and ran his ideas past Alexander Pontitoff, the founder of Ampex, a pioneer in the magnetic tape field. "I tried to put eight tracks on a quarter-inch tape," Pontitoff told him. "You can't do it. Just can't squeeze that much information on it." Emboldened by the apparent challenge,

Lear invented just such a tape, the Stereo Eight, and began installing the play-ers on his Learstar corporate jets. He also lobbied the automobile companies to offer the eight-track as an option on their new car lines.[97]

Magnetic tape, then, was popularized by outsiders who prodded an ambiva-lent music industry to adopt the new technology as a recording medium. Muntz was known for his cars and televisions, and Lear for his planes. The Madman conceived of his tape player as an add-on for cars. RCA only signed on to pro-vide music after Lear pitched a hard sell to Ford, arranging for Lear Jet to make the cartridges, and Motorola, the car stereo equipment.[98] The other record com-panies were hesitant at first. "The remaining three of the Big Four in recorded music (Columbia, Decca, Capitol) have made no big move yet," *Business Week* reported in 1965, "but all are watching with interest."[99] Three years later, labels looked with fear and suspicion on yet another new format—Philips's compact cassette—much as it had the tape cartridge before it.[100] Golden, for one, believes that the record industry was indifferent. "Muntz was able to license so many duplication deals from record companies during the early sixties at unbeliev-able prices because they . . . said that consumer tapes were a passing fancy and that *nothing* would ever replace vinyl records," he wrote. "So much for corporate forecasters."[101]

In any case, Ford, Lear, and Motorola brought the first effective, user-friendly tape cartridge to a mass audience. To persuade Henry Ford II, Auld installed a tape player into the executive's Lincoln Continental.[102] At a Detroit auto show in 1965, Ford showed off a car with a tape player and radio combo that fit into a conventional radio slot, eight inches wide, three inches high, and six and a half inches deep. Consumers could also get the tape player attached underneath the dashboard. The tapes—rectangular, plastic, and palm-sized—played eighty minutes of music, and Lear had tapered the end of the cartridge so motorists could tell which way to insert the tape without looking. The company planned to install as many as 100,000 players in 1966.[103] That year, car buyers could order a sedan, wagon, Mustang, Thunderbird, Mercury, or Lincoln with an eight-track player built-in. The option cost $128.49. Lear built the tape cartridge, Motorola manufactured the radio and stereo speaker components, and RCA sold prere-corded tapes for prices starting at $4.95.[104]

While Philips had made no deals with Detroit, its launch of the compact cas-sette in 1964 further complicated the burgeoning magnetic tape business. The cassette was smaller than open-reel tape or the various cartridges, and Philips initially deemed its sound quality better suited for dictation than for listening to prerecorded music.[105] The electronics firm offered a free patent license to any company that would maintain the same basic specifications of the original tape, allowing competitors to develop better cassettes while preserving compat-ibility. The press at first expected the compact cassette to be used for recording nonmusical sounds, while the four-track or eight-track cartridge delivered pre-recorded music in the car or home. These two uses eventually converged in one device, but that outcome was not apparent in 1966. The compact cassette, with its facility for both playing and recording, won out in the long run, surpassing vinyl record sales in 1983.[106]

In the late 1960s, though, chaos prevailed in the market. "The rise of the cassette...has added to the great buzzing confusion that characterizes the cartridge tape business," *Business Week* reported in 1968. Lear's eight-track had won the support of some record companies and the automakers, but the tug of war continued. Muntz won the right to manufacture tapes of 75,000 Capitol recordings in 1967, but no one system emerged as the clear favorite in a crowded field, and other companies had new formats slated for release, each supposedly superior to all the others.[107] "Retailers, who must now stock the same musical selections on monaural and stereo discs, reels of tape, several types of cartridge, and cassettes, are beginning to get that hunted feeling," *Business Week* said. "Enough, they say, is enough."[108]

The great tangle of different tape formats in the late 1960s resulted in supply gaps when one medium fell into disfavor. The record companies, unsure of which horse to bet on, were willing to pull their support if one type of cartridge began to lag in sales. The *Los Angeles Times*' profile of Muntz implied that he was gaining the upper hand in 1967, but as soon as four-track sales slipped, the record companies abandoned him and backed the eight-track tape instead. Muntz ended his tape business in 1970, eventually turning to the nascent cell phone industry a decade later. As a result, the supply of four-track tapes dried up and left consumers who had Muntz's players in a bind.[109]

Donald Koven, a Canadian migrant who sold stereo equipment and tapes in Los Angeles, had difficulty supplying his customers even before four-tracks were discontinued. "It would take so long for a factory tape from the record companies to come out," Koven recalled. "A hit record would appear, but the tape came out months later. I had to supply my customers with tapes, somehow." Other electronics stores were making their own four-track tapes from the already available vinyl records, leading Koven to purchase quality equipment and compete with them. When record companies stopped making new four-tracks, he expanded his operation. The cost of machinery led Koven to manufacture continuously, in order to maximize his investment, and the resulting oversupply of tapes motivated him to branch out by wholesaling to other stores. "There were millions of four-track machines," he said. "How could the public get four-track tapes? What the hell are you supposed to do? What's the public to do?...I was forced to give my customers good service."[110]

Koven was also forced to plead "no contest" when he ended up in court in 1971. California had passed a law in 1968 prohibiting the unauthorized reproduction of sound recordings—the first state to do so after New York. Koven and other entrepreneurs in the tape field formed the Tape Industries Association of America to defend their activities, and they aimed to overturn the antipiracy statute as unconstitutional. Copyright was the federal government's job, they said, and Congress had excluded sound recordings from any legal protection. The California state government was thus intruding on an area that Congress preempted. Their campaign would eventually reach the Supreme Court in the landmark *Goldstein* decision of 1973, which upheld state antipiracy laws, but for the moment, one aspect of the case is most relevant: pirates such as Koven responded to the record industry's inability to cope with the technological disorder of the late 1960s in much the same way as the Hot Record Society and Dante Bollettino had done before. When consumers wanted a product, and the established industry could not or would not provide it for them, someone else stepped in and connected supply with demand.

Koven's rationale strikes one as more self-serving than Bollettino's. Koven had to start pirating in order to keep up with his competitors, and then he had to build a bigger manufacturing operation to stay profitable. He could not turn to the cultural preservation defense that jazz pirates had used, since he copied commonly available contemporary music. Still, the case bears a similarity to the bootleg boom of the early 1950s: periods of technological transformation and uncertainty can foster a sort of market failure, in which the official offerings of industry fall especially short of the desires of consumers. In the late 1940s and early 1950s, when the music business moved away from the shellac record, bootleggers pressed LPs of older recordings that stood little chance of being issued in the new vinyl format. In the late 1960s, record companies were divided in their allegiance to four-tracks, eight-tracks, and other formats, meaning that not all music was available in each medium. When one type of cartridge stopped being made, consumers could either choose to trash their now-obsolete players or turn to a pirate like Koven who would sell them the latest hit in the medium of their choice.

This clash of formats mirrors the conflict over technology and property rights in the early twenty-first century, when file-sharing networks such as Napster or Limewire made music available free of charge to Internet users in new, digitally compressed file formats such as the MP3. The record industry stuck to selling compact discs, until online services like iTunes provided a legal means for listeners to purchase audio files in the new medium. Likewise, bootleggers in the early 1950s furnished collectors with copies of old recordings that had not been released in the new format of the vinyl LP. Piracy filled the shortfall between established media and technological means.

The struggle over magnetic tape as a form of sound recording resulted from the convergence of postwar consumer goods—cars and music—when the baby boom generation began to come of age. It is no surprise that the first version of magnetic tape to gain widespread popularity was built for a car, nor that a teenager put in touch the two men who made magnetic tape into a mass medium. When *Business Week* spoke of a "Music Maker for the Masses" in 1968, it pictured a bearded boy placing a microphone in the face of young folk-singing girl, strumming her guitar; two teenagers dancing on the beach with tapes scattered around a portable player; a girl lying down, recording the sounds of a radio; a war reporter sticking a microphone into a foxhole; a barbershop quartet harmonizing into a tape recorder; and a businessman dictating on an airplane.[111] One can imagine a middle-class man purchasing a hi-fi system in the 1950s; a decade later, his son might have a four-track player installed in his Mustang, or his daughter might have taken Philips's Norelco Carrycorder to a rock concert. New formats for sound recording proliferated in the 1950s and 1960s—first the LP, then the four-track, Stereo Eight, and compact cassette   creating a confusion not seen since the days when discs, piano rolls, and wax cylinders vied for supremacy as a vehicle for sound. In the era of new media, though, the ever greater investment companies made in producing and promoting a record was undermined by the ease of appropriating that investment with the push of a button.

"It's All Done with Tape Recorders"

Whereas Joe Gould kept his ears open and a pen and paper handy as he documented the sounds of New York, William Burroughs relied on the tape recorder. In his 1967 essay, "The Invisible Generation," the Beat novelist urged readers to exploit the full range of subversive possibilities presented by magnetic tape. He emphasized the medium's ability to capture and replay sounds that are normally not studied closely, like the sounds of the street or idle chatter around the office. "Record your boss and co-workers," Burroughs advised. "Analyze their associational patterns learn to imitate their voices oh you'll be a popular man around the office but not easy to compete with."[112] On the other hand was the medium's capacity for distorting sound, slowing it down, speeding it up, and rearranging it, to reveal new meanings not detected on hearing a sound the first time. Burroughs touched on the same theme of deception raised by classical bootleggers who attributed a performance of Wagner's *Ring* cycle to a made-up festival, or Eli Oberstein's invention of generic blues singers to sell records in grocery stores. But Burroughs's renegade was something of a mild-mannered spy:

> this is the invisible generation he looks like an advertising executive
> a college student an american tourist doesn't matter what your cover
> story is so long as it covers you and leaves you free to act you need a

philips compact cassette recorder handy machine for street recording
looks like a transistor radio for playback playback in the street will show
the influence of your sound track in operation of course the most unde-
tectable playback is street recordings people don't notice yesterday
voices phantom car holes in time.[113]

Burroughs did not merely catalogue a variety of unconventional uses for a new
media technology. He also touched on a number of distinctive characteristics of
magnetic tape as a medium. The cassette recorder was small enough to be portable and easily concealed, allowing for sounds (such as concerts) to be recorded
without knowledge of the authorities. It could be erased and re-recorded on,
permitting freer play of experimentation. That magnetic tape was divisible and
editable meant that Burroughs could reassemble conversations to preserve the
best or worst parts, but it also meant that a bootlegger who recorded a live opera
performance could revise the weaker elements of a performance before making
the recording available to the public.

Burroughs also spoke of "the efficient generation." The technologies that
he believed could subvert received wisdom and break "obsessional association
tracks" had been developed for business and military applications. The techniques were effective for processing information as computer development
made great strides in the postwar period and the metaphor of "information processing" became commonplace for describing human consciousness, especially
in the emerging field of cognitive psychology.[114] The conversion of sound into
magnetic traces prefigured the general inclusion of all "information"—whether
moving images, genes, music, poetry, or anything else—under the rubrics of
"intellectual property" and "content."[115] (The latter term, ever more popular in
the early twenty-first century, suggests that knowledge is a fluid, homogeneous
substance that could fill a container of any size.) The pamphlet that inspired
Masaru Ibuka and Akio Morita to develop Sony's first tape recorder suggested
the use of magnetic recording, not just for music or even dictation, but for capturing traces of any measurable phenomenon—any kind of data. *999 Uses of the
Tape Recorder* informed Ibuka and Morita that "Magnetape recording can be
applied to any phenomenon that can be converted into a varing [sic] voltage,
current, resistance, pressure, opacity, humidity, viscosity, temperature, transpar-
ency, impedance, torque or speed."[116]

In the 1950s and 1960s people spoke more and more of sound as a matter of information—of how many tracks, or how much information, could be
crammed onto a magnetic strip of a certain size.[117] The manipulability of tape—
its capacity for slowing down, speeding up, fast forwarding, rewinding, editing,
and rearranging—meant that recorded sound was a more fluid and malleable
medium than ever before. The Supreme Court in 1908 could not accept the

notion that a pattern of holes in a piano roll qualified for copyright, since the mechanical inscription was not a human expression that could be understood with the naked eye, unlike all previous drama, fiction, music, photography and poetry had been. Even when Congress addressed the thorny issues raised by the court's decision, it recognized only the underlying written composition as deserving copyright protection. The unintelligible representation of music in the grooves of a disk record or wax cylinder, the perforation of a piano roll, or the pattern of magnetic particles on a tape or wire would not qualify under federal law as a protectable expression until 1972. By then, pressure to recognize all information, including sound and music, as copyrightable (and economically valuable) expression had risen to a fever pitch.

PART TWO

THE LEGAL BACKLASH, 1945–1998

4

Counterculture, Popular Music, and the Bootleg Boom

As a boy in Germany the filmmaker Wim Wenders loved American rock and roll, even though he could not understand the lyrics. "For the longest time," he recalled, "I thought the words 'Be-Bop-A-Lu-La' actually meant something."[1] Geza Ekecs had much the same problem when he worked as a DJ for Radio Free Europe in the 1960s. Beaming Western music into the Communist bloc, he struggled to find a way to explain what the song "Too Pooped to Pop" would mean in Hungarian. Translation problems aside, young listeners continued to tune in. Those who could get their hands on a tape recorder would copy their favorites from the radio. However, Communist authorities considered Western music, especially jazz and rock and roll, to be decadent, preferring to provide the masses with classical music.[2] Tape recorders being scarce in the Communist world, diligent listeners had to find another way to copy music that was unavailable or forbidden: they collected discarded x-ray plates from hospitals, rounded the edges, and recorded music from the radio onto the images of human skeletons. "X-ray plates were the cheapest and most readily available source of necessary plastic," Artemy Troitsky recalled. "People bought them by the hundreds from hospitals and clinics for kopeks, after which grooves were cut with the help of special machines (made, they say, from old phonographs by skilled conspiratorial hands)." The records became known variously as "ribs" and "bones," and were circulated under the table and played at secret dance parties.[3]

Unauthorized reproduction takes many forms. For instance, these Hungarians could be seen as pirates of a sort. Like jazz and classical buffs in America, they copied music from the radio and traded it outside the bounds of the law, in samizdat fashion. As Troitsky notes, the sound of the bones was often quite bad, but people eagerly settled for it. Both the capitalist and communist pirates sought to acquire or make available music that was hard to get, only in America the recording company would not manufacture it (nor let anyone else do so) and in Hungary the Communist Party disallowed it. Ekecs reported the copying of rock hits in Hungary in 1965, and a few years later Americans were also reproducing popular music without permission—albeit not with x-ray plates or, necessarily, tapes.

The bones story shows that technological capacity does not determine whether people will disregard the rules and copy music. There must be a will, and there must be some conceivable sort of means, but the former may be more important than the latter. Many observers have credited the advent of the cassette tape recorder as the cause of a surge in bootlegging during the 1960s and 1970s, but this explanation ignores the fact that most bootleggers actually made and sold vinyl LPs, at least at first. For most listeners, the Bob Dylan "basement tapes" that touched off the bootleg boom in 1969 were not tapes at all. When a curious customer inquired about them at the local record shop, the clerk would pull one or two vinyl discs, usually in a plain white sleeve, from under the counter. Recorded in a hotel room or basement, or copied from the radio, these recordings may have come into the world on magnetic tape, but the vast majority of early bootlegs—of Dylan, the Beatles, the Rolling Stones, the Who—reached consumers as conventional LPs.

Popular music now joined the underground market, which had been dominated by bootlegs of classical, folk, and jazz recordings prior to the late 1960s. A practice that had once been confined to a small niche, catering to minority tastes, abruptly moved onto the turf of platinum-selling rock stars and the image-makers who sold them. Several cultural, economic, and technological trends converged in the 1960s to make this bootleg boom possible. Advances in recording technology made it easier to get copies of music out of the studio and to sneak tape recorders into concerts, while the availability of independent plants and custom pressing services allowed entrepreneurs to convert their recordings into vinyl records. Meanwhile, a generation of young listeners seized on the new technology to circulate every utterance they could find of iconic artists such as Bob Dylan or the Beatles, animated by the zeitgeist of the counterculture and social rebellion.

Predecessors like Dante Bollettino or Boris Rose had aimed to serve fans of less popular genres by reproducing the vanishing traces of America's musical heritage, but the new bootleggers wanted to liberate the music of the moment. Some flaunted their products and personal images in the media, insisting that they were blazing a trail for a new way of producing music. Record companies soon discovered that they could not curb the unauthorized reproduction of their products with the old remedies of injunctions and civil suits. In response, Congress would pass a reform of copyright law that the recording industry had desired since 1909.

Piracy in the Heyday of Rock and Roll

The growth of piracy was only one of many changes that shook up the American music industry in the years after World War II. The period saw the rise of new technologies, new genres, and new firms that challenged the power of the dominant record labels, especially with the breakout success of rock and roll in the mid-1950s. The 1950s were a time of growing diversity in the music industry, when independent record labels popularized rock and roll, and radio stations shifted from costly network and syndicated programs to playing mostly pre-recorded music. The popularity of cheap transistor radios also expanded the potential listening public. Radio stations responded to renewed competition by catering to musical niches, rather than treating listeners as a single mass audience. Labels released fewer cover versions of hit songs, which companies had traditionally viewed as less risky than recording new material, while the number of new artists doubled over the course of the decade. Independent labels benefited most from the rock and roll sensation, but the majors also capitalized on the popularity of new artists, songs, and styles.[4]

The growth of consumer electronics opened up new possibilities for producing and enjoying music. Independent studios and pressing plants served people who had made recordings on magnetic tape and wanted to share the music in a more commonly used medium. As Edward Tatnall Canby pointed out in 1951, a church group could afford to record and press its Christmas cantata if it could count on selling a few hundred copies. In the 1950s, tape remained an adjunct to disc recording, but the music and broadcasting industries rapidly adopted it as a basic means of capturing sounds. "The introduction of magnetic tape in recording studios, to replace the cumbersome wax masters, put recording technology in everybody's hands. Records could now be made almost anywhere—local radio stations, basement studios, homes—just as long as a pressing company was available to produce the discs for sale," Pekka Gronow observed. "The introduction of cassettes and cartridges in the late 1960s removed even this obstacle."[5] Its flexibility and affordability, compared to wax and vinyl, meant that more music could be recorded, and the greater volume of production made it likelier that copies or alternative takes of recordings would leak out of the studio. "Imperfect rehearsal recordings—ones that an artist ordinarily does not want released for sale—may be stolen, duplicated, and made quietly available," *Business Week* observed. The author went on to chide *New York* magazine's music critic for praising the pirates who had made an obscure Off-Broadway musical available on tape.[6]

Often, the complicity of workers in the entertainment industry allowed officially unreleased recordings to reach the public. Some live bootlegs were so good that critics believed they must have been recorded on the soundboards by the concert staff, rather than a bootlegger with a briefcase. "Are these bootleg tapes from someone onstage involved with their sound equipment?" Greil Marcus asked of *LIVEr Than You'll Ever Be*, the first rock live bootleg to make a splash and, in his opinion, the best Rolling Stones album ever released.[7] Bob Johnston, a longtime producer of Leonard Cohen and Bob Dylan, said he had enough unreleased material in his possession to make twenty great albums for either artist. "I've been offered a check for $200,000 for some Cohen tapes I have, and a blank check for Bob's," the producer said. "It's all locked away in Nashville, and I've got the key!"[8]

Johnston valued his relationship with Dylan, Cohen, and Cash and was unlikely to endanger it by leaking music they chose not to publish. However, other producers could not have been so conscientious if the flood of unreleased music by major stars is any indication. Sound engineers and other staff could be tempted to take acetates and tapes out of the studio, whether to "liberate" the music, make some extra money, or stick it to their employer. A 1952 essay by Hot Record Society alum Charles Edward Smith suggests that this practice had a long history: "The collector must rely upon the never quite infallible ear of the critic, to tell him whether this is the first master, the second master, or the acetate test that the office boy filched from the wastepaper basket."[9]

Even without the assistance of a sound engineer, getting music out of the concert hall was easier than before. As early as 1901, Lionel Mapleson was lugging his wax cylinder recorder all over the Metropolitan Opera House, searching for a place where he could keep the cumbersome machine out of view. Not everything had changed by the 1960s; a cartoon in *Stereo Review* shows a woman in a fur coat trying to enter an opera house with a microphone sticking out of her extravagant hat. However, those with the money or ingenuity could do a much better job of concealing their equipment. They snuck into concerts, especially as tape recorders became more compact, flexible and effective. The most advanced organizations would send an agent into a concert with a microphone that transmitted to a van, where tape was rolling a quarter of a mile away. Small-scale success allowed ambitious bootleggers to invest in better equipment. One could start with a simple tape recorder costing $40 and work up to a $100,000 stereo system. "Music-trade publications and underground newspapers carry ads for the machines," *Time* observed in 1971, "and many an Aquarian-Ager has been able to convert his basement into a tape factory."[10] Michael "Dub" Taylor used his profits from a Bob Dylan bootleg to move up from pilfering studio outtakes to producing high-quality concert recordings; he was spotted in 1971 at a Faces concert with a $3,000 microphone hidden in a suitcase.[11]

Law enforcement began worrying about the penetration of bootleggers into concerts before there were even laws to enforce. Congress would extend copyright to sound recordings in 1971, and North Carolina did not pass its own antipiracy law until 1975, yet high school students in Charlotte reported police monitoring at a Jimi Hendrix concert in 1969. An officer asked one attendee if his movie camera was a tape recorder—apparently, a concert video was acceptable, but a sound-only recording was not. The policeman then asked his friend about a suspicious case:

Cop: What's in that case under your chair?
Friend: A poloroid [*sic*] camera.
Cop: Do you have a tape recorder?
Friend: No.
Cop: Open up the case.
Friend: Do you have a search warrant?
Cop: Open it up.
Friend: I don't believe I have to without a search warrant.
Cop: (grabbing him by the arm) Step outside.
Friend: (by this time a uniformed pig appeared) Am I not entitled to a search
    warrant by the Constitution?
Cops: Step outside son.[12]

That summer, the first major rock bootleg began to circulate in Los Angeles: a passel of tunes by Bob Dylan, recorded in hotel rooms, radio and record studios, and, most famously, the basement of Dylan's home in Woodstock, New York. The bulk of these basement tapes consisted of covers and new folk songs performed with members of the Band during the period between the singer's motorcycle accident in 1966 and his return with *John Wesley Harding* in late 1967.[13] Word leaked of an unreleased set of Dylan songs, written and performed in the fashion of his early 1960s work, while many fans had greeted his just-released country album, *Nashville Skyline*, with dismay. Reviewers in the *Berkeley Barb* and other left-leaning independent magazines expressed disgust at Dylan's innocuous musings on "country pie" while the Vietnam War dragged on and student rebellion raged. Even as the Top 40 format imposed uniformity on many radio stations and DJs, the emergence of "free form" radio on the West Coast allowed hosts to air new, unreleased, and soon-to-be released music at will, culled from review tapes sent out by labels to critics or recordings ferreted out of local recording studios.[14]

The album of Dylan's "basement tapes," *Rolling Stone* reported in 1969, "was collected, pressed and currently is being marketed by two young Los Angeles residents both of whom have long hair, a moderate case of the shakes (prompted by paranoia) and an amusing story to tell." The young men went by the names of Patrick and Vladimir, until both interviewer and interviewee found the latter too difficult to spell and opted instead for Merlin. By hook or crook, the two

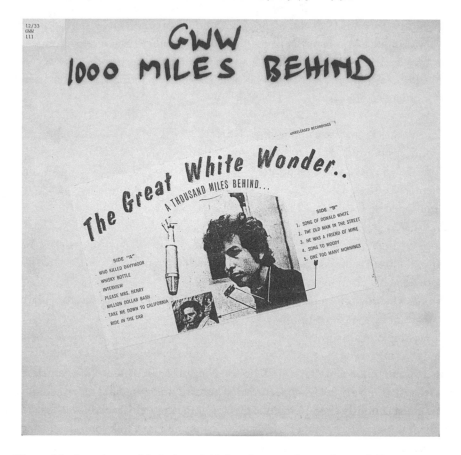

Figure 4.1 An unknown label released this bootleg record, one of many different compilations of Bob Dylan's "basement tapes" to circulate under the title the *Great White Wonder,* beginning in 1969. It has the same blank aesthetic as many of the *Great White Wonder* records, with a paper label listing the album title and the song tracks glued to the front of the sleeve. *Source:* Courtesy of Music Library and Sound Recordings Archive, Bowling Green State University.

had obtained tapes of unreleased Dylan songs, including recordings made in hotel rooms, a few off-the-cuff "rap sessions," and a live TV performance with Johnny Cash. Lacking their own vehicle, they had to borrow cars to deliver the records to the Psychedelic Supermarket and other local retailers. Although they struggled to keep their names and addresses secret, many people had already approached them with other "secret tapes" for future release. "He's got all these songs nobody's ever heard," Patrick said of Dylan. "We thought we'd take it on ourselves to make this music available." Jerry Hopkins ended the interview with this question: "Do you know what will happen if you get away with it? Why, if John Mayall or anybody opens at the Whisky tonight, there'll be a live recording of it on the stands by the middle of next week."[15]

Figure 4.2 The cover of this 1970 bootleg of the San Francisco band It's a Beautiful Day features only text handwritten with a black marker—prefiguring the way listeners labeled "burnt" CDs later in the twentieth century. *Source:* Courtesy of Music Library and Sound Recordings Archive, Bowling Green State University.

These earliest rock bootlegs were minimalist by default, with plain white covers that gave little or no indication of what was contained inside. When a woman from Brooklyn saw the Dylan album and expressed interest in hyping it back in New York, she told the boys it needed a name. Based on its presentation, she suggested *Great White Wonder*. Subsequently, Patrick and Merlin stamped each release with the letters "GWW." According to *Rolling Stone*, "Some [stores] objected to the simple packaging—a white double sleeve with 'Great White Wonder' rubber stamped in the upper righthand corner—they said, while others indicated they were afraid of how Columbia might react."[16] Many other versions of these recordings followed, as entrepreneurs imitated the style of the original and either tried to improve the sound quality of the material or offered a slightly different assortment of live recordings and demos.

The blank design of the early *Wonder*s recalled what became known as the Beatles' *White Album*, released the year before. Designed by pop artist Richard Hamilton, the 1968 record originally featured a plain white cover, the lack of adornment mirroring its simple title: *The Beatles*. In other words, it was just the band, with no fanfare or addenda. (It was also the first album they released on their own label, Apple Corps.) While a blank album cover might be expected to stand out on the record shelves—Hamilton wanted its militant abstraction to resemble "the most esoteric art publications"—Apple still added the stamp "The Beatles" on the cover to ensure that fans knew what the record was.[17]

Great White Wonder stood in contrast with standard music industry product much as the *White Album* did, as a plain container filled with an unalloyed volume of the artist's work. Packaging design is an aspect of marketing, a central piece of the campaign to tantalize the public into purchasing any musical product, and thus represents a portion of the investment in production and promotion that record companies accused pirates of appropriating. The earliest bootlegs, however, exploited this investment only indirectly; pirates may have benefited from the attention already generated by the promotional machine, but they did not copy the graphic design of the product. In the case of *Wonder*, they were not even copying an actual major-label release. Alan Bayley of GRT Corp., which manufactured tape versions of albums for major labels, urged the music industry to adopt an industry-wide trademark to distinguish legitimate recordings, but *Business Week* observed that in most cases the difference was already evident: "Authentic tapes are nicely packaged with full-color illustrations whereas bootleg tapes generally have a plain printed label listing the performers and songs and no maker's name or address."[18]

Aesthetics aside, the plainness served more practical purposes. The two young men who first published *Great White Wonder* lacked the resources to create a more elaborate production, even with the funds they scared up from a local businessman known only as "the Greek." Further, Patrick's desire to get the basement tapes into the hands of frustrated fans required forgoing much attention to detail in terms of presentation. Plain white packaging might have prevented police or other authorities from recognizing a record as the work of an artist on a major label, at least until the design became well known enough for the public to associate it with bootleg music.

If nothing else, leaving the sleeve blank could keep anyone from tracing the record to a particular bootlegger—unless, of course, he had the album manufactured at Columbia Records' own pressing plant in Los Angeles. A young man named Michael O made this mistake, issuing his own edition of *Great White Wonder* after being displeased with the original release. His was also packaged in a white sleeve, distinguished only by one low-budget touch—a drawing of a flower by his girlfriend on each of the 200 releases, which led to its being dubbed *Flower* by retailers. Michael found his mother at home one afternoon, fuming because a Columbia rep had come by and insisted that the boy buy back whatever records he had sold and turn them over to Columbia. Another entrepreneur in the area took a stab at perfecting the basement tapes, releasing a ten-track record in another blank sleeve. Like *Flower*, it also got its name from retailers, who saw the letters TT inscribed on the disc label and called it *Troubled Troubadour*.[19]

As the summer and fall of 1969 wore on, multiple versions of the basement tapes circulated. Retailers expressed astonishment that young people would buy up any bootleg available, with no sure knowledge of what it contained or whether it duplicated another record they owned. Recorded music came unmoored from any kind of fixed identity; fans could no longer assume that a recording was one of a definite sequence of releases by a particular artist in a label's catalog, recorded and packaged for sale at a definite moment in time, nor could they be sure whether the sounds had appeared elsewhere in slightly different form. Sound became free-floating and promiscuous, like the motley mix of recordings by any artist that one might find on a spindle of "burnt" CDs or a computer hard drive in the twenty-first century. The music's provenance, its release date, even the identity of the performer was far less certain than those of a glossy, well-designed LP released by a legitimate label. The tireless effort of record companies to build the stardom and image of their performers crumbled in the face of widespread duplication.

Despite their unpredictable content and quality, bootlegs became a premium item. *Great White Wonder* sold for between $6.50 and $12.50, while stores in New York asked $9.98 on average. Street vendors near Columbia University and other campuses got $20 for the product.[20] *Protean Radish*, an activist rag published in the college town of Chapel Hill, North Carolina, noted that bootleggers had "liberated" the unreleased Dylan music at prices that were often higher than a regular Columbia records disc. (Price is what distinguishes bootleg collectibles from pirated or counterfeited versions of existing recordings, which were often sold for less to undercut an official release.) According to the *Radish*, small record shops in Durham and Chapel Hill sold *Great White Wonder* for $10 and *Troubled Troubadour* for $5; meanwhile, peddlers were selling *Wonder* in Washington Square Park for $15 in October 1969. "If Columbia goes through with its intention to sue all store[s] carrying the album," the paper noted, "they would be suing themselves, as one of the record chains selling the album is owned by Columbia."[21]

It soon became essential to distinguish one product from another. Since bootlegging was an activity of dubious legality, an "anything goes" attitude prevailed. In other words, since bootleggers were already copying the work of recording artists, their competitors felt free to copy each other's products. "Uncle Wiggly," a twenty-six-year-old Los Angeleno who pursued an MBA on his profits from piracy, said his team was hard at work on a new Janis Joplin LP but that they would have to move the product quickly once it was perfected. "We're taking orders, and then we're going to deliver them all in the same 24-hour period," Wiggly told *Time* in 1971. "You see, if we don't do it that way, somebody will get hold of an early copy, duplicate it and start competing with us."[22] Wiggly's struggle recalls the competition among American publishers to pirate foreign works in the 1820s and 1830s. "The first step in 'The Game,' as it was called, was to secure a copy of a desirable work," according to historian Aubert Clark. When one publisher saw his offer of £100 for an advance copy of *Nicholas Nickleby* turned down, "he gave up further negotiations simply because he could not afford to pay more for a few hours' advantage."[23] However, time was not the only factor for the bootleggers of the early 1970s. As some labels sought to offer higher-quality recordings, they wanted customers to be able to tell their products apart from those of inferior copycats, who would often make a copy of a copy.

The best way to assert an identity in the market was to cultivate a trademark, a recognizable image. Bootleggers did this by inventing logos, such as Trade Mark of Quality's (TMQ's) cigar-smoking pig or the Amazing Kornyfone Record Label's Dr. Terrence "Telly" Fone, and using a characteristic style of art for their album covers. William Stout's artwork, similar in style to Robert Crumb's underground comics, was an extension of the music; his covers depicted scenes from the album's lyrics. The images were both a representation of the music and a comment on it, sometimes satirical. The cover of a Dutch Dylan bootleg, *Little White Wonder*, featured a cartoon for each of the album's thirteen songs. Several of the images allude to the chameleonic singer's roots: at the top, a masked Dylan is back on the farm in Minnesota, the caption "Bob Zimmerman," referring to his original name. Nearby, a winged Star of David flies by with a musical note inside. In others he is a lascivious character. He stands on the sidelines of a parade shouting "Don't forget to flash!" in the picture for "Million Dollar Bash." The last picture shows Dylan seated in a cluttered apartment, with a leering expression on his face as he mouths the song title, "You Ain't Goin' Nowhere," like an overly friendly host insisting that his guests stick around. The downside, of course, was that such calling cards made it easier for the authorities to track down particular companies (and the quality packaging cost more, especially if the illustrations were in color). TMQ's Deep Purple disc, *Purple for a Day*, may not have been an official band release, but a sticker on the plain white jacket guaranteed that it was a "Genuine Trade Mark of Quality Disc," pig and all.[24]

Trade Mark of Quality used its brand to distinguish itself among numerous peddlers of unreliable quality, but the name also caricatured the ways corporations present themselves. It resembled the bland monikers used by fly-by-night tape pirates, like Custom Recording or Super Sounds, and the label's mascot was a cigar-smoking pig—not unlike the iconic image of a cigar-smoking capitalist. Ze Anonym Plattenspieler (ZAP) was another paradoxical trademark, meaning, "The Anonymous Record Players." Another venture of Dr. Telly Fone, ZAP tried to have it both ways, cultivating an identity for itself in the market *and* mocking the business of musical commodities. Each ZAP record promised "A High Standard of Standardness!" As a one-liner, it was a cheap shot at mass production and marketing, but as a bootleg slogan, it highlights the awkward position of an entrepreneur in a marginal line of business: ZAP sought to assure consumers that a certain level of quality could be associated with its name and logo, as with any company. However, identities were just as likely to be stolen as music in the bootleg market; smoking pigs showed up on records by people unaffiliated with TMQ, and nine inferior albums were released with the Kornyfone label in 1975.[25]

Perhaps the most notorious brand to emerge in the heady days of the early 1970s was Rubber Dubber. A sort of capitalist commune, this outfit recorded live performances by the likes of Jimi Hendrix and James Taylor, quickly evolving from white covers to albums adorned with striking monochromatic art and photography—and, of course, the Rubber Dubber logo. Dubber offered not just a trademark or recognizable design, but also a media persona. The group sent review copies to *Rolling Stone* and other critics, with the note, "Yours Truly, Rubber Dubber," and Columbia Records threatened to withdraw advertising revenue when music magazines began reviewing the records as though they were regular albums.[26] Soon the agents of up-and-coming artists were trying to get in touch with Dubber, hoping the firm would bootleg their clients and show that they were good or at least popular enough to be copied.[27] Dubber's mysterious leader told reporters that they connected artists directly with fans, without the intermediary of a record company. His description of their egalitarian operation recalled Karl Marx's description of the well-rounded socialist individual in *The German Ideology*: "Everybody in Rubber Dubber has to work, but nobody has to work all the time, and nobody works the same job every day. Each person knows how to do every facet of the operation, so if somebody gets sick or wants to take a vacation, somebody else can take over."[28]

Bootlegging and Counterculture

Rubber Dubber was one of numerous bootleggers who espoused a radical creed. Not everyone put forward a blueprint for a different economy, but many aligned themselves with a general insurgency against the establishment. "Many of our salesmen would otherwise be pushing drugs," Uncle Wiggly argued. "We give a lot of money to the free clinic and to the peace coalition. I don't think there's anything illegal about this."[29] *Rolling Stone* claimed that the original purveyors of *Great White Wonder* had fled to Canada to avoid the draft.[30] "It was the mentality of the time, the Vietnam war," one bootlegger recalled. "There was such an anti-establishment feeling in the air."[31] Michael O concurred: "It was the psychedelic era and people did a lot of goofy things to break the rules."[32] Producer Dennis Wilen argued that the youth were enamored with the ideal of "bringing music directly to the people without having to go through the bureaucracy of the music industry."[33]

> The romantic aspect is the most compelling attraction. People can't go fight in the Spanish civil war any more, and the day of the desperado, of Robin Hood, is over. So they strike out at the fat cats of the music companies this way. It's an existential romantic trip.[34]

If anything, most bootleggers were taking from the rich—a record label or a famous rock star—to give to the middle class. The pirates who copied major label products to sell at lower prices might lay a better claim to the mantle of Robin Hood, but almost no one ever praised them.[35]

For the true believers, bootlegging offered an avenue for creating an alternative music industry, one uninfected with marketing glitz and commercial caution. This *truly* free market would provide more of the rough-hewn, political, folky protest music that Bob Dylan had made early in his career—not the Bob Dylan that Columbia wanted to foist on the public, nor even the version that the singer himself chose to present. The first round of rock bootlegs focused on unreleased songs by Dylan, but copiers soon turned to raiding the studio material of other artists.[36] The Beatles made for a prime target for several reasons. Besides their immense popularity, the Fab Four had also logged countless hours in the studio experimenting with the sounds that became *Sgt. Pepper* and *Revolver*, and it was widely known in 1969 that the band's follow-up to the *White Album* had languished in limbo for much of the year.

Though the Beatles publicly expressed support for the Left and the peace movement, the unreleased songs from these sessions reveal a political side the band's surviving members have so far chosen to hide. More than anything, they demonstrate an acute sense of the racial conflict that rocked American and British society in the late 1960s. Sung partly in a stuttering Elvis croon, "Back to the Commonwealth" skewers "dirty Enoch Powell," a Conservative politician who warned in an infamous speech that "rivers of blood" would flow if the United Kingdom did not cut off immigration. "Enoch Powell said to the immigrants," Paul McCartney sings, "you'd better get back to your Commonwealth homes.... If you don't want trouble, you better go back to home." Such a topical song might not have translated well for the band's audience outside the United Kingdom, and it might have offended some British listeners who knew Powell and supported him. The song "White Power" on *Sweet Apple Trax* further illustrates the band's political caution. The extended jam lists the names of black notables, such as James Brown, Cassius Clay, and Malcolm X, and juxtaposes them with the likes of Richard Nixon and white soul singer Dusty Springfield. The tune resembles "Dig It," which later appeared on the official *Let It Be* LP and also consisted of a list of names; however, that short track packed less political punch, as John Lennon free-associated, "CIA, KGB, BBC, BB King..."[37]

The new album, tentatively titled *Get Back*, was intended to be a return to the simpler rock and roll of the Beatles' early days. The band released many of the recordings from these sessions as part of *Let It Be* in December 1969, but bootleg versions hit the streets of San Francisco in the form of *Kum Back* months earlier.[38] Fans who obtained a copy of the bootleg realized that the original version of the song "Get Back" was very different from what listeners were hearing on the radio. The official version speaks of cross-dressing Loretta Martin and Jo-Jo, who "left his home in Tucson, Arizona for some California grass"; the lyrics imply that bad things will happen to both characters if they do not "get back to where [they] once belonged."[39] Bootleg editions reveal that the original lyrics dealt with immigration, speaking of Pakistanis in the United Kingdom and Puerto Ricans in the United States. On an alternate version that bootleggers called "No Pakistanis," McCartney sings, "Don't dig no Pakistanis taking all the people's jobs." If released on a major label, the tune might indeed have damaged the band's carefully cultivated image; instead, it appeared on illicit records like the 1969 *Kum Back* and Kornyfone's 1976 compilation *Tanks for the Mammaries*.[40] "No Pakistanis" still circulates on file-sharing networks in the twenty-first century, but the Beatles never opted to publish it officially, even when their *Anthology* series released several new—and unremarkable—songs from the vault in the mid-1990s.

Unauthorized releases provided an avenue for risqué material to reach the public, even if only a tiny portion of the mass audience heard it. For example, the best-known Patti Smith bootleg, *Teenage Perversity and Ships in the Night*, featured a strikingly different version of the song "Birdland," which appeared on her landmark 1975 debut *Horses*. On *Teenage Perversity*, a concert recording, Smith prefaces the song with a comic monologue about aerosol cans and the ozone layer, which slips into a tale of a young boy being molested by his father. Her telling becomes poetic and rhythmic, and then turns to singing; gradually, the audience learns that the father in the story is Wilhelm Reich, the controversial German psychologist whose theories about sexuality and "orgones" landed him in prison, where he died in the 1950s. The lyrics are graphic enough to make the executives at any major label blush, whereas the album version of "Birdland" is much less explicit.[41]

This alternative channel for music distribution proved useful for Smith and other early punk-rock artists, whose work was too provocative for a chary music industry. Television, for instance, was a seminal New York band whose work circulated on bootlegs in the 1970s; concert tapes remain the only surviving documents of some short-lived and ever-changing groups of the period.[42] Smith seemed to support the bootleggers who disseminated her live performances, Clinton Heylin says, as she "sometimes [introduced] 'Redondo Beach' as a song from *Teenage Perversity*."[43]

The labels that circulated (potentially) controversial records did not neatly fit the model of the "collectors' pirate" who dominated the jazz and classical underground in earlier years. In the early 1970s, sociologists R. Serge Denisoff and Charles McCaghy distinguished this zealous new breed of bootleggers from earlier copiers like Dante Bollettino, who had justified their sales of unreleased or out-of-print material as a service to listeners. The commercial scale of pop music and the tug of youth rebellion put the bootleg boom of the late 1960s in a different context, both economically and culturally. "First, the demand for their products was much greater, hence potentially more profitable," Denisoff and McCaghy noted.[44] Opera piracy might have been a minor irritation to record companies, but bootlegs of the Beatles or Bob Dylan were harder to ignore.[45] Second, "counterculture pirates" went far beyond the archiving and service functions espoused by jazz or classical bootleggers. Their ideology was, according to Denisoff and McCaghy, "a complex amalgam drawing upon both Marxist and utopian socialist writers and translated into the rhetoric of the New Left."[46]

Historian Doug Rossinow's attempt to define both "counterculture" and the "New Left" can help us understand where bootlegging fit in the broader environment. In his book *The Politics of Authenticity*, Rossinow argued that the young rebels of the 1960s sought to expand "the scope of 'politics' after several decades in which political activity was understood…merely as the attempt to influence governmental institutions and the social allocation of resources."[47] They refused to restrict social change to setting the tax rate one percent higher or lower, insisting that revolution must encompass every level of daily life. Slogans such as "the personal is political" and "the revolution is about our lives" exemplified this attitude toward political struggle.[48] If the revolution was about one's life, then it could be as much about music as about civil rights or war.

How could popular music—the product of capitalist media—fit into the schema of radicalism, though? The musicologist Nadya Zimmerman has written about tensions that shaped the San Francisco counterculture of the late 1960s, in which young people, inspired by novelist Aldous Huxley and Buddhist writer Alan Watts, among others, desired to reject consumerism and embrace a more "natural" way of life. But as Zimmerman cautions, we ought not assume that opposition to materialism or conformity necessarily meant that radicals eschewed all interest in consumption or pop culture.[49] Bootlegging was a form of rebellion that scrambled the anti-corporate, anti-consumerism, and anti-technology tendencies of the counterculture, existing alongside the back-to-nature aspirations of those who "dropped out" of mainstream life to form rural communes, as well as the more conventionally political goals of activists.[50]

As Rossinow suggests, it is fruitless to try to pin down one definition or even one counterculture, since Americans of many stripes fought against one perceived establishment or another. After all, the most successful rebellion of the time may have been that of conservative Americans who rallied to support Richard Nixon in 1968 and 1972.[51] This "silent majority" also saw itself as oppositional, defying the establishment elite, albeit in the spirit of patriotism and the work ethic. Defining a counterculture requires not just identifying a group or movement that opposes the status quo, but also determining what it is about the prevailing society that people oppose. Rossinow argues that the New Left and the hippie counterculture shared a search for "authenticity," yet opposition to capitalism was also an important unifying thread. Not every participant in these movements hated consumption, markets, or property rights, as the flourishing market for hippie paraphernalia attested, but an inchoate desire to resist the domination of American society by business and bourgeois values was central to much of the counterculture.[52]

Indeed, the commercial success of rock and roll bootlegs and the attention given to them in left-leaning media indicate that many critics of the establishment did not blush at consumption (of a kind). This style of opposition was displayed in the 1968 debate between activist-showman Jerry Rubin and Fred Halstead, presidential candidate of the Socialist Workers Party. While dour spectators looked on in despair, Rubin rebutted Halstead first by playing "I Am the Walrus," and then by burning two dollar bills. A socialist hooted, "If you have no goddam [sic] use for those dollars then give them to us!" "I wouldn't burn $100," Rubin drily replied. "It's just a symbol. I believe in the end of personal property and all the capitalist dollar thing."[53] Property—whether in the form of money or music—was outdated and irrelevant in Rubin's eyes, but the music possessed a political value in its own right.

The counterculture to which bootleggers ascribed themselves did seek to build alternative ways of life, and did oppose capitalism, at least as it was understood at the time—bureaucratic, corporate, industrial. However, just as Rubin later grew rich in the yuppie era of the 1980s, the bootleggers' new world ran the risk of looking a lot like the old one. Writing in *Harper's*, Ed Ward recognized that "your run-of-the-mill headshop/waterbed/record-store" often amounted to "the same old thing with longer hair," but he believed that the Rubber Dubber organization constituted a genuine alternative model of capitalism.[54] One bootlegger told *Rolling Stone* that "profits from bootleg albums are more equally distributed to employees than are major company profits which are often funneled up to parent conglomerates."[55] Here, the pirate drew a distinction between the bootleg labels, which clearly sold goods for consumption on the market, and big business. However, dissension within some enterprises casts doubt on such claims of egalitarianism. In 1971, two employees reported Los Angeles tape

Figure 4.3 The title of this recording of punk artist Patti Smith performing live on New York radio station WBAI captures the paradox of the countercultural ethos—freeing music from capitalist control while still selling it as a market commodity. *Source:* Courtesy of Music Library and Sound Recordings Archive, Bowling Green State University.

copier Donald Koven to the authorities when he refused to give them a raise, and Rubber Dubber's warehouse of albums, cover art, and equipment was given away by an informant, most likely from within the secretive group.[56]

Piracy, counterculture, and capitalism made strange bedfellows, yet the centrality of desire (including, but not limited to, the desire to consume) unified them. The title of a Patti Smith bootleg, *Free Music Store*, neatly combines the rhetoric of anti-capitalist liberation and liberatory capitalism.[57] Here was consumerism, freed from almost all constraints—consumerism with the gloves off, so to speak.

Ironically, pirates could give consumers what they wanted in part because they did not operate within the complex web of relationships that labels traditionally used to bring records to market. They did not have artist and repertoire (A&R) representatives to identify promising talent; they had no promotional staff to cajole DJs and program directors to give recordings precious airtime, nor did they have to work out arrangements with distributors, record clubs, or rack jobbers (merchandisers who selected only the most popular and profitable recordings to place on racks in variety shops and grocery stores, with the option of returning unsold copies to the labels).[58] In fact, retailers complained about the deals the labels offered consumers through record clubs, arguing that the low prices undercut sales in stores; certain small dealers did not feel much remorse when they purchased cheaper bootleg tapes to sell instead of label-sanctioned merchandise.[59]

With no allegiances within the industry, most bootleggers were like Uncle Wiggly—they simply raced to bring the most desired music to listeners as quickly as possible, with the ability to produce in smaller batches with much lower overhead than Columbia or Warner Brothers could manage. They knew that fans would snap up their albums without the marketing push of t-shirts, buttons, advertisements, and payola that left most major label releases still failing to break even. A bootleg of a concert performed one day could appear in a record store or the back of a van a week later. In this way, the bootleggers offered a desired product faster than the established industry's structure would allow— a prototype of fast, flexible capitalism, however radical the pirates' rhetoric or their convictions might have been.

Craftsmen or Criminals?

Indeed, some on the Left challenged the radical credentials of music copiers. North Carolina's *Protean Radish* saw piracy as evidence that music could be distributed without the involvement of the record labels, even though pirates were not using this alternative system for revolutionary purposes. They used other people's music to antagonize the Man *and* to turn a profit. "You have to sort of admire them for taking one [*sic*] the Columbia and fucking them," Edd Taub opined. "But at the same time these outlaw capitalists are responsible for placing the people's music in the hands of the people with money, a lot of it."[60] Note that Taub said "the people's music" and not "the artist's." He felt that bootleggers were only secondary copycats, following the original mimics—white rock stars like Bob Dylan and Elvis Presley, who were quite literally "great white wonders." "Now the class that gave birth to the music can't afford to buy it back in the form of Dylan," Taub argued, "who has created higher levels of this culture by using musical forms from the Black and white working class experience."[61] The reality of many bootlegs as sought-after rarities capable of commanding high prices contrasts with the role of outright counterfeits, which were (and still are) usually sold at bargain prices. Often, bootlegging for collectors and fans was seen as more admissible than a parasitic, entrepreneurial piracy. From Taub's perspective, however, the latter sort of copying could be understood as making music more affordable for the masses.

Most journalists felt sorrier for the artist than for the lumpenproletariat that had inspired what was now a high-dollar collectible. A reporter from the *Los Angeles Press* clandestinely met with a bootlegger who wore a Columbia University sweatshirt and a paper bag over his head. "I interrupted him to ask about Dylan's share," the journalist wrote. "Wasn't he entitled to royalties on his own material?" The man in the bag at first evaded the question, declaring that *Great White Wonder* was better than the "shit" Columbia Records chose to release. He then turned into a populist: "In a sense, we're liberating the records and bringing them to the people, not just the chosen few." Finally, the man admitted that paying Dylan was "a dream we here have long held and will continue to cherish." Less disingenuously than some other pirates, this one did not feign a sincere concern for the artist's royalties. He would send Dylan a little of the profit some day, but in the meantime dreams of outselling *Nashville Skyline* consumed his thoughts.[62]

Ralph Gleason, a music critic and executive at Fantasy Records, ridiculed the professed mission of bootlegging and foretold its demise, as record companies stopped tolerating unauthorized reproduction and pushed Congress to change the copyright law.[63] The prosperity of the 1960s, he said, "allowed quack Robin Hoods like the Rubber Dubber to pose as public benefactors, in a sense, giving the public a chance to get some more of what they wanted when the artists themselves (and the companies) were unable or unwilling to supply the demand." These Robin Hoods liked to say they circumvented the big, bad corporations by giving the people what they wanted and sending royalty checks to the artists. Even if they did—and Gleason doubted it—they gave nothing to the session musicians who made the music. He noted that the record companies were going after stores that sold unauthorized merchandise, especially pirate tapes: "These are usually made by straight criminal types who are into some kind of hustle as opposed to bootleg LPs, where the implication—though even this isn't sure—is that a counter culture dude does them." Overall, Gleason rejected the notion that bootlegging meant cultural liberation, suggesting it was only free in the sense of a free market. "It is the same kind of self-justification that a pimp employs or the manager of a stag show or a porny movie house," he concluded. "After all, we are performing a public service. So is a bull."[64]

In other words, even the Mafia can claim to be true adherents of laissez faire. Indeed, Gleason's criticism gives a sense of where the musical black market was headed in 1971. As was seen in the crackdown on illegal jazz records in the early 1950s, bootleggers who expanded beyond small-scale operations ran afoul of the law. As record copying became bigger business in the 1970s, the market drew the attention of both the major labels and organized crime. The days of 1,000-copy batches of Louis Armstrong reissues were gone, as the potential profit of this quasi-legal activity began to attract professional criminality and violence.[65]

The line between entrepreneur and criminal was often hard to draw, though, especially since the legal status of recordings remained unclear. "I wasn't exactly representing the nicest people in the world," admits Francis Pinckney, an attorney who worked for several pirates in the late 1960s and 1970s. Still, there were many players in the business he refused to represent. "There were really some shady characters in it, who just surreptitiously copied these things and sold them out of the back of trucks," he recalled. "They would be in South Carolina until the law started catching up with them, then they'd move to North Carolina."[66] When a friend asked Pinckney about copying sound recordings, he assumed that it could not possibly be legal. The friend said that a man in Atlanta had gotten legal advice that there was a loophole in the copyright law, and he decided to go into business selling his own tapes of popular music.

The Charlotte attorney looked into it further and discovered, as so many had before him, that sound recordings were not copyrightable. Technically, it seemed, one could copy existing recordings and pay song publishers the flat royalty for their compositions created by the 1909 Copyright Act. Before letting his clients proceed, though, Pinckney wrote a letter to the major record companies, explaining his theory about the loophole and offering to pay an additional royalty to the labels in exchange for the permission to use whichever recordings they wanted. He even suggested a proviso that would bar his clients from taking more than half the songs from any given album, to prevent the copiers from identically replicating the original release:

> The idea was that they were going to take the top 10 songs, and put them on one tape, and it was going to be a great product. Instead of having to go out and buy ten records, each one of them had one of the top ten songs, instead you'd have them all on one cassette tape....I never heard from any of them. I thought I'd at least get one response that says, "Go to Hell."[67]

Pinckney's legal and ethical take on piracy reveals much about a certain breed of copier in this period. Disliking the pejorative term "pirate," they preferred to call themselves "anti-monopolists." They thought that consumers should be able to obtain the recording they wanted without having to buy it in the form the record company determined—for instance, as part of a full-length LP. Just as any artist could record a cover of any song they chose, thanks to the compulsory license system, other firms would be able to sell the product on their own terms, while paying both the songwriter who composed the music and the record company that recorded it separate royalties.[68]

In 1971 Pinckney and several other lawyers representing the pirate firms proposed such a system to Congress. All the while, they aspired to present the pirates as respectable businessmen. "The clients which we represent have known places of business, open to the public, are advertised, and anybody can come and see them and talk to them," attorney Thomas Truitt told lawmakers, speaking on behalf of G&G Sales, Eastern Tape, and several others. Truitt held up a tape, telling the copyright committee, "This is an example of their product. It states on its face who makes it and where you can come and find those people."[69] Pinckney had insisted that his clients include their name and address on the tapes; though they had done so reluctantly, they soon discovered that the practice helped them sell the product: "They would go into a 7/11 and say, 'We've got these tapes we want to sell,' and the guy would say, 'There ain't no way I'm gonna buy those things'...And they'd say, 'Look, here's our name and address. Come by and see our place of business. If it weren't legitimate, we wouldn't be doing it.'"[70]

Unlike the hippie bootleggers, who sought to liberate live or unreleased music, this group of pirates focused on making "mixes" of readily available songs. "You can't buy a legitimate product with songs by all the top artists, because they have exclusive contracts with different companies," Bruce Weber observed in *Billboard*. "So the illegal operator picks selections from several leading albums, puts them together on a tape and offers all the hits in one."[71] One could find this product in unconventional outlets such as gas stations and flea markets. *Time* noted in 1971 that "nearly every city has record stores, gas stations and supermarkets with selections of bootlegged tapes and records, which are usually packaged in unadorned boxes and albums with plain white covers."[72] Jan Bohusch, for instance, sold music mixes with his partner at the Wisconsin state fair in the early 1970s, raking in large sums of money for anthologies that were calibrated to particular tastes. After he abandoned the business, E-C Tape, he testified before a 1974 hearing called by New York attorney general Louis Lefkowitz. "E-C Tape did issue royalty checks to copyright owners [composers and publishers], the vast majority of which were uncashed," he said.[73]

Bohusch: E-C was a unique pirate because they did not take any existing record albums. They took simply cuts from albums and combined them into anthologies.
Lefkowitz: Made a contribution with some talent in other words?
Bohusch: Yes, I would say.
Lefkowitz: A little high class.
Bohusch: We were the highest class of pirates. Yes, generally I would say that we also had the audacity to charge $7 for the product.
Lefkowitz: Which cost you what, $1.11?
Bohusch: Under a dollar. We were the only people in the entire nation selling 8 tracks for the full list price.[74]

Bohusch took pride in what he had done, even if he had come to believe it was unethical. Other tape pirates produced a product with bad sound quality, or simply copied existing albums track for track, with no creative input. "The quality runs from absolute trash to good," Bohusch recalled. "[E-C] was garbage, but it was the best garbage."[75]

Some pirates built on Bohusch's idea of anthologizing popular music by using the mix as an opportunity to satirize the material, while making a unique product available. One wag at a bootleg label promoted a mythical John Denver compilation called *Wish I'd Been Born a Deer*.[76] Other albums might qualify as a sort of conceptual art if they had been presented in a gallery or university rather than on the black market. Released in 1982, *Elvis' Greatest Shit!!* combined the dregs of the King's catalog with a package designed to insult his most obsessive fans. Although this bootlegger usually used the name "Richard Records," he attributed the *Greatest Shit* album to "RCA Victim," a dig at the RCA Victor label. A slogan on the front cover asserted, "50,000,000 fans can be wrong!" Worst of all, the album brought together the most inexplicable and embarrassing tunes from Presley's career, including "Fort Lauderdale Chamber of Commerce," "Dominic the Impotent Bull," and "Song of the Shrimp."[77]

The project inverted the perennial record label tactic of squeezing a few extra dollars out of the audience for an over-the-hill artist by adding one or two new tracks to a collection of his or her best-known hits. The record openly presents itself as an artifact of corporate greed, with the slogan "A New Rip-Off Repackaging Job" emblazoned across the top. (Except, perhaps, for Joni Mitchell, who released both a *Hits* and a *Misses* collection, the greatest hits formula has rarely been modified.) Further, Richard used the album to tweak the whole logic of collecting upon which bootlegging largely depended. Most hardcore fans would want to vacuum up any odds and sods by their favorite artist, even if the material were utter dross and the packaging mocked their affection. If nothing else, *Greatest Shit* presents an alternative view of the artist that would not be apparent from looking at a greatest hits collection or any other individual item in his catalog—a sort of remix on a larger scale.[78]

Not everyone shared this sense of craft, and here the lines between above-the-board entrepreneur, radical bootlegger, and pure opportunist became the most muddled, revealing a drift toward organized, professional profiteering. Godzilla's American Phonograph Record Export Service, based in Glendale, California, made its economic intentions about as plain as could be in the early 1970s. The group sold TMQ records like *Great White Wonder* and *LIVEr Than You'll Ever Be*. Jumbling familiar Beatles hits with outtakes, its *Renaissance Minstrels* album showed how impure the mission of bringing unreleased music to the people often was. "We offer these high quality original productions at the lowest and most competitive prices possible," Godzilla's catalog promised. "This enables your firm to have a substantial profit margin when reselling this product." They also nodded and winked at the notion of counterculture: "We might add, this profit margin is much greater than that of legitimate albums and, due to the nature of being 'underground,' is very easy to sell on the wholesale and retail levels."[79] Up to ninety-nine albums could be purchased at a unit cost of $2.10 each, and orders of between 100 and 499 could be had for $1.95 each. Likewise, a Houston-based group called Music City Distributing sent out catalogues promising top albums for $2.75 a piece. The accompanying letter was signed, "Your friendly bootlegger."[80] *Business Week* claimed that large bootleg outfits were rapidly outstripping "'mom and pop' thieves" like Bohusch. They ran their own factories, put display racks in gas stations, printed catalogues, and dispatched salesmen around the country.[81]

One such salesman was Tom Brown, an idealistic young musician who worked with bootleggers in Texas and California during the early 1970s.[82] His story reveals some of the dangers involved in bootlegging, especially as legal suppression loomed. Tom got involved with the illicit market in the summer of 1970, when he found a "day gig" with a group called the Record Plant in Grand Prairie, Texas. He spent the day making labels for Jimi Hendrix and Led Zeppelin records; he claimed to be unaware that the products had not been authorized by the bands or record companies. Management soon recruited him to be an ambassador to the hippie stores in the Dallas–Fort Worth area. "The owner offered to front me a few albums and promised me half the profit on sales," he recalled. "I didn't know much about artists' royalties at the time and figured the artists were getting paid." Tom started pulling in $2,000 a month, and the managers sent him and his friends on a mission through Illinois, Kansas, Missouri, and Oklahoma. When the boys reached Chicago, policemen looked at the Texas plates on their truck and figured their cargo must be marijuana from Mexico. "They were still uptight from the '68 SDS riots at the Democratic Convention," Tom surmised. Unable to find the contraband they were looking for, the police dumped the guitars, bongos, and boxes of records in the street and arrested the youths for possession of illegal weapons (a pocketknife and a starter pistol). After watching the police abuse and humiliate two drag queens in jail, they were released on a $25 bond and ordered to get out of Chicago in twenty-four hours. "To this day I have never met anyone else who was ever kicked out of Chicago like my brother and I were," Tom said.[83]

Soon, Tom joined the actual Rubber Dubber organization. He came home one day to find the Record Plant's secretary waiting for him with a "big, burly and tall hippie looking character, who introduced himself as Chuck Kane." The man claimed to be one of the founders of Rubber Dubber, and he said the Texans had been selling his company's products without permission. What difference did it make, though, if the Record Plant stole from Rubber Dubber, since Dubber was

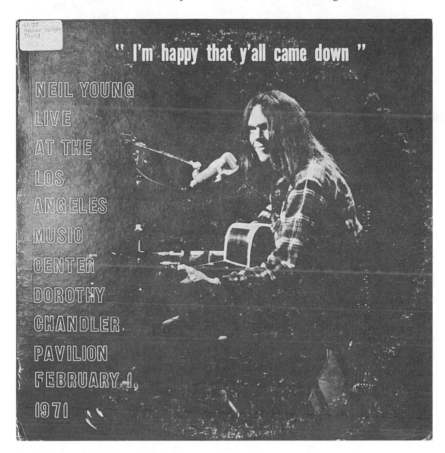

Figure 4.4 This recording of a Neil Young concert is typical of many Rubber Dubber records, which documented performances by Jimi Hendrix, Elton John, and others in the early 1970s. Recorded in 1971, this disc was made eight months before a bill providing federal copyright protection for sound recordings was passed by Congress. *Source:* Courtesy of Music Library and Sound Recordings Archive, Bowling Green State University.

stealing from Hendrix? The difference, Kane said, was that his people believed in paying royalties to artists. "This impressed me because I considered myself an emerging artist at the time and I didn't want any bad 'karma' to come back on me," Tom recalled. In any case, Rubber Dubber wanted to take advantage of his midwestern sales base, and Tom soon found himself working for the company in Los Angeles. The group back in Grand Prairie folded, as workers in Los Angeles printed, shrink-wrapped, and mailed records to their former clients in the Midwest.

In California, Tom worked in sales and recording, capturing performances by artists such as Elton John, James Taylor, and Neil Young.[84] Rubber Dubber made sure to snap up tickets for the best seats in the house as soon as they were available. Chuck Kane would carry a high quality reel-to-reel tape recorder to the concert in his backpack, while Tom had to maneuver with a long microphone stuck in his pants. Although it looked awkward, no one ever bothered him about it. "One person would limp in with a shotgun mic down one leg," Tom said. "That was never noticed because of all the returning Vietnam vets with injuries." Although the sound quality was not excellent, the recordings captured the feel of the live performance. The Rubber Dubber gang saw this product as having more value than the pirated tape of an album that was already a hit. "We did not put ourselves in the same category as them," Tom said. "We were selling something that was totally new and captured from the 'air.'" At the time, he believed that they were giving the fans something they wanted and paying the artists for their work; although he began to suspect that what they were doing was illegal, everybody seemed to win.

Like many things with Rubber Dubber, the truth differed from the image. According to Heylin, Dubber's leader was the scion of a Dallas crime family who wandered away from the family business.[85] The evidence suggests that he did not stray very far. Terry Conklin, a Laguna Beach drug dealer, had ponied up funds to get the organization going, and some participants pulled in additional cash from credit card scams. Of course, as Tom said, the group's leaders could afford to be "very generous, as they never paid for anything." When Ed Ward asked Rubber Dubber's leader, "How do you expect to make money?" he responded that they had no need for profits. The group divided up its proceeds equally, and looked after the rent, health insurance, and Social Security of its employees.[86] However, the reality was not so communist; the sales staff, for example, worked on commission. Tom insists that the workers never got a share of the profits, nor did the artists ever receive a dime. "It didn't take long to see through those guys," he says. "They were only in it for personal gain."[87]

By late 1971 time was already running out. A bill providing federal copyright protection for sound recordings passed Congress in August, and Rubber Dubber rushed to sell off as much of its stock as possible.[88] After its Crosby, Stills and Nash bootleg hit the shelves, David Crosby hired detectives to monitor the group, although the investigation turned into a farce. Several gumshoes followed a trail all the way to a school for the deaf in Texas, which Rubber Dubber had led them to believe was a bootleg factory. Meanwhile, in Kansas, another team of detectives banged on the door of a man they were sure was the group's leader at four in the morning. "After he'd listened to them trying to serve the subpoena on him, he ripped it into shreds and threw them in jail for disturbing the peace," Ward wrote. "He was the county sheriff."[89] A more serious encounter soon followed. US Marshalls descended on the Dubber headquarters, deep in the warehouse district of East Los Angeles. Kane had to keep the lawmen occupied in the office while Tom and the other employees removed all the contraband from the warehouse and drove away. "It fell apart after the raid and never really recovered," Tom said. "By that time, the idealists like me had already moved on."[90]

Many of the bootleggers got out of the business after the new copyright law went into effect in February 1972. For example, Rubber Dubber's leader quit after a few close brushes with the law, although he landed in jail on a murder charge years later. Tom Brown went to Oregon to seek spiritual enlightenment shortly after the US Marshals showed up. Jan Bohusch turned on his former partner and testified about their activities at a public hearing in New York in 1974. Some, like Bohusch's partner, kept on copying, in part because the 1971 law only banned the reproduction of recordings copyrighted after the statute went into effect. Some used the same tactics as Boris Rose and the Bronx baker, who put out each record on a different label to cover their tracks. For example, one bootleg group in the mid-1970s issued each of its records under names like Hen, Led, and Steel Records.[91]

After the law changed and the fervor of the late 1960s faded, rock bootlegging reverted to much the same form as the jazz and classical piracy before it, continuing to provide live performances and other rarities to a devoted fan base. No longer making splashy statements about changing the system, these bootleggers were, in Denisoff and McCaghy's terms, essentially collectors' pirates. A countercultural tendency did persist, perceptible in the role of bootlegs in spreading the word about punk rock and hip-hop. Throughout the 1970s, record companies, musicians, and politicians struggled to squelch the growth of unauthorized reproduction through increasingly punitive copyright reform and new kinds of law enforcement; during the same period, piracy endured and evolved in response to legal suppression at the state, federal, and ultimately, international levels.

5

The Criminalization of Piracy

Even as war, riots, and rock and roll shook the United States in the 1960s, Congress continued to fiddle with copyright reform. When *Great White Wonder* appeared in 1969, lawmakers were considering yet another proposal to give the record industry what it had wanted for sixty years: a separate copyright for sound recordings. The numerous legislative false starts of the era forced labels to look elsewhere for help in dealing with the surge of music piracy, first with renewed litigation on the grounds of unfair competition, and then by lobbying state governments to pass their own antipiracy laws. Lawsuits proved costly and ineffective, as pirates found it easy to dodge injunctions and other penalties, often by leaving one state and setting up shop across the border. And state laws raised constitutional questions about whether the states were creating an unlimited quasi-copyright, thus intruding on the federal government's turf.

California's 1968 statute, one of the first and one of the strictest, was challenged at the state and federal level, leaving the debate open until the Supreme Court's 1973 *Goldstein v. California* decision.[1] By then, Congress had already responded to the bootleg boom by extending copyright to sound recordings. When that reform failed to quash piracy, lawmakers strengthened fines and enforcement and ultimately passed a measure in 1976 that changed the terms of copyright for decades to come.

Stirrings of Reform, 1955–1964

Why did Congress decide to take up the issue of copyright again in 1955? Dante Bollettino and other bootleggers had made headlines in the early 1950s by copying rare and out-of-print jazz recordings. Record companies used these incidents to remind lawmakers of the shortcomings of the last major copyright revision, passed in 1909. Indeed, the 1920s and 1930s saw lawmakers attempt to bring US law in line with the Berne Convention, an international agreement signed in

1886, but each effort failed because of discord among publishers, record companies, broadcasters, and other interests. Congress abandoned the revision project in 1940 to handle the more pressing concerns of war.[2]

With the return of peace, politicians turned their attention to copyright once more and attempted to assess the role of the media and culture industries in the booming economy. Economic growth meant that consumers had money to spend on nonessential goods, whether a bootleg of New York's Metropolitan Opera or an old Jelly Roll Morton recording. Pirates could take advantage of consumers' greater disposable income and the youth market by satisfying a demand unmet by the major record companies. Television and radio provided more material for bootleggers to copy and sell, and advances in recording technology made it easier to do so.

The first signs of friction over unauthorized reproduction emerged soon after World War II. The entertainment capital of Los Angeles passed the first criminal law forbidding piracy in 1948, and California would be one of the first states (second only to New York) to approve a similar statute in 1968.[3] Music labels formed the Recording Industry Association of America in 1952 to protect their interests, which consisted largely of maintaining the compulsory license system (which permitted them to record songs by paying a low fixed royalty) and stopping the illicit reproduction of records. Never known for its celerity, Congress began to reconsider the issue in 1955, funding a series of studies on copyright and related industries; a stopgap measure to provide copyright for sound recordings would arrive sixteen years later, and the long-awaited comprehensive revision came only in 1976.

Congress passed the first Copyright Act in 1790, and major revisions ensued about every forty years—in 1831, 1870, and 1909. Judging by this pattern, an overhaul was due by the 1950s. Reporting to Congress, economist William Blaisdell calculated that various industries had generated $6.1 billion from the use and sale of their copyrighted products, out of a national income of $299.7 billion. The aggregate of radio stations, newspapers, record stores, and related businesses earned more than banks, mines, or utilities, and slightly less than the auto industry, even in the 1950s heyday of General Motors.[4] Blaisdell's study showed Congress that various media represented a sizable share of the nation's economic output, but the qualitative changes were at least as significant as the quantitative ones. Radio and television broadcasting did not even exist when the 1909 act was passed, and the film and recording industries were then only beginning to take shape.[5]

In 1961 the Register of Copyrights, Abraham Kaminstein, made a series of recommendations that addressed looming controversies in music and publishing, among other industries. He proposed ending the compulsory license for musical compositions, which would allow songwriters to license their work selectively, like any other copyrighted item. Publishers were eager to see the existing system terminated, since they hoped to negotiate higher prices for the use of their songs than the flat rate fixed by Congress. Record companies, on the other hand, wanted to be able to record any song without negotiating deals with individual composers or publishers.[6] Kaminstein also hinted at the brewing conflict over "new techniques for reproducing printed matter," such as the Xerox machine, an increasingly vital tool in labs, libraries, and offices throughout the country. A long and bitter conflict over "fair use" would play out during the 1960s and 1970s, pitting academic publishers against the National Institutes of Health, whose libraries regularly photocopied articles from science journals in large numbers for researchers throughout the country.[7] Before the mêlée broke out, the Register recommended that a library be restricted to making a single photocopy of an item in its collection, with specific guidelines to be worked out later. As for music piracy, Kaminstein was cautious: "This report…favors the principle of protecting sound recordings against unauthorized duplication, but makes no specific proposals pending further study."[8]

Indeed, over fifty years of experience failed to yield a solid answer about what to do with recordings. There still was no consensus about whether a mechanical reproduction of music was a "writing" apart from the song on which it was based, or, if it was, then who the writer was. The Constitution allows an author to benefit financially from his writings, but the first Congress included only books, maps, and charts in this category, to which legislators added (written) music in 1831 and photographs in 1865.[9] As the Supreme Court noted in its controversial 1908 *White-Smith* decision, Americans had only attributed copyright to works that were visually perceptible. One could understand letters, musical notes, and images, whether printed, painted, or photographed with the naked eye. To Justice William Day, the grooves on a phonograph disc and the holes in a piano roll were not the same thing. They were more like the gears in a clock than the words in a book. Machines could be patented on the basis of what they did, not what they meant, and patents had to reach a higher standard of novelty than the standard of originality for copyrighting an expression.[10] Congress could have decided to take the unprecedented step of recognizing a mechanical application of expression under copyright, but, as we saw in chapter 1, lawmakers chose not to recognize the recorded performance as a copyrightable expression, separate from the song itself.

Numerous media developments in the first half of the twentieth century undermined this idea that a visual expression was necessary for copyright protection. Film, radio, and television all provided new examples of meaning conveyed by technological means quite distinct from the palpable, visual world of print and paper. Still, lawmakers and judges found ways to square the circle; a movie could be understood as a series of individual images, thus fitting into the precedent of copyright for photographs. Advances in computer technology, especially during and after World War II, posed much thornier dilemmas. For instance, should a string of ones and zeroes or a microchip qualify as a novel mechanical achievement, worthy of patent, or a meaningful cultural expression, deserving copyright?[11]

The growing use of media such as magnetic tape added to this confusion. A motion picture can be viewed as a series of individual images, which were already copyrightable, but a recorded performance was fundamentally different and distinct from the written composition on which it was based. Authorities thus found it easier to fit film into the old copyright paradigm than musical recordings; the record possessed elements of creativity that could be found only among its vinyl grooves or magnetic particles, not on the written page. At Congressional hearings in 1962, the American Guild of Authors and Composers (AGAC) argued that "all forms of authorship creation, visual and aural (whether on disk, electronic tape, or otherwise) should be deemed to be copyrightable 'writings.'" The AGAC went on to note that, with the increasing use of recording technology, the "initial expression" of a work often first occurred in an electronic form—for example, a poet speaking into a tape recorder, or a jazz band improvising in the studio.[12]

Such works did not start with written symbols and then get inscribed in an electronic medium. Indeed, legal scholars Harriet Pilpel and Morton Goldberg pointed out that certain types of electronic music could not even be transcribed in any conventional notation, thus denying them any chance for copyright protection.[13] Record producer Herbert Kanon explained the problems he faced with his own "sound effect" recordings, which he could only copyright in the form of a book that described the sounds. The AGAC concurred: "Often, the only full of expression of a work—a musical composition as performed or a motion picture—consists of a fixation by such form of recording."[14]

The AGAC's term "authorship creation" is telling. This vaguely industrial-sounding expression alludes to the creation of something and implies that some kind of authoring occurred, but who authored what is unclear. Although the phrase did not enter general usage, one can assume that the AGAC chose "authorship creation" carefully in preparing its testimony. The author is easy to find when one imagines a literary genius pecking away at a typewriter, but media like radio and film almost always involved the creative contributions of numerous workers. One could say the screenwriter was the author of the Hollywood blockbuster, but countless decisions separated the script's creator from the final product, the series of images on the screen. Was the gaffer or the key grip an author? What about the cinematographer, the person who actually pointed the camera and determined what the images would look like? By convention the film director has won the honor of a byline in the movie business, but even this person (usually) works for the movie studio, and "works for hire" were owned by whoever put up the money and did the hiring.[15]

Not everyone at the hearings, at least in the early 1960s, was convinced that the problem of who authored or owned a recording could be resolved. Organized labor worried that reform would result in a record company, rather than the performers, receiving the copyright. Even songwriters and their publishers were unsure about the revision; the record companies could end up possessing a stronger copyright than the composers, who had limited control over who could record their work and only received a flat rate for each copy of a recording. The Music Publishers Association's Philip P. Wattenberg explained the problem:

> Music publishers have always been against copyright of records. They have difficulty in understanding just how this can be done. For example, if we take a musical composition "Begin the Beguine," it has been copyrighted as a composition, which has been published in printed form, assume we now license RCA Victor to make a record of "Begin the Beguine" in exactly the same series of notes that we have in the printed form. In other words, there is no arrangement. If RCA Victor were to try to copyright that record under the title "Begin the Beguine," in whose name would that copyright be? Certainly it could not be RCA because the basic work is copyrighted in the name of the publisher. This can only lead to confusion and a dilution of the rights of the original copyright owner, which is the publisher.[16]

If the recording is merely a note-for-note transcription of the sheet music into sound with little in the way of interpretation, what is the record company's claim to a copyright? It can only consist of hiring a musician, buying the studio time, and paying for the production and promotion of the record. In other words, it is a monetary and technical investment in this hypothetical scenario, involving almost no degree of interpretation or artistry. The record companies thus wished to obtain a copyright for their capital.

Wattenberg's example is an extreme one, but the possibility that individual interpretations *would* be unique (and copyrightable) also raised concerns. In 1962, the lawyer Julian Abeles insisted to lawmakers that sound recordings were not sufficiently original to merit copyright. Even if they were, the result would be a logistical nightmare, at least from a legal and economic perspective. "If every time an artist rendered a composition that rendition would be subject to copyright, then we would have innumerable copyrights of every composition, because each artist would claim copyright for his or her purported original rendition," Abeles said. One performer might sing the song in a particular tone of voice; claiming a copyright for that rendition, he or she might try to stop someone else from recording it a similar style. How the engineer recorded or mixed a performance might be copyrighted as a unique interpretation. Critics of a copyright for recordings wondered how courts could possibly sort out the claims of those who "owned" certain sounds. Technology seemed to open up new avenues for individual expression, but how those expressions would be handled individually was far from clear.[17]

Given profundities of this kind, as well as the lack of unity within the music industry on the subject, Congress backed away from providing copyright for sound recordings in the early 1960s. Instead, lawmakers tried to formulate a more limited bill that would make counterfeiting illegal. Support for such a modest step was more forthcoming. "Sound recordings should be protected against physical reproduction, i.e., dubbing, for a limited term comparable to the term of copyright," the Author's League allowed. "However, copyright protection is not required for this purpose and, in fact, could cause serious disadvantages. A simple prohibition against dubbing would serve the purpose."[18] In contrast, Barbara Ringer, who worked in the Copyright Office and later became Register of Copyright, believed that any such prohibition would have to be based on copyright law. How else could dubbing be banned except on the grounds that someone else's creative expression was being unfairly exploited—the purpose of copyright? As introduced in April 1961, the bill forbade anyone from selling and distributing a counterfeit record over state or national lines "without permission of the owner of the master recording."[19]

Ringer's view won out, however. Congress realized that prohibiting people from copying and selling a record was tantamount to giving it copyright, and that lawmakers might as well resolve the issue directly rather than indirectly. The resulting bill, passed in 1962, focused instead on duplication of the packaging of the record, rather the music inside it. "The bill was limited to dealing with what was then the rather pernicious practice of simply duplicating everything, the trade dress, the appearance of the label and album cover," Ringer recalled in 1971, "so that you could not tell the legitimate record from the counterfeit."[20] She also noted that pirates got around the law simply by forgoing any effort to mimic the original package.

Taking the Battle to the States

Congress revisited copyright reform in 1964, shortly after two landmark Supreme Court decisions set a new precedent for limiting property rights.[21] In the 1940s and 1950s, courts had zigzagged from Learned Hand's cautious approach to an expansive view of copyright in *Metropolitan Opera v. Wagner Nichols* (1940) and *Capitol v. Mercury* (1955). In *Sears* and *Compco* (1964), however, the court held that one company could not be prevented from copying the look of another's light fixture, since the design was not a unique invention or a work explicitly protected under copyright. Since copyright was the prerogative of Congress, and it had specifically listed what items could be protected, state governments and the courts had no power to create additional property rights. Such "quasi-property rights" not only impinged on the supremacy of Congress but also opened up potentially unlimited rights that, under copyright law, would have been limited to a fixed number of years. Kaminstein warned that the industry could end up with *stronger* rights if Congress neglected to provide clear guidelines for sound recording, and Ringer echoed this concern. "In the absence of Federal legislation," she said, "performers and record producers have what amounts to a complete monopoly under state law."[22]

In yet another turn, though, virtually every subsequent court ruled that *Sears* and *Compco* did not permit the copying of sound recordings. They determined that the rulings could not extend all the way from the design of a lighting fixture to a record, in which much time and money had been invested. According to this view, the two decisions permitted copying or imitating someone else's work but not directly appropriating it through piracy.[23] The distinction is fine but significant: "copying" referred only to imitating the look or sound of another product, while "appropriating" meant taking the product itself—in this case, a recorded performance—and selling it as one's own. Just months after *Sears* and *Compco*, in the case *Capitol Records v. Greatest Records*, the New York Supreme Court enjoined Greatest Records from selling two albums and a single by the Beatles that were originally released by Capitol Records.[24] The court determined that *Sears* only concerned the "copying of an idea," while pirating a Beatles record amounted to taking and profiting from someone else's actual product.[25]

Five years after the *Greatest* case, the California Court of Appeals agreed that reproducing a sound recording amounted to outright theft.[26] A company called Phoenix sold tape copies of recordings by the Lettermen, taking care to remind consumers on the packaging that they were in no way affiliated with the group's label, Capitol Records. The difference in design would protect them from prosecution under the 1962 anti-counterfeiting law, Phoenix thought, and the disclaimer would prove that they were not "palming off" their tapes as Capitol's products—a tactic that had consistently failed since the heyday of Wynant Van Zant Pearce Bradley in 1909. Phoenix had also changed the order of the tracks on the tape, perhaps to show that they were not selling the exact same product. "It is obvious that Phoenix is able to sell the cartridges at such lower price, and still gain substantial profit, because Phoenix circumvents the necessity of expending skill and money in acquiring the artists and recording their performances," Justice Park Wood wrote for the court. "Thus, Phoenix unfairly appropriates artistic performances produced by Capitol's efforts, and Phoenix profits thereby to the disadvantage of Capitol."[27]

Phoenix was guilty of unfair competition, having taken advantage of not just the artistic performance acquired by Capitol but also the popularity of the recording. Recall that the doctrine of unfair competition grew out of trademark rulings in the nineteenth century that prohibited a company from taking advantage of the reputation of a competitor by deceiving customers into associating its own products with another firm's well-regarded name.[28] In the twentieth century, this notion gradually expanded to address cases in which a pirate unfairly profited from the popularity of a recording artist by copying his or her works— as when Wagner-Nichols put out recordings of the Metropolitan Opera without the organization's permission. While Phoenix had not attempted to pass itself off as Capitol, it did sell a hit by the Lettermen that had not become popular by accident. Justice Wood noted that Capitol had spent $10,000,000 producing master recordings since 1965, and over three times as much to advertise them.[29]

Record companies enjoyed an unbroken string of successful litigations in the mid to late 1960s, yet several factors suggest that these were Pyrrhic victories. A lawyer who defended tape copiers on numerous occasions won only one such case, when a South Carolina judge declined to grant an injunction against his clients. Even then, the decision was subsequently overturned on appeal. On at least one occasion a judge in North Carolina forbade a defendant only from copying the plaintiff's records,[30] and the defendant went on merrily pirating music by all the other companies. Meanwhile, the record industry told anyone who would listen that the cases were easy to win but costly to pursue and difficult to enforce. Sometimes the penalties imposed by a court barely deterred an especially prosperous pirate. The Recording Industry Association of America (RIAA) complained to Congress that a pirate was fined only $500 in the case *Capitol Records v. Frank D. Campoy, Jr.,* an amount the offender was able to absorb as a "minor, incidental expense."[31]

The industry watched as copyright reform idled in Congress, courts yielded empty successes, and piracy grew more widespread and flagrant in the late 1960s. Its next strategy was to lobby the state legislatures for measures that would be more punitive than the common law of unfair competition. New York, a center of the entertainment industry, was the first state to pass a law against piracy. Governor Nelson Rockefeller signed the bill, which went into effect on August 2, 1966.[32] California caught up with New York by passing its own far more stringent law in 1968. No further state laws appeared until 1971, when Arkansas, Florida, Pennsylvania, Tennessee, and Texas outlawed unauthorized reproduction.[33] Of these, only Tennessee and Texas could be described as having a homegrown music industry, and Tennessee's Governor Winfield Dunn signed the bill in a photo-op, flanked by Nashville music stars.[34] The New York law that started it all was among the weakest, at least in its first iteration. Whereas Tennessee threatened pirates with a $25,000 fine and between one and three years in prison for the first offense, New York mandated a $100 fine and up to a year in prison.[35] Both forbade "transferring" sounds without the consent of the owner, as well as distributing and selling such sounds.[36]

Such a law, of course, presupposes that the owner can be clearly identified. The owner of the sounds could be the performer or the record company, but the state laws seemed to side with the label that produced the original master recording of a performance. During debate over the New York law, the RIAA's Henry Brief insisted that the record company's right to its recordings was well established, thanks to the precedents set in the *Metropolitan, Capitol v. Mercury* and *Fonotipia* decisions.[37] The court in *Metropolitan* had ruled that Wagner-Nichols had interfered in a contract by making its own records of the Met Opera from radio broadcasts, because the Opera had already arranged with another company to put out recordings of its performances. The *Fonotipia* decision rested partly on the fact that the public got an inferior product when Wynant Van Zant Pearce Bradley made his own copies of Italian arias originally released by another company.

It may seem like a fine distinction, but none of these decisions actually declared that the record company possessed an inviolable right to control how its products were used. Rather, the rulings condemned various instances of copying that were harmful to the public or to the parties in an existing contract, or that otherwise smacked of ill-gotten gains. Though the courts said that one should not reap where one has not sown, they never issued a categorical approval of the notion that the record company, and the company alone, *owned* the recording. Even if the courts had wished to provide such a right, their ability to do so was constrained by the ambiguity in copyright law. Further, the performers whose sounds were actually contained on the record could also make a persuasive claim for ownership. Indeed, in its report on the bill, the New York legislature's Committee on Penal Law and Criminal Procedure condemned pirates for failing to pay the proper dues to "the performer or issuing company," leaving open the possibility that either party could be the owner of the recording.[38]

By lobbying for the New York law, the RIAA aimed to have the state legislature decisively endorse its own claim about ownership, which was based on its investment in the product. "Many hours of planning and work and the investment of much capital go into the production of a phonograph record," Brief argued. "The end result is a combination of artistic skill and mechanical ingenuity."[39] The right to ownership, it seemed, lay in the combination of creativity and capital, courtesy of management. "The master recordings are carried as assets by recording firms," the lobbyist went on to say. "They have a dollar value, and the rights to use them have been sold, leased, traded and exchanged both domestically and on an international basis."[40] In other words, record companies wanted their de facto property to be recognized as de jure.

The industry had the labor movement and consumer advocates on its side in this campaign. Max Arons of the American Federation of Musicians expressed his support for the bill to the governor, commenting that his union's members had been harmed by the growth of piracy.[41] Meanwhile, state attorney general Louis Lefkowitz and his staff pushed hard for the bill. His Bureau of Consumer Frauds investigated illicit copies in New York's record stores and found that some recordings listed a different performer or performance than was actually contained on the disc or tape. In the Bureau's view, piracy was a problem chiefly because the consumer was deceived into purchasing a low-quality imitation of the official record company product.[42]

Opposition to the bill came from two sources: broadcasters, who feared that the ban on unauthorized copies would outlaw the practice of making temporary copies of music to be played on the air, and collectors, who made the perennial argument in favor of copying out-of-print records. In a telegram to the governor, NBC president Thomas E. Ervin warned that making temporary copies of sound recordings was necessary for the everyday functioning of radio and television stations.[43] Ervin avowed his opposition to commercial piracy of recordings but urged Rockefeller to veto the bill, unless a provision permitting ephemeral copies was allowed for broadcasters. He maintained that the record industry supported such an exception. Radio disc jockeys sometimes taped programs that blended their own words and sounds with musical recordings to air at a later time, and the broadcasters argued that this practice was harmless compared to the copy and sale of pirate recordings.[44]

Record collectors, in contrast, appealed to the ideal of preserving scarce recordings. Representatives from ABC and NBC based their arguments on the practical needs of broadcasting, while the collectors made a broader claim that the public's right to its cultural heritage overruled whatever ownership that a legislature might permit a record company to enjoy. Like Dante Bollettino in the early 1950s, the New York lawyer and archivist Payson Clark believed that the public should not be denied access to a recording because the company that originally produced it no longer found it profitable.[45] "Properties which are gravely affected with the public interest, in which society has artistic and cultural rights of enormous significance (although no one has yet found them materially rewarding to reproduce) are being locked away from posterity out of a misdirected zeal to keep 'The Beatles' recording royalties from being diluted," Clark wrote to Governor Rockefeller.[46] "Let us defend The Beatles right to riches, if that pleases the Legislature, but *not* by forever suppressing the immortal recordings of America's creative musicians of the 1920's and '30's whose playing has been felt and heard around the globe."[47]

Clark sounded an alarm that other critics would ring in the years to come, as the scope of property rights inched ever outward. He noted that the ban on copying records conferred on record companies an open-ended right of ownership, whereas federal copyright could only last for a limited amount of time. (The term was a maximum of 56 years in 1966.) "No nation, to my knowledge, confers a *PERPETUAL proprietary right* in the author or inventor, but rather fixes a reasonable term (sometimes with a renewal privilege which is similarly limited in duration) at the expiration of which the work enters the public domain," Clark observed. "The grave danger in this proposed New York statute is that it employs *criminal sanctions* to confer a unique form of aural or *audio copyright which is vested in perpetuity* in a manner greatly inimical to the public interest."[48]

Several non–New Yorkers also wrote to urge Governor Rockefeller not to sign the bill. A New Orleans lawyer who collected old jazz records, Harry Souchon, apologized for intruding on the internal affairs of another state. He commented on the law, however, because he suspected that "whatever action is taken by the State of New York may well influence similar action in other states." Souchon commended the intent of the bill—to curb piracy—but said the bill as it was written would be "very detrimental to record collectors in all fields."[49] The collectors argued that the world of the antiquarian had nothing to do with the market for popular music, and that scholars had no interest in profit when they copied and exchanged "obscurities out of the ancient past."[50]

This quest for an exception in the law might have been noble enough, but none of the collectors explained how the state could allow small-scale copying of old records while forbidding commercial piracy. If bootleg labels copied truly obscure music for the most esoteric tastes, would the state or the record companies bother to penalize them? Naturally, the collectors did not want to have their activities classified as illegal, even if they were not actively suppressed. The case of Jolly Roger in the early 1950s raises the real question. One could imagine a system that permitted copying and distribution of music on a nonprofit basis, keeping in circulation records for which no viable commercial market existed. Or, as James Goodfriend suggested in *Stereo Review*, the government or the libraries could undertake a custom mail-order service on a noncommercial basis.[51]

But what if business got too good? What if Blind Lemon Jefferson or Tampa Red's Hokum Jug Band experienced a renewed vogue with the public, and the small outfits started selling reissues like hotcakes? Undoubtedly, the record company that first released these performances would seek to prove it had the exclusive right to distribute them, if the original label still existed. People could be allowed to copy only those out-of-print records that had been produced by defunct companies, for which no legal claim could be made or copyright holder found—so-called "orphan works."[52] However, the performing artist or his descendants would still have to be considered. Devising a workable system that would satisfy collectors while forbidding commercial exploitation posed many logistical problems, and no one at the time tried to lay out a plan.

In any case, Henry Brief roundly rejected the arguments of Clark, Souchon, and others. "Mr. Clark charges the record industry with a conspiracy to keep consumers from obtaining out-of-print recordings for their collections," he wrote to Rockefeller. Record labels were making a good faith effort to provide the public with reissues of old recordings, and Brief insisted that they would sell records if demand for them existed.[53] However, if there were no market for such goods, then how could piecemeal reproduction threaten the industry? Clark argued that it was precisely these tiny demographic groups whose desires either could not or would not be met by regular record companies. "The fact remains that the greater number of ancient phonograph recordings can never be made economically available by the few companies dominating the industry today," Clark proposed. "The demand is too infinitesimal, and the profit is non-existent."[54]

In the end, the legislature disregarded the collectors and placated the broadcasters. Clark and Souchon's legislative influence was ultimately as inconsequential as they claimed their economic impact to be. Meanwhile, Lefkowitz assured broadcasters that the bill would not interfere with their normal operations.[55] The New York bill paved the way for subsequent state legislation, but, more importantly, it established the first clear-cut legal precedent that record companies owned their recordings. Congress had retreated from this position during its consideration of the 1962 anti-counterfeiting bill, preferring to forbid only the mimickry of packaging rather than the copying of the sounds contained on a record. The 1966 law can be seen as a model for the historic act passed by Congress in 1971, which would put to rest the long-running debate over ownership with the force of federal supremacy.

The Long-Awaited Copyright Reform of 1971

Despite several close brushes with accomplishment, Congress continued to postpone and procrastinate throughout the late 1960s. The House of Representatives managed to pass a copyright reform bill on April 11, 1967, but the legislation bogged down in the Senate over questions about the new medium of cable television. Senator McClellan (D-AR) kept the bill alive as the Judiciary Committee kept deferring it through the next several sessions of Congress.[56] A comprehensive reform still had to wait until 1976. In the meantime, growing awareness of music piracy prompted Congress to separate the issue of sound recordings from many other thorny problems, such as the legal status of cable

TV or the price level of the compulsory license for songs. What had been a slug-gish and halting legislative process was about to pick up pace in the early 1970s.

With the rise of tape copying and countercultural piracy, Congress found the record companies' familiar cries of suffering much more persuasive. "Anyone working with this on a day-to-day basis cannot fail to be impressed with the enormous growth in [piracy] over the last 5 years or so," Barbara Ringer told Congress in 1971. She attributed the growth to the "ease of tape duplication" and the "lack of clarity" in the law.[57] While lawmakers in Washington squab-bled, California had made it a felony to copy someone else's record, no matter how many years had passed since the work was published. Ironically, Congress's refusal to extend copyright to recordings resulted in a far greater property right at the local level. Court rulings on unfair competition were similarly open-ended. "These are not limited in time," Ringer observed. "There are no formalities. They don't have to put a copyright notice on them. They do not have to register or deposit anything. They just sue and win."[58]

Despite all the laws and lawsuits, the music industry continued to face an enemy that could make a similar product at a lower price, investing next to nothing and possessing an endless variety of hiding places. Jack Grossman of the National Association of Record Merchandisers (NARM) lamented that law enforcement might harass pirates in Manhattan, but they soon moved to Long Island or New Jersey. "There are many basements and garages in which they can hide," he said.[59] Ralph Gleason, the critic and Fantasy records executive who denounced bootleggers in the pages of *Rolling Stone*, conceded that the threat of legal reprisal could prevent the record stores and big chains from selling bootleg product, but "it's hard to get at all the service stations and places selling tapes along with stoplights and rearview mirrors."[60]

Of course, industry representatives went to great lengths to demonstrate to lawmakers that pirate recordings were technically inferior, pointing out the cheapness of the equipment used by pirates, bringing in sound engineers to tes-tify to the difference between legitimate and bootleg products, and even playing tapes in court to show their poor quality. Some copies must have come very close to the quality of the originals, for record companies also complained of having to reimburse retailers for unsold tapes, only to discover later that they were not authentic. Also, if an expert technician was required to explain the difference between a real and pirate recording, then the shortfall was probably less than significant. In any case, youngsters who wanted to listen to "Yummy Yummy Yummy" might not be looking for sonic virtuosity. What they wanted were hits. Pirates could supply the hits by putting all the most desired songs on one tape, even if they were by different artists who recorded for different labels.[61]

The recording industry knew that this product would be highly desirable, and they strenuously opposed it.[62] Allowing consumers to get any song they wanted in any format would undermine the entire basis of the industry, which involved hyping one song to stoke the public's interest in other recordings by the same artist on a full-length LP or tape. Representative Richard Fulton, the self-styled Congressman of "Music City, U.S.A." (i.e., Nashville), argued that the revenue from popular records made it possible for the industry to invest in new artists and money-losing products. Nine out of ten records fail, Fulton said, and the profits from the few big hits subsidize the rest of the industry.[63] If pirates were allowed to shave off the benefits of a record that finds public favor, then record companies would be less able to take a chance on other artists, with the result of less diversity in the market. The RIAA's Stanley Gortikov echoed this point: "The pirate skims the cream of what artists and record companies offer except for one particular ingredient, which he avoids like the plague ... our risks."[64]

According to Gortikov, recording a typical album cost $55,000. By the time the record landed in the stores, a company had spent $180,000 to $200,000, meaning that manufacturing, distribution, and promotion cost $145,000. Pirates spent money on manufacturing and distribution, so the difference lay in recording and promotion. "The pirate can go into business for as little as $500," Gortikov said. "Yet, we can't even take one artist into one studio for one hour for $500."[65] In a written statement to Congress, the RIAA claimed that a Crosby, Stills, and Nash album cost $80,000 to record and another $200,000 to promote.[66] This figure was the only specific reference to advertising expenditures during the 1971 hearings, and it reflects the difficulty of making a really big hit, not to mention the extent to which the pursuit of hits cost more than other aspects of production and distribution.

Pirates appeared to jeopardize the entire music business. "Victims of this unconscionable racket are many," Representative Emanuel Celler (D-NY) declared in 1971. "They include song writers and publishers, record manufacturers, distributors and dealers, recording artists and musicians, manufacturers of phonographs, and, last but not least, the U.S. government."[67] Organized labor was now on board with the record industry's position on copyright, which it had doubted in the past. "Large incalculable amounts were lost by various trust funds maintained by the AFM," union president Hal C. Davis testified, "trust funds that are dependent upon royalties from sales of legitimate recordings and that are used to provide employment for musicians and free concerts for the public."[68]

For artists who had long been taken advantage of by the industry, backing the record labels in their quest for copyright could not have been easy. Labels said the pirates cheated them out of their royalties, wages, and benefits, yet the record companies had a long record of abusing musicians. Upon signing a contract, recording artists typically received an advance against future royalties, meaning they did not make any money until a variety of costs—for recording, promotion, and the signing bonus—were recouped by the label. Since only a few hits went on to make big profits, many artists remained in debt even if their records enjoyed moderate success. As one artist complained, "You can have a number one record and still not earn a f—king cent!"[69] Yet because debt was only paid down by the artist's royalties, which were a small percentage of revenue from sales, labels could still earn money on records that "failed." Labels were also notorious for finding ways to underreport or otherwise dodge royalties; for instance, contract provisions allowed them to pay reduced royalty rates for sales to record clubs, foreign sales, and "cutouts," unsold records that were returned by record stores and subsequently resold at deep discounts. The process lent itself to creative accounting, and artists often found it impossible to determine if all sales were properly recorded.[70]

Performers had their own interest in the rights to the recordings they created. Since the 1940s, musicians had argued that they should hold the copyright for a recording, not the label, or that the law at least guarantee royalties for performers when their records were played on the radio. (Composers' groups such as ASCAP held the right to collect payment for the use of their songs by broadcasters.)[71] However, the mounting problem of piracy threatened to destroy the industry upon which the union depended for work and benefits. "In the long run, gentlemen, the consumer will not benefit if pirating activities are not halted," Grossman warned. "For a while he may get a somewhat inferior product at a lower price, but, in time, the goose that laid the golden egg will be killed and new performers and new talents will not be available to him."[72]

But was the golden egg music itself, or just a hit song? In other words, did piracy threaten the existence of the music industry as a whole, or just the prevailing model for making and selling music? Did $200,000 need to be spent to inform the public about a particular recording, and persuade them to like it and buy it?

In fact, hype and promotion had been integral to the music business ever since publishing companies paid vaudevillians to play their songs and Victor invested heavily in creating the mystique of its Red Seal records. Despite routine denials, the industry indulged in "payola" since at least the 1930s, bribing stations to play particular records and retailers to situate them prominently in their stores. "Payola was the greatest thing in the world," record executive Hy Weiss enthused. "You didn't have to go out to dinner with someone and kiss their ass. Just pay them, here's the money, play the record, *fuck you*." Indeed, labels courted DJs and radio station program directors with money, liquor, gifts, and drugs ("drugola") and threw lavish parties for musicians and industry insiders. Such tactics were part of the titanic effort of labels to privilege their products by buying up territory in the public sphere—the price of access to the airwaves, the shop windows, and the ears of listeners. As the German critic Theodor Adorno argued in the 1940s, much of the appeal of popular music lay in a bandwagon effect, where songs became popular because they were ubiquitous and familiar. This notoriety made up no small part of the commercial value of a sound recording, and the labels were determined that their costly efforts not go to waste.[73] A song cannot be liked if it is not heard, after all.

Though the industry portrayed itself as the victim of lawless predators, it too bore the taint of criminality. Rumors of mob connections trailed artists such as Frank Sinatra for years, and industry players like Morris Levy, the wealthy and powerful founder of Roulette Records, relied on friends in organized crime to advance their business interests. In the 1970s, labels deepened their entanglement with unsavory figures, as "independent promotion" emerged as a substitute for the direct bribes of payola. Promoters sold their services to labels, guaranteeing that singles ended up in rotation on a given station. These well-connnected middlemen policed access to the stations that they controlled with the help of colorful "characters" from organized crime, as journalist Fredric Dannen revealed in his groundbreaking study *Hit Men*. This system reached its fullest expression after 1971, but promotion was already central to the arguments that labels advanced in Congressional hearings over piracy. What listeners heard and which songs became popular depended on money, drugs, and sometimes even violence, and the value of this "investment" was, in part, what pirates threatened.[74]

Only the pirates themselves stepped forward to present the case against the industry. They proposed a compulsory license system for sound recordings, patterned after the system set up for songs in the Copyright Act of 1909. "At minimum, the safety valve of a statutory royalty provision must be provided so as to guard against extortionate prices for copyrighted sound recordings," asserted Thomas Truitt, a lawyer for G&G Sales and several other pirate firms. "Since 1909, the recording companies have had the advantage of such a proviso in their dealings with composers and authors, and in simple justice, their competitors should enjoy similar rights."[75] Charles Schafer, owner of the Custom Recording Company in South Carolina, had been experimenting with the magnetic tape business since the mid-1950s, recording services for funeral homes and outfitting hearses with cartridge players. He warned that providing a copyright to record companies would foster monopoly, diminishing competition and leading to higher prices.[76]

A few Congressmen did doubt the necessity of handing property rights to the record companies, but the sort of zesty contention found during the Progressive Era debates over copyright was not to be found. Representative Abner Mikva, a Democrat from Chicago, expressed concern that prices would go up if record companies enjoyed exclusive control of their products, and he asked

Gortikov why the RIAA rejected a compulsory license system as an acceptable alternative:

> Gortikov: It would provide inadequate income to the record company, for the covering of its costs.
> Mikva: I do not follow you.
> Gortikov: Well, to the compulsory license, it would yield to the record company inadequate income to recover the cost for the product, and there would be no income from our hit product. We would have no source of income to recover the costs of maintaining our business, since about one out of 10 records only make money.
> Mikva: You could not build into a licensing agreement, a figure, that would be sufficient to cope with that?
> Gortikov: No; we need the distribution of everything we produce, so that the public has ample opportunity to make a choice, as to which product is to become a hit. If we are denied access to distribution, we have no skill in developing only hits.[77]

"Only hits" is key. Gortikov believed that record companies needed to monopolize the use of their creations in a way that a songwriter could not, in order to recoup, if at all possible, the investment in producing and hyping hit records. Treating sound differently from written music would have significant consequences in the years to come; musicians could record their own versions of a composition, for instance, without seeking permission, but artists could not use samples of recorded sound to create new works without negotiating licenses at often prohibitive costs.[78]

Senator Philip Hart (D-MI), known to his admirers as the "Conscience of the Senate," was the most outspoken opponent of the bill, and he particularly objected to Gortikov's reasoning. He supported the idea of compulsory licensing as a way to limit the record companies' power, and questioned whether the label should be treated as an author.[79] "Presumably, this committee believes record piracy imperils the investment of risk capital.... Neither the patent grant nor the copyright grant were intended to protect the separate interest of an entrepreneur's investment of risk capital," Hart argued. "They are limited to the protection of authors and inventors for the purpose of encouraging the disclosure of inventions and the publication of writings."[80]

Hart did not view protection of corporate investment as the same thing as an incentive to create and publish, but the bill's proponents did. A compulsory license offered sufficient incentive for songwriters to compose and release their music to the world, but record companies demanded greater protection to reap a return on their investments. The industry asked Congress to protect a business model based on hyping a few major songs, lest pirates imperil the worth of vast sums spent on advertising. They persuaded lawmakers to think of a work like a rock LP as a store of value created by a corporation. Sound was a form of information that could be fixed in vinyl grooves, magnetic particles, or any other technological medium. The new law would protect the authorship not just of the musicians but also of "the record producer responsible for setting up the recording session, capturing and electronically processing the sounds, and compiling and editing them to make the final sound recording," *Congressional Quarterly* reported.[81] Thus, copyright law recognized the label's role in creating the record as much as, if not more than that of a singer, songwriter, or musician.

The passage of the Sound Recording Act marked a turning point in American thought about culture, technology, and property. The Senate passed a bill providing the first US copyright for sound recordings by voice vote on April 29, 1971, and the measure passed the House with similar ease on October 4. President Richard Nixon signed the bill into law on October 15.[82] Courts had long struggled with the problem of how to protect a business's legitimate investment in making a good or desirable product when copyright law technically did not provide any exclusive right to sell a recording. The idea of a quasi-property right gradually emerged to recognize and protect that investment in the absence of copyright, and the growth of piracy in the late 1960s pushed lawmakers to encode this view of the purpose and nature of copyright into federal law.

The traditional American preference for limiting copyright as much as possible had begun to ebb. American copyright had always been utilitarian in nature, designed to "promote the Progress of Science and useful Arts" by giving creators an incentive to make their works known to the world. The new way of thinking emphasized protection of capital outlays, of established businesses like record labels, rather than incentives. By reinterpreting copyright in this way, Congress showed a willingness to view whatever was good for business as being good for copyright and the public in general. This could mean strengthening penalties, extending the term of protection, or adding other products, such as software, computer games, and genetic code, to the list of protected works.

Indeed, the reform was merely part of a broader shift toward stronger property rights in the late twentieth century. Trademark law also grew stronger and more expansive during this period; whereas courts had traditionally focused on deception, penalizing firms that tried to pass off their own products as those of a competitor and unfairly profit from another firm's good name, they increasingly condemned any activity that could *dilute* the value of a trademark.[83] Defendants could be held responsible for infringing when their names or logos vaguely resembled those of a competitor, not just when they plainly copied. Similarly, a record company did not want the capital it had invested in signing Bob Dylan to a contract and promoting his records to be freely exploited by someone else, even if the bootlegs did not directly compete with any of Dylan's officially released records. The law had long forbade firms from freeloading on the "good will" that a competitor generated by providing a quality product or service. By the 1970s, however, the notion of good will had mutated into popularity, as the doctrines of unfair competition and trademark law provided the intellectual basis for protection of the social value of a hit.

Goldstein and Beyond

The Sound Recording Act only protected records made after the law went into effect on February 15, 1972. Congress did not wish to interfere with existing contracts or state laws, which meant that antipiracy statutes would remain in effect in the seven states that had already passed them—Arkansas, California, Florida, New York, Pennsylvania, Tennessee, and Texas. Before passage of the federal reform, three tape pirates in North Hollywood, California, faced 140 counts of tape piracy under the state law. Among the trio were Donald and Ruth Koven, whose disgruntled employees tipped off the police about their pirate enterprise, as well as Donald Goldstein, whose name became synonymous with a landmark court decision on copyright.[84] The pirates were convicted and appealed through the California courts without success, but the US Supreme Court agreed to hear their case in 1972.

To the pirates, the state's antipiracy law violated the Constitution. Copyright was a responsibility of the federal government, and the historical record showed that Congressmen had consciously excluded "mechanical reproductions" (i.e., sound recordings) from protection under the 1909 act. Moreover, the California law indefinitely barred the unauthorized reproduction of a sound recording, providing the presumed owners of the recordings—record companies—an open-ended monopoly that surpassed the rights enjoyed by creators or owners of works under federal copyright law. This permanent property right, the pirates argued, violated the Constitution's mandate that ownership should last only for "limited times." Though bankrupt, Goldstein enlisted the help of attorney Arthur Leeds, who had persuaded several veterans of pirate defense to help him argue the case in California. Leeds believed that fighting a criminal prosecution would be the best strategy to undermine the antipiracy laws, since a jury might shy away from imposing so severe a penalty (prison) for the act of copying tapes.[85]

The court ultimately endorsed a capacious view of states' rights in a 5–4 ruling. Citing Alexander Hamilton, Chief Justice Warren Burger argued that the states could only be constrained from doing something under three conditions: first, if the Constitution gave that power exclusively to the federal government, as in matters of foreign policy. Second, an action would be illegitimate if Congress specifically forbade the state governments from taking it—for instance, if Congress had stated that mechanical reproductions of music were *ineligible* for copyright in the 1909 law, rather than simply leaving them out. Third, a state could not act in a way that was "contradictory and repugnant" to a similar federal policy. Burger admitted that the California antipiracy law might fall into this category, but he reasoned that the Constitution had not specifically barred the states from writing their own copyright laws.[86] The chief justice pointed to states such as Massachusetts and South Carolina that had granted their own patents in the late eighteenth century. He also dismissed Leeds's argument that the open-ended, unlimited property right created by California was contrary to the constitutional requirement of copyright "for limited times." That restriction only applied to federal copyright, Burger said.[87]

The majority also rejected the notion that *Sears, Compco,* or any other precedents should stand in California's way. Decisions such as *White-Smith* and *RCA v. Whiteman* specifically refused to turn sound recordings into intellectual property, but Burger and his allies sided with the line of cases, such as *Metropolitan,* that protected a company's investment. In fact, with the important exception of *Sears* and *Compco,* American courts had drifted in this direction for some time, given the reversal of *Whiteman* and the series of rulings against tape piracy in the late 1960s. Burger argued that *Sears* and *Compco* involved potentially patentable objects (light fixtures) that failed to qualify for patent, while sound recordings had been out of the federally defined ambit of copyright altogether. Therefore, the states were free to protect these goods in whatever way they saw fit. The chief justice brought up Louis Brandeis's dissent in the 1919 *Associated Press v. International News Service* decision, in which the progressive jurist suggested that "the noblest of human productions—knowledge, truths ascertained, conceptions, and ideas—become, after voluntary communication to others, free as the air to common use."[88]

Burger disagreed. "There is no fixed, immutable line to tell us which 'human productions' are private property and which are so general as to become 'free as the air,'" he said.[89] Lacking such a line, the court preferred to err on the side of property. *Goldstein v. California* came down on the side of property rights and state power, to the detriment of the public domain and federal supremacy. Better to give property the benefit of the doubt, Burger seemed to say, unless such rights were explicitly denied by Congress or the Constitution. A Los Angeles record company enjoyed stronger rights than a songwriter in Little Rock, and the investment of capital got surer protection from the state and federal governments than the labor of a writer or inventor. *Goldstein* can in part be attributed to the conservative shift of the Burger court; it followed soon after the departure of Earl Warren, whose judiciary had favored federal power over the state and local governments in cases such as *Brown v. Board of Education, Griswold v. Connecticut,* or, for that matter, *Sears* and *Compco.*[90]

The dissenters—Harry Blackmun, William Brennan, William Douglas, and Thurgood Marshall—believed that the creation of quasi-copyrights by the states would undermine "national uniformity," which they considered a top priority of federal policy. In his dissent, Douglas sounded the once-familiar cry of monopoly, which moved the Supreme Court in 1973 no more than it had Congress in 1971. The justice, an appointee of Franklin Roosevelt, pointed out that federal law may create a monopoly in the form of copyright, but it was a limited one, quite unlike the right created by California law.[91] Meanwhile, three Nixon appointees—Burger, Lewis Powell, and William Rehnquist—sided with the state of California, joined by Potter Stewart and Byron White.

The *Los Angeles Times* reported approvingly of the court's move to protect the performers and composers of California's "vast record industry."[92] Chief Justice Burger argued in his opinion that states had a legitimate interest in protecting their local businesses that other states (and the federal government) might not share. If piracy deterred record companies—"a large industry in California," as Burger pointed out—from making new recordings, then the state had every right to pass laws to stop it.[93] In such a way did the Supreme Court understand its treatment of music and property in 1973. Congress had considered a ban on pirate recordings to be unworkable little more than ten years earlier. In that short span of time, ensuring the recording industry could recoup its investments became accepted as a matter of economic necessity for local and federal authorities. Copyright became a safeguard and a symbol for the capital invested in creative works, and the lines between copyright and other property rights, formerly stark, became increasingly blurred in the move toward stronger, longer forms of protection. The recording industry accomplished this political feat through a decade of intense lobbying and litigation, but persuading law enforcement to enforce these measures posed even greater challenges in the decades that followed.

The Politics of Enforcement

The Sound Recording Act took effect on February 15, 1972, but tangible results did not materialize right away. Offenders had to have the opportunity to break the new law, and it took time for federal law enforcement to track the offenders and build cases against them. In the meantime, the RIAA took advantage of the Supreme Court's mandate in *Goldstein* to press state and local authorities to enforce existing antipiracy laws and to pass them where they did not exist. Twenty-seven states had passed such statutes by 1975, but the coverage was patchy. In the Midwest, for instance, Indiana and Nebraska had barred unauthorized copying of sound recordings, but Illinois, Iowa, Michigan, and Wisconsin had not, making it easy for pirates to evade criminal prosecution or civil suits.[94]

Pirates of pop hits carried on much as before, retailing their tapes in outlets where music was not conventionally sold. As Max Arons of the American Federation of Musicians observed, "In New York State every garage and everywhere else, every drug store they can get it."[95] The *Chicago Tribune* found them in "gas stations, laundromats, convenience food stores, and the like."[96] Mom-and-pop pirates relied on mom-and-pop outfits such as the local drug store to sell their products without anyone important noticing; the small business also represented a poor target for an industry lawsuit, unlike a record store chain like Sam Goody.[97]

RIAA agents had to explain to many policemen that pirates were actually violating the law. Francis once spent several hours at a precinct in downtown Manhattan, explaining to the secretary that he had found several stores around town selling pirate tapes. She eventually decided to transfer him upstairs, where he explained to two detectives that New York had a state law against piracy. "One of the detectives was willing to listen and the other fellow felt it was too much trouble to pursue an obscure misdemeanor and suggested some other bureau handle it," Francis said. Following a call to the assistant district attorney's office, he ended up recounting the story twice more to several other detectives that afternoon.[98]

If police in downtown Manhattan had not been informed of the antipiracy law, how much easier would it be to violate the statute in some remote hamlet upstate? Unless the FBI stepped in to enforce federal copyright, record companies had to rely on state laws that were carried out by city, county, and state police. Where states had only made record copying a misdemeanor, police departments seldom placed a high priority on seeking out pirates or following up on complaints.

The case of Jack and Julius Kessler suggests that pirates had begun to coordinate such operations nationwide, consciously choosing production sites they believed were beyond the reach and attention of law enforcement.[99] From 1971 to 1972, the Kesslers worked with Leonard Lockhart, owner of a dress manufacturing company called Playgirl Industries, to produce tape anthologies of pop music such as *Janis Joplin's Greatest Hits* and *The Best of Rock, 1970*. They did attempt to meet their obligations under the compulsory license system, sending out $95,578.65 in checks to publishers and songwriters, of which $53,000 were not cashed. (At least some songwriters were accepting the payments.) The business operated out of a "windowless white concrete building in a secluded area in Elk Mills," according to the Maryland Supreme Court. Piracy was not yet a criminal offense in Maryland.[100]

Lockhart, described as "the proverbial 'sad but wiser' man" in the ruling, defended their activities with a critique of the music industry that was familiar to many pirates and their lawyers. "You see, Atlantic and Columbia have a great gimmick in what they do," he testified. "They put two good songs on and six bad ones and they will sell it for $6.95. Now, very honestly, what we did was we put eight good ones on and they were sold to the market for $3.00. So that it was a value to the kids around the country and it serves a purpose, in my mind."[101] In any case, the pirate enterprise ceased operation in March 1972, less than a month after the new copyright for sound recordings closed the loophole that Lockhart and his friends sought to exploit.[102]

The decision to call it quits suggests that the Kesslers had learned their lesson, but Jack soon ran afoul of the law on the other end of the country. Going by the name Jack Fine, he was indicted in Los Angeles in December 1973 for his bootlegging activities, on grounds of tax evasion—the result of an IRS investigation. Like most pirates, he and his partner Martin Stern worked with cash and hid their actual profits from the government.[103] "Most of them don't even pay their employees by check," the RIAA's Jules Yarnell observed, emphasizing the harm of such practices to ordinary citizens. "They pay all in cash... There are no social security deductions or payments. There are no unemployment insurance payments, no health or other benefits, and the general public has to bear that additional burden."[104]

Local officials in Los Angeles launched a crackdown against piracy the same month that Fine and Stern were indicted, focusing on retailers. The city government enlisted the help of the Latin American Record and Tape Association (LARTA), in part because police raids found pirated tapes in many stores that catered to the Latino community. LARTA president Osvaldo Venzor formed the group after finding that bootleg recordings were being sold throughout Oklahoma and Texas. "We hope to make a dent in Southern California and then move on to the northern part of the state," Venzor said. "Then we will move east."[105]

Both the state and federal operations reveal a collaboration between law enforcement and corporate lobbying, in what might be called a public-private partnership. The RIAA started a twenty-four hour hotline for tips on the sale and production of illicit records, although an industry spokesman implied that the number got few rings. Meanwhile, the group's Anti-Piracy Intelligence Unit functioned as the music industry's own spy agency. "Part of our job is to disseminate information and acquire information on pirates all over the country," Jack Francis told Louis Lefkowitz, the New York attorney general. "It's a very clandestine operation. When something happens in New Jersey they know about it in Columbus, Ohio, two hours later."[106]

Of course, all that information could only lead to more tedious civil suits unless local or federal authorities were persuaded to act, and the industry's representatives had to train police to do their bidding. "We finally educated the state police up there and they being aware, there have been two subsequent arrests since then on their own without anyone's help," Francis said. "They know a pirate tape when they see one." Joel Schoenfeld, an intern with Lefkowitz's office, teamed up with RIAA counsel Jules Yarnell to scour the five boroughs of New York for evidence of pirated recordings, and then reported the information back to the police.[107] (Schoenfeld went on to become a major RIAA spokesman.) Likewise, LARTA assisted the Los Angeles police in pursuing pirates.

This collaboration resulted in ever more elaborate sting operations by local law enforcement. At the initiation of the RIAA, the District Attorney's Office in Manhattan began investigating piracy in the city, and detectives soon identified All Boro Records and Tapes as a wholesaler of counterfeits. Police raided the firm's office at 156 Fifth Avenue and called in label representatives to determine whether the recordings were copies. The experts said they were, but the sound quality was so high that prosecutors feared they could not persuade a jury that the wholesaler definitely knew he was dealing in counterfeits.[108]

As a result, the NYPD began using informants, undercover agents, and surveillance. The police used these tools, including wiretaps, to arrange deals to purchase 35,000 recordings from Premier Albums of 10 W. 66th Street, posing as retailers. Delbert Green, the owner of All Boro, had taken the precaution of moving his enterprise to Farmingdale, Long Island, where he stored records in a car wash. Premier Albums got its products from Green and "a source in Pennsylvania," Assistant District Attorney Roy Kulcsar said. On the day Premier Albums delivered the shipment to the detectives, police carried out simultaneous raids on the car wash in Farmingdale and a warehouse in Long Island City, Queens. Along with Green, Michael Javits and Phillip Vaudevehr of Premier pled guilty in February 1974, and the New York County district attorney pressed hard for jail sentences. The maximum penalty would have been one year in prison and a $1000 fine, but the judge only imposed fines on the men. All the work it took to nab these three pirates hardly seemed worth it.[109]

Even with a federal copyright for sound recordings, reams of favorable rulings, and an array of state laws, the record industry found itself in much the same spot as in the 1950s and 1960s. Piracy continued, and its trade group still had to pressure the government for further protection. Continued litigation such as the Missouri case *NBC v. Nance* (1974) and *A&M Records v. MVC Distributing* (1978), which reached the Sixth Circuit Appeals Court, suggests that the new statutory penalties had inadequately deterred copiers.[110] Jan Bohusch or Rubber Dubber might have gotten out of the business with the passage of the federal act in 1971 or the *Goldstein* decision two years later, but some players persisted, and others joined in the game.

Bohusch's old partner at E-C Tape, David Heilman, also carried on, despite having his stock confiscated by the FBI in May 1975. E-C Tape sold mixes tailored to those with a taste for "Early Beatles" or "Revolutionary Beatles," and nostalgia collections such as "Return of the Big Bands" and "Country & Western Classics."[111] Heilman moved the business from Wisconsin to California, where it ran afoul of A&M Records and the state antipiracy law. According to court records, Heilman's earnings from 1971 to 1975 amounted to $4,300,000, of which he personally collected $200,000. He broke several injunctions against continuing his business, and defied a ruling of unfair competition by the Superior Court of Los Angeles. Heilman went on plead the reproducers' case at hearings for the Copyright Act of 1976, but his appeal to the Supreme Court was denied in January 1978.[112]

The ease of entering the piracy business tugged the curious into what was now an unambiguously black market. Pirates could begin with a small investment and reap large profits. One Maryland man set up a pirate factory in his living room, with a turntable connected to five tape recorders. Beyond the initial capital costs, he only needed blank tapes and an LP to use as a master recording. This kind of operation might seem small to the point of preciousness, an RIAA spokesman said, but he urged the public to consider the output. The man could turn out five tapes every forty minutes and fifty tapes a day.[113] When a record shop bought pirate recordings at $2 apiece, such a small-scale business could gross $700 a week. By comparison, a professionally run pirate venture with printing presses, warehouses, and a large staff could make a better product and pull in $500,000 during the same time.[114]

Bootleggers, of course, were not alone in skirting the law. They could make a better product when they used a record company's own original recording rather than copying the mass-produced consumer LP. The availability of these masters hinted that some pirates had links to both the Mafia and the industry itself. The allegation of mob involvement in piracy was nothing new; in 1959 organized crime was held responsible for flooding the market with illicit 45s of Bobby Rydell's hit "Ding-A-Ling," and many observers had cited the use of pirated records in jukeboxes, through which the Mafia laundered funds.[115] In 1973 a grand jury in Los Angeles looked into accusations that record labels used drugs to bribe radio DJs and retailers, shook down artists for prized bookings in Mafia-linked clubs and casinos, and even collaborated with pirates. Meanwhile, warehouses and other buildings owned by record companies in Los Angeles were going up in flames; FBI investigators suggested darkly that someone was "trying to bring people into line."[116] Two years later the *Chicago Tribune* reported bombings at bootleg facilities in Michigan.[117]

Such scandals had a habit of "coming with uncanny timing in relationship to proposed legislation," the sociologists R. Serge Denisoff and Charles McCaghy observed in 1978. Just as Congress was considering whether to extend or enhance the 1971 Sound Recording Act, allegations of payola and other unethical practices once again hit the music industry.[118] The music business could not shake off its seedy public image. As the *Chicago Tribune*'s Bill Anderson observed in 1972, "The flamboyant lifestyles of singing stars generated little public sympathy from buyers and the small businessmen who began stocking bootleg tapes in gas stations, laundromats, convenience food stores, and the like."[119] Indeed, poor publicity may have contributed to the record industry's inability to achieve its legislative goals for such a long time.[120]

However, the record industry had little trouble influencing lawmakers in the 1970s. The 1971 bill was a stopgap measure that provided copyright protection for new sound recordings only until 1975, on the assumption that a comprehensive reform of copyright law would be passed by then. The RIAA lobbied Congress to extend the law and to beef up penalties, and the House Judiciary Committee approved an increase in fines in September 1974. The Sound Recording Act of 1971 imposed a $100 fine on a first-time offender and $1,000 for repeated convictions. In contrast, the new bill increased fines to $25,000 and $50,000 respectively—a 250 times increase for the first offense. The prison term, previously one year, became two, and the law passed in December 1974.[121] "I feel we now have the tools to go after them," Jules Yarnell said. "Whether the government will use them depends on the individual U.S. attorney in each area."[122] Then again, the industry simultaneously pushed for New York and other states to make their own statutes more severe.

The campaign to stop piracy reached its most spectacular dimensions in 1978. Early that year two fresh-faced young men opened a record store in Westbury, Long Island, with hip disco interiors and the name Modular Sounds. People in the neighborhood could not believe the bargains they found at Modular. Nobody expected the boys to stay in business long, but they snapped up the deals while they lasted. You could buy a 99-cent tape for 79 cents. To the landlord, Bobbie and Richie were just "nice kids" who did not know how to run a store, although they always paid their rent on time. The two daydreamed most of the day, left early, and had little traffic from customers.[123] Transactions must have occurred there, at some time of day or night, because the FBI had identified 400 suspects when it hung up the "For Rent" sign at Modular months later.[124] Bobbie and Richie had been undercover agents all along. They made contact with over fifty underground merchants, who brought them pirate recordings to stock the store.[125]

The ruse allowed the FBI to get an inside look at the networks that distributed bootlegs across the country. On the December morning Modular closed in 1978, the FBI simultaneously raided four plants in Suffolk County, New York; one in Albany; one in Mount Vernon; two in Georgia; three in Connecticut; four in New Jersey; and eight in North Carolina. The investigation had gone on for two years and had uncovered significant ties between the Tar Heel state and Long Island. Facilities on the Island manufactured both tapes and packaging, and the labels—a lighter and more discreet cargo than recordings—traveled to Charlotte, where workers pasted them onto locally produced records and tapes.

In fact, investigators identified a Charlotte businessman, Jerrold H. Pettus, as the kingpin of both the North Carolina and New York operations.[126] His company, General Music, also sold tapes to retail stores in the Midwest.[127] Pettus denied the FBI's claims of big takings. "The figures are grossly exaggerated," he said. "I don't think we have that much inventory in stock." He and his brother-in-law, Ralph "Buddy" Phillips, claimed to have legitimate invoices for all their merchandise. However, music industry men and store owners around Charlotte expressed little surprise at Pettus's legal troubles. In 1971 he settled out-of-court with four major record companies over reproducing recordings without permission, and in 1974 the FBI raided his company Sound Duplicating Systems.[128]

Back in New York, the paper trail led to some interesting dead ends. Newsday dug up tax records for two of the illicit manufacturers on Long Island, Ramart Printing and BCF Productions. The companies had formed in 1975 and 1976, respectively, and the documents only mentioned the names of the lawyers who incorporated them. "Each said he could not remember the names of the principals in the respective firms," journalist Steve Wick reported. The third pirate site, Marta Printing, did not have any records on file. Wick then turned to the Suffolk landlords who owned the plants and warehouses and came up with the name of one suspected pirate: Chris Colon. John Perrotto began renting a warehouse at 9 Drayton Avenue in Bay Shore to Colon in 1975. As far as he knew, the tenant ran a printing press that manufactured cake boxes and labels for eight-track tapes. Curiously, Colon closed his press, packed up his family, and moved to Puerto Rico three weeks before the raids. When FBI agents descended on the warehouse, they found a blank space. "They came down like a ton of bricks," Perrotto said. "Afterwards, I took two Rolaids and a Tums." He must have reconsidered Colon's recent departure, so sudden and practically timed as it was. Was he a criminal? Did he learn of the sting operation somehow and abandon his coconspirators? Perrotto remembered the mystery entrepreneur as "hardworking and loyal."[129] On the other side of the law, the FBI's landlord at Modular Sounds regretted the loss of such good clients. "I wish I could get some more," Mario Eliseo said.[130]

Copyright Reborn: The 1976 Law

These raiders were armed with the Copyright Act of 1976, which went well beyond the sound-related reforms of 1971 and 1974 to transform the nature of all aspects of copyright. Congress acted on the question of sound recordings in the early 1970s only because the music industry insisted that the piracy crisis was too pressing for lawmakers to wait until they had sorted out every single copyright issue, from the regulation of cable television and jukeboxes to the pricing of the compulsory license for music. Everyone agreed that manifold disputes about new technology made an update of the Copyright Act of 1909 urgent, yet this complexity also made such an overhaul all the more difficult to enact—and easy to postpone.

It took almost seventy years, but the petitioners of 1909 finally got much of what they had originally sought.[131] In the Progressive Era lawmakers declined to extend copyright to the life of the author plus fifty years, as numerous artists, publishers and writers had requested; they retained instead the old model of a twenty-eight year period, which could be renewed once for another twenty-eight years. The 1976 act adopted the life-plus-fifty-years standard, which many other nations by then were using. Only the Philippines had a copyright term as short as the United States, and its law had been fashioned after America's. For works for hire—that is, most corporate products—the new copyright would last seventy-five years from publication or 100 years from the time of creation, whichever ended first. Supporters of this reform supposed that the old model of two twenty-eight year terms had been based on the lifespan of earlier Americans. Since people were living longer in the late twentieth century, some authors survived to see their works go into the public domain.[132]

Lawmakers also believed that changes in technology warranted greater copyright protection. "The tremendous growth in communications media has substantially lengthened the commercial life of a great many works," a Senate committee concluded. "A short term is particularly discriminatory against serious works of music, literature, and art, whose value may not be recognized until after many years." The senators did not consider the possibility that the public might benefit from "serious works" being freely and cheaply reproduced. Lawmakers also argued that the new system would be less time-consuming to administer, because "the death of the author is a definite, determinable event, and it would be the only data that a potential user would have to worry about"— as opposed to the date when the copyright was registered or renewed.[133] Throughout the debates over the 1976 act, legislators favored reforms that conferred copyright automatically, making protection less contingent on compliance with legal requirements. The public domain, not copyright, had become the necessary evil.

Indeed, Congress fundamentally changed the nature of copyright by no longer requiring creators to register their works with the Copyright Office to receive protection, as had been required since 1790. Under the new law, copyright existed as soon as the ideas were expressed in tangible form, whether printed, visual, or electronic. In other words, everything is copyrighted. In doing so, Congress aimed to replace the so-called "dual system" that protected unpublished works through common law copyright, which was enforceable only through a civil suit. Under the old system, authors received the full force of federal protection only for those works that they published and registered with the government. The Senate committee considered this arrangement "anachronistic, uncertain, impractical, and highly complicated."[134]

Publication had always been the main determinant of eligibility under federal copyright law, but by the late 1970s, it was harder to say exactly when a creative expression was published. If a song was performed on the radio or television, did that constitute publication? Should a writer have to register a poem with the Copyright Office if it were to appear in a zine with a print run of 50 copies? Instant copyright protection, backed by federal law, would alleviate this confusion and facilitate international trade, since no other nation had such a complicated system of protection. In the committee's view, the uncertainty of legal status impaired the export of creative works abroad and put the United States at a disadvantage.[135]

This simple but fundamental provision best exemplifies the shift toward expanding rather than restraining property rights. No longer would copyright protection depend on the author's registration of the work with the Copyright Office. This innovation suggests that copyright is an inherent quality of an expression, something that the author and his heirs can exploit for the rest of his life and well beyond, just by the act of creation. The old system, in place since 1790, had treated the author's monopoly as a temporary legal arrangement with the state, dependent on the filing of a claim. Otherwise, the work defaulted to the public domain, and anyone else could make use of it. ("Your rights are purely statutory," as a Congressman reminded music publishers seventy years earlier.)[136] After 1976, by contrast, every recorded utterance became a new piece of property, and virtually none of an author's contemporaries would likely live to see the day that copyright expires on his work.

The new policy also solved the problem of registering and regulating every single copyrighted work, the former task of the Copyright Office, the rare government agency that paid for itself (through the collection of registration fees). One difficulty in devising a right for sound recordings had been figuring out how to manage a separate right for each rendition of a song, no matter how minutely different one was from the other. If one had higher treble in the mix, and another was sung in a lower octave, but they were otherwise identical, would one be an infringement of the other? Could every different take recorded while the tape rolled in a studio be registered for a separate copyright? As the age of tape recorders, personal computers, and desktop publishing dawned, the challenge of cataloguing every bit of intellectual property would dizzy even the most fastidious librarian. The automatic conferral of copyright in the 1976 act eliminated the issue in one fell swoop.

These broad changes affected all rights owners, but the lion's share of debate over the bill dealt with balancing the demands of those who made and used copyrighted material in various media. In the field of music, for example, broadcasters, composers, performers, and record companies traditionally wrestled over who would get the biggest share of the entertainment dollar. Broadcasters wanted to pay less for the music they aired. Composers wanted to charge more for labels to record their songs. Labels wanted jukebox companies to pay more for the use of their music. Performers had long sought recognition and remuneration for their creative contribution to a sound recording, a question that had vexed judges and lawmakers for years.[137] The 1971 Sound Recording Act created a copyright for records, but the right belonged to the record company. A recording was typically a work for hire; the company that paid for and managed the contributions of singers, musicians, and producers owned the final product, just as a publisher who hired scholars to write entries for an encyclopedia would control rights to their work.

The unions had backed the record industry's effort to get a copyright and fight piracy in 1971, but they now sought a bigger piece of the pie. "It must be obvious that using a person's labors and talents to enrich oneself without compensating that person is less than ethical," said Sanford Wolff, of the American Federation of Television and Radio Artists. The union pushed for broadcasters to pay a royalty to musicians and singers who perform on sound recordings. Since radio stations turned from airing live music to records in 1950s, Wolff said, more and more musicians were employed as session musicians in recording studios. The RIAA backed musicians in their quest for greater compensation. Speaking on behalf of the record industry, Stanley Gortikov noted that "the sound recording is the *only* copyrighted creative work for which a royalty will not be paid when it is performed by others." The new bill required cable companies to pay royalties to broadcasters for use of their programs, and composers were to receive a new royalty for the use of their songs in jukeboxes. The musicians who actually gave sound and shape to these recordings, though, were the only ones not getting paid for the continued use of their work. For Wolff and his fellow musicians, the question in 1976 was how to deal with the problem leftover from 1971: if we can agree that a recording is a creative work, why is the only party that seems to make no direct creative contribution (the record company) the one getting the copyright?[138]

The few critics who opposed expansion of copyright at the hearings found an unreceptive audience. Representative Robert Kastenmeier (D-WI), one of the bill's champions, lost patience with the "duplicators," who frequently interrupted him and other Congressmen as they urged the legislators to rescind the copyright for sound recordings. The Independent Record and Tape Association (IRTA), a group of small retailers and tape copiers based in Vermont, revived the idea of a compulsory license for recordings, which would have allowed competitors to make and sell their own copies of another company's records for a standard fee, much like the system for recording different versions of a musical composition. Their pamphlet, "The Great American Rip-Off," might have sounded too shrill a note, though; the cover showed a pirate and his sidekick opening a treasure chest, with the words "The United States House of Representatives Copyright Revision Bill" inside it, just below "Rip Off."[139] Were the pirates implying that the Congressmen were ripping people off? Or were they saying that the mainstream record companies were the buccaneers, and the bill was the treasure they sought? "We are amazed that the House of Representatives is considering a bill that will enable the multi-billion dollar music conglomerates to reap unconscionable profits," the IRTA declared, "all at the expense of the consumer and the small recording companies." David Heilman railed against "the mechanical trust" which sought to control "the majority of major copyrights in the United States," vertically integrate the writing, recording and sale of music, keep out competitors, and drive up prices.[140] His was the only mention of a "mechanical trust" during the hearings, and, unlike earlier in the century, the word "monopoly" rarely came up.

In an era of inflation, critics also cited the rising price of music as an argument against exclusive copyright for sound recordings. "When Congress granted relief with Public Law 92–140, the suggested retail price of records was $3.98," Heilman said. "Now, it is $6.98. You were told that if the pirates or re-recorders were put out of business, prices would drop. Have you or your family purchased a $3.98 record recently?"[141] This observation seemed to vindicate the fears of Representative Abner Mikva, who predicted that giving copyright protection to recordings would lead to higher prices.[142] However, the industry argued that pirates were siphoning off its profits, forcing companies to charge more to recoup their investments. The industry blamed piracy for higher prices, and pirates blamed copyright, but the price of most goods rose during this period. It is little surprise, then, that consumers turned to a cheaper product in a time of high prices and stagnant employment.[143]

In the end, Congress preserved the property right it gave to record companies in 1971, and the performers' royalty failed because of opposition from broadcasters. The Copyright Act required the negotiation of many difficult compromises, and lawmakers did not consider the performers' right worth ruining the whole project.[144] As Barbara Ringer commented, "It is a source of wonder that somehow all of this succeeded in the end."[145] Perhaps the bill survived the long process of negotiation because it offered certain benefits that all copyright holders were eager to see, such as the longer term of protection. The resulting law capped a long process of reform that began in 1955, resulting in an anti-counterfeiting law, a copyright for sound recordings, a longer period of protection, and tougher penalties.

Source of wonder or not, the final bill passed easily in Congress. Reforms that artists, composers, musicians, publishers, record labels, and so many others had pursued for seven decades won resounding approval, facing only minor objections. As with the Copyright Act of 1909 and the Sound Recording Act of 1971, the legislation did not divide lawmakers along partisan lines. The bill passed the Senate in February 1976 with ninety-seven votes in favor and none against.[146] Senator Abourezk (D-SD) proposed an amendment limiting the length of copyright to the author's life or fifty-six years, whichever was longer, but the measure was overwhelmingly rejected by a 14 to 78 vote moments before the bill as a whole was passed.[147] When the bill was approved by the House Judiciary Committee, only one member— Representative Joshua Eilberg (D-PA)— opposed it, on the grounds that a new requirement for cable television providers to pay copyright fees would disadvantage rural communities, where cable had compensated for inadequate access to television broadcast signals.[148]

Ringer had good reason to be surprised that it all came together in the end. After all, when her career in the Copyright Office began in 1949, a copyright for sound recordings remained an implausible proposition.[149] State and federal statutes did not yet provide long-lasting or open-ended property rights for the ownership of creative works, but the antipiracy law of California, the Supreme Court's *Goldstein* decision, and the Copyright Act of 1976 cast aside the cautious tradition of limiting copyright protection in the public interest. The political ground had shifted toward an embrace of copyright in the early 1970s; however, the apparent ineffectiveness of antipiracy enforcement, combined with continued anxiety over the nation's economic health, led to the pursuit of ever-stronger and more sweeping copyright measures, of which the 1976 act was only the most prominent.

6

Deadheads, Hip-Hop, and the Possibility of Compromise

In 1978, the Doobie Brothers paid a visit to the Watts high school attended by three of their biggest fans—Raj, Dwayne, and Rerun. The three youngsters were dying to get tickets to the show, a fundraiser for their school's music program. Unfortunately, Rerun's perennial weakness for hamburgers distracted him on the way to the ticket line, and by the time he arrived the seats were sold out. The only way the boys would get to hear the Doobies now, Raj told his friends, was by popping a quarter in the jukebox. Music had to be paid for.

There was, however, another way. A seedy gentleman and his muscle-bound friend overheard the boys' conversation. The men offered to give Rerun and his friends tickets if they agreed to tape the show, and Rerun naively accepted. (As part of the deal, he even got "a professional soundman's pay for a day"—four dollars!) Later that day, Rerun and his friends managed to finagle an interview with the band. "What's your biggest problem?" Raj asked. "What gets you the craziest?" The Doobies did not hesitate to answer—bootlegging. In perfect afterschool-special style, they went on to explain to the boys what the word means. "That's where someone illegally records our concerts and sells it to the public," bassist Tiran Porter said. "Yeah, what happens is the record company doesn't make any money, we don't make any money, and the public gets a pretty bad recording," said another member. Also, they added, the bootlegger ran the risk of going to jail "for a *long* time."[1]

Rerun was understandably terrified. The boys tried to back out of their deal, but the thuggish bootlegger threatened them. Through a series of comic shenanigans, Rerun's tape recorder was exposed during the concert, and the Doobies confronted the boys. It turned out that the bootlegger was Al Dunbar, a "low-life" serial pirate who had been taping the band's shows across the country. The Doobies proceeded to ambush the venal bootlegger, who lived such a lavish existence that he tried to order a filet mignon and a shrimp cocktail at the local soda shop moments before their arrival. In a final irony, the tape Rerun recorded was revealed to consist almost entirely of crunching sounds. Rerun's appetite got the better of him again. "You mean to tell me I'm going to jail for a *long* time," Dunbar lamented, echoing the Doobies, "and all I have to show for it is a tape of a fat kid eating popcorn?" The police took him away. The band and their fans cheered, and there were high fives all around.

Airing in February 1978, this episode of *What's Happening!!* was as much a long commercial for the Doobies' new album as it was a public service announcement about the evils of piracy. As an allegory, the episode portrays both consumers and artists as the victims of a parasitic con man. It casts the bootlegger in the mold of a pimp or drug pusher—an entrepreneur who operates in the shadows, fulfilling a demand in the marketplace that is ultimately harmful to everyone but himself.

The reality of bootlegging in the aftermath of 1970s copyright reform was often less sleazy. Even as the record industry won one new protection after another, people continued to reproduce recordings in a variety of different ways. Some may have been two-bit con artists who dined on filet mignon as they robbed artists and defrauded the public, but many others were simply sharing tapes with friends and like-minded members of underground music scenes. The novelist Nick Hornby, punk musician Thurston Moore, and many others have mused on the cultural significance of personal mixtapes, the individualized assortments of songs recorded on cassettes and shared among a small circle of friends. The word "mixtape" took on a different meaning in the 1970s and 1980s, when hip-hop DJs combined sounds from various records to create a new type of sound collage that gradually became an underground commodity and a vital part of the hip hop music industry in New York, Atlanta, and elsewhere. Meanwhile, collectors and entrepreneurs continued to bootleg live and unreleased tracks by rock artists, albeit in a less showy fashion than predecessors such as Rubber Dubber.[2]

Bootleggers raised legitimate questions about whether such copying and exchange really threatened the survival of the music industry. For every commercial outfit seeking to counterfeit mainstream pop at cut-rate prices, there were numerous examples of fans who copied music that did not directly compete with the offerings of record labels. Cassettes were a key means by which punk rock reached new audiences, a medium that allowed an aspiring band to put out its own recordings on the cheap and its followers to spread the word through unauthorized reproduction. Followers of artists as different as Kraut, the Grateful Dead, and Brucie Bee became part of a new distribution structure for music; in the case of hip-hop mixtapes, the artists themselves often pushed records that incorporated their own words and music with sounds borrowed from others, outside the normal conduits of the record business. In doing so, these listeners and artists showed how the industry might accommodate itself to a degree of copying, especially if it could profit from this unpaid promotion. Such a model called into question the necessity of the antipiracy laws that labels and their copyright allies had fought so hard to obtain. Piracy may have persisted in spite of the reforms, but the law still put power in the hands of rights holders. Like the Doobie Brothers, they could decide how vigorously they wanted to pursue pirates—or let Rerun off the hook.[3]

Tape Trading among the Dead

As in the past, pirates and bootleggers evolved to fit the new legal conditions and persisted in the face of criminal prosecution. The 1962 anti-counterfeiting law led pirates to wrap their copied recordings in new packaging to avoid allegations of "palming off" their knock-offs as the originals. Ten years later, the inclusion of sound recordings in copyright law encouraged pirates to go deeper underground, distributing their goods in less-regulated sites such as gas stations and independent record stores. The 1976 Copyright Act reinforced the effects of the 1971 law, imposing stiffer penalties and giving pirates greater incentives to cover their tracks, but it fell far short of stamping out piracy altogether. While large corporate retailers became more vigilant about keeping counterfeits off their shelves, independent record stores continued to stock bootlegs, and counterfeiting of cassettes continued apace.[4]

The bootlegging of the 1970s shifted away from the radical sensibilities of Rubber Dubber and Trade Mark of Quality, resembling more the cautious, low-profile copiers of jazz and classical music in the 1950s. Legal scholar Louis Holscher described a "secondary market" of record conventions, mail-order catalogs, and swap meets that catered to collectors and largely evaded the attention of state and federal law enforcement.[5] This group of consumers resembled the earlier generation of collectors who recorded and traded copies of hard-to-find jazz records and opera performances within the limits of a small subculture. Greg Shaw, collector, critic, and impresario of the seventies rock magazine *Bomp!*, remembered a period of interpretation and archiving not unlike the effort led by jazz critics in the 1930s. "The early '70s was a formative lull in pop culture, a depressing hangover after the previous decade's wild party, but also a time when the fan network of true music lovers began taking shape, largely via magazines like *Bomp*," Shaw recalled. "Esoterica that's now widely known thanks to garage-psych compilations started to be discovered and classified."[6]

Of course, the collectors of this period did not focus purely on the esoteric and obscure. The devotees of Bob Dylan and Bruce Springsteen shared a key quality with the countercultural pirates who flourished in the late 1960s and early 1970s: they trafficked in recordings by popular, bankable stars, and the established music industry still viewed them as a greater nuisance than the jazz aficionados who copied long out-of-print recordings by artists who were lesser known to the public at large. In short, the rock bootleggers of the 1970s combined the aesthetic and musical tastes of the fading counterculture with the business model of the old-fashioned collectors' market.

Pirates like Jerry Pettus and Julius Kessler, seduced by the easy money offered by a tape deck and a hit record, had come under serious scrutiny by the authorities, but the collector-oriented bootleggers also had their own share of run-ins with the law. Many labels, such as Rubber Dubber, got out of the business before the federal government criminalized their activities in 1972. Numerous others, such as Dittolino Discs, Immaculate Conception Records, Kustom Records, Phonygraf, and Pig's Eye were also defunct by the late 1970s. The FBI shut down two significant outfits, Wizardo and Hoffman Avenue Records, in late 1976. Wizardo swung back into operation in 1977 but again ran afoul of the law.[7] "Legal hassles have been few since our last edition," the editor of *Hot Wacks*, a bootleg guide based in Ontario, reported in 1979. "While there were major busts on the east coast for counterfeit records, bootlegs came only under minor attack."[8] The most recent busts rounded up 500 copies of a Beach Boys record called *The Hawthorne Hot Shots* in California, while the FBI raided a "bootleg warehouse" in New York. *Bomp!* magazine reported that the Amazing Kornyfone Record Label had folded, but the organization had in fact adopted a common tactic of bootleggers, periodically changing the name on its products to avoid notice. The fact that Kornyfone shed its name—one of the best-known "brands" in the seventies bootleg scene—suggests that it had come under renewed legal scrutiny.[9]

Publications such as *Hot Wacks* (founded 1975) and *Goldmine* (1974) developed a discourse among collectors and bootleggers that mirrored the ideas of their predecessors in *Stereo Review* and the Hot Record Society's *Rag*. One bootlegger, calling himself Harry the Bastard, voiced the traditional complaint of collectors that the industry was trying to prevent them from capturing sounds for posterity. "In the Middle Ages, the church controlled all the artists," Harry said. "If some work of art didn't fit in with their religious doctrines, the church would put it away or destroy it. That's what record companies are doing—destroying history."[10] The writers and readers of these periodicals viewed collecting as a way of documenting the past and honoring the output of the artists they revered. While not all agreed on the legitimacy of bootlegging—"Ban Bootlegs From Record Shows!" declared *Goldmine* in 1991—the illicit market made rare and unreleased recordings available to fans who did not believe they were hurting the artist by purchasing them.[11]

Supporters of bootlegging always drew a bright line between their activities and the profit-seeking efforts of pirates. "Collectors often suffer the injustice of having all illegal recordings labeled as 'bootleg,' but this fails to take account of crucial differences of production and consumption within the sphere of 'piracy,'" says Lee Marshall, a scholar who has written extensively on the culture of bootlegging. Pirates and counterfeiters copy popular recordings to take advantage of the music industry's business, while bootleggers, he argues, do not directly compete with the products sold by record labels. "The vast majority of this officially unreleased material contains either recordings of live concerts or 'outtakes' (studio recordings of songs which did not make it onto finished albums, or alternative versions of songs that were released)," Marshall says.[12] Similarly, *Hot Wacks* maintained that bootlegs were different from pirate or counterfeit records, since the so-called "underground record" documented such ephemera as concerts and radio and television performances.[13]

Bootleggers, then, claimed that they made more music available to the public without impinging on the music industry's bottom line. *Hot Wacks* chose the soundtrack of *The Sound of Music*—a massive hit that sold over ten million official copies—as its example of a counterfeit, highlighting the distinction between a pirated mainstream product and the alternative fare preferred by bootleggers. Such counterfeits directly hurt the established companies by fooling consumers into purchasing a nearly identical knock-off instead of the official release. Most importantly, *Hot Wacks* argued that bootlegging did not contribute substantially to the $200 million a year in losses claimed by the RIAA in the late 1970s: "Bootleg records, with an average run of 2,000 copies, should not even be included in this figure as the record labels do not lose revenue on a record which is not their catalog."[14] The economists Alireza Jay Naghavi and Günther G. Schulze lend tentative confirmation to these claims in their study of the economic impact of bootlegging, suggesting that bootlegs are not substitutes for officially released albums. "It is neither clear that they are cheaper," the economists suggest, "nor that they crowd out official sales."[15] According to this view, the typical purchaser of a bootleg is a fan who also buys all the official releases by his favorite artist, thus causing no direct financial damage to the performer or the record company.

Some musicians considered recording by fans to be harmless. The trading of concert tapes helped spread the word about many musicians in the punk movement of the 1970s, lifting the fortunes of Patti Smith and the band Television in particular.[16] British punks the Buzzcocks reportedly knew of the *Times Up* bootleg and even owned a copy; they did not inform the authorities, but the British Phonographic Industry trade association took action against the pirates. "I'd like to have some kind of royalty from bootleggers," the manager of singer-songwriter Elvis Costello conceded in the late 1970s. "100 albums wouldn't be a lot to ask. But it's the record companies who stand to lose most out of it—which tells you something interesting about the whole record industry."[17]

Figure 6.1 This mid-1970s recording consists of live performances by the punk artist Patti Smith. Released on the label Ze Anonym Plattenspieler, it illustrates how bootlegging persisted after the passage of federal copyright protection for sound recordings in 1971. *Source:* Courtesy of Music Library and Sound Recordings Archive, Bowling Green State University.

Most notoriously, Bruce Springsteen openly endorsed bootlegging early in his career. For example, when "the Boss" became entangled in a contractual dispute that prevented him from making new recordings, he took to the stage to deliver his music to the public. He arranged to have five concerts aired on the radio in 1978, in hopes that the music would be recorded and circulated among his fans nationwide. On stage, Springsteen celebrated "the magic of bootlegging" for making his music available to fans, and one night he even called out, "Bootleggers, roll your tapes, this is gonna be a hot one!"[18]

Springsteen initially viewed concert recordings as a matter of fans' devotion. "You find out most of the time that, number one, they're fans," he told an interviewer in 1978. "I've had bootleggers write me letters saying, 'listen, we're just fans,' that's their story." At this stage in his career, he also subscribed to the theory that bootlegs did not reduce overall sales because they appealed primarily to fans who would buy his official recordings: "The kids who buy the bootlegs buy the real records too, so it doesn't really bother me. I think the amount of money made on it isn't very substantial. It's more like a labor of love."[19] Springsteen was a fair-weather friend of the bootleggers, though, eventually coming to resent the appropriation of his work. Just a year later, Springsteen and his label sued Vicky Vinyl, a legendary bootlegger in California, for copyright infringement and a host of other offenses, including illegally using his name and likeness.[20] He later told *Rolling Stone* that "in some way, the song is bein' stolen," expressing indignation at bootleggers who made big profits from albums with poor sound quality. His staff continued to work with the RIAA and legal authorities to pursue charges of copyright infringement in the 1980s and 1990s.[21]

The Grateful Dead provides perhaps the best-known example of a popular group that accepted bootlegging and even incorporated it into its way of doing business, much as Springsteen attempted to harness unauthorized reproduction with his radio shows of 1978. The "Deadheads" who followed this quintessential jamband around the world devoted themselves to capturing every trace of the group's meandering improvisations, night after night. Their zeal for documentation recalls the classical copiers of the 1950s and 1960s, who yearned to record the subtle nuances of each unique performance of a beloved opera singer, just as jazz fans valued every iteration of a composition by a virtuoso musician as worthy of preservation. "The Dead...is a compilation, every night, of every show that went before," taper Dan Hupert averred. "Without a tape, what they played in Laguna in '68 is nothing more than past history.... If you see two shows a year, or five, or seven, they are individual concert experiences. If you see twenty-five and listen to tapes of most of the others, it is no longer an individual experience or a set of them. It is a continuing process."[22] This mode of perceiving the band's work—hearing it live, listening to and comparing the tapes—would be impossible without the creation of an ongoing record of the music.

The Dead also served as a link between the rebellious cultural milieu in which pop bootlegging first flourished in the 1960s and the stable pattern of underground collecting that developed in the following decade. The band emerged in 1965 in the midst of the countercultural fervor in San Francisco, embracing an antiestablishment ethos that advocated both hedonism and collectivism. Band members described their followers as "a community, tribe, family, and traveling circus," in which "the audience is as much the band as the band is the audience."[23] The recording and trading of concert tapes rapidly became a part of this shared experience, beginning in the late 1960s but becoming truly widespread in the following decade.[24]

When the band issued an official policy on taping in 1985, it codified and regulated activities that had long occurred (literally) under the performers' noses.

Taper David Cooks recalled hauling his reel-to-reel tape machine into concerts by the Quicksilver Messenger Service, one of the Dead's psychedelic contemporaries, starting in 1968, and no one tried to stop him. "Occasionally they'd question me," he said, "then they figured I was just recording them [for personal use] and let it go at that."[25] Cooks did not run into another taper, though, until 1972. Tape trading did not take off until the early 1970s, when fans began to organize clubs to share their recordings.[26] New advances in consumer electronics sped the development of this hobby, exemplified by the shift from Cooks's reel-to-reel set-up in 1968 to cassettes as the currency of trading in the 1970s. When Harvey Lubar and Jerry Moore made a pivotal early bootleg in 1970, they still used a small Uher open-reel tape deck.[27] By 1974, taping experts were recommending Sony's 152 SD cassette recorder to beginning bootleggers.[28]

Interest in taping grew as seven high-quality tapes recorded by the Grateful Dead's technical support during a series of shows in 1968 and 1970 made the rounds among fans. Unlike the live bootlegs of Rubber Dubber, which captured the likes of Jimi Hendrix and Elton John on tape but distributed the sounds of vinyl, these recordings remained in tape form and reached listeners in samizdat fashion. The tapes also contributed to the growing lore about the Dead's prowess in live performance. "Listening to the Dead's albums is fine, but the studio cuts are to their live sets as hamburger is to steak," Charlie Rosen wrote in the early 1970s. "They are theoretically composed of the same ingredients, but a sirloin is juicier, more delicious, more nutricious [sic] and far more filling than a Big Mac. There are also several bootleg albums to be had, but the quality of sound is so inconsistent that forking over all that bread is almost like playing the ponies."[29] Rosen proposed that the document of a live performance contained a value that could be found nowhere else, qualities that no one who missed the concert could access unless the sound was recorded and preserved. The paucity of recorded live material in the early 1970s inspired many concertgoers to start making their own recordings and assist in the project of documentation.

The launch of Les Kippel's fanzine *Dead Relix* in 1974 also spurred interest in recording among fans. The writers in *Relix* sang the praises of the Grateful Dead and tirelessly discussed the minutiae of recording—how to sneak recording equipment into concert venues, what kind of tape to use, the etiquette of copying and distributing tapes to other fans, and so on. Just as the band itself did not oppose audience recording, the management of most venues did not seem especially concerned about taping either. "Hiding it [recording equipment] under your coat or a girl's skirt is out," one fan explained, "because it will bulge and bouncers are always suspicious of bulges. What they are looking for, however, is bottles. As long as you can convince a heavy that what you are carrying is not a glass container, your [sic] O.K. Because, while heavies are supposed to confiscate recording equipment, they seldom see it and are not looking for it."[30] In 1974, the smuggling of alcohol—the original inspiration for the term "bootlegging"—still mattered more than smuggling a tape recorder. The author even suggested that one could get a device past a bouncer by saying that it was only a tape *player*, not a recorder. "They are usually dumb," he said.[31]

Relix offered a forum for nascent tape-trading networks to connect with other potential participants. In a handwritten advertisement, Jerry Moore promised "the finest tapes available," but added "trade only, *no* sales" and "quality recording a *must*!" The tapers embraced a number of artists who shared the Dead's propensity for improvisational and experimental music, particularly those who blended folk with psychedelic rock. For example, Harvey Lubar of the Bronx invited readers to join his Hell's Honkies Tape Club, announcing both the recordings he had to offer and the ones he was seeking. "We got Dead (lots), NRPS, Q.M.S., Airplane, Zappa, Floyd, and much, much more!!!" he wrote. "We want more of the same—and any OLD Frisco music."[32] Similarly, Mike Tannehill of Fort Worth, Texas, advertised recordings by a similar range of taper's favorites, including King Crimson, Bob Dylan, New Riders of the Purple Sage, Traffic, Frank Zappa, and, of course, the Grateful Dead. Although these preferences reflect the taste of a generation weaned on sixties rock, they also show how bootleggers and collectors continued to favor music that emphasizes improvisation (like jazz) and the virtuosity of live performance (like opera).

In 1985 the Dead took a new approach to the great number of tapers who showed up at their performances. They explicitly condoned audience recording—as long as the tapes were used for strictly noncommercial purposes—and they set aside a section of each venue near the stage for tapers, who could order special tickets for this area through the mail. The decision brought some order to the bustle of recorders jockeying for the best positions at shows and introduced a degree of quality control by granting tapers an advantageous place to do their work. Bootleggers made copies available to other fans, often through a tape-trading "tree"; the possessor of a sought-after bootleg was a "branch," who would mail copies of the original recording to other fans, the "leaves," who supplied a blank tape and paid postage. The system was meant to maintain the sound quality of copies and operated on the basis of good will and reciprocity, rather than profit.[33]

The Dead's policy attempted to square the circle of music copying by fans— an ethical puzzle that lawmakers, listeners, and labels had never been able to solve. Collectors in the 1960s had urged the New York legislature to provide an exception in new antipiracy laws that excluded the "antiquarians" who copied and traded rare recordings in obscurity. However, no one had ever explained how bootleggers who catered to a small group with esoteric tastes could be distinguished from pirates who copied and sold the hits. Was it not necessary to bar the sale and distribution of unauthorized copies across the board? What if the small-scale collector's bootlegger made a profit? The Grateful Dead and its loyal following of Deadheads, however, presented a case of fans individually recording, copying, and trading music, with an avowed commitment to noncommercialism.

For the trading market to work, participants had to police their behavior themselves. "To mention or believe in a large-scale for-profit 'bootleg tape industry' is to seriously offend any true Deadhead and show yourself to be an outsider," Melissa McCray Pattacini learned when she interviewed the band's followers.[34] In its maiden issue, *Relix* declared in no uncertain terms that taping and trading would be permitted, but for-profit piracy would not: "The publisher and the editor of this magazine in no way advocate the duplication of live recordings for purposes other than free exchange. We do not condone unauthorized duplication for sale. We will not accept subscriptions or take advertizing [*sic*] from known bootleggers."[35] The magazine even had a feature called the "Shit List," devoted to shaming errant members of the trading community who took music from others without reciprocating. "Lets say you record five tapes for Dale Crook...and you mail them off to him (insured mail)," the column proposed. "Eagerly you await the return of five tapes from Dale."[36] The victim in this scenario goes to great lengths to get in touch with the rogue, who never sends the tapes back. *Relix* presented itself as a means of recourse:

> We will try to locate him and find out what happened. If we cannot locate him, we will print a note in this magazine asking him to get in contact with us. If we get no reply, we will print your letter, outline our efforts to contact him, and his reply, if any.... It will be up to each reader to make his own opinion whether or not he wants to trade with Dale Crook of Seattle.[37]

Relix also offered to chastise traders who continually supplied others with tapes of inferior quality. "Let's hope for honesty," they concluded. "After all, tape trading is based upon HONESTY!"

By regulating the mores that underpinned exchange, the Deadheads anticipated the development of mechanisms like seller ratings on eBay, Amazon, and similar websites. Anyone can try to sell a car on eBay, but potential purchasers have to determine whether they can trust the seller to describe the condition of the car honestly and provide the agreed-upon goods upon the completion of a sale. "Remarkably, eBay offers no warranties or guarantees for any of the goods that are auctioned off," sociologist Peter Kollock observed in 2008. "Buyers and sellers assume all risks from the transaction, with eBay serving as a listing agency. It would seem to be a market ripe with the possibility of large-scale fraud and deceit, and yet the default rate for trades conducted through eBay is remarkably small." Kollock attributes this level of cooperation to "an institutionalized repu-tation system" called the Feedback Forum, in which participants can evaluate the trustworthiness of buyers and sellers for the benefit of others. Whether in a tape-trading network or online auction, each individual is potentially a producer, seller, and buyer, and mutual understandings must prevail for the participants to convey goods to each other in a peer-to-peer fashion.[38]

The legal scholar Mark Schultz cites a tradition of reciprocity as the basis for the voluntary adherence of almost all Deadheads to the social norms—sharing and noncommercialism—that the band mandated. Pointing to political scientist Robert Axelrod's work on "tit-for-tat" situations in game theory, Schultz argues that a latent human tendency for cooperation can be fostered under the right conditions, namely, "the possibility for mutually beneficial exchange, repeat interactions among actors, knowledge of how actors behaved in the past, and the ability to withhold cooperation from actors who had failed to cooperate in the past."[39] The Deadhead subculture fulfilled each of these conditions, as trading allowed each participant to get a desired good and the practice of fans touring with the band made "repeat interactions" possible. Moreover, the 1985 taping policy merely endorsed the practices of sharing that listeners had cultivated in the preceding decade—the self-monitoring networks of tapers and traders had already established their own norms and expectations when the Grateful Dead officially incorporated such activities into their live performances.

The arrangement worked out well for the Grateful Dead. Fan John R. Dwork recalls that the band's concert audience multiplied after the 1985 decision. "More tapers meant more tapes and more tapes mean more folks getting turned on to the Dead," he said.[40] In Schultz's words, the pro-taping policy "let the fans do some of the work"—a practice that the legal thinker Yochai Benkler calls "peer production."[41] The Dead allowed recordings of their music to circulate for free, while fans paid ticket prices for an endless series of shows that permitted them to record, manufacture, and distribute copies of the music to other followers of the band. In return for serving as the Dead's unofficial distribution system, the tapers reaped the "symbolic capital," in anthropologist Mark Jamieson's phrase, of knowing the most about the band and having the fullest tape collection. Lawyer and collector Cason Moore noted the upside of this voluntary mode of production: although the Dead never sold many albums, they were still recorded and listened to a great deal. "The Grateful Dead rarely received much radio play, and they only had one Top Ten hit in 1987 with 'Touch of Grey,'" he observed. "Yet by the time 'Touch of Grey' climbed into the top five of the singles chart, the Grateful Dead had already attracted tens of thousands of loyal fans and had gone on some of the highest grossing tours of all time."[42] Lyricist John Perry Barlow remarked that the taping policy was a major source of the band's success, "one of the most enlightened, practical, smart things that anybody ever did."[43]

From Counterculture to Free Culture

Barlow eventually became a gadfly of the burgeoning anti-copyright movement. In 1990 he co-founded the Electronic Frontier Foundation, a group that has opposed new copyright restrictions and eventually defended online file sharers, and in 1994 he wrote an influential piece for *Wired* magazine entitled "The Economy of Ideas." In it he quoted the slogan "Information wants to be free," which was coined by hippie impresario Stewart Brand in the 1980s. This mantra sums up an approach to intellectual property shared by jambands and computer hackers alike.[44] Journalist John Markoff credits the late 1960s counterculture for indirectly inspiring innovations such as the personal computer and the iPod, as well as the open-source software movement, which advocates the free distribution and modification of software, unencumbered by copyright concerns. Scientists in the San Francisco area challenged the idea that computing had to be centrally controlled by corporations and governments; they proposed that computers could be easily manipulated and freely available for the public's benefit. These pioneers dabbled in the region's radical politics, its heady atmosphere of experimentation and, indeed, its drugs. Apple founder Steve Jobs long maintained that taking LSD was one of the key events of his life; the psychedelic pulses and swirls on the iTunes music player's Visualizer function certainly attest to this influence.[45]

The Grateful Dead provided the soundtrack of the California cultural milieu that shaped such entrepreneurs as Brand and Jobs. That scene prompted not just new ways of thinking about computers, but a broader rethinking of the relationship between property rights and creativity. Indeed, the Dead's support for bootlegging reveals how the 1960s counterculture helped spawn a new politics, at once communal (with an emphasis on sharing and a suspicion of property rights) and libertarian (an opposition to bureaucracy and any limits on creativity or individual expression). In its subterranean form, that politics has expressed itself as piracy—a diffuse and often unarticulated resistance to copyright committed by anyone who copies, shares, and sells culture without asking permission, for fun or profit. Its ideological offshoots include the copyright-skeptic groups the Free Software Foundation and the Creative Commons movement, as well as the "cyberlibertarianism" that imagines innovation and the free market as the solution for all problems, an ethos best exemplified by *Wired*. For some of the counterculture's heirs, liberty meant freedom from the legal restrictions of copyright as well as any other kind of government regulation.[46]

The techno-utopianism of *Wired* was congenial to big business in many ways, but the legacy of the 1960s contained other, more radical impulses. Corporations, of course, found it easy to repackage nonconformity and individualism to sell soap, and former radicals like Jerry Rubin were more than willing to accommodate themselves to a hip new capitalism by the 1980s. However, real ideological affinities existed among bootleggers and hackers, reflecting a shared desire for a free or communal approach to culture. For example, the Dead formally endorsed copying and sharing by fans in 1985, the same year that programmer and activist Richard Stallman founded the Free Software Foundation. The band's policy on concert recordings resembles Stallman's own concept of a "general public license," or GPL. Stallman introduced the GPL in 1989 to permit software developers to distribute programs outside the bounds of copyright law, mandating that anyone could use, copy, and alter the software as long as they agreed to adhere to certain limitations defined by the original creator. Most often, these mandates forbade using the software for commercial purposes and placing copyright restrictions on any new, modified versions of the program made by subsequent users. In the early 2000s, this open and noncommercial spirit inspired the founding of Creative Commons, an organization that encouraged artists, musicians, and other creators to adopt such qualified licenses for their own work, in the hope of reducing the barriers to remixes, sampling, and other forms of appropriation.[47]

The Grateful Dead created a model that anticipated the ideas and strategies of Creative Commons, the Electronic Frontier Foundation, and other copyright activists. The band's vast and interconnected following of traders formed its own kind of information-sharing network, employing cassettes, zines, and the postal service to do what the Internet would later make much easier. The tape-trading system shares some of the economic qualities of a decentralized network such as the World Wide Web. Broadcast television and other types of mass media cater to a large, passive audience, while a website or a tape-trading network relies on a higher level of engagement from a smaller number of participants. Music distribution through a freewheeling gift economy favors artists who can sustain the commitment of their audience, rather than a star whose label can drive up CD sales through advertising and hype.[48]

At the same time, not every artist can inspire the intense devotion of such a large number of listeners as the Grateful Dead or Bob Dylan, nor can each performer be equally adept at exploiting multiple revenue streams. A DJ may play live sets, but other types of electronic musicians and composers may be less likely to succeed through performing. Such a business model would almost certainly disadvantage some artists. Some musicians may prefer to earn their income by selling recorded works, rather than hawking t-shirts or touring. Others simply may not desire to see every sound they make documented, replicated, and distributed far and wide.

In other words, decentralized reproduction was not going to be a boon for everyone. Indeed, the Grateful Dead represents only one extreme in the range of artist and business responses to bootlegs. Profiteering so angered the

Replacements that band members raided a record store in the 1980s, personally destroying illicit albums. "There are so damn many of them," said Paul Westerberg, lead singer of the influential Minnesota rock band, in 1991. "I'm not opposed to people hearing them, and I don't mind when somebody trades them, but to think that somebody's making money off them irritates me."[49] In a sense, the band's own label was among those "making money off them [bootlegs]." Shortly before the Replacements moved to a major label in 1985, their original company, Twin/Tone Records, rushed out a cassette-only copy of a bootleg tape that a roadie confiscated from a fan during a 1984 show. *The Shit Hits the Fans* documents one of a series of performances in which Westerberg and his crew deliberately played poorly when talent scouts from major labels were in the audience.[50] With its patchy sound and tape-only format, the album represents a curious intersection of fan recording and legitimate product—an "official bootleg" in the truest sense of the phrase.

As the Replacements' rage suggests, bootlegging was not restricted to artists like the Grateful Dead or Phish, whose fans gobbled up every twenty-minute guitar solo that was captured on tape. In the 1980s, copiers circulated recordings by popular contemporary artists such as Bon Jovi, Guns & Roses, and R.E.M., as well as sixties standbys like Cream, Pink Floyd, and the Rolling Stones. These bootlegs, increasingly issued on CD in the late 1980s and early 1990s, included live performances, B-sides of singles, and unreleased studio tracks. According to the RIAA, police confiscated 95,000 bootleg CDs in 1990—twelve times more than the year before.[51] Prince's 1987 *Black Album* is often cited as the most bootlegged album of the period, having been pulled by the artist at the last minute, when he decided the record's treatment of sex and violence was too dark. The withholding of the record made it all the more attractive to fans, and the existence of a small number of advance copies ensured that the album would become available to those who sought it out. As with Bob Dylan's basement tapes, widespread pirating led to the album's eventual release several years later.[52]

The uptick of piracy in the late 1980s resulted from both legal and technological changes. The United States received a wave of imported bootlegs from Europe due to a legal quirk—the so-called "protection gap" that allowed European copyrights to lapse on many recordings that were still protected in the United States. Previously unreleased Beatles recordings known as the Ultra Rare Trax series helped spark interest in imports upon their release in 1988.[53] The eighties also witnessed the zenith of the easily recordable cassette's popularity, as the vinyl LP declined and the music industry promoted the new compact disc. In New York, Los Angeles, and other American cities, vendors sold bootleg tapes on the street for half the price of a regular cassette. Rapper Joseph "Run" Simmons of Run-DMC reacted to sidewalk pirates in much the same way that Westerberg responded to bootlegs in a record shop: when a vendor set up shop right outside the offices of his Manhattan record label, selling copies of the album *Back from Hell* a week before it was even released, Simmons exploded. "I just took it from him," the rapper said. "He was taking money out of my pocket."[54]

The Hip-Hop Mixtape as a Bootleg Medium

A pirate copy of *Back from Hell* was not the only place one might find Run's voice. Starting in the 1970s, hip-hop DJs produced and distributed mixtapes—hodgepodges of recordings by various artists that circulated in the underground hip-hop scene of New York City. The initial tapes captured the unique combinations and sequences of borrowed sounds that DJs assembled in live performance, much as tapers documented the improvisation of the Grateful Dead. The pioneers of hip-hop used new media to disseminate music at the same time that rock fans developed their tape-trading communities. As Jeff Chang observed in his history of hip-hop:

> Live bootleg cassette tapes of Kool Herc, Afrika Bambaataa, Flash and Furious 5, the L Brothers, the Cold Crush Brothers and others were the sound of the OJ Cabs that took folks across the city. The tapes passed hand-to-hand in the Black and Latino neighborhoods of Brooklyn, the Lower East Side, Queens and Long Island's Black Belt. Kids in the boroughs were building sound systems and holding rap battles with the same fervor the Bronx once possessed all to itself.[55]

Such recordings were doubly bootleg. The tapes documented the performance of the DJs who played records at parties and the emcees who rhymed over the music—but they were also copies of the artists whose recordings were chopped up and recombined by the DJ. The result was a new mélange of music that could shade from one song to the next almost imperceptibly. In the process, the early performers of hip-hop were bootlegged even as the records they used were also bootlegged. What began as a local phenomenon of recreation and live entertainment became an art form in its own right, for the DJs who spun records as well as the vocalists who accompanied them. Word of hip-hop spread out of the Bronx—at first informally, in the form of bootleg "party tapes," and later as mainstream entertainment, particularly with the success of the Sugar Hill Gang's 1979 single, "Rapper's Delight," in which a trio rapped over a rhythm copied from the funk band Chic's hit "Good Times."[56]

Neither the Bronx nor any particular technology can be said to have spawned the musical innovations of hip hop. Sound systems, rapping, remixing—each had roots in the musical culture of Jamaica in the 1950s and 1960s, where the genesis of reggae furnished the practices that would later evolve into hip-hop in New York City. The saga of sound systems began when Arthur "Duke" Reid set up a record player and a battery of speakers in his Kingston, Jamaica, liquor store, hoping to lure customers with the sounds of American R&B music. Reid loaded the system on to his truck and began winning fame and fortune by playing at parties around the country in the late 1950s.[57]

Reid used his profits to build a recording studio in 1964, and there a seminal cultural event occurred by accident three years later. Sound engineer Byron Smith forgot to add the vocal track to a recording of "On the Beach" by the Paragons, and Reid's partner, Ruddy Redwood, played the disc at a party later that night. Redwood realized that they could use the instrumental track as a B-side for their records, instead of spending money on recording a whole new performance. Different singers subsequently performed over the same sounds, while DJs and sound engineers tweaked the track to make their own distinctive versions, leading to the spacey, producer-driven genre of music known as "dub," made famous in the 1970s by eccentric personalities such as Lee "Scratch" Perry.[58]

These ways of reusing records migrated from Jamaica to New York—literally, as a twelve-year-old boy brought his experience with sound systems to the Bronx when his family moved there in 1967. The boy was Clive Campbell, who won fame DJing parties as Kool Herc in the early 1970s. Herc noticed that people particularly enjoyed dancing to the brief instrumental breaks in songs, where often only bass and drums remained in the mix. He realized he could prolong those portions of the songs by playing the two copies of the same record simultaneously, on two turntables; as a few seconds of rhythm ended on one record, he started from the beginning of the same passage on the other, building an ongoing beat out of one short segment of a recording. This method, known as the "Merry-Go-Round," created the musical framework of hip-hop, providing an intense, repeating rhythm over which DJs and MCs would speak, shout, and rhyme.[59]

As other DJs copied and improved Herc's techniques, some began to tape their performances. Grandmaster Flash started recording his live performances in 1973.[60] Spinners such as Harlem's Brucie Bee and the Bronx's Starchild began recording their live performances and selling tapes of the sound collages they had created to promote their talent as DJs. Handwritten labels on cassettes often listed the occasion for the recorded sounds, such as "Doug E. Fresh Birthday Party, Vol. 1."[61] Some took cash for agreeing to shout out someone's name on the mic during a night of spinning records. Whether sold or circulated for free, mixtapes helped build a DJ's fame, bringing people out to his shows. Afrika Bambaataa's mother gave him two turntables upon his high-school graduation, and the hip-hop pioneer made his debut mixing records at the Bronx River Community Center in November 1976. Bambaataa's performances melded together sounds from diverse sources, beginning, for example, with the theme music of TV's *The Munsters* before blending in a James Brown recording or switching to the beat of the Rolling Stones' "Honky Tonk Woman."[62]

The first hip-hop recordings formally released by record labels captured this playful recycling of music and other popular culture. Sugar Hill Records scored the breakthrough 1979 hit "Rapper's Delight" after co-owner Sylvia Robinson heard about a young man named Henry "Big Bank Hank" Jackson, who managed several rappers in New York and was known to rap over bootleg hip-hop tapes at the New Jersey pizza parlor where he worked his day job. Jackson was also employed as a bouncer at several clubs in the Bronx. Svengali-style, Robinson recruited two other amateur rappers to record with Jackson; on the resulting single, which clocked in at fifteen minutes yet still became a huge radio hit, the trio was accompanied only by an imitation of Chic's funk hit "Good Times," already a live favorite of rappers and DJs when Robinson orchestrated the recording of "Rapper's Delight."[63]

The recording succeeded because it captured the zeitgeist of a critical moment: the pivot when hip-hop metamorphosed from live party music into a recorded art form. Many rappers and fans in New York wondered how an improvised, hours-long DJ performance could be compressed into the length of a regular disc or tape. In fact, "Rapper's Delight" achieved almost unprecedented radio success for a track of its length, yet followers of the nascent hip-hop scene were more surprised that the music could actually be cut so *short*.[64] The record's content also embodied the difficulties of translating hip-hop to the studio. Over the years, numerous scholars and journalists incorrectly identified the instrumental accompaniment of the song as a direct sample from Chic's recording, but Robinson insisted that her house band re-performed the rhythm of "Good Times" in the studio. Bernard Edwards and Nile Rodgers, the songwriters behind Chic, still sued Robinson's Sugar Hill Records on the grounds that "Rapper's Delight" violated their copyright for the written composition of "Good Times," and they ultimately won songwriting credit for the hip-hop breakthrough that recreated their sound.[65]

The advent of digital samplers in the early 1980s soon made it easier to construct elaborate collages of recorded sounds, borrowing not just a song's rhythmic break but also snatches of melody and other sound effects. One of the earliest digital samplers, the Emulator, was released in 1981 by E-mu Systems, a synthesizer manufacturer based in California. By storing and replaying small sections of recorded sound, the sampler allowed artists to "loop" a sound over and over—accomplishing what Herc had done manually with his turntables, and permitting the simultaneous layering of many different sounds.[66] Bambaataa's landmark 1982 recording "Planet Rock," for instance, combined the synthesizer melody of "Trans Europe Express," a recording by the German electronic group Kraftwerk, with the rhythm of Captain Sky's 1978 funk hit "Super Sporm." Starting with the familiar hip-hop pattern of a repeating snatch of rhythm, producer and DJ Arthur Baker decorated the track with electronic video game–like noises and distorted voices that intoned, "Rock, rock with the Planet Rock," as Bambaataa repeated the phrase "the rock it don't stop," producing a sound that was staccato, foreboding, and exuberant   an echo of the spontaneous concoction of sounds created by DJs and MCs in live performance.[67]

Most histories of hip-hop devote little space to the role of mixtapes in the development of the genre throughout its evolution. Bruce Bee, Starchild, and other mixtape pioneers are not easy to find in these works, as the narrative arc moves swiftly from the experiments of Herc to the mainstream success of "Rapper's Delight," and from the initial popularity of mid-1980s acts like Run-DMC to the rise of "gangsta rap" and the commercial empires of moguls such as Puff Daddy in the 1990s. The move is, thus, from the music's modest but innovative birthplace in South Bronx parties to its acceptance and ultimate co-optation by established corporate interests in the music industry. As a persistent offshoot of rap's disorganized origins, mixtapes do not figure prominently in this story. Journalists Jeff Chang and S. H. Fernando make occasional reference to the importance of bootleg tapes in spreading the word about innovative performances by Herc and Bambaataa, when the infant genre of hip-hop had not yet seen the inside of a recording studio. However, scholars, journalists, and filmmakers have recently begun to study the cultural influence of mixtapes in the wake of the more recent success of artists such as Funkmaster Flex, DJ Clue, and DJ Drama.

Mixtapes continued to be made in the intervening period, cultivating new talent and providing an outlet for experimentation in hip-hop as multimedia conglomerates began to exploit the profit potential of rap music, especially with its rising popularity in the 1980s and near-universal acceptance in the following decade. "While I was home it was only me, Kid [Capri], Star Child and Star Ski that I knew of," Brucie Bee recalled. Brucie did a brief stint in prison, and when he got out the scene had changed. "When I came home in 1993 there was all these other D.J.s. It was Doo Wop, Triple Cee and Buck Wild."[68] Both mainstream commercial hip-hop and the New York mixtape market were booming. His friend Kid Capri won a record deal and issued his first official album, aptly titled *The Tape*, in 1991. In the same period when Dr. Dre, Snoop Doggy Dogg, the Notorious B.I.G. and other rappers found massive popular success, the *Village Voice* observed:

> Mix tapes... have changed the soundscape of New York City in recent years.
>
> Their fast-chat patter and aggressive shout-outs ('Big up to my G's from the Polo Grounds uptown! Big up to my real niggaz in Brooklyn!')

have become a striking element in the noisy urban mix Mayor [Rudolph]
Giuliani wants to muffle.[69]

Indeed, B.I.G., or "Biggie," secured a record deal after his own demo tape circulated among the editors of *The Source* magazine and executives at Uptown
Records in 1992.[70]

Originally rare documents of fleeting performances, the tapes gradually
became commodities that circulated outside the scope of copyright law, an
adjunct to the urban economy of parties and live performance. They were one
piece of a larger complex of jobs and businesses that New York youth created
for themselves, whether it meant starting a record label, getting a record deal,
mixing music at clubs and parties, or selling bootleg tapes on the street. "Hip
hop has ... created a lot of jobs that otherwise wouldn't exist," Kool Herc argued
in 2005.[71]

Scholars have sometimes romanticized the idea of sampling and mixing as
natural responses to conditions of poverty, yet DJing and producing hip-hop
tracks were hardly cheap enterprises.[72] It could be as simple as the two turntables and a speaker used by Herc in the early 1970s, but successful artists started
small and reinvested their earnings in technology. An E-mu sampler in 1986 cost
at least $2,745.[73] "'They were too poor to get instruments.' Yeah, right," said DJ
Kool Akiem of the Micranots in 1999. "They were too poor for classes.... Man,
those samplers were [expensive] back then! I mean, you gotta have money, some
way, to put your studio together...I mean deejaying, if you're serious, you're
gonna have to spend a thousand dollars on your equipment. But then every
record's ten bucks. Then you got speakers and blah, blah, blah."[74]

While the technology needed to assemble samples into one fluid collage
could be costly, the physical object of the recording itself was often unpolished.
The early mixtapes were, like bootleg cassettes of hit albums, cheaply produced
and packaged. "As cult objects go, they're not much to look at: primitive graph-
ics printed on cheap paper and handwritten track listings, frequently inaccu-
rate and incomplete," the journalist Frank Owen observed in 1994. "They're
scruffy-looking yet highly prized artifacts sold out of small stores in the East
Village or record shops uptown."[75]

The content of mixtapes signaled shifting tastes in hip-hop. DJs anticipated
the next big hits and brought attention to new artists by mixing their words and
music with those of other, better-known rappers.[76] The DJ served as a tastemaker,
connoisseur, and opinion leader. In his work studying British fans of American
soul music in the 1970s, anthropologist Mark Jamieson has shown how DJs
exercised cultural authority through their knowledge, good taste, and access to
prized recordings. Similarly, buyers of mixtapes valued the maker for his judgment in selecting classic R&B and funk tracks, which formed the basis of many

remixes, as well as his acumen at finding the most desirable new music before anyone else. Taxi drivers sought out the best mixtapes, since certain well-heeled customers would pay for a "hold call" just to listen to the work of certain DJs. "A Hold Call is where a person who had some money would want to get into this particular vehicle and do just basically nothing, sort of just ride around for hours and hours," Grandmaster Flash remembered. "If [the driver] had the hottest tape he would get all the Hold Calls across the [taxi dispatcher's] radio."[77]

Unregulated and entrepreneurial, the mixtape market contained a variety of different patterns of production, distribution, and profit making. Some DJs, like Brucie Bee in the 1980s, sold their tapes directly to people who loved the music they played. "I would spend a day in my house just making tapes," Brucie recalled. "I would come out with about 100 tapes and then go into everybody's block that was getting money... I would just jump in a cab and go up in they block."[78] Other DJs simply released the tapes as free promotional materials, which bootleggers in turn copied and sold on the street. Hiding behind a sticker that said "For Promotional Use Only," DJs insisted that mixtapes were just a noncommercial showcase of their mixing skills, knowing that the work would be replicated and sold by others. DJ Clue, who climbed to the top of the New York scene in the 1990s by mixing together the most sought-after new music on his tapes, claimed not to distribute mixtapes at all. He would simply record the mix and send free copies to athletes, record shops, and clothing stores to ensure that the right people were hearing them. DJ Whoo Kid described the multitiered structure that had evolved in New York by 2003. "I take it to the main [wholesale] bootlegger and he does his thing and kills the streets," he said. "The main bootlegger has about 300 bootleggers [that he works with]. They all know each other. They all got their own portable pressing machines. It's not only them, it's regular people. My main thing is to get it bootlegged."[79] Journalist Shaheem Reid reported that other DJs sold their mixtapes to stores on consignment. Some made money by naming their mixes after commercial sponsors. "We used the bootleggers as our own personal street team," remarked Lloyd Banks of the group G-Unit.[80]

By the 1990s, mixtapes became more than a vehicle for DJs to show off their talents. The genre also became a tool for aspiring rappers to distribute their own work on the streets in the absence of a record deal, or for enterprising DJs to leverage their own personal connections and marketing savvy to act as cultural arbiters within the hip-hop scene. DJ Clue was among the first to distribute "mixtapes" in the form of CDs in the early 1990s, and his knack for delivering the newest, most sought-after music became a model for future mixtapes, as much a showcase for cutting-edge music as for DJing virtuosity. Some artists suspected that Clue maintained his competitive advantage by sneaking a digital audiotape (DAT) device into studios and capturing the music before it was even released. Clue used his connections with sound engineers and industry insiders to get new recordings before anyone else. DJ Kay Slay admitted to finding the "grimi-est intern" at a label, who was so underpaid that he would provide Slay access to fresh music in exchange for $75 or $100. "I had one of these at every label," Slay said in 2005.[81] DJs like Clue and Slay followed in the footsteps of 1960s bootleggers, who tried every method of persuasion, including bribery, to obtain unreleased recordings from stars like Johnny Cash and Leonard Cohen.

Such tactics violated copyright law, since DJs rarely cleared the use of sound samples on the tapes with the owners of the recordings, but in time, successful DJs like Funkmaster Flex began releasing official mixtapes through established labels. Flex's 1995 *The Mix Tape: 60 Minutes of Funk* was among the first DJ com-pilations released as a legal mainstream product, consisting entirely of borrowed sounds from other rappers. The recording resembled the sonic pastiche he furi-ously constructed on air for Hot 97, a New York radio station, including freestyle raps by Erick Sermon and Busta Rhymes alongside a single by Yvette Michelle, a singer whose career was cultivated by Flex.[82] The DJ was partly a promoter, plugging himself and pushing new artists like Michelle. He also served a kind of variety-show host, appearing occasionally to comment on the proceedings and introduce artists, who praised the master of ceremonies in their lyrics: "1996 in your ass, Funkmaster Flex, compilation freestyle album, in your ass, we got lyrics for years for all you fuckin' peers," Redman and Method Man free-associated on one track. "Who's that nigga smokin' buddha on the A train? It's the Funkmaster Spock rock the spot."[83]

Kid Capri, Funkmaster Flex, and others began producing legally acceptable recordings like *The Tape* and *60 Minutes of Funk* in the 1990s, but DJs continued to release mixtapes in the same informal fashion as ever. Many rappers coveted a spot on a popular DJ's tapes, freely volunteering their work in order to reach a large audience. Mixtapes also offered an alternative path of distribution and promotion for artists without record label deals. Jadakiss remembered being in awe of DJ Clue's prestige: "We used to sit around the house and listen to Clue tapes and be like, 'He'll call us one day.' So we sat and sat and sat and waited. Eventually he called." Both DJ Clue and Jadakiss's group, the LOX, vaulted to mainstream success on the strength of their mixtape fame. As Shaheem Reid notes, the popular rapper 50 Cent's "debut" *Get Rich or Die Tryin'* was prob-ably his twentieth album in circulation when Aftermath Records released it in 2003. Cent had already put out numerous mixtapes with titles like *50 Cent Is the Future* on the street, striving to build his reputation. He even inked a deal with Columbia Records in 2001, but the label stopped returning his calls when it learned that he had been shot nine times. He then turned to the informal arena of the streets to make his comeback and land another deal. He stood outside radio stations with business partner Sha Money XL, trying to get their mixtapes played on the air, and in time they were.[84]

Soon after, 50 Cent became one of the most commercially successful record-ing artists of the early twenty-first century, a clear example of the trajectory from mixtape obscurity to mainstream fame. No less an arbiter of conventional wisdom than *USA Today* declared in 2006 that 50 Cent helped bring mixtapes to the attention of the mainstream. "The often unlicensed and frequently boot-legged collections of exclusive advance tracks, hot street jams, diss songs and freestyles—available for sale via the Internet, small retail shops and street ven-dors, or as free downloads and file swaps—aren't just for hardcore fans anymore," Steve Jones reported.[85] Though technically infringing copyright, the bustling trade in bootleg sound collage served as a useful complement to the official record industry—a sort of disorganized minor leagues for cultivating talent. "You run the mixtape game, you have a chance at the mainstream industry," the rapper Jedi observed in 2005.[86] The medium provided an alternative network for new performers to introduce themselves to listeners and build their reputations, forming what media scholar Jared Ball calls "an African American underground communication and press."[87] As Ball points out, mixtapes occupied a peculiar place in the music industry, perceived as a threat by record labels that also stood to benefit from the artists who emerged from the mixtape scene.[88]

In the new millennium, hip-hop continued to be a participatory medium, a stratified market, and an arena for unpunished piracy. When Ball spoke of mix-tapes as an "underground press" he perhaps consciously evoked the political rap-per Chuck D's 1990 description of rap music as "a CNN that black kids never had."[89] Similarly, DJ Red Alert referred to mixtapes as "underground radio on tape" in 1994.[90] Anyone with a tape deck or CD burner could become a de facto record label, and the recording industry found ways to take advantage of this spontaneous activity, in much the same way that major labels learned to pluck the most successful rock bands from independent labels.[91] While police some-times raided stores that sold mixtapes, the RIAA considered outright piracy a much higher priority. "We try to focus most of our attention at the higher levels of distribution before it gets to retail," the group's antipiracy czar said in 2006. "We leave it for the most part to local police to enforce state laws.... We have trained police in terms of what to look for."[92]

In a way, the exuberance of the mixtape culture in the 1990s and early 2000s pushed back against the legal regulation of mainstream hip-hop. Siva Vaidhyanathan decried the effect of copyright enforcement on rap music in his 2001 book *Copyrights and Copywrongs*, documenting how the threat of litigation forced rappers and their labels to obtain costly copyright clearances from rights owners for the sound samples they used in constructing new tracks. "The legal implications of sampling has created a subsidiary industry within rap, fattening the pockets of lawyers, older artists, defunct labels, and sample clearinghouses, who conduct the actual busywork of acquiring rights and negotiating fees," journalist S. H. Fernando observed in 1994. "It has also meant that, in the studio, artists do not have the carte blanche to create as freely as they once did."[93] The formerly freewheeling collage and pastiche of hip-hop ran up against a high wall of rents paid to the established industry when rappers signed to major labels and reached mainstream audiences, but DJs in the informal mixtape market blithely disregarded the procedures of copyright compliance, slapping together old beats with the words of new artists and disavowing involvement in the commercial reproduction of their creations.[94]

But the meaning of the DJ's work as a cultural impresario remained open to interpretation. As a gatekeeper to commercial success, a well-regarded DJ wielded power not unlike that of a record company; like a record executive, DJs profited from music recorded by others, exploiting everyone from the much-sampled funk musician James Brown to the aspiring rapper who *wanted* to have his music exploited. A hip-hop producer could make a career out of collating and rearranging recorded sounds, winning awards, ad revenue, jobs on the radio, and prestige.[95] He became like the curator at a famous museum; in this way, his work mirrored the appropriation art of Richard Prince and others, who rose to prominence in the 1970s and 1980s by collecting things—photos from biker magazines, cigarette ads, pulp magazine covers—and simply putting them on display.[96]

The musician and theorist Ian Svenonius argues that, like the appropriation artist, the DJ's skill was not *making* a new expression but simply choosing among goods, in this case recordings. His work resembled "the new role of the bourgeoisie as stockbroker/trader/designator-of-worth and handler-of-commodities," Svenonius declared in his 2006 polemic *The Psychic Soviet*.[97] For Svenonius, the traditional recording artist was the counterpart of the industrial worker, an iconic figure of the twentieth century who superseded the individual craft of the painter or sculptor through the power of mass production. By the end of the century, he suggested, the DJ was pushing out the rock star or singing sensation by removing labor from the equation entirely. He became the ideological and artistic equivalent of the financier, the reigning king of a deindustrialized America: "Like the rulers on Wall Street, he has no actual talent except to play with other people's labor. His talent is his impeccable taste and his ability to turn junk into gold, like his stockbroking masters."[98]

The DJ's defenders would no doubt agree—the young people who first assembled the bricolage of hip-hop in the Bronx did indeed "turn junk into gold." As apartment buildings burned and drugs, poverty, and violence wrecked lives, New Yorkers of the 1970s seized on whatever tools were available to create a billion-dollar industry. At the same time, hip-hop reflects a broader aesthetic of appropriation that characterized American culture in the late twentieth century, from the exhibitions of the Museum of Modern Art down to the derivative remakes of films, TV shows, and comic books that stream out of Hollywood. The question here is how an unregulated, informal aspect of that culture—bootlegging—related to the whole. Constructing a mixtape required more creative input than recording a rock concert or making identical copies of commercially released albums, since the DJ cleverly selected and juxtaposed parts of different recordings in the mix, creating a new kind of composition. They put a personal stamp on what they assembled, to a greater extent than the rock or jazz bootlegger who designed the packaging of a live recording. On the other hand, producing and *selling* a mix of other people's sounds was far less permissible under American copyright law than recording and trading tapes of the Grateful Dead, even though some rappers wanted their music to be bootlegged, as did the Dead.

The partial tolerance of jamband tape trading and the mixtape market suggests a modus vivendi could exist among artists, fans, pirates, and the record industry. So long as it did not directly cross the path of the established labels, music copying was a peripheral—sometimes even helpful—nuisance. Record companies had looked on with indifference when the Hot Record Society copied and distributed out-of-print jazz recordings in the 1930s, yet the greater popularity of Jolly Roger and other labels elicited legal retaliation in the early 1950s. Likewise, mixtapes have served as a practical adjunct to the official industry, at least until the trade gets too big. Concert bootlegs and mixtapes can stimulate sales of officially released products for rock bands, rappers, and their labels. Devoted fans with disposable income will buy the "real" CD, concert tickets, and merchandise while illegally downloading unreleased tracks or buying a DJ's remix on the street.

The mainstream industry reaped the benefits of the buzz generated by mixtapes for its artists, but it did not hesitate to crush competition from petty capitalists like DJ Drama, who was arrested in Atlanta on racketeering charges for selling his Gangsta Grillz mixtapes in 2005. At the time, the trade publication *Billboard Biz* acknowledged the industry's dilemma in a throwaway line, noting that the arrest "calls into question whether major labels will continue to utilize mixtapes as promotional tools."[99] The mainstream record companies could not decide whether mixtape DJs were their competitors or informal partners. When Def Jam and other labels leaked MP3s of vocal and instrumental tracks before an album's release, they implicitly encouraged DJs to circulate the music. The labels also benefited from DJs doing the work of their own artist and repertoire (A&R) agents, who traditionally found and signed promising new talent. Mixtape success signaled which rappers and DJs would be successful in the mainstream. As one rapper put it, for music to succeed, "You gotta get some opinion from the streets."[100] The mixtape trade thus became a valuable source of the "collective intelligence" described by Italian autonomist thinkers such as Franco "Bifo"

Berardi and Tiziana Terranova, because companies could exploit street buzz as a type of market research.[101]

Although the industry still turned often enough to the copyright cudgels it had won since the 1970s, some artists and businesses accepted unauthorized reproduction as a fact of life, especially where profit could be made from the publicity generated by a popular mixtape, file sharing, or word-of-mouth. *Spell My Name Right,* the title of a 2008 official release by the rapper Statik Selektah, an alum of numerous mixtapes, hinted at the underlying principle, evoking a classic saying by Broadway impresario George M. Cohan: "I don't care what you say about me, as long as you say something about me, and as long as you spell my name right."[102] Distributing mixtapes was not unlike plugging in the early twentieth century music industry, when song publishers *wanted* their tunes to be widely and freely performed in public to drive up sales of sheet music.[103]

Such a model does not work so well when piracy in developing countries is concerned. With a few exceptions, American artists and businesses cannot expect to piggyback profitably on the unauthorized copying of their products abroad. Poor consumers who buy bootleg CDs and DVDs in Asia do not necessarily have the ability or the opportunity to buy a concert ticket or officially licensed merchandise; they buy the recording at a price they can afford, perhaps a tenth of the price charged in the United States. Global piracy served as the latest intellectual property panic in the 1980s and 1990s, presenting an adversary that seemed even more intractable and potentially fatal for America's entertainment, fashion, and technology industries than the homegrown pirate.

The Global War on Piracy

Reporter: What do you think of secret recordings?
Cynthia Hawkins: It's a theft, a rape. I despise them.

— Diva (1981)

A celebrated opera singer, Cynthia Hawkins was notorious for her refusal to allow herself to be recorded. "Music comes and goes," she told a gaggle of reporters. "You don't try to keep it.... Commerce should adapt to art." However, commerce was about to force the artist to adapt instead. An earnest young fan, Jules, managed to sneak a tape recorder into Hawkins's Paris performance, creating a bootleg for his own personal pleasure, but a shadowy syndicate of Taiwanese record pirates was bent on obtaining the tape. They planned to use it to blackmail Hawkins into signing an exclusive recording contract; otherwise, they would pirate the performance and break the singer's career-long embargo against the market. Hawkins's manager, Mr. Weinstadt, had tolerated the unusual path she had chosen to take in her career, but his patience was running out. Since Taiwan had not signed on to international copyright agreements, there was nothing Hawkins could do to stop them. "They have us by the throat," Weinstadt said. "They use the recording to print a record in their country. They flood the market, with no guarantees on the quality and no profits for us." He understood her "scruples," but he also demanded that she act like a "responsible artist" and start recording.[1]

Though fictional, the story of Jean-Jacques Beineix's 1981 film *Diva* perfectly encapsulates the conflicts of art, technology, law, and commerce that characterized the world economy in the early 1980s. Hawkins stood against the forces of new media, clinging to the conviction that a performer should be able to set the terms of how her work was experienced. She refused to let any record company, bootlegging fan, or pirate take advantage of her voice, yet the film suggests that such control was nearly impossible.

Beineix presented a world in which almost any cultural good was free for the taking, and he contrasted various types of theft to make the point. In one scene, a young woman slips an LP into her art portfolio and evades the watchful eye of a record store clerk. Later, she gives Jules a pilfered Rolex watch, prompting him to ask, "Do you steal a lot?"—even as the bootleg recording that he, in a sense, stole from Hawkins plays in the background. Is taking an LP from the record store shelf worse than taking the singer's voice from the concert hall without her permission? Given the technological capabilities of tape recorders and personal computers, is there any way to prevent someone on the other side of the world from copying one's work, and is there any limit to the amount of that work in circulation? As Weinstadt suggested, the market resisted any regulation of quality or quantity; it enforced its own will upon artist and listener alike.

So far, the story of music piracy in the United States has involved a variety of individuals and groups who advanced different rationales for how recorded music ought to be produced and regulated. Record collectors wanted to distribute copies of old and out-of-print recordings, and fans of opera and rock and roll captured concert sounds that otherwise would never have been fixed in a physical form. In decade after decade, record companies lobbied to pay the lowest possible royalties for the songs they recorded, while seeking protection from slippery enterprises that copied and sold their recordings without permission. Meanwhile, those enterprises devised ingenious legal strategies to justify repackaging another company's sounds as their own—whether Wynant Van Zant Pearce Bradley's off-brand arias in the early twentieth century or David Heilman's mixtapes in the 1970s.

Throughout, judges had to wrestle with these competing claims. Like Learned Hand, they had to identify the elements of value in a sound recording; like the Supreme Court of Warren Burger, they had to determine the economic importance of music and the degree of control a record company could exert over its products. Musicians might follow the path of jazzman Clarence Williams, who collaborated with the Hot Record Society when it prepared a reissue of his music in the 1940s. In contrast, artists as different as Louis Armstrong and Metallica chose to pursue legal action against their copiers. All the while, consumers bought live bootlegs, copied records for their friends, sought out unreleased music leaked from the studio, and opted for cheap pirate editions of hit records.

The worldwide proliferation of piracy broke from these patterns in the 1970s. In the two preceding decades, bootleggers in Sweden, Argentina, and other countries had satisfied much the same demand as the Dante Bolletinos or Boris Roses of the United States, copying blues, folk, jazz, and classical music for a small, scattered minority of fans. The global boom of piracy that followed looked much more like the profit-driven reproduction of popular recordings like *Saturday Night Fever* or *Grease* in the United States, both of which were also smash hits abroad. Moreover, illicit copying of American goods multiplied at a moment when business and political leaders in the United States noted with growing unease the economic competition of the Third World.

It was no coincidence: piracy in developing nations piggybacked on industrialization, as expanding markets made it possible for consumers to gain access to equipment for recording and playing music, while many people remained too poor to pay the price for the legitimate copies of recordings sold by American and European companies. As musicologist Peter Manuel observed, piracy often disadvantaged local music companies at least as much as their Western competitors, if not more so.[2] At a certain stage of development, governments had little incentive to deny their citizens cheap access to books, movies, and music; unlike the United States, which was becoming increasingly protective of its domestic "information industries," these countries had not yet cultivated entertainment or publishing sectors that were large enough to warrant energetic enforcement of intellectual property rights.

In the cast of characters in this new world economy, one could find a left-wing Pakistani leader with a demagogic streak telling his countrymen to copy Western textbooks freely, on the grounds that a too-high price deterred education and development.[3] Poorly paid policeman in many countries could be "persuaded" not to enforce whatever copyright law was on the books, and judges were reluctant to impose serious penalties on local businessmen for selling pirated music. The representatives of Western corporations and trade groups could be found investigating pirate markets in Thailand or Singapore, while dodging death threats. Meanwhile, a new generation of political leaders, including Ronald Reagan and Margaret Thatcher, sought to protect exports of copyrighted music, patented medicines, and computer software to the outside world, taking an aggressive stance in trade deals with emerging economies such as South Korea.

US policymakers worried about both the decline of American manufacturing and the ability of the nation's "post-industrial" industries, such as entertainment and information technology, to sell goods and services in the developing world. While multinational corporations either built or contracted with factories in places like Taiwan and Thailand, entrepreneurs in these countries took advantage of new media to copy sounds, images, texts, codes, and formulas.[4] "Movies, computer programs and recordings can be stolen by merely copying, in ways that a shipment of logs or soybeans cannot," the *Journal of Commerce* warned Western businesspeople in 1990. "Continued losses in the long run undermine the incentive to invest capital in research and the ability to develop new products."[5] Piracy threatened to dilute demand for the goods that the most technologically advanced nations exported to the rest of the world, creating an imbalance between the manufactured goods that countries such as the United States imported and the compact discs and videotapes they attempted to export.

The threat was real enough. The United States had benefited from exploiting foreign culture and technology as it developed its own manufacturing capacity in the nineteenth century, eventually surpassing the nations whose copyrights and patents it had pirated.[6] By the 1970s, American hegemony was no longer unquestioned; Western Europe and Japan had recovered from the devastation of World War II, and less developed nations throughout Asia, the Middle East, and Africa began to industrialize in earnest. In 1971 the United States began buying more goods from other countries than it sold, and this trade deficit has, with very few exceptions, expanded ever since.[7] In the remainder of the twentieth century, business and political leaders, both in the United States and Europe, worked hard to develop the rest of the world on their own terms, encouraging export-led manufacturing in poor countries while attempting to lay the groundwork for the authorized sale of Western goods and services in these markets.

New media sped the growth of trade—licit and illicit—throughout the world, raising the twin specters of deindustrialization and piracy as the causes of economic woe in the United States and other wealthy countries. Nations such as Taiwan, the United Arab Emirates, and Liberia might have broadly differed in their degree of development and influence in the emerging global economy, but they formed ties with each other as entrepôts within complex networks of trade. In response to the global spread of piracy, a variety of business interests, ranging from software companies to record labels, coalesced behind the idea of "intellectual property," which became a priority in US trade negotiations for the first time in the 1980s. The antipiracy movement won significant legal and dip- lomatic victories in the ensuing years, yet piracy remained nearly as common as ever in many parts of the world.

Crisis at Home, Growth Abroad

The economic crunch of the late 1970s hit the music industry in the United States and Europe hard, ending a period of prodigious growth that had coin- cided with the coming of age of the postwar generation. In the United States, the dollar value of the domestic production of records and tapes grew by 112 percent between 1972 and 1977, whereas it increased about 55 percent between 1977 and 1982.[8] The recording industry hit a record sales high of $4.1 billion in 1978, shortly before music sales started to tank. "Some industry analysts even suggested that a recession in the general economy was good for the music

Table 7.1 **Estimates of Pirate Recordings Seized in Selected Countries, 1980–1985**

Year	Country	Number of recordings seized
1980	Japan	4,500
	Germany	50,000
	Spain	300,000
1981	Australia	14,000
	Egypt	25,000
1982	United States	6,000
	Chile	8,000
	Australia	12,000
	India	27,000
	Peru	50,000
1983	Australia	2,000
	Netherlands	250,000
1984	United Kingdom	1,000
	Mexico	10,000
	Cameroon	140,000
	Benin	195,000
	France	350,000
1985	Canada	50,000
	Sweden	52,000
	Ivory Coast	200,000
1981–1983	Singapore	460,000
1984–1985	Nigeria	460,000

Source: Publishers Association and Federation of Phonogram and Videogram Producers Association, *International Piracy: The Threat to the British Copyright Industries* (United Kingdom Anti-Piracy Group, 1986).

industry because people would stay home more, thereby increasing the need for music," economist Laurence Kenneth Shore observed in his 1983 study of the industry.[9] Europe's domestic recording industry also enjoyed substantial growth in the 1970s, as record sales grew at an average of 11 percent per year in the European Economic Community (EEC) between 1971 and 1978. The industry was shocked to find that sales dipped in most of Europe for the first time ever in 1979, and observers worried that the decline would continue in the new decade.[10]

Growth stalled in the late 1970s and early 1980s for a variety of reasons. Recession struck, most severely in 1981, and consumers no longer tolerated the steady rise in the cost of records. The average LP cost $4.98 in 1975 and $7.98 in 1978; the phenomenal growth in sales figures during the decade partly resulted from the fact that the record industry simply charged more per unit, and until 1979, inflation-weary consumers appeared willing to pay more.[11] Indeed, the increase in record prices was roughly equal to the rate of inflation between 1977 and 1982, which suggests that record companies could no longer inflate their prices as energetically as they had in the early to mid-1970s. The high price of oil increased shipping costs, which made records, like so many other products, more expensive. In May 1979 *Billboard* estimated that 700 record company staff had been let go, and the cuts continued all along the chain of production.[12] The number of workers who made records and tapes in the United States declined by 26 percent between 1977 and 1982.[13]

Economic conditions were not solely to blame. New media such as video-cassette recorders (VCRs) offered consumers alternative ways to spend their entertainment dollars. Industry executives worried that video arcades and home gaming systems such as Atari siphoned off the disposable income of the youth market.[14] Lastly, consumers turned to tape recorders to share copies of albums— an appealing option in the face of steadily rising prices. The RIAA began campaigning in the mid-1970s for a tax on tape recorders and blank cartridges, the proceeds of which would flow to the record industry to compensate for its hypothetical losses. This idea also took root in Europe, but in the United States the proposal never became law.[15]

Given this inauspicious climate, record companies began looking abroad for growth, but the burgeoning world market soon supplied the industry's next big headaches. US executives worried that the domestic market had reached a "saturation point" as the seemingly unstoppable growth of the early 1970s tapered off. "Just as people are unlikely to read many more newspapers next year than today," musicologist Pekka Gronow speculated in 1983, "they perhaps already buy as many records as they need."[16] The recording industry sought to squeeze more sales out of the domestic market by introducing new products, such as the compact disc, that might tempt consumers to re-purchase recordings they already owned on vinyl or tape. However, the "CD boom" was necessarily temporary—once consumers upgraded their record collections by purchasing their old recordings on the new format, sales leveled off once again.[17]

Both the technological fixes and the turn toward the world market reflected the extent to which record companies had become part of huge, multinational

Table 7.2 **Sales, Employment, and Investment in the US Recording Industry, 1972–1982**

	1972	1977	1982
Value of product shipments (millions of dollars)	537.3	1,138.7 (1,181.7)*	1,768.9
Employees (thousands)		23.1	17.1
Payroll (millions of dollars)		244.6	292
Value added by manufacture (million of dollars)		727.3	1,189.5
New capital expenditures (millions of dollars)		29.8	36.4

*The 1982 census offered a different estimate of the value of shipments in 1977 (noted in parentheses).

Source: US Department of Commerce, *1977 Census of Manufactures, Volume II: Industry Statistics, Part 3. SIC Major Groups 35–39* (Washington, DC: US Government Printing Office, 1970), 36D-20. US Department of Commerce, *1982 Census of Manufactures: Subject Series General Summary, Part 1. Industry, Product Class, and Geographic Area Statistics* (Washington, DC: Bureau of Census, 1982), 1–16, 1–17.

corporations that sold all kinds of entertainment goods and services. Dutch electronics giant Philips, having introduced the compact cassette in 1964 and the compact disc in the early 1980s, also owned Mercury Records and other labels. Warner Communications International formed in 1981, consolidating the record companies Atlantic, Elektra, Reprise, and Warner under one corporate umbrella with toy, video game, soft drink, publishing, and television interests. The Japanese company Sony bought up CBS Records in 1987 and Columbia Pictures in 1989, becoming a purveyor of both hardware and software. The company's Walkman, a compact cassette player designed for portability, helped revive the flagging music industry of the early 1980s by boosting sales of both players and cassettes. CBS and RCA already made 50 percent of their sales overseas in 1977, and by the 1990s, it was typical for American music publishers, record companies, and film and television producers in general to earn 50 percent of their revenues from foreign sales.[18]

Record companies, then, paid greater attention to foreign sales in the late 1970s and early 1980s as a way to overcome the stagnation of domestic markets in the United States and Europe, a crisis which provoked the reconstitution of ailing firms in large multinational conglomerates with an increasingly global focus. Previously, labels in the United States and Britain looked at overseas profits more as a bonus than an essential source of revenue, yet record label RSO actually made more money on foreign sales of the *Saturday Night Fever* soundtrack than it did in the United States. The most records were still sold the United

States, Australia, West Germany, and other wealthy nations, but less-developed markets in countries like Brazil and Mexico were approaching the level of sales seen in Europe and the United States.[19]

Record companies built up infrastructure abroad to capitalize on these new markets in the developing world. Large new pressing plants opened in Nigeria and Venezuela, where burgeoning oil profits propelled economic growth during the 1970s. As Nigeria became a bigger market for recorded music in the 1980s, it also became a hotbed of piracy and a chief target of music industry investigators. In fact, expanded access to tape recorders during the oil boom hastened so much unauthorized reproduction of foreign music and movies that multinational corporations began to abandon efforts to sell their official recordings in the Nigerian market.[20]

As the international market for music expanded well beyond the frontiers established by the recording industries of America and Europe, illicit recordings spread across new terrain like an advance guard for the multinational record companies. For example, *Grease* hit the market in Turkey before the film or soundtrack were officially released there.[21] In Saudi Arabia, substantial oil wealth and the complete lack of copyright laws made for a bustling sale in foreign movies and music, whether licit or illicit. The fact that the Saudi kingdom was impoverished in terms of cinema and television also made piracy an appealing option. Similarly, the sounds of *Saturday Night Fever* went where the Bee Gees and the label RSO could not go: across the borders of communist states such as Vietnam and North Korea.[22]

Indeed, tape recorders served the purposes of both entertainment and politics. Revolutionaries in Iran used audiocassettes to circumvent state media and disseminate their radical message to the people, and tapes of Islamic sermons subsequently became popular throughout Africa. Iranian pilgrims smuggled recordings of the Ayatollah Khomeini's sermons and phone conversations from Iraq, where the radical leader was exiled prior to founding the Islamic Republic of Iran. Khomeini bootlegs were even reported in the Communist republics of Central Asia after the Soviet Union invaded Afghanistan. While distinct from the music market, these uses paralleled the flows of pirate product that brought American popular culture into the Islamic world. Media scholar Douglas Boyd noted that *Rambo* was popular in Syria, even though it was "hardly a U.S. client state."[23]

The Sylvester Stallone action hit circulated behind the Iron Curtain as well, along with the films *Gorky Park* and *Moscow on the Hudson*.[24] Soviet authorities condemned capitalist films for celebrating the "three s's—sex, supermanism, and sadism," although some intellectuals acknowledged the quality of films such as *Straw Dogs, Apocalypse Now,* and *The Godfather*.[25] (Not surprisingly, all these works focused on the ills facing capitalist society.) Much like foreign guest workers in the Persian Gulf took tape recorders home to South Asia, some Soviet citizens snuck VCRs and audiocassette players into their home country after traveling abroad. The bolder ones made big profits by screening Western films in their homes and copying tapes to sell for the equivalent of hundreds of dollars a piece.[26]

Similarly, the People's Republic of China experienced an influx of foreign music despite its long struggle to control what the Chinese people could see, hear, and say. By the early 1980s, some of the prodigious flow of bootleg tapes from Taiwan and Hong Kong crossed into China, as the Communist government opened up "special economic zones" along the eastern coast to foreign trade. In the early 1980s, the Chinese authorities felt it necessary to issue a booklet called "How to Distinguish Decadent Songs," which warned against music with a "quavering rhythm," "a frenzied beat, neighing-like singing and a simple melody." It singled out jazz, rock and roll, and disco for their perverse qualities and damaging effects, while declaring that the Chinese pop music of Hong Kong and Taiwan celebrated "deformed love in a colonial or semicolonial society." While the government condoned the sale of Yugoslav folksongs and agitprop like "Medical Teams in Tanzania," Chinese listeners looked for "Puff the Magic Dragon" and *The Sound of Music*. Most of these recordings were pirated, since foreign companies were not allowed to distribute such decadent material in China. Ironically, in the early 1980s, the Chinese government took the sort of proactive steps to suppress piracy that Western leaders later implored the Communist state to take in the 1990s. Customs officials in Shenzhen began confiscating cassettes, records, and videotapes smuggled in from nearby Hong Kong, while the administration of Qinghua University demanded that students turn in all foreign recordings. Officials at another school in Beijing requested that students register their records and tapes with the authorities.[27]

Networks and Flows

Nearby Taiwan was one of the vectors of piracy in the world economy, although it would largely cede that role to other developing countries later in the 1980s. The island's bootleggers were just as eager to export their wares as the legal manufacturers who had begun to supply cheap labor and goods to the West, and counterfeit sales were driven both by rising incomes in Taiwan and demand from abroad.[28] Buyers came from the Middle East, Africa, America, and India to browse for pirated books, hair dryers, motor parts, and, of course, sound recordings. Meanwhile, Taiwanese law allowed judges to consider their own "moral convictions" in sentencing, and many were reluctant to condemn entrepreneurs for copying foreign trademarks, copyrights, and patents. Most convictions carried a six-month jail sentence, which was frequently commuted to a small fine; many infringers could simply factor these costs into their bottom line. Like fines, bribes could also be a matter of operating cost for pirates. "One counterfeiter was unable to pay a bribe to turn things his way in a civil law case because he had exhausted his resources on bribery to head off a previous criminal prosecution," journalist Jonathan Fenby reported in 1983.[29]

Whomever a pirate bought protection from, local authorities showed a general attitude of indifference or even tacit support for pirate industry, well into the early 1980s. Vincent Siew, the director of Taiwan's Board of Foreign Trade, compared his nation to Japan in the 1960s. "Twenty years ago," he said, "Japan was branded as a major source of imitations. Now Japan has burst through that period to produce its own designs and technology.... It becomes inevitable for developing countries in this stage to imitate in order to learn."[30] Siew condemned counterfeiting of all kinds, but he also suggested that Taiwan had a legitimate need to catch up in the process of economic development, regardless of property rights claims from abroad. Singapore's prime minister, Lee Kuan Yew, echoed this sentiment. The Japanese, he said in 1979, "learnt, they imitated; they were poor imitators at first; they caught up, they surpassed. The Koreans are doing likewise and Brazil and Mexico are making the grade. And they could make the grade better and faster if the industrial countries and their governments were not so self-centred and took a longer view in terms of one interdependent, inter-reacting world."[31]

Lee spoke broadly of imitating the West, of acquiring its technologies and learning its ways of production; in other words, he likely did not mean his remarks to refer narrowly to copyright infringement or music piracy. His comments imply, though, that industrializing countries had to reach a certain level of economic or technical sophistication before they could afford to adhere to Western copyright laws. Singapore's position in the world economy was not unique. The UK Anti-Piracy Group cited the "developing and newly-industrialized countries" of Asia, such as Indonesia, Malaysia, and Taiwan as the biggest culprits, suggesting that piracy flourished in neither the wealthiest nor the poorest countries.[32] In the rich world, more energetic enforcement of copyright law and the inclination of affluent consumers to buy the real thing kept piracy to a reasonable, if persistent, minimum. In the very poorest countries, cassette recorders and other new media had not disseminated fully enough to support a brisk pirate trade. But in rapidly industrializing countries, the technical means were easily at hand, and growing consumer markets beckoned throughout the Third World.

Industrialization had proceeded furthest in East Asian nations like Singapore and Taiwan, where entrepreneurs seized on available technologies to set up tape mills and export counterfeit copies to less-developed countries throughout

Africa and Asia. Pirates in Singapore shipped tapes to the United Arab Emirates, which were in turn sold in Saudi Arabia, and then resold in poorer countries like Egypt, Somalia, and Yemen. Taiwanese book pirates sent "trade delegations" to Nigeria. Antipiracy investigators from the International Federation of Phonograph Industries (IFPI) caught up with one of their shipments in Nigeria in 1983; raids the next year nabbed containers of pirate books in Benin, Cameroon, and Ivory Coast. The shipments subsequently entered through Liberia, which had no copyright laws. Nigeria had been the main point of entry into West Africa, where books and tapes passed through traditional commercial towns to a network of smaller settlements through the countryside.[33]

For instance, the city of Kano in northern Nigeria offered consumers a wide variety of Hollywood blockbusters, Bollywood musicals, and Islamic sermons in local markets, while entrepreneurs reproduced a new genre of Hausa "videofilms" on the same rickety tape decks used to pirate foreign works. For centuries the city had functioned as a trade center for a region that stretched from Cameroon to Ghana, and this network of exchange became part of a larger circuit that connected Taiwan and Dubai to peddlers and nomads in West Africa. A man in rural Nigeria could watch a Jean Claude Van Damme film with Chinese dialogue superimposed over Arabic subtitles. The name and fax number of a pirate in Abu Dhabi might scroll across the screen; if the farmer watching it understood English, he might be amused to see the warning "Demo tape only. Not for rental or sale. If you have rented or purchased this cassette call 1-800-NO COPYS" appear every few minutes.[34]

The phenomenal growth of this shadow market since the 1970s had paradoxical consequences. Nigerians were more connected to the world market and foreign culture than ever before, yet the anthropologist Brian Larkin observes that the country has "become progressively disembedded from the official global economy (with the single exception of its oil industry)."[35] Piracy, the drug trade, and even online scams reflect Nigerians' engagement with a broader world, albeit on illicit terms. The state, which controlled important systems such as telephone and radio in the early years of independence, encountered new media that it could scarcely control. The sociologist Manuel Castells described the growth of the black market as the result of "perverse integration," suggesting that unofficial and often criminal enterprises were a central feature of globalizing capitalism. While multinational corporations linked certain parts of the world—say, Taipei and Tokyo in the 1980s or the high-tech industries of Bangalore, India, more recently—other regions became less connected to flows of capital, labor, goods, services, and communication. Such neglected areas provided bases of operation for criminal enterprises, as drug cartels, arms dealers, and human smuggling rings formed international networks and exploited the same technologies relied upon by multinational corporations.[36]

Perverse integration, though, was not always so perverse. It comes as little surprise that the widening scope of global trade brought with it not just "legitimate" foreign investment by multinational corporations but a range of underground transactions such as bootlegging. Whether one was more perverse or detrimental than the other depends on the commerce in question. In an age of globalization, criminality progressed by degrees, from the criminal mischief of Nigerian e-mail scams to violent operations like human smuggling, from Union Carbide to Pablo Escobar and back again. Along this spectrum, piracy occupied a kind of middle point. Selling bootleg tapes was in many ways a prosaic act in the marketplace, like selling newspapers or fruit. But piracy also tied in at times with the organized criminal empires that colonized the world alongside Western corporations. In its varied forms as small and big business, underworld enterprise and agent of the spread of Western pop culture, piracy connected people to technologies, sounds, and images from beyond their borders. It showed how culture and technology traveled not just from the wealthy nations to the countries they hoped to "develop" but through a variety of channels that crisscrossed the developing world, as production and trade proceeded apace in ways that Western powers could not fully control. As Brian Larkin suggests, it was part of the "infrastructure" of globalization—a globalization made by many hands, in many places, for often contrary purposes.[37]

The Antipiracy Movement Goes International

Copyright interests did not merely resign themselves to a global pirate pandemic, nor did their political allies stand idly by. The 1970s saw international organizations take a series of tentative steps to stem the rising tide of piracy around the world. The United Nations World Intellectual Property Organization won the support of numerous countries for the Phonograms Convention, which did not create new rights but instead mandated that signatories reciprocally recognize each other's copyright laws for sound recordings and work to stop piracy.[38] Thirty-four countries signed onto the Convention by the end of the 1970s; the United States, United Kingdom, Australia, and France had joined earlier on, while India was the first large developing nation to join, in 1975. South Korea and China waited until 1987 and 1993, respectively, to sign, once they had experienced significant pressure from the United States and Europe.[39] However, such agreements were not worth the paper they were written on if the signatories did not take enforcement seriously. Peter Manuel's study of "cassette culture" showed that piracy in India flourished long after it signed the Convention, and numerous scholars and journalists have documented the copying of everything from music to "razors, soap, and cornflakes" in China, regardless of its participation in international agreements.[40]

Anyone who has paid attention to the opening minutes of a VHS tape or DVD will likely recognize the next step taken by the international community in its fight against piracy. The warnings that precede most movies (even bootlegs) warn viewers of the declaration by Interpol, the International Police Organization, of its opposition to "audiovisual piracy" at a meeting in Stockholm in 1977. The police group said it was mindful of how piracy hurt national economies, sapping businesses of revenue and fostering unemployment, and it pledged to coordinate efforts between states to stop unauthorized reproduction of movies and sound recordings. Interpol planned to keep governments apprised of international pirate activities and to convey information between the police forces of its members. It also promised to encourage countries to join international agreements such as the Phonograms Convention and to pass new legislation that would allow for adequate copyright protection.[41]

Beyond these measures, Interpol could not go; by its very nature, the organization served chiefly to coordinate activities between national law enforcement agencies. Problems such as smuggling, terrorism, and the high-seas piracy of ships occupied far more of the group's attention in the 1980s.[42] Indeed, apart from the declaration's ubiquity on VHS, Interpol's commitment to fight piracy barely figures in the group's history, and little has changed in the twenty-first century. In 2000, the IFPI pressed for a "global police response" to international piracy, which it said "thrives on weak legislation and poorly coordinated law enforcement across national borders," and *Billboard* magazine noted that the IFPI had been "actively liaising" with Interpol for over a year.[43] Twenty-three years after Interpol added music piracy to its list of concerns, global police protection for intellectual property was still a new idea.

Interpol's 1977 declaration was more a reflection of anxieties in developed countries over ills such as unemployment and sluggish economic growth than of purposeful policy. The United Kingdom, for instance, hoped to remedy the problem by updating its 1956 Copyright Act. When the Whitford Committee took up copyright reform in 1977, it focused on concerns that American legislators would have found familiar: how to regulate photocopying in libraries, schools, and businesses; how to prevent commercial piracy and home taping from harming the music industry; and how to fit computer programs into the existing copyright law. The Committee proposed that libraries and other institutions in the United Kingdom pay a blanket licensing fee to publishers that would allow their users to copy freely—much like the compensation that restaurants and radio stations pay ASCAP in order to play music in the United States.[44]

The idea of imposing a tax on copiers was appealing to many in Europe and North America. The Whitford Committee proposed a fee on all tape recorders that would compensate the music industry for sales lost to home recording. It cited surveys showing that 88 percent of respondents in Belgium said they copied recordings, while prerecorded tapes accounted for only 22 percent of cassettes owned by consumers. Presumably, the other 78 percent of sales were blank tapes that consumers used to duplicate and share copies of the original albums.[45] As early as 1965, West Germany had imposed a levy on recording equipment that provided compensation to composers, record companies, and performers whose works were presumably being copied with tape recorders.[46] When the Council of Europe met in 1980 to debate cultural policy, speakers recommended both lower sales taxes on recordings and a levy on blank cartridges that would funnel revenues to the record industry—in essence, shifting the burden of taxation onto consumers and away from the music business, which would also reap a windfall from the sale of products it did not make. Their own products would become cheaper to consumers, and they would get a cut of the blank tape business. What was not to like?[47]

The consensus was not absolute, though. A few participants at the Council of Europe's conference expressed the oldfangled notion that consumers might benefit from lower prices and more competition in the music industry. Gillian Davies, a British intellectual property lawyer who attended the proceedings, remarked ruefully on these ill-informed views. "The opinion was voiced by one or two speakers that piracy and private copying of phonograms were activities to be encouraged, on the ground that it was in the public interest that consumers should have access to recorded music as cheaply as possible," she said. "Indeed, a surprising ignorance of the principles of copyright law was demonstrated by the speakers."[48] Davies took for granted that strong copyright served the public interest, much as the Whitford Committee had chided those who failed to recognize the importance of property rights in its report to the UK government: "It is always hard for those brought up to believe in competition as the most beneficent market force to realize that the exclusive rights which are granted by national copyright, patent, trade mark and design laws are granted because it is in the public interest to grant them."[49]

The more property rights were disrespected, the Committee assumed, the worse off consumers would be. Property rights trumped free competition as the prime consideration for safeguarding the public interest. Anyone who thought that the state should not restrict the way people used creative works was just ignorant; so was the person who thought that lower prices would benefit consumers. The Whitford Committee presented strong copyright protection as good and wholesome, suggesting that stronger copyright is always better copyright—more of a good thing.

From Bootlegs to Bullets

Conferences, conventions, and committees did not stop people all over the world from pirating music. In the 1980s, the IFPI and other representatives of the record industry took a more aggressive approach to fighting copyright infringement, acting as intellectual property police where local governments refused to do so. Investigators traced the movements of bootleg tapes and seized shipments believed to contain illicit goods, while lawyers pushed for prosecutions under whatever local copyright laws existed. "Working with 10 investigators, the federation identifies shops selling pirated tapes and brings them to the attention of the police," reporter Steve Erlanger wrote of Thailand in 1990. "Unfortunately, enforcement varies with the part of town and the susceptibility of the officers to outside inducements."[50] Seeking redress in foreign courts could be costly and even dangerous. According to the International Federation of Phonogram and Videogram Producers, prosecutions in Pakistan sometimes dragged on so long that plaintiffs had to appear in court dozens of times, while exposing themselves to intimidation and even retaliation.[51] One industry representative in Thailand claimed to have received "four bullets in the mail" and refused to give his name when speaking to the New York Times in 1990.[52]

If they can be believed, the IFPI's figures for the early 1980s reflect an impressive campaign to suppress piracy. The group claimed to have confiscated a million and a half cassettes in raids throughout Southeast Asia, though adding that the amount was "a small percentage of the total."[53] Seizures in 1980 were confined to wealthier countries: 4,500 recordings were seized in Japan and 50,000

Table 7.3 **Percent Change in Size of the US Recording Industry, 1977–1982**

	Difference between 1977 and 1982 (%)
Number of employees	−25.97
Payroll amount	+19.38
Value added by manufacturing	+63.55
New capital expenditures	+22.15

Source: US Department of Commerce, 1977 Census of Manufactures, Volume II: Industry Statistics, Part 3. SIC Major Groups 35–39 (Washington, DC: US Government Printing Office, 1978), 36D–20; US Department of Commerce, 1982 Census of Manufactures: Subject Series General Summary, Part 1. Industry, Product Class, and Geographic Area Statistics (Washington, DC: Bureau of Census, 1982), 1–16, 1–17.

in West Germany. Spain, which was poorer than some of its neighbors, turned up 300,000 bootlegs. Investigators seized 25,000 records in Egypt the next year, and Chile, India, and Peru came under target in 1982. As the decade went on, various operations in the developing world made ever-greater gains in their pursuit of pirates; raids in Benin, Cameroon, Ivory Coast, Nigeria, and Singapore netted hundreds of thousands of tapes in the mid-1980s. The most developed countries posted big figures as well, even as antipiracy campaigners turned their attention toward illicit markets abroad. The Netherlands saw 250,000 recordings confiscated in 1983, and 350,000 were found in France the following year. The bigger the figures they announced, the more dramatic the problem looked to policy makers and the public.[54]

By 1985, these legal efforts began to show scattered success. Singapore won the title of "biggest pirate" in the international press, as the *Economist* claimed that the small island nation produced $150 million of bootleg tapes—half of an estimated $300 million world market. Despite this sizable output of illicit music, the first notable victory for outside copyright interests did not actually deal with recordings. Rather, a group of British publishers won a judgment against a bookseller, Ng Sui Nam, for selling copies of books originally published in the United Kingdom by the Royal Academy of Music, among others. The Singaporean court ruled that British copyright law was still in force in the city-state, even though it had gained independence from the United Kingdom in 1963. Antipiracy campaigners thus turned to a vestige of colonialism to prop up their claim to protection in Singapore, which had not yet fully recognized copyright protection for foreign works. At the time, the US government of Ronald Reagan joined European powers in urging Singapore to pass tough new legislation and join the Berne Convention or another treaty. The ruling was an early sign that Lee Kuan Yew's government might be ready to play by the West's rules. "Singapore wants eventually to become a net exporter of information," the *Economist* noted, "but in the meantime it wants to continue to import knowledge on the cheap."[55]

Government and business groups began to make some inroads in foreign pirate markets, particularly in East Asia, during the 1980s. Chemical giant Monsanto happily reported that Taiwan was exporting fewer bootleg insecticides, while the government cracked down on factories that imitated General Motors auto parts. Indonesia banned pirate tapes in 1988, giving in to pressure from the United States and the European Community, and it agreed to adopt a patent law the following year. Indonesians swamped the markets in Jakarta to snap up tapes before the cassette ban went into force in June. "Our sales have tripled," Andi Suhalan said of his music store. "Some people are buying 40, 50, or even 100 tapes at a time."[56]

One wonders what a customer planned to do with forty copies of *Thriller*. The Europeans demanded to know how the local tape producers would dispose of an estimated three million tapes remaining in stock, as well as two million that had already shipped to the Middle East. Whenever new laws were enacted, the same problem arose: how could the traces of such a widespread practice as bootlegging be scrubbed from everyday commerce, even if local authorities genuinely wished to do so? "There may still be some unauthorized reprints in the bookstores or pirated cassettes in video stores, but they are disappearing," trade negotiator Hwang Doo-Yun said of South Korea. "It still takes time to educate our people."[57]

Taiwan, at least, seemed to get the message. In 1989 the *Wall Street Journal* observed approvingly that retailers in Taipei's shopping areas stopped openly selling counterfeit Rolex watches, although knock-offs of Gucci and Polo remained available on the street. Many upwardly mobile Taiwanese chose to buy legitimate goods in department stores such as Sogo and Sunrise, but rising affluence did not push bootleg products off the market entirely. Three main steps moved Taiwan and other countries toward compliance. First were the aggressive investigations funded by foreign companies. Apple Computer, for instance, hired a former narcotics agent to spearhead an operation against imitators who gave their knockoffs cheeky names like "Orange" and "Pineapple," setting up fake businesses and hiring local people to pose as buyers of pirate goods, thus ensnaring sellers in criminal transactions and raids. Apple's elaborate stings in Taiwan in many ways resemble the FBI's ruse of setting up the Modular Sounds record shop to bust pirates up and down the East Coast in 1978.[58]

Antipiracy campaigners then had to pool their resources and organize to attain political clout in the developed world. Whether they made computers, pharmaceuticals, or sound recordings, corporations shared not just tactics but a larger interest: protecting all their products under the umbrella of "intellectual property." Though they did not create the term out of whole cloth, it was still fresh enough in 1989 for the *Wall Street Journal* to refer to "a continuing U.S. war against thievery of so-called intellectual property."[59] Indicative of this shift was the formation in 1984 of the International Intellectual Property Alliance (IIPA). The group melded together a range of interests, including the Association of American Publishers, the Business Software Alliance, the Entertainment Software Association, the Independent Film and Television Alliance, the Motion Picture Association of America (MPAA), and the RIAA.[60] A revolving door developed between the executive branch and industry. Gerald Mossinghoff, for instance, was both an assistant US trade representative and assistant secretary of commerce before heading the lobbying group Pharmaceutical Research and Manufacturers of America (PhRMA); the group was later led by former Louisiana congressman Billy Tauzin.[61]

Once constituted, these groups pressured the US government to take up the cause of intellectual property worldwide. Lobbyists rallied together to awaken uncomprehending minds in Washington to the importance of preventing handbags, records, and pills from being copied around the world. Working for Monsanto in the late 1970s, Jim Enyart found that some government officials did not believe that issues of copyright and patent belonged in international trade negotiations. "Everyone said: 'Oh gee, patents are highly technical, very esoteric things. What do they have to do with trade?'" he said. "And we pressed them and said: 'Look, intellectual property is property. It costs money and time to create; it has commercial value, and if people steal it, it's like stealing any other kind of property.'"[62]

Meanwhile, companies such as Chanel, Gucci, and Izod banded together in 1978 to form the International Anti-Counterfeiting Coalition, which aimed to get the matter of trademark protection into the Tokyo Round of negotiations over the General Agreement on Trade and Tariffs. (The GATT system was established after World War II to foster international exchange by reducing tariffs and other barriers to trade.) The Tokyo Round ended in 1979 without attending to the intellectual property issue, but the copyright, trademark, and patent forces were sure to press on when new negotiations began in 1982.[63] By 1989, the Reagan administration had "more than a dozen senior officials in the White House and the State and Commerce departments" working on intellectual property negotiations around the world, according to the *Wall Street Journal*.[64]

The United States and its allies forced copyright onto the agenda of trade negotiations in the face of stiff resistance from developing countries. Indeed, poorer nations showed much greater willingness to fight the extension of copyright as a group than, say, Singapore or South Korea did in individual negotiations with the United States or United Kingdom. Argentina, Brazil, Egypt, India, and Yugoslavia held to their opposition during talks in 1985, while President Reagan warned that the United States would press for greater copyright protection in bilateral negotiations if GATT did not provide adequate progress. In 1986 the United States and Japan proposed that GATT take on the issue of intellectual property as a whole, not just counterfeit goods in particular. This time, a "group of 10" stepped forward and argued that intellectual property was not any of GATT's business; the faction consisted of Argentina, Brazil, Cuba, Egypt, India, Nicaragua, Nigeria, Peru, Tanzania, and Yugoslavia.[65]

Intellectual property was a fundamentally new consideration for GATT, whose main purpose over the years had been to prohibit restrictive trade practices. Member countries agreed to lower tariffs and avoid discriminating between trading partners, but they could regulate their domestic economies as they wished—including matters of intellectual property enforcement.[66] Thus, the "new issues" of the Uruguay Round, such as copyright and trade secrets, were an extension of the push for active enforcement of property rights in the United States during the 1980s. The US strategy was clear: offer developing countries tariff reductions and access to its markets and services in exchange for enforcement of intellectual property rights abroad.[67]

The Uruguay Round negotiations ran into several dead ends between 1987 and 1994, but the Americans' determined lobbying ultimately produced the Agreement on Trade Related Intellectual Property Rights (TRIPS). Many leaders in developing countries remained unconvinced that curbing piracy was in the best interests of all, believing that antipiracy measures would privilege American corporations and inhibit their own development. The stubbornness of both sides in the debate stalled progress, as everyone argued over the basic premises of the negotiation. The Americans threatened to push bilateral deals across the board if talks at GATT failed. The process broke down in 1990, but GATT director-general Arthur Dunkel revived it the following year with a new proposal, the so-called Dunkel Draft, which lowered tariffs on a wide variety of goods and mandated stronger protections for intellectual property.[68]

By this time, resistance to the prospect of a new intellectual property regime had softened somewhat. Leaders in the developing world began to see that multinational corporations looked favorably on nations with better intellectual-property protections as candidates for investment, and GATT officials believed that poorer countries were willing to accede to US demands to keep the North American giant at the negotiating table. Concessions on intellectual property could be a reasonable price to pay if the United States reduced barriers to foreign agricultural products, textiles, and other goods.[69]

Ironically, business interests in the United States began to have their own doubts by 1990. Some in the American entertainment industry worried that Dunkel's proposal would prove less effective than bilateral negotiations, which had allowed the United States to pressure other nations into accepting its terms of intellectual property protection. Movie studios complained that the agreement would allow the French to use levies on blank tapes to subsidize their own national film industry, and they also viewed the European practice of setting 51 percent of television time aside for European programs as a restraint of trade.[70] Jack Valenti, the tireless MPAA campaigner, did not sleep for three days and even went a day without eating as he fought such provisions. "If these quotas exist," he said, "this is Armageddon time. I'm on the Hill in a New York minute bringing out every patriot missile, every F-16 in our armory, leading whatever legions we can find to oppose this agreement."[71]

Despite these "North-North" struggles, the so-called South still saw the Dunkel Draft as a victory for intellectual property interests in the First World. The proposal required developing countries to accept the fundamental premise that copyrights, patents, trademarks, and trade secrets deserved protection throughout the world. It required them to develop procedures for enforcing property rights that were more efficient than the legal mechanisms antipiracy campaigners had encountered in countries like Pakistan and Nigeria. The agreement also urged customs officials to hold on to pirate goods seized at borders and stated that piracy "on a commercial scale" should be treated as a criminal, rather than a purely civil, offense. Finally, the deal went beyond setting standards for copyright law, which some countries might formally adopt but fail to carry out. The agreement set up a Dispute Settlement Body that would handle cases of alleged noncompliance through the World Trade Organization (WTO), a new body established to weigh trade disputes between nations.[72]

The Dunkel Draft also contained concessions to various interests in the developed countries. The United States insisted on an exception to the mandate for "moral rights," a European concept that recognized the inherent right of an artist not to see his work altered, even when ownership of the work changed hands. The American model of copyright included no such right, allowing whoever purchased the rights to control the fate of the work in question, regardless of the wishes of the original creator. Japan also managed to include in TRIPS an exception for its popular system of renting compact discs. The United States had banned rental of sound recordings (1984) and software (1990), but in Japan, music rental shops were commonplace.[73]

Developing nations, particularly Brazil and India, attempted to limit the new agreement's effect on their economies. While acquiescing on the basic issue of intellectual property, the developing bloc pushed for differential treatment for poorer countries and the most limited standards in matters of copyright, patent, and trademark. India's prime minister Narasimha Rao faced political risks at home; while the Americans pushed tough international standards, many Indians opposed any compromise in the country's position on intellectual property. Everyone from the Communists to the conservative Bharatiya Janata Party viewed the agreement as bad for the country.[74] Though it still raised the ire of many Indians, the Dunkel compromise ceded some ground to critics. TRIPS provided a multitiered system of compliance in which most developing nations would have five years to conform their legal systems to the new standards, while the poorest countries would have a ten-year period to update copyright laws and enforcement mechanisms.[75]

Rao was not the only head of state to worry about getting the result of the Uruguay Round approved at home. President Bill Clinton also contended with enemies on the left and the right when the agreement reached Congress in 1994. Conservatives Patrick Buchanan and Senator Jesse Helms worried about ceding sovereignty to the WTO—or any other international organization, for that matter—while labor unions, environmentalists, and consumer advocates warned that the WTO could strike down economic regulations as unfair restraints on trade. Hollywood was disappointed with the pact, despite the provisions that bound developing nations to protect its intellectual property, in large part because Europeans retained the right to limit broadcasts of foreign television.[76] California's Republican governor, Pete Wilson, faxed a warning to Clinton: "We must walk away from a bad GATT agreement."[77]

The measure passed because of several factors, not the least of which was a concerted, focused effort by other business advocates to cement the gains made during the Uruguay Round. Pharmaceutical lobbyist Gerald Mossinghoff described the operation as "a full-court press," with daily lobbying of senators and representatives. Although some liberals were uneasy with the direction of US trade policy, GATT had the support of every key Democrat—the House and Senate majority leaders, the Speaker, and the president—and Clinton's energetic support helped ensure its passage. If nothing else, certain doleful Democrats could vote for the Uruguay Round Agreements Act when it passed in December 1994, fearing no further electoral consequences. The Republican Party had swept the elections in November, and many Democrats would not be returning to Congress in 1995.[78] "It wasn't a huge fight," recalled Clinton aide George Stephanopoulos. "We all had bigger problems after that election."[79]

The Persistence of Piracy under the New International Regime

Battles over piracy continued both during and after the passage of TRIPS. Several Asian governments scrambled to do more to curb piracy as the diplomatic debate remained unresolved in the early 1990s, because the United States was determined to enforce property rights one way or the other, within GATT or without. "Southeast Asian countries are worried about the Clinton stand," an official for the record company EMI (Asia) said in 1993. "A year ago piracy was a disaster. Now I think we are rounding the corner." That year Thailand fired the director of the antipiracy agency that had been set-up under US pressure in the 1980s. He had been doing too little to stifle the illicit trade. Taiwan was still raiding pirate factories, capturing 16,000 compact discs in February 1993. Bilateral negotiations with South Korea were also making progress.[80]

However, the battle lines shifted once again, as the antipiracy campaigners encountered a foe that was much harder to push around than Singapore or Thailand: China. The IFPI warned in 1994 that China's pirate factories could produce 60 million recordings a year, a number so great that the Chinese could export bootleg discs and tapes throughout the region.[81] The turnabout was ironic: Hong Kong and Taiwan had exported bootleg music to China in the 1980s, and now the People's Republic was providing Hong Kong with the illicit records it could no longer produce. By 1995 the *Economist* claimed that China consumed 25 percent of the world's bootleg discs, and many of its pirated discs ended up in Hong Kong, where authorities had worked hard to curb domestic piracy.[82]

Despite their political accomplishments, antipiracy crusaders failed to strike a decisive blow against the global illicit market. Yes, many countries had signed on to the 1971 Phonograms Convention. Interpol (ostensibly) joined the fight against audiovisual piracy in 1977. The United States passed one tough copyright law after another and persuaded other countries to do much the same, while the entertainment, fashion, pharmaceutical, and technology industries won the long battle over GATT and TRIPS. They did not, however, vanquish piracy in the developing world. The *Economist* reported in 1995 that pirate recordings were, at least, "no longer on open display" in Thailand, although a visitor to Bangkok in the early twenty-first century can find pirate CDs and DVDs widely available on the street. In Pakistan, the *Economist* estimated that 92 percent of 1994 sales were illicit.[83] Pakistanis could get the latest Madonna CD for less then a dollar; and if they did not want all twelve tracks by the Material Girl, they could go to a local shop, pick out the songs they liked best, and have a personal CD or tape mixed. These services were affordable, available, and popular, while a legitimate market for music barely existed. Little had changed by the twenty-first century, as the IIPA estimated that 90 percent of recordings sold in the country during 2003 were illegitimate. "There are no legitimate licensees producing in Pakistan," an IIPA report said, "or licensed to produce such product in Pakistan…Legitimate domestic demand in Pakistan is dwarfed by the number of discs being produced, meaning Pakistan's production is destined for export."[84]

The Philippines provides an example of a developing nation where licit and illicit markets emerged side by side. Recorded music could be found in the stalls of street markets and the Tower Records in an upscale urban shopping mall. In the early 2000s, anthropologist Jonas Baes noticed how vendors and consumers haggled over pirate CDs on the street in front of the SM City supermall, while other bootleggers sold their goods within sight of the police department. The singer Martin Nievera exhorted consumers to buy the "real" thing in a 2002 TV interview, arguing, "You actually miss out on a lot of things when you buy that garbage." This expectation—that all Filipinos could easily choose to buy the "orig" CD over the bootleg one—defied reality there as it did in Pakistan or Nigeria. As one teenager told Baes, "I would never be able to buy a beautifully packaged CD of my favorite bands from Tower Records in Makati, but I was able to buy that album I wanted from the stacks of [pirated] CDs in Quiapo."[85]

A young man in Queens, New York, echoed the same sentiment twelve years earlier. Holding up a bag of tapes, local resident Marc Anthony told a reporter, "I got five of them here. For those who can't afford the $9.99 tapes, this helps them out." He was standing outside a record store on Jamaica Avenue that had just been raided by the police, minutes after he had made his purchase. Another bystander disagreed. "The rappers are getting robbed real bad," said Eric Petty. "The police got to bust the whole avenue because we got them on every block." Petty had invested a lot of money in his car stereo system and considered it pointless to play inferior pirate tapes on it. The raid was spurred by the RIAA, which lobbied the state legislature to toughen antipiracy laws and pestered the police to enforce them. Lawmakers ratcheted up penalties for piracy in November 1990, making it a felony to sell or possess 1,000 or more pirate recordings. The NYPD said it had bigger problems to deal with, but it continued to act on tips from the RIAA, which had been investigating piracy in New York's discount stores and flea markets for more than six months.[86]

The RIAA estimated that piracy cost the music business $400 million in 1989. Did that mean that customers like Marc Anthony would have bought $400 million of legitimate recordings at the regular price if cheaper pirate tapes were unavailable? A New York street vendor sold Run-DMC's *Back from Hell* for $5 in 1990, whereas the record company charged $10 for the cassette. When Anthony visited the store in Jamaica, he walked away with five tapes, saying that he could not afford to buy them at full price. According to the RIAA's logic, Anthony would have sprung for two $9.99 tapes if he could not get five cassettes for $5 a piece. In this sense, the industry's astronomical figures might have had some basis in reality.

However, the same principle did not apply for the teenager in the Philippines; her street purchase did not necessarily substitute for a potential sale that Tower Records could have made. Piracy filled a niche for the poor around the world, whether in New York City or Quezon City, providing a product that would otherwise have been less available or completely unavailable. Piracy might have made it easier for Marc Anthony to purchase *more* music, whereas it made it possible for his counterpart in Pakistan to acquire any recordings at all. The latter impulse was always going to be harder to deter than the former.

Perhaps one might better understand the recording industry's claims of "lost sales" in the developing world as the potential loss of future sales. The majority of Nigerians or Pakistanis might not have been able to purchase an American CD at full price in the 1990s, but American firms wanted to secure the exclusive right to sell their music, movies, and software if and when those nations attained a greater degree of affluence. As the Philippines example suggests, multinational corporations also wanted to build legitimate markets that could sell high-priced goods to the middle and upper classes in developing countries, without interference from lower-priced, pirate alternatives. While failing to squelch piracy, TRIPS and other trade agreements ensured that, going forward, Western nations could appeal to institutional protection for their output of information technology and intellectual property—and, by doing so, they could attempt to preserve their commanding position in these fields relative to developing countries.

In other words, US leaders did not want to depend on imports for manufactured goods while seeing their own country's potential exports of entertainment and technology freely reproduced elsewhere, undermining both the incentive for capital investment in these industries and, in the long run, America's competitive advantage. The US foreign trade deficit doubled between 1973 and 1980 and continued to grow in the following decades, as the nation imported shoes and shirts from developing countries, as well as higher-value products such as cars and televisions from Japan and South Korea.[87] The anxiety over declining manufacturing in the United States and Europe masked the fact that Western firms drove industrialization in the developing world, building facilities abroad or contracting with sweatshops to bring cheaper goods to the affluent countries. As a companion to new technologies and economic growth in the developing world, piracy was a problem to be managed from afar; the dispersal of manufacturing throughout the world created the possibility that American music or software would be exploited by the very people whose labor was exploited by American capital. The businesses that rallied behind the banner of intellectual property successfully prodded US politicians to push for stringent restrictions on piracy in trade negotiations, hoping to maximize the benefits of globalization while minimizing its apparent cost—piracy.

Yet theirs was a puzzling kind of success. Indeed, the entire fracas over global piracy from the 1970s to the new millennium had a funhouse mirror quality to it. Interests in fashion, film, music, pharmaceuticals, and software deplored the devastating effect of piracy even as they prospered. *Saturday Night Fever* and *Thriller* may have been among the most bootlegged records in the world, but they were also among the most profitable hits in the history of the industry. The fact that people listened to them from North Korea to North Carolina attested to their world-dominating success. Record companies conjured the image of a vast, debilitating pirate nemesis, whose size might have been incalculable except for its opponents' lust for citing astronomical figures—pirate sales in the millions, industry losses in the billions, and each only a fraction of an unknowably large problem. Even the industry's claims of how many pirate records its agents had confiscated around the world bolstered the image of an industry under siege. Similarly, rich countries like the United States may have exacted concessions from their poorer trading partners, but promises to fight piracy were honored most often in the breach. If anything, the result of struggles over GATT and TRIPS resulted in freer trade and less regulation for multinational corporations, not the draconian copyright enforcement that developing countries feared. The music industry seemed to be winning imaginary victories against imaginary enemies.

   Piracy remained widespread, but it did not cripple the corporations that extended the reach of American pop culture and technology throughout the world at the end of the twentieth century. The temporary downturns of the record industry were likely the result of broader recessions in the late 1970s and early 1990s, although advocates of stronger copyright were quick to blame piracy. The familiar pattern recurred in 2001, when another recession struck and the rise of online file sharing took the blame for faltering record sales. However, the market for recorded music did not recover in the new century as it had so many times before. The newest blowup over piracy soon provoked the record industry to a round of panic and recrimination of unprecedented proportions.

Conclusion
Piracy as Social Media

> I remember buying blank cassette tapes and recording music from the radio. No one said it was illegal, I wasn't afraid of getting sued and everybody I knew did it. The only difference in downloading from the internet and recording on tape is the type of media you are using. Record companies are gluttonous vultures, stealing money, and music rights from talented, inexperienced artists. Screw their so called loss. If it were impossible to download music, people who download music now would still not buy your $25 cd's. They download it because it's there.
>
> —"Jo Jackson" (2011)

Internet commenter Jo Jackson could not quite believe it. In the history of the record industry's long love affair with hyperbole, there had never been anything like the $75 trillion dollars in damages that thirteen record labels sought in their suit against the file-sharing network Limewire in 2010.[1] That Limewire could be liable was not much of a stretch; in the previous decade the courts had held companies like Napster and Grokster responsible for "contributory infringement," or enabling and encouraging Internet users to violate copyright on a massive scale. But the sum sought by these record companies left nearly all observers in disbelief—including federal district court judge Kimba Wood in Manhattan. Quoting the defendants, Wood observed that the labels wanted "more money than the entire music recording industry has made since Edison's invention of the phonograph in 1877." Other critics asked if there was even $75 trillion in the world.[2]

The labels could be forgiven for asking for the sun, moon, and stars, since American courts had showed remarkable fealty to intellectual property interests in the new millennium. For example, in the 2005 decision *Capitol v. Naxos*, the New York Court of Appeals arrived at the curious conclusion that *no* sound recordings were currently in the public domain, no matter how old they were. Not the Beatles, not Jelly Roll Morton—not even the earliest etchings of sound on tinfoil in Thomas Edison's laboratory in the 1870s.[3]

The case arose when the label Naxos decided to remaster and sell classical recordings originally released by Gramophone (an earlier incarnation of EMI) in the 1930s. Since the compositions performed were already in the public domain, the case depended solely on the copyright status of the recordings themselves. The Sound Recording Act of 1971 only gave copyright protection to recordings released after 1972, and the Copyright Act of 1976 confirmed that common law protections for pre-1972 recordings would remain in place even as it did away with the so-called "dual system" of federal and common law copyright going forward. Previous federal law provided authors with rights only once their work was published, whereas common law copyright protected an author's private, unpublished work from exploitation by others.[4]

When EMI's Capitol division sued Naxos, claiming the sole right to sell copies of these recordings, it actually lost the first round of the legal fight. New York's Southern District Court determined that the copyright on the recordings had already lapsed in the United Kingdom, where they were first made, and that no other rights remained. The Court of Appeals, however, disagreed. New York's state constitution held that common law rights were perpetual unless otherwise limited by federal law; Congress, realizing that the 1970s copyright reforms created a situation where pre-1972 recordings might never go out of copyright, passed a measure ensuring that any remaining common law copyrights for recordings would lapse by 2067. But works could only retain common law protection as long as they were unpublished, and the Court of Appeals in *Capitol v. Naxos* ruled that manufacturing and selling copies of records did not qualify as "publication." As one legal observer concluded, *Naxos* meant "there is arguably no way to 'publish' sound recordings."[5]

Here was a reductio ad absurdum worthy of a $75 trillion payout. According to *Capitol v. Naxos*, the public domain literally does not exist for sound recordings, because a novel interpretation of the word "publication" allowed one of the oldest and most powerful record companies (EMI) to stop a younger upstart (Naxos) from re-releasing performances from the early twentieth century, many of which were out-of-print. As Barbara Ringer feared in the early 1970s, the battle over piracy resulted in the invention of nearly unlimited property rights. The *Naxos* decision was one more step in a breathtaking expansion of rights in areas where, for much of the twentieth century, most experts doubted if rights existed at all.

From Betamax to Facebook

The legal and political victories may look overwhelming, but popular skepticism about intellectual property continued to undermine the power of rights owners. Jo Jackson, for instance, viewed the trillions in damages the labels sought as the perfect symbol of their boundless avarice. Its unreal quality seemed to confirm suspicions that a business long held in dubious esteem by the public was exaggerating or even lying about the harm caused by file sharing. Jackson remembers the 1980s and 1990s as a time when listeners were free to copy and exchange music more freely, but she may be too young to recall the battles over copying in those decades. The British Phonographic Industry tried hard to persuade listeners not to copy with their "Home taping is killing music" ad campaign, which was parodied by a variety of artists in the United Kingdom and the United States.[6] ("Home taping is killing record industry profits!" leftist punk rockers the Dead Kennedys printed on a 1981 cassette. "We left this side blank so you can help.")[7] Record labels won a ban on sound recording rentals in 1984, on the grounds that rented discs could be easily copied and returned to stores, crippling sales.[8] The same year, though, the Supreme Court weighed in to the debate with a landmark decision that affirmed the right of consumers to use the Betamax video system to make personal, non-commercial copies of television programs and movies—over the howls of Universal Studios and other Hollywood interests, which viewed home recording as an insidious form of piracy.[9]

Online file sharing threatened the compromise forged by the Court in 1984, as individual users could share copies of their recordings not just with a few friends or family but with millions of strangers around the world. Jo Jackson believed the difference between tape recording and file sharing was purely technical— simply a question of "the type of media"—while the record industry argued that the scale and scope of file sharing meant that such uses were no longer personal or private in any meaningful sense. Worse still, the designers of file-sharing software stood to profit from trafficking in the labels' intellectual property—if, of course, the makers of Napster, Kazaa, or any number of other networks could figure out a way to make money before the courts shut them down.[10]

By the mid-2000s, a wave of new technologies, dubbed "social media," embraced the Napster model of peer-to-peer sharing but recast it as social networking. From Friendster to Facebook, these websites consisted largely of images, texts, and sounds copied and distributed among users, whose free and uncoordinated labor generated a value that a handful of discerning entrepreneurs learned to exploit.[11] The term "social media" may seem redundant—after all, media are inherently social, a fact immortalized in AT&T's slogan "Reach out and touch someone." Yet these new media harnessed the social relationships among people ("peers") to generate profit, enabling users to distribute copies of works to each other. This way of distributing creative works looked a lot different from the mass production or broadcasting model of twentieth century media.[12] File-sharing and social networks brought out into the open patterns of exchange that had evolved in private and underground among bootleg labels, record collectors, tape traders, DJs, and, yes, outright pirates over the past century. At stake in the debate over copying and sharing was a set of questions that had bedeviled Americans all the way back to the debates of 1906: was the state obligated to protect businesses from their competitors? Was it in the public interest for creative works to be freely copied and exchanged? Should consumers be constrained in what they do with a book, movie, or sound recording after they purchase it?

The answers to these questions changed over the twentieth century. Lawmakers in the Progressive Era denied composers and publishers the right to control how their compositions were used, saying that music lovers were (more or less) free to do what they wished with a song or recording once they purchased it. They could loan it to a friend, like a piece of clothing or farm equipment. Throughout the New Deal era of the 1930s and 1940s, courts still vacillated over how much record companies could constrain the use or reproduction of their recordings, reflecting a preference for free competition and a reluctance to expand monopolies that persisted into the 1960s, as recordings continued to lack federal copyright protection.

From the 1970s onward, though, American politicians were far more solicitous of rights owners. This political and legal shift can be seen in legislation, ranging from stiffer penalties for infringement to longer copyright terms. Lawmakers added protection of sound recordings to the law in 1972, toughened the consequences of piracy in 1974, and overhauled the entire statute in 1976, elevating copyright infringement to a felony offense. Infringement had once been a misdemeanor, punishable by a $1,000 fine and one-year prison term, yet in the 1990s pirates could expect to pay $250,000 and spend five years in prison for the first offense.[13]

Such measures reflect a conviction that more copyright is always better copyright, since tough rules protect vital industries. The 1976 act adopted a standard term of the life of the author plus fifty years, and the Sonny Bono Copyright Term Extension Act of 1998 added an extra twenty years onto all copyrights. Representative Mary Bono recalled that her late husband wanted copyright to last forever, although such a law would violate the constitutional requirement of protection for "limited times." Movie industry spokesman Jack Valenti was willing to compromise—he suggested a copyright term of one day less than forever.[14] The additional two decades may seem arbitrary, unless you happened to own the copyright on a profitable work that was about to enter the public domain in the late 1990s. Critics called the bill "the Mickey Mouse Protection Act," since it prevented copyrights for the earliest Mickey cartoons (created in 1928) from lapsing.[15]

The shift can also be seen in the rise of this very critique. Whereas only a few pirates spoke out against copyright reform in the 1970s, a diverse movement among scholars and activists emerged to counter the perceived excesses of intellectual property law in the early twenty-first century. Groups such as the

Electronic Frontier Foundation and Creative Commons have fought against over-zealous copyright claims and proposed alternatives to traditional property rights, while a raft of critics from academia, such as the musicologist Joanna Demers, legal scholar Lawrence Lessig, and cultural historian Siva Vaidhyanathan, have offered intellectual heft to the movement to curb copyright.[16]

Both the push for stronger rights and the pushback against intellectual property originated in the social world of music itself, in the emergence of a wide array of copying practices that transformed music into a terrain for new kinds of political conflict. From the mixing of sounds by DJs on a turntable or laptop, to the personal mixtape or playlist; from the reproduction of live recordings to the sharing of files and links through social media, music has been the stuff of exchange, the currency of social discourse. These practices are not unique to the late twentieth or early twenty-first centuries. Early recording artists found their works pirated in the 1890s, while Lionel Mapleson made some of the first concert bootlegs at the Met in 1901. Fan communities took up the task of copy-ing and curating the recorded legacy of jazz in the 1930s, prompting battles in the courts and Congress over who should control music in subsequent decades. These early struggles not only foretold the larger conflicts over copyright that would follow in the late twentieth century; they also remind us of an era when the prerogatives of property were not so readily accepted in American political culture.

Piracy as Aesthetics

Copying and property have always functioned in dynamic tension. The music or movie industry may like people to believe that the morality of copyright is absolute and self-evident—"You wouldn't steal a car," they say, so why would you steal a movie?—but history tells us that what is acceptable one day may be wrong the next.[17] What is "free as the air" today, as Justice Louis Brandeis put it in 1918, may be property tomorrow.[18] A vendor may sell t-shirts featur-ing 50 Cent's face at a flea market in North Carolina without expecting reprisal for using the photographer's intellectual property or the rapper's likeness. The same vendor may run afoul of the law for selling bootleg CDs of his music, even though "Fiddy" himself rose to prominence by hawking borrowed sounds on the streets of Queens and Manhattan.

A degree of copying will always be permissible, within certain limits. As Vaidhyanathan, Demers, and others have taken pains to point out, all creativity involves referencing or riffing off of the ideas of others, whether it means quoting a line or borrowing a chord progression or incorporating a sample from another work. Just as importantly, some uses will always fly under the radar, failing to attract the interest of intellectual property owners who are too busy litigating against more lucrative offenders. The record industry paid little attention to jazz bootleggers until their success revealed the commercial viability of reissues, while hip-hop labels tolerated the use of unauthorized samples on DJ mixtapes as long as the free publicity seemed to justify a policy of benign neglect.

Such skirmishes tend to muddy the lines between the sanctity of property rights and the moral turpitude of piracy. Some copiers are profiteers, but others are not. Businesses and rights owners often seek to squelch unauthorized use of their works, but sometimes they look to piracy for cues about new sources of value and even potential benefits from the circulation of sound. These ambiguities, say critics, mean that intellectual property law itself is fundamentally flawed. Demers, among others, has pressed the case for "transformative appropriation," suggesting that some uses of recorded sound should be permitted under the law as recontextualizing or otherwise changing the works they draw upon, unlike the commercial pirate who merely counterfeits a work that is already widely available. Lee Marshall has argued that bootlegging—meaning, in this case, copying live recordings—should be viewed differently than outright piracy, since bootlegs cater to fans and supplement the market for music with a product that does not already exist. They do no harm, in this view, and they arguably do good by documenting music that would otherwise never be heard again.

Both arguments have their merits, but they ignore conceptual and technical difficulties that resist easy resolution. Should judges—or even worse, lawmakers—get to decide which uses are creative and which are merely exploitative? When rapper Biz Markie sampled Gilbert O'Sullivan's 1970s hit "Alone Again, Naturally," the Southern District Court of New York held him liable for copyright infringement, while 2 Live Crew found that their use of Roy Orbison's "Pretty Woman" in a raunchy rap song qualified as a creative form of parody in a landmark 1994 Supreme Court case. Is one a "transformative appropriation," and the other theft? The difference between the two cases shows the sometimes arbitrary nature of copyright. Markie used the actual sounds of O'Sullivan's recording, whereas the music publisher Acuff-Rose targeted 2 Live Crew only for infringing Orbison's written composition. Lifting the signature melody and riff from "Pretty Woman" for the purposes of parody was more acceptable than copying sounds directly from a recording—a distinction that reflects, in part, the less privileged status of written music in copyright law.[19]

Critics of intellectual property law see both examples as "transformative," suggesting that musicians should be no more limited in quoting from other recording artists than I am from quoting another author in this text. But where does transformation begin and end, and how can the demands of rights owners and sound users be reconciled? A mixtape or pirate record may reveal the unique touch of the person who chose the track sequence, picked a title, and designed a cover, without necessarily transforming the sounds contained on the CD, LP, or tape to a great extent. The history of bootlegging contains many examples of pirates who imprinted their own sense of humor or critical perspective on records that contained live performances or merely rearranged previously released tracks in a new context. Does this creativity deserve respect, as well as legal sanction?

The satirical newspaper the *Onion* ribbed defenders of sampling in 1997, when it reported a bogus story about rapper Sean "Puffy" Combs sampling Michael Jackson's "Billie Jean" for a song called "Tha Kidd (Is Not My Song)." The joke was that Puffy did not simply use part of the Jackson hit in his new song. "When I was in the studio mixing and recording, I decided 'Tha Kidd' would work best if I kept all the music and vocals from the original version and then didn't rap over it," Combs said. "So what I did is put in a tape with 'Billie Jean' on it, and then I hit record. The thing turned out great."[20] The article, of course, poked fun at the rapper's penchant for lifting famous bits from artists like Diana Ross and the Police to make his own hits. Would he have been more of a pirate if he copied "Billie Jean" note for note? Appropriation artists like Sherrie Levine and Kenneth Goldsmith have made a name for themselves by copying works as different as the photographs of Walker Evans and an issue of the *New York Times* to create "new" works that are nearly identical to the originals, receiving praise for "recontextualizing" the works of others. Why not Puffy?[21]

Piracy as Economics

These examples merely go to show that distinctions between transformative and exploitative copying are highly subjective, defying easy categorization. The culture of piracy has been too protean, too varied, and too multifaceted for critics of copyright to easily define some uses as good (sampling in hip-hop) or bad (commercial piracy), or for supporters of property rights to defend their preferred position that all copying is always bad. Battles over piracy have polarized businesses, musicians, politicians, and listeners into camps that admit little in the way of mutual recognition, diminishing the potential for a discussion about how copying and copyright have historically constituted each other. If, as the anarchist philosopher Pierre-Joseph Proudhon said, "property is theft," it may be true that theft is also property—or rather that theft produces the need for property rights. Property only exists as a creature of the contests over resources that produce law and legislation. Piracy prompted record companies, musicians, and music publishers to push for new rights, and its persistence continues to shape how the intellectual property regime evolves, for good and ill.

Piracy also shows the demand for products that the market might not otherwise produce, while pioneering new ways in which music can be distributed and experienced by listeners. Playing records on the radio was, after all, a kind of unauthorized reproduction of sound. The medium not only offered new outlets for sound to be reproduced and heard for "free," it also provided musicians a means for finding audiences and record labels for promoting their recordings, although the industry at first feared that the medium would substitute for record sales, rather than supporting them.

Unauthorized reproduction expanded in the early twenty-first century on a scale that equaled or surpassed even the potential of radio to mass produce sound. Whether in the form of MP3s attached to e-mails, torrents on file-sharing networks, or uploads to YouTube, this ceaseless churning of sound reveals two key points: music is more abundant than ever before, and the demand for it remains huge, despite the flagging fortunes of the record industry. The thirteen labels that filed suit in 2010 for $75 trillion based their figure on collecting damages for every infringement—that is, counting every time someone downloaded or uploaded a file from Limewire as an offense, just as an earlier pirate might have paid damages for every copy of an unauthorized record pressed and sold. The figure, of course, far outstrips the number of legitimate record sales during the same period, or any period in the history of the record industry. It reflects not just the industry's penchant for exaggerating figures, but the power of new media to make a wider variety of music available at a greater order of magnitude than earlier technologies. Compared to the solitary efforts of a musician and the mass production of the record-pressing plant, this new media infrastructure is even more prolific.

Piracy, then, heralded a move from mass production to mass reproduction. Pirates always multiplied the offerings of the market, whether they used home disc engravers in the 1930s, custom-pressing services in the 1940s, or a battery of tape decks in the 1970s. Listeners captured opera and jazz performances from the radio and shared them with friends, creating new "products" that neither the radio station nor the performers intended to produce. Sound engineers could make money on the side by leaking tapes of unreleased recordings from sessions with popular performers, and these outtakes—alternative renditions of songs officially released or new compositions that the artist or company chose not to market, for whatever reason—went into circulation, held under the counter at record stores or sold out of the backs of vans next to college campuses. Concert performances became recorded documents and new commodities. These records often took on a plain, unadorned quality that resembled "burnt" CDs, the homemade discs labeled by listeners with Sharpie pens.

Bob Dylan's *Great White Wonder* was the quintessential model of the blank, homemade bootleg aesthetic, and his "output" in the 1960s tells the story. In 1968 the following Bob Dylan albums were on the market: *Bob Dylan, The Freewheeling Bob Dylan, The Times They Are A-Changin', Another Side of Bob*

Dylan, Bringing It All Back Home, Highway 61 Revisited, Blonde on Blonde, and *John Wesley Harding.* With the bootleg boom of 1969, these eight records were joined by *Great White Wonder, Flower, Stealin', The Gaslight Tapes,* and numerous other samizdat works. There were literally more records on the market than before, more than a single profit-maximizing label would release in so short a time. Record companies believed that the value of their official releases was diminished by competition from cheaper, pirated versions, and they worried that the availability of additional works (such as live bootlegs) would dilute the value of their contracts with artists.

By exploiting the productive capacities of new media, pirates and bootleggers threatened to swamp the market with more music, lowering prices and lessening the incentive for labels to sign the stars and hype the hits. The perennial business model of the music industry—scoring one hit for every nine flops—depended on heavily promoting the popular artist to the public, by means both legal (advertising) and illegal (payola). In 1971, the industry seriously worried that the practice of spending over $500,000 to record and market an album could not survive in the face of widespread unauthorized reproduction by consumers and pirate competitors.[22]

Record labels and pirates presented two very different ways of making and distributing music, and scholars have attempted to describe this difference in terms of a broader change in economic production since the 1970s. The twentieth-century recording industry was a perfect example of a Fordist mode of production that relied on economies of scale to provide a standardized product to a mass audience. Advertising was key to creating the celebrity performer with the giant following and platinum record sales. In contrast, piracy exemplifies the new forms of production that emerged in the late twentieth century, organized around small batches of goods that were often customized to fit demand. Toyota, for instance, introduced its just-in-time system that eschewed mass-producing parts ahead of time in favor of a leaner, faster system that only produced goods as they were needed.[23]

File-sharing networks function in much the same way—particular, customizable, and flexible, affording greater choice and diversity than is available on the established market for music. Research by Big Champagne, a company that monitors online file sharing, shows that most users have only a few songs by each artist on their computers, but the range of artists runs the gamut from old to new, from Led Zeppelin to Lil Wayne and TI to Tim McGraw. Some users have dozens or hundreds of songs by a particular artist, while dabbling in the catalogs of numerous musicians who would rarely be heard on the same radio station or found on the same store shelves. The US Government Accountability Office estimated in 2010 that only one in five illegal downloads actually substituted for a potential record sale, which suggests that as many as 80 percent of downloads involved music that users would not otherwise purchase. The system suits both the casual listener, with a broad but shallow interest in many artists, as well as the "completist" who seeks every single work by a particular artist.[24]

Piracy actually anticipated these innovations in production and distribution. Bootlegging in the 1930s and 1940s demonstrated some of the qualities that theorists later attributed to the post-Fordist economy, yet these practices occurred in the heyday of mass media and standardized factory production. Enterprises like the Hot Record Society and Jolly Roger offered consumers more-specialized products, produced in smaller runs than RCA-Victor, a large, vertically integrated firm considered profitable in the 1950s. In this sense, bootlegging prefigured the "Long Tail" concept that former *Wired* editor-in-chief Chris Anderson introduced in 2004. Anderson pointed out how online retailers Amazon and iTunes could afford to make books and music available that would appeal to only a very small number of consumers; whereas traditional stores maximized profit by allocating scarce inventory and shelf space to the biggest selling goods, the lower costs of stocking and distribution enjoyed by iTunes permitted its parent corporation, Apple, to reap additional income by catering to a wide array of small niche interests. Each additional audio file hosted or sold on iTunes poses little marginal cost to the company.[25]

These new business models are only new in the sense that the established music industry has begun only recently—and reluctantly—to embrace them. Businesses such as iTunes provide a greater variety of choices than a Target or Tower Records could manage to stock on their shelves by exploiting economies of scope, answering the complaints long voiced by collectors and other enthusiasts that record labels and retailers saw little to be gained by providing the obscure music that they desired. For much of the twentieth century, piracy fulfilled this demand, making up for the inadequacies of the legitimate market. Similarly, pirates made music and other goods available in the developing world to consumers who otherwise could not obtain them. In both instances, piracy filled in the cracks between official supply and real demand.

The Politics of Information

The record industry has, of course, more often attempted to squelch this demand rather than cater to it. It won political support for punitive antipiracy measures by arguing that government had to protect sectors such as music and film in the interest of promoting economic growth, at a time when manufacturing was beginning to decline in the United States. Judith Stein and other scholars have examined the political ascendance of post-industrial interests in the 1970s and 1980s, documenting how policy makers embraced tax reforms, deregulation, and other programs that benefited industries in the FIRE (finance, insurance, and real estate) sector. The rise of an important political coalition behind intellectual property rights was but one part of this ideological and rhetorical shift toward an "information society" that favored certain kinds of businesses to the diminution of manufacturing.[26]

The idea of an information revolution first appeared in the early 1960s, soon after journalists and scholars began to speculate about a post-industrial society. Promoted by Madison Avenue, the revolution was eventually embraced by academics, policy makers, and technology giants such as IBM. The future of the American economy did not lie in heavy industry and mass production, but, rather, in automation, computers, and the production of information—the copyrights, patents, and other forms of knowledge that made it all possible. While some optimists looked forward to a day when automation allowed Americans to create more with less labor, and thus enjoy greater leisure, the central premise of information politics was the greater importance of information over labor, manufacturing, or any other concerns. This assumption—widely accepted yet rarely questioned—has become an article of faith among academic theorists, as in Manuel Castells's influential formula of the information society as "a specific form of social organization in which information generation, processing, and transmission become the fundamental sources of productivity and power." In an oft-cited 1977 study, economist Marc Uri Porat estimated that 53 percent of Americans already worked in information jobs (according, of course, to his own categorization). If one accepts the premise that information is the key to the entire economy and that a majority of workers' jobs depend on it, then taking measures to protect information or intellectual property makes plain sense.[27]

Only in the 1960s, though, did lawmakers and jurists at every level begin to view the economic imperative of protecting investments made by record labels and other entertainment companies as paramount. A few politicians, such as Rep. Abner Mikva (D-IL) and Sen. Philip Hart (D-MI), questioned whether stronger copyright would actually favor consumers, but skepticism about copyright was much scarcer in the 1970s than before. The change in attitudes occurred as rock music, magnetic tape, and the counterculture set off the bootleg boom of the late 1960s. It was also the result of a subtle shift in the understanding of property rights that had evolved during the long period when sound recordings were not protected by copyright, as jurists sought an alternative rationale for protecting records that focused on the value companies had already invested in producing and popularizing records. The argument for protecting recordings depended on the investment of time, labor, and money into the product itself, not on the concept of a limited incentive that had traditionally shaped copyright. It committed the state to preserving what later generations would call "brand value."[28]

Representatives of a so-called copyright industry pitched stronger prop-erty rights as a vital tool for economic development. Movie studios and record labels, in particular, have routinely pressed Congress for stricter protection of their goods. For example, in 1982 Congress considered a bill to stiffen the penalties against piracy of music and movies. The deliberations over copyright infringement occurred against the backdrop of a wrenching recession in 1982, when jobs involving services and information technology were among the only sectors showing signs of growth.[29] Copyright interests positioned their own businesses as vital to the nation's economic well-being. Disney's Peter F. Nolan argued to Congressman Barney Frank (D-MA) that his company depended on a long-term return on its investment in animated films, which it re-released for new audiences of children every few years. Piracy threatened this business strat-egy. "You can see that a lot of jobs and a lot of investment capital are riding on your bill," he concluded.[30] Politicians increasingly linked strong enforcement of intellectual property rights to the economic health of an emergent information economy, and in the 1990s Bill Clinton made growing "information-based jobs" a key priority of his administration.[31]

The ascendance of intellectual property coincided, ironically, with the success of politicians like Clinton and Ronald Reagan, who decried "Big Government," as well as a substantial expansion of government intrusion into the lives of Americans. This twist in American political culture reflects the strange heritage of the 1960s—a continued tension between the emerging New Right, with its focus on the economic prerogatives of business, and the anarchistic, hedonistic idea of liberation that germinated in the era's counterculture, of which piracy was one exuberant part. The rhetoric of the "free-market" imagined freedom as low taxes and deregulation, while a distinct subculture flourished in Silicon Valley that emphasized liberation through technology, championed by boomer activists such as Richard Stallman and John Perry Barlow, the former Grateful Dead lyricist who helped popularize the slogan "Information wants to be free." Although the conservative freedom agenda has experienced greater legislative success, the free-information movement has found expression through influ-ential outlets like *Wired* magazine and political vehicles such as the Electronic Frontier Foundation (EFF).[32]

In fact, the conservative economic program—known to scholars as "neoliberalism"—has been misunderstood by many of its critics as being fun-damentally antistatist. Intellectual property law was only one dimension of an American state that increasingly intervened in citizen's lives during the 1980s and 1990s. In theory, neoliberalism represents the small-government platform of Reagan, Thatcher, and Bush, politicians who espoused the greater virtue and effi-ciency of the private sector over the state. In practice, neoliberalism has become a catch-all category for all things opposed by the Left, even as "neoliberal" leaders pursue a jumble of policies seemingly unrelated by a central theme; consider, for example, the administration of President George W. Bush, which endorsed "small-government" policies like tax cuts and privatization while expanding military spending, government surveillance, and federal intervention in education. Neoliberalism often represents "a further blurring of the line between the state and the economy rather than a rolling back of the public sector," journalist Daniel Ben-Ami observed in 2011. "Indeed, in some respects it involves an extension of state involvement in businesses."[33]

Ben-Ami is right not to take rhetoric of small government and free markets at face value. Far from ushering in the death of the state, the neoliberalism of the late twentieth and early twenty-first century pruned the functions of government in some ways, such as social welfare, but bolstered them in others— providing subsidies for favored taxpayers and businesses, protecting sectors such as finance and entertainment, and controlling the bodies of workers and consumers in newly invasive ways. Its policy prescription amounted to "state protection and public subsidy for the rich, market discipline for poor," as Noam Chomsky observed in 1995. Lawmakers passed more stringent penalties for copyright infringement at the same time that laws regulating drugs and immigration became vastly more punitive. People who trafficked in certain goods and services could expect to face years in prison, thanks to mandatory minimum sentencing and other measures designed to "get tough" on crime. Congress considered one of the earliest mandatory minimum bills the same year it passed the seminal Copyright Act of 1976.[34]

Drug dealers and pirates, of course, were likely not the people politicians had in mind when they lauded small business. Indeed, poor communities and people of color have borne the brunt of the push for more aggressive law enforcement, yet few scholars have looked at the intensification of intellectual property law as part of the same repressive zeitgeist.[35] One need look no further than the case of Ousame Zongo, an immigrant from Burkina Faso who in 2003 was shot dead in New York after being wrongly suspected of hiding pirate CDs in a Chelsea storage locker, for confirmation of how real the regime of copyright enforcement has become.[36]

Zongo's murder was remarkable, even atypical of the war on piracy—more the result of racism and a culture of police violence than of overzealous copyright enforcement, perhaps. Yet it speaks to the tragic futility of a debate that has raged from the days of piano rolls and wax cylinders to global struggles over trade, the Internet, and intellectual property rights. Political action put the state squarely behind the protection of copyright by the 1970s, and law enforcement has labored to curb piracy without ever fully stopping it. Unauthorized reproduction continues—not just online or in Pakistan or Nigeria, but on the counter of an Atlanta gas station that sells clearly bootlegged copies of Nicki Minaj CDs for $3.99 a piece, in full view of the police officers who frequent the store. When a friend tells me about some new music she has, she says I can "steal" it from her, meaning I can connect a USB drive to her laptop and transfer the files to my own computer. "Stealing" has taken on a humorous and altogether ordinary connotation in the context of music. Piracy is, of course, less amusing when a man senselessly loses his life in the quest to protect the record industry's property rights and revenue.

Like the War on Drugs, the war on piracy has fallen far short of its goals. The gap between laws and norms is especially disquieting, as Lawrence Lessig has argued.[37] Despite strong legal sanctions against drug use, studies suggest that Americans are more likely to smoke marijuana than citizens of the Netherlands, with its notoriously permissive drug laws.[38] The behavior lacks the social stigma that policy makers might have wished for when they passed laws forbidding the production and sale of cannabis. Similarly, strict intellectual property laws did not deter millions of Americans from copying music, file sharing, or buying bootleg CDs. Cynicism about the music industry lingered with the public, as some users of online file sharing continue to express little guilt about piracy, seeing it as a way of "getting back" at record companies.[39] Piracy is a problem that may not be solved by law or moral exhortation.

A compromise remains possible between the desires of listeners and the interests of rights owners, particularly artists. Since 2001 the organization Creative Commons has promoted the use of alternative licenses, which allow artists and companies to opt out of copyright law by permitting others to use their work in any number of carefully defined commercial and noncommercial ways. Another opt-out system prevails on sites such as YouTube, which contain numerous creative works that have not been cleared for use by copyright owners. Rights owners can ask the site's managers to remove their material if they wish. A good deal of live concert footage, TV clips, music videos, and other work remains online in any case, since some artists may not oppose their performances being available and some companies may not notice or care that the material is posted.

Fittingly, the innovations of social media arise, at least in part, from the world of music. Piracy prefigured the emergence of online social networking, as evidenced by the web of relationships through which Grateful Dead fans have recorded, copied, and exchanged tapes since the 1970s. These practices are rooted in an ancient, yet oft-forgotten, dimension of musical experience that is primarily social. People see musicians as part of an audience, sing as part of a choir, listen to records or the radio together, and share music to forge relationships and signify their own tastes and identities.[40] In some ways, the rise of recording diminished these social, interactive aspects of music, in much the same way that recording made individual musicianship less essential for people to be able to experience music. Music becomes private; one can sit and listen to a record in a room alone, with no presence other than the sound of the absent musicians. Music historian William Howland Kenney argued that this private aspect of recorded music should not be overemphasized, though, as people continued to encounter music as part of a group experience through radio, jukeboxes, and other media.[41]

Yet the music industry has long wished to control how consumers used its products, preferring an ideal relationship in which the purchaser is the only one licensed to enjoy the written or recorded music he purchased. As a congressman summed up the industry's viewpoint in 1906, "The property itself does not carry the right to use it."[42] Music publishers lobbied to deny churches the right to share sheet music with each other in the early twentieth century; labels sought to bar the playing of records on the radio in the 1930s; and the industry later warned consumers that copying and sharing tapes was illegal, even when it was not. If nothing else, piracy has catered to a desire to connect with others through music—a desire that swelled and broke out into the open in the age of Napster and YouTube.

Such networks showed that people could produce, distribute, and consume creative works without the traditional intermediaries of talent scouts, record executives, or broadcasters. Without the help of a label and its promotional budget, obscure artists could cultivate followings by presenting their music online as individual tracks or videos, which circulated through music blogs, social networks, and video hosting sites. These developments undercut much of the rationale for record companies' ownership of recordings, which was based on the notion that money spent on production and promotion created a value that the companies alone deserved to exploit. Songwriters, musicians, radio stations, and other interests had long contested the right of labels to own recordings and act as arbiters of access to music, and they only acquiesced to this right in the face of rising piracy in the 1960s and 1970s. As new forms of music distribution supplant the role of labels, unauthorized reproduction may yet prove to be the undoing of those rights.

Not all artists view sharing as bad. They may want their music to be heard, like the music publishers of the early twentieth century who paid pluggers and vaudeville artists to familiarize audiences with their songs by playing them.[43] Hip-hop DJs sometimes saw bootleggers as the unofficial manufacturers of their work, ensuring that mixtapes ended up on the streets and in the hands of retailers, radio stations, and other important audiences. When the Supreme Court considered the case against the file-sharing network Grokster in 2005, numerous artists on small labels expressed concern that they would lose an outlet for their music. "I look at it as a library," Jeff Tweedy of the band Wilco said, "I look at it as our version of the radio."[44] Wilco freely offered recordings on its website for months before releasing a new album, and, like the Grateful Dead, the band favored taping of concerts by fans. A 2007 study of file sharing tentatively suggested that such networks helped independent musicians overcome their lack of promotion and distribution by making their music more easily accessible. The result was more recordings from independent labels making it onto the charts.[45] "If anecdotal evidence is correct in suggesting that minor labels have utilized file-sharing networks to popularize their albums," the study's authors surmised, "then the majors have an added incentive to fight file sharing."[46] For a small artist or firm, "piracy" could be just another word for "distribution" or "promotion."

Early in the twenty-first century, the record industry sought to quash competitors such as Limewire, MP3.com, and the maker of the first MP3 player, Diamond Multimedia, each of which offered different vehicles for bringing music to listeners. Some of these firms worked out deals with independent artists and labels, offering free MP3 downloads to curious listeners and valuable exposure to little-known performers. In 1999, MP3.com even began working with the group Emerging Artists and Talent on a deal that would give musicians a 50 percent royalty on any CDs sold through the site, a much higher rate than most artists received from the major labels. However, litigation soon ended these experiments as MP3.com and the file-sharing networks that followed it were steadily dismantled.[47]

A subsequent wave of new enterprises emerged to resolve the conflict between rights owners and file-sharing networks. Online streaming services such as Pandora and Spotify create the same sensation of free music— choosing anything you want, the surprise of getting something for nothing—that Napster once provided, except with the consent of record labels. In Spotify's case, it took two years for the service to clear legal hurdles in the United States after becoming available in Europe.[48] Such services offer a diverse supply of music to listeners as an ad-supported free service or without ads for a monthly fee. If the music industry is the thesis and piracy is the antithesis, social media and online streaming sites offer a kind of synthesis—driven by user choices, and based on a model that does not necessarily involve the sale of a good but instead the provision of a service that makes music readily and widely accessible. The idea of the information economy, as advanced by businesses and politicians, maintained that sound must be protected from theft just as a book on a bookstore shelf is, whether by antipiracy mechanisms or the threat of prosecution. In the emerging media environment of the early twenty-first century, however, selling a disc or even an MP3 may not be the dominant way that people receive and experience music or that artists make money. A new model may look more like radio, offering free access to sound, than the traditional recording industry that manufactured and sold sound as a scarce good.[49]

Such a reorganization of the industry has profound implications not only for how music is produced and distributed, but what kinds of music survive and prosper. For much of the last century, conventional wisdom held that nine out of ten records failed to make a profit. This arrangement meant debt and oblivion for many artists and, for labels, pandering to the lowest common denominator in the hope of scoring a hit. Some independent artists could make a living by setting up their own miniature version of a major label, as folk singer Ani Difranco did with her Righteous Babe Records in the 1990s, yet they still faced the same barriers of access to reaching radio listeners and consumers. A service-oriented music business at least holds the potential for a broader, more diverse array of musicians to find an audience, without relying as much on record labels and hype to survive.[50]

Yet nothing is assured. The likes of Spotify may fail in the marketplace or the courts, and new middlemen may emerge to take advantage of artists in new, innovative ways. Jazz polymath Herbie Hancock expressed this worry amid the Napster controversy in 2001, when the outcome of the RIAA's lawsuits remained unknown. "*Excuse me*," he declared, "*but* just because record executives give artists a bad deal doesn't mean everyone else can then go and do worse [emphasis in original]."[51] Music blogs that review and distribute free MP3s may exploit the free labor of emerging artists for profit, and companies such as Pandora may take the place of record labels and radio stations as the gatekeepers of popular culture.[52]

Whatever shape the industry itself takes, the history of recorded sound suggests that unauthorized copying and sharing will persist in its own unpredictable and shifting ways. In 1995 the Clinton administration hoped to stop copying entirely, worrying that "just one unauthorized uploading of a work onto a bulletin board … could have devastating effects on the market for the work," yet the idea of preventing any item from ever being shared is unrealistic in the context of a culture and an economy that thrive on the unencumbered communication of ideas and expression.[53]

Legal scholar James Boyle has described the expansion of intellectual property rights in the twentieth century as a "second enclosure movement," comparing new laws to the privatization of the countryside in early modern England that denied peasants their traditional right to share and use the land as a commons.[54] Indeed, when corporations asserted new kinds of property rights, they resembled the politicians, foresters, and landowners who fenced in the backwoods of the American South in the late nineteenth and early twentieth centuries—land that rural people previously used as an open territory for grazing hogs and cutting timber to support their modest, isolated homesteads. Felling a tree did not constitute stealing when the land under it belonged to no one in particular, and the land became property only when others saw a potential value there and put a fence around it. In his work on the Southern countryside, historian Jack Temple Kirby showed how law ultimately extinguished a whole social world of shared resources, mutual aid, and self-sufficiency.[55] The way of life of many rural Southerners was gone, supplanted for the prerogatives of those who desired orderly, efficient production for the market.

Like any analogy, a comparison between the fencing in of the countryside and the growth of intellectual property is neither perfect nor exact. A creative work "belongs" to an artist more plainly than a patch of land belongs to any interested party—the artist made the song but the property owner did not make the land. But the battle over piracy does resemble historic examples of enclosure in the sense that it placed a logic of economic utility and property rights against an array of spontaneous and organic relations of production, exchange, and consumption. In the case of recorded sound, anti-piracy efforts attempted to curtail the web of social relations through which so much of the meaning and value of music emerges—the desire for it, the sharing of it, and the surprises piped through illicit and unofficial channels of sound. Fighting piracy, home taping, and file sharing means fighting demand, rather than satisfying it.

Such an outcome is not just an instance of market failure. It is also a failure of political imagination. Uncritical support for intellectual property rights places private interests high above those of the public. When an individual's or corporation's right to maximize profit becomes the only goal of public policy, any stake the broader community may hold in the vast store of human creativity, whether music, art, writing, or technology, disappears from view. Hence the odd argument that copyright should last forever, or almost forever—a rightful inheritance that should endure like a family heirloom or estate. In such a scenario, we would have to seek out the descendants of Shakespeare for permission to perform *All's Well that Ends Well*.[56] The value that culture holds for other artists, seeking inspiration and borrowing ideas, for students seeking affordable access to music and literature, or for any citizens to draw on the legacy of the past appears irrelevant. Copyright interests in the late twentieth century supposed that people should not learn, feel, or experience any expression without money changing hands. Pirates suggested otherwise.

Piracy was present throughout the history of the record industry, a fact of life that was ignored, accepted, or resisted, depending on the circumstances. In its various permutations, from the jazz era to the heyday of rock and the rise of hip-hop, unauthorized reproduction pointed the way to different ways of making and enjoying sound, a nascent set of productive relations that grew in tension with mass culture and copyright law. Lawmakers and judges recast copyright as a bulwark against a rising tide of piracy since the 1950s, yet stronger property rights failed to thwart the industry's pirate nemesis—and the traditional sectors of the music business stumbled into an unprecedented decline in the early years of the twenty-first century. Music remains as abundant as ever, as file sharing and new businesses provide access to a broader range of music than was available to most people for most of the industry's history. Piracy might not kill music, but history may record that it killed the twentieth-century record industry.

NOTES

Introduction

1. J. Cole, *Friday Night Lights*, November 12, 2010, http://www.jcolemusic.com/us/music/friday-night-lights-mixtape, accessed May 12, 2011.
2. Lorenza Munoz, "Anti-Piracy Swords Drawn in Theaters," *Los Angeles Times*, March 3, 2003, http://articles.latimes.com/2003/mar/03/entertainment/et-munoz3, accessed February 3, 2011; Jason Silverman, "Anti-Piracy Campaign Gets a Laugh," *Wired*, February 9, 2004, http://www.wired.com/entertainment/music/news/2004/02/62197, accessed February 3, 2011. House Committee on the Judiciary, *Prohibiting Piracy of Sound Recordings: Hearings on S 646 and H.R. 6927*, 92 Cong., 1 sess., 1971, 53.
3. Adrian Johns, *The Nature of the Book: Print and Knowledge in the Making* (Chicago: University of Chicago Press, 1998), 622; Siva Vaidhyanathan, *Copyrights and Copywrongs: The Rise of Intellectual Property and How It Threatens Creativity* (New York: New York University Press, 2001), 37.
4. Edward Samuels, *The Illustrated Story of Copyright* (New York: Thomas Dunne Books, 2000), 31.
5. Aubert J. Clark, "The Movement for International Copyright in Nineteenth Century America" (PhD diss., Catholic University of America, 1960); Lisa Gitelman, "Reading Music, Reading Records, Reading Race: Musical Copyright and the U.S. Copyright Act of 1909," *Musical Quarterly* 81 (1997): 272; Mildred Hall, "Copyright Revision Passage Unlikely in Current Session," *Billboard*, May 13, 1967, 12.
6. Gitelman, "Reading Race," 265–79. On the problem of dividing up rights among composers and various performers, see House Committee on the Judiciary, *Copyright Law Revision Part 2: Discussion and Comments on Report of the Register of Copyrights on the General Revision of the U.S. Copyright Law*, 88th Cong., 1st sess., 1963, Committee Print, 11–12.
7. For a look at the post-industrial paradigm, see Michael Hardt and Antonio Negri, *Empire* (Cambridge, MA: Harvard University Press, 2000), 280–9; and Yochai Benkler, *The Wealth of Networks: How Social Production Transforms Markets and Freedom* (New Haven, CT: Yale University Press, 2006), 2–7.
8. Benkler, *Wealth of Networks*, 31–2; Ernest Mandel, *An Introduction to Marxist Economic Theory* (Chippendale, Australia: Resistance Books, 2002), 41.
9. William Howland Kenney, *Recorded Music in American Life: The Phonograph and Popular Memory, 1890–1945* (New York: Oxford University Press, 1999), 3; Benkler, *Wealth of Networks*, 369. For one example of music as a medium of mutual exchange, see the study of tape trading among "metalheads" in the Middle East in Pierre Hecker, "Heavy Metal in the Middle East: New Urban Spaces in a Translocal Underground," in *Being Young and Muslim: New Cultural Politics in the Global South and North*, ed. Asef Bayat and Linda Herrera (New York: Oxford University Press, 2010), 338.

10. For academic and popular typologies of piracy, see Mark Jamieson, "The Place of Counterfeits in Regimes of Value: An Anthropological Approach," *Journal of the Royal Anthropological Institute* 5 (1999): 1–2; and Pamela G. Hollie, "Piracy Costly Plague in Record Industry," *New York Times*, March 10, 1980, D5.
11. Lee Marshall, *Bootlegging: Romanticism and Copyright in the Music Industry* (Thousand Oaks, CA: Sage, 2005), 81.
12. Grace Lichtenstein, "Tape 'Bootleggers' Still Active," *New York Times*, June 5, 1971, 3; Peter Goodman, "Your New Tape May Be Phony," *Newsday*, December 8, 1978.
13. "Bittorrent Goes to Hollywood," *Infoworld*, January 1, 2007, 11.
14. John D. Zelezny, *Communications Law: Liberties, Restraints, and the Modern Media* (Boston: Wadsworth, 2011), 357–9; Rob Arcamona, "What the Viacom v. YouTube Verdict Means for Copyright Law," *Mediashift*, July 2, 2010, http://www.pbs.org/mediashift/2010/07/what-the-viacom-vs-youtube-verdict-means-for-copyright-law183.html, accessed February 6, 2011.
15. David Lowery, "Meet the New Boss, Worse Than the Old Boss? Part 1," *The Trichordist*, April 8, 2012, http://thetrichordist.wordpress.com/2012/04/08/meet-the-new-boss-worse-than-the-old-boss-part-1/, accessed June 20, 2012.
16. AmericanCountryMan, "'taliban song'—toby keith," http://www.youtube.com/watch?v=7hPjatgRjL4, accessed December 29, 2010.
17. RABOD, "Ben Folds Five—Mitchell Lane," http://www.youtube.com/watch?v=fVhZPbyn3is, accessed December 31, 2010.

Chapter 1

1. "Stenographic Report of the Proceedings of the Librarian's Conference on Copyright 1st Session, in New York City, May 31-June 2, 1905," in E. Fulton Brylawski and Abe Goldman, eds., *Legislative History of the 1909 Copyright Act, Volume 1* (South Hackensack, NJ: Fred B. Rothman & Co., 1976), 12.
2. Griffin Hall, *The Bogus Talking Machine; or The Puzzled Dutchman*, arr. by Charles White (Chicago: Dramatic Publishing Company, 1876), 3.
3. Hall, *Bogus Talking Machine*, 5–6.
4. Reebee Garofalo, "From Music Publishing to MP3: Music and Industry in the Twentieth Century," *American Music* 17 (1999): 325; Geoffrey Jones, "The Gramophone Company: An Anglo-American Multinational, 1898–1931," *Business History Review* 59 (spring 1985): 79.
5. Allan Sutton and Kurt Nauck, *American Record Labels and Companies: An Encyclopedia (1891–1943)* (Denver, CO: Mainspring Press, 2000), 228–9.
6. David Morton, *Off the Record: The Technology and Culture of Sound Recording in America* (New Brunswick, NJ: Rutgers University Press, 2000), 1. Ironically, AT&T later suppressed the development of magnetic recording by Bell Labs in the 1930s because of fears that the ability to record telephone conversations easily would raise public suspicion about the company and damage its image. See Mark Clark, "Suppressing Innovation: Bell Laboratories and Magnetic Recording," *Technology and Culture* 34 (July 1993): 516–38.
7. H. S. Maraniss, "A Dog Has Nine Lives: The Story of the Phonograph," *Annals of the American Academy of Political and Social Science* 193 (September 1937), 8–13; William Howland Kenney, *Recorded Music in American Life: The Phonograph and Popular Memory, 1890–1945* (New York: Oxford University Press, 1999), 54–5; Charles Bernstein, "Making Audio Visible: The Lessons of Visual Language and the Visualization of Sound" *Text* 16 (2006): 279.
8. Lynn Bilton, "The Talk of Ohio," April 1991, http://www.intertique.com/The%20talk%20of%20Ohio.htm, accessed March 3, 2007, 1; Allan Sutton, "The Leeds & Catlin Story," http://www.mainspringpress.com/leeds.html, accessed February 26, 2007, 1.
9. Allan Sutton, "Early American Record Piracy," *Mainspring Press*, http://www.mainspringpress.com/pirates.html, accessed February 11, 2009. For example, Arthur Collins and Byron G. Harlan, *Alexander's Ragtime Band* (Universal Talking Machine Copy, c. 1911).
10. "High Standard Records (ad)," *Phonoscope*, October 1897, 2 (all caps in original).
11. "The Original 'Michael Casey' (ad)," *Phonoscope*, November 1896, 3.

12. "A Little Spice Now and Then Is Relished by the Wisest Men (ad)," *Phonoscope*, October 1897, 2.
13. "General News," *Phonoscope*, April 1897, 9.
14. "The Globe Phonograph Record Co. (ad)," *Phonoscope*, December 1896, 17.
15. Joanna Demers, *Steal This Music: How Intellectual Property Law Affects Musical Creativity* (Athens: University of Georgia Press, 2006), 19; Edward Samuels, *The Illustrated Story of Copyright* (New York: Thomas Dunne Books, 2000), 168–9.
16. "Letters," *Phonoscope*, May 1897, 14.
17. "Original 'Michael Casey' (ad)," *Phonoscope*, 3.
18. "Notice," *Phonoscope*, 17.
19. Walter Leslie Welch, Leah Brodbeck Stenzel Burt, and Oliver Read, *From Tinfoil to Stereo: The Acoustic Years of the Recording Industry, 1877–1929* (Gainesville: University Press of Florida, 1994), 74.
20. Fred Gaisberg, *The Music Goes Round* (New York: Macmillan, 1942), 19.
21. "Original 'Michael Casey' (ad)," 3.
22. R. R. Bowker, *Copyright, Its History and Its Law: Being a Summary of the Principles and Practices of Copyright with Special Reference to the American Code of 1909 and the British Act of 1911* (Boston: Houghton Mifflin, 1912), viii.
23. Bowker, *Copyright, Its History and Its Law*, x. On the quest to universalize copyright law, see Aubert J. Clark, "The Movement for International Copyright in Nineteenth Century America" (PhD diss., Catholic University of America, 1960).
24. Samuels, *Illustrated Story of Copyright*, 34–5.
25. *White-Smith Music Pub. Co. v. Apollo Co.*, 209 U.S. at 2 (1908).
26. Victor Herbert, "Canned Music," *New York Times*, December 19, 1907, 8.
27. "Music Test Case Argued," *Washington Post*, January 17, 1908, 2.
28. David L. Morton, Jr., *Sound Recording: The Life Story of a Technology* (Baltimore, MD: Johns Hopkins University, 2006), 18.
29. Ibid., 25, 35.
30. Ibid., 31.
31. "Music Test Case Argued," 2.
32. *White-Smith*, 209 U.S. at 17; Lisa Gitelman, "Reading Music, Reading Records, Reading Race: Musical Copyright and the U.S. Copyright Act of 1909," *Musical Quarterly* 81 (1997): 265. In 1978 author John Hersey dissented in the decision of the Commission on New Technological Uses of Copyrighted Works, appointed by Congress, that computer code should be covered by copyright. Hershey argued that a series of ones and zeroes in a computer program could not convey any meaning to a human reader, as traditional artworks do. See John C. Lautsch, *American Standard Handbook of Software Law* (Reston, VA: Reston Publishing Company, 1985), 109–10.
33. "Music Test Case Argued," 2.
34. *White-Smith*, 209 U.S. at 19; Nicholas Henry, *Copyright—Information Technology—Public Policy* (New York: Marcel Dekker, 1975), 53.
35. John H. Wigmore described Day's assertion that the "musical tones are not a copy that appeals to the eye" as "philistine and unimaginative," in Wigmore, "Justice Holmes and the Law of Torts," *Harvard Law Review* 29 (1916): 610. At the time, though, the *Harvard Law Review* said "the decision reached by the court is logical, and is supported both in England and in this country," in "Recent Cases," *Harvard Law Review* 19 (1905): 134; see also "Perforated Music Rolls Not Sheet Music within Meaning of Copyright Law," *Yale Law Journal* 15 (1906): 141.
36. *White-Smith*, 209 U.S. at 2.
37. "Stenographic Report," vii.
38. Ibid., 7.
39. Ibid., 46.
40. Ibid.
41. Adrian Johns, "Pop Music Pirate Hunters," *Daedalus* 131 (spring 2002): 68.
42. "Stenographic Report," 12.
43. Johns, "Pop Music Pirate Hunters," 68.

44. "Stenographic Report," 12.
45. "Hearings before the (Joint) Committees on Patents, June 6–9, 1906," in E. Fulton Brylawski and Abe Goldman, eds., *Legislative History of the 1909 Copyright Act, Volume 4* (South Hackensack, NJ: Fred B. Rothman, 1976), 26.
46. Ibid., 28–9.
47. Ibid., 28.
48. Ibid., 27.
49. Ibid., 28.
50. Andre Millard, *America on Record: A History of Recorded Sound* (New York: Cambridge University Press, 2005), 37.
51. "Hearings Before the (Joint) Committees on Patents, June 6–9, 1906," 27.
52. Ibid., 27.
53. Ibid., 25.
54. Kenney, *Recorded Music in American Life*, 52–3.
55. "Hearings before the (Joint) Committees on Patents, June 6–9, 1906," 31.
56. U.S. Const. art. I, § 8, cl. 8.
57. Henry, *Copyright—Information Technology*, 51.
58. Neil Weinstock Netanel, "Copyright and a Democratic Civil Society," *Yale Law Journal* 106 (1996): 294.
59. "Arguments before the Committee on Patents, May 2, 1906," in Brylawski and Goldman, *Legislative History of the 1909 Copyright Act, Volume 4*, 20.
60. "Stenographic Report," 42.
61. Ibid., 43.
62. Roger W. Erickson, "Copyrights—Mechanical Reproduction of Musical Compositions—Liability of Non-Manufacturing Seller of Unauthorized Recordings," *George Washington Law Review* 26 (1958): 746; a comprehensive guide to the licensing system can be found in Harry Henn, *The Compulsory License Provisions of the United States Copyright Law* (Washington, DC: US Copyright Office, 1957).
63. "Arguments before the Committee on Patents, May 2, 1906," 15.
64. Ibid., 8.
65. Samuels, *Illustrated Story of Copyright*, 37.
66. "Hearings before the Joint Committee on Patents, December 7–11, 1906," in Brylawski and Goldman, *Legislative History of the 1909 Copyright Act, Volume 4*, 307.
67. William Lichtenwanger, "94–553 and All That: Ruminations on Copyright Today, Yesterday, and Tomorrow," *Notes* 2nd ser. 35 (1979): 813.
68. Russell Sanjek, *American Popular Music and Its Business: The First Four Hundred Years Volume III: From 1900 to 1984* (New York: Oxford University Press, 1988), 16–9.
69. Herbert, "Canned Music," 8.
70. When Senator Reed Smoot (R-UT) proposed consideration of the bill, only Senator Charles Allen Culbertson (D-TX) objected, demanding more information on the minor differences between the House and Senate versions of the bill. Despite this snag, Smoot again brought the bill to the floor later in the day, and it passed without amendment or objection. Congress, Senate, *Congressional Record*, 60th Cong., 2d sess. (1909), 3744–7.
71. Ibid., 3744.
72. "Arguments before the Committee on Patents, May 2, 1906," 22.
73. "Stenographic Report," 28.
74. Ibid., 3.
75. Bilton, "The Talk of Ohio," 1.
76. Sutton and Nauck, *American Record Labels*, 56.
77. Roland Gelatt, *The Fabulous Phonograph: 1877–1977* (New York: Macmillan, 1977), 60.
78. *Fonotipia Limited et al. v. Bradley*, 171 F. 951 (U.S. App. 1909) at 953.
79. Ibid., at 955–6.
80. Sutton and Nauck, *American Record Labels*, 56.
81. *Fonotipia*, 171 F. at 957.
82. Ibid.
83. Ibid., at 956–7.

84. Ibid., at 954.
85. "Is Deception a Necessary Ingredient of Unfair Competition?" *Harvard Law Review* 30 (1916–1917): 168.
86. *Fonotipia,* 171 F. at 957.
87. *International News Service (INS) v. Associated Press (AP),* 248 U.S. 215 (1918).
88. Ibid., at 239.
89. *Metropolitan Opera Association v. Wagner Nichols Recorder Corp.,* 199 Misc. 786, 101 N.Y.S. 2d 483 (Sup. Ct. 1950).
90. *INS,* 248 U.S. at 240. Justice John H. Clarke did not participate in the case.
91. David Suisman, *Selling Sounds: The Commercial Revolution in American Music* (Cambridge, MA: Harvard University Press, 2009), 114–21.
92. *Feist Publications, Inc., v. Rural Telephone Service Co.,* 499 U.S. 340 (1991); *Sears, Roebuck & Co. v. Stiffel Co.,* 376 U.S. 225 (1964); *Compco Corp. v. Day-Brite Lighting, Inc.,* 376 U.S. 234 (1964); Arthur R. Miller, "Copyright Protection for Computer Programs, Databases, and Computer-Generated Works: Is Anything New Since CONTU?" *Harvard Law Review* 106 (March 1993): 978–9.
93. *INS,* 248 U.S. at 262–3.

Chapter 2

1. "Music Copyright Legislation Develops New Battle Fronts at Third of House Hearings," *Billboard,* June 14, 1947, 4; "Copyright Act Overhaul Move Seen in Offing," *Billboard,* January 31, 1948, 34; Mildred Hall, "AFM Charges Revision Gives Short Shrift to the Musicians," *Billboard,* July 10, 1965, 8; Russell Sanjek, *American Popular Music and Its Business: The First Four Hundred Years Volume III: From 1900 to 1984* (New York: Oxford University Press, 1988), 130.
2. David Diehl, "'Call It Bootlegging but It's Legal': Eli Oberstein and the Coarse Art of Indie Record Production," *ARSC Journal* 31 (fall 2000): 282.
3. Allan Sutton and Kurt Nauck, *American Record Labels and Companies: An Encyclopedia (1891–1943)* (Denver, CO: Mainspring Press, 2000), 214.
4. "Petrillo Perplexed," *Time,* June 28, 1943, 76.
5. Sutton and Nauck, *American Record Labels,* 305.
6. Ibid., 214.
7. Ibid., 161, 208; media scholar Jacob Smith has written extensively about the content of the "party records" or "blue discs" that attained limited popularity in the late 1930s and early 1940s. Jacob Smith, "Filling the Embarrassment of Silence: Erotic Performance on 'Blue Discs,'" *Film Quarterly* 58 (2004): 26–35.
8. "Mr. Big," *Time,* February 19, 1940, 59.
9. Sutton and Nauck, *American Record Labels,* 208.
10. David Diehl, "Risque," *The Blue Pages,* August 11, 2008, http://www.hensteeth.com/risque.html, accessed February 20, 2009.
11. "New Hearing Is Set on Disk Called Nazi," *New York Times,* October 27, 1959, 11; David Diehl, e-mail correspondence with author, February 20, 2009.
12. Jeremy Rifkin, *The Age of Access: How the Shift from Ownership to Access Is Transforming Modern Life* (London: Penguin, 2000), 24; see also Benjamin B. Hampton, *History of the American Film Industry: From Its Beginnings to 1931* (New York: Dover, 1970).
13. Charles Edward Smith, "Background to Bootlegging," *Record Changer,* January 1952, 3.
14. Wilder Hobson, "Le Jazz Jubilant," *Saturday Review,* August 25, 1951, 41.
15. David Suisman, "The Sound of Money: Music, Machines, and Markets, 1890–1925" (PhD diss., Columbia University, 2002), 208.
16. Eric Porter, *What Is This Thing Called Jazz: African American Musicians as Artists, Critics, and Activists* (Berkeley: University of California Press, 2002), 47.
17. Alan Lomax, *Mister Jelly Roll: The Fortunes of Jelly Roll Morton, New Orleans Creole and "Inventor of Jazz"* (New York: Pantheon Books, 1993), 282–3.
18. J. R. Taylor, "Jazz Periodicals" in *H.R.S. Society Rag* (Westport, CT: Greenwood Press, 1977), 1.
19. Porter, *What Is This Thing Called Jazz,* 48.

20. Stephen Duncombe, *Notes from Underground: Zines and the Politics of Alternative Culture* (London: Verso, 1997), 3.
21. Stephen W. Smith, "Hot Collecting," in *Jazzmen,* ed. Frederic Ramsey and Charles Edward Smith (New York: Harcourt Brace, 1939), 292.
22. Dick Reiber, "First Thrills in Beulah Land," *H.R.S. Society Rag* 1 (July 1938): 9.
23. Reiber, "First Thrills in Beulah Land," 11.
24. Smith, "Hot Collecting," 290.
25. Ibid., 291.
26. Ibid.
27. A useful comparison can be found in anthropologist Mark Jamieson's work on collectors of doo-wop, northern soul, and other genres, for whom the prestige and originality of bootlegs were important; Jamieson, "The Place of Counterfeits in Regimes of Value: An Anthropological Approach," *Journal of the Royal Anthropological Institute* 5 (1999): 1–11.
28. Smith, "Background to Bootlegging," 4.
29. See "⁵dub," in *Webster's Third New International Dictionary of the English Language* (London: Encyclopædia Britannica, 1966), 698.
30. George Hoefer, "Few Discerys Cash in on Bechet's Popularity," *Downbeat,* June 16, 1948, 12.
31. Russell, "Boogie Woogie," in Ramsey and Smith, *Jazzmen,* 192.
32. On the decline of the cylinder, see Gelatt, *Fabulous Phonograph,* 158–71.
33. Hammond "was born in the kind of family and educated at the kind of school and given the kind of accomplishments, accent (slightly Hahvud) and clothes that mean the future is assured and just cushy. He didn't choose to be an expensive lawyer like his father, or anything else respectable and gilt-edged that his Westchester family might have wanted." Otis Ferguson, "John Hammond," *H.R.S. Society Rag* no. 2 (September 1938): 2.
34. David L. Morton Jr., *Sound Recording: The Life Story of a Technology* (Baltimore, MD: Johns Hopkins University, 2006), 98.
35. S. J. Begun, *Magnetic Recording* (New York: Murray Hill Books, 1949), 220.
36. Morton, *Sound Recording,* 98.
37. Ashley Kahn, liner notes in Various Artists, *Billy Crystal Presents: The Milt Gabler Story* (New York: Verve Records, 2004).
38. Charles Delaunay, "Untitled," *H.R.S. Society Rag* no. 5 (September 1940): 6.
39. Smith, "Background to Bootlegging," 4.
40. Ibid.
41. "H.R.S. Members—Attention!" *H.R.S. Society Rag* no. 1 (July 1938); Otis Ferguson, "John Hammond," *H.R.S. Society Rag* no. 3 (January 1939): 1–7; Frank Norris, "Wilder Hobson," *H.R.S. Society Rag* no. 3 (January 1939): 1–4.
42. Frederic Ramsey Jr., "Grand Lama of Jazz," *H.R.S. Society Rag* no. 4 (August 1940): 4.
43. Norris, "Wilder Hobson," 2. The unusual usage of the word "philatelist"—a stamp collector—suggests that Norris conceived of the relatively new practice of record collecting in the familiar terms of established hobbies, as if collecting jazz records were essentially similar to pressing stamps in a book.
44. "Records—How Experts Rate Them," *H.R.S. Society Rag* no. 4 (August 1940): 30–1.
45. "Hot Society," *Time,* May 17, 1937, 50.
46. Porter, *What Is This Thing Called Jazz,* 51.
47. Paul Starr, *The Creation of the Media: Political Origins of Modern Communications* (New York: Basic Books, 2004), 336.
48. *Herbert v. Shanley Co.,* 242 U.S. 591 (1917); Starr, *Creation of the Media,* 339.
49. Susan J. Douglas, *Listening In: Radio and the American Imagination* (New York: Times Books, 1999), 85–6.
50. Ibid., 90–2.
51. Melville B. Nimmer, "Copyright Publication," *Columbia Law Review* 56 (1956): 185–202.
52. "Piracy on Records," *Stanford Law Review* 5 (1953): 446.
53. *RCA v. Whiteman,* 114 F.2d 86 (U.S. App. 1940), at 4.
54. *RCA v. Whiteman,* 28 F. Supp. 787 (U.S. Dist. 1939), at 6–7.
55. *RCA,* 28 F. Supp. 787, at 15.
56. Ibid., at 12.

57. Ibid., at 11.
58. Melvin Garner, "The Future of Record Piracy," *Brooklyn Law Review* 38 (1971): 409–10.
59. *RCA v. Whiteman*, 114 F.2d 86, at 5.
60. Ibid., at 6.
61. Ibid., at 5.
62. Ibid., at 13.
63. Ibid., at 7–8.
64. Learned Hand, *The Spirit of Liberty: Papers and Addresses of Learned Hand* (New York: Knopf, 1952), 189–90.
65. *Metropolitan Opera Association v. Wagner-Nichols Recorder Corporation*, 199 Misc. 786, 101 N.Y.S.2d 483 (Sup. Ct. 1950).
66. Ibid., at 796.
67. Ibid., at 796–7.
68. Ibid., at 791.
69. Ibid., at 793.
70. Vaidhyanathan, *Copyrights and Copywrongs*, 19.
71. *Metropolitan v. Wagner-Nichols*, at 797–8, 800.
72. Ibid., at 796.
73. *Jacobellis v. Ohio*, 378 US 184 (1964).
74. Frederic Ramsey Jr., "Contraband Jelly Roll," *Saturday Review*, September 30, 1950, 64; as for the baker, Ramsey observed, "Jelly Roll, who once split a vaudeville bill with an entertainer who boasted he was Sweet Papa Cream Puff, would be happy."
75. Ramsey, "Contraband Jelly Roll," 64.
76. Thom Holmes, ed., *The Routledge Guide to Music Technology* (New York: Routledge, 2006), 172, 277.
77. Wilder Hobson, "Le Jazz Jubilant," *Saturday Review*, August 25, 1951, 41.
78. "LP Jazz Reissues Squeeze Bootleg Diskers on Old Collector Items," *Variety*, May 9, 1951, 42.
79. Alan Lomax, *Mister Jelly Roll: The Fortunes of Jelly Roll Morton, New Orleans Creole and "Inventor of Jazz"* (New York: Duell, Sloan, and Pearce, 1950), 298.
80. Smith, "Background to Bootlegging," 3.
81. *Shapiro, Bernstein and Co. v. Miracle Record*, 91 F. Supp. 473 (N.D. Ill. 1950).
82. Ibid., at 474.
83. Ibid., at 475.
84. *RCA v. Whiteman*, 114 F.2d at 89.
85. Russell, "Boogie Woogie," in Ramsey and Smith, *Jazzmen*, 194.
86. "Chi Court Ruling on Copyright Status of Recorded Music Stuns Industry," *Variety*, June 14, 1950, 57; "Music Biz Maps Midwest Action Vs. Diskleggers," *Variety*, June 18, 1952, 41.
87. "Victor Presses Bootlegs!" *Record Changer*, November 1951, 6. As evidence, the magazine published an RCA invoice that showed 466 copies of a Jolly Roger record composed entirely of performances originally released by Columbia.
88. "Victor Presses Bootlegs!" front cover.
89. Ibid., 6.
90. "Fox Called in on Disk-legging," *Variety*, August 15, 1951, 43.
91. "RCA Cracks Down on Disk-legging in Policy Switch," *Variety*, September 26, 1951, 131.
92. "Victor Presses Bootlegs!" 6.
93. Cripple Clarence Lofton, *Boogie Woogie and Blues* (Pax, 195-?), New York Performing Arts Library, Rodgers and Hammerstein Archives (RHA-NYPAL).
94. For example, see notes by Charles Edward Smith of Hot Record Society on Eureka Brass Band, *New Orleans Parade* (Pax, 195-?), and Hoefer's notes on Jimmy Yancey, *Yancey's Mixture* (Pax, 195-?), RHA-NYPAL.
95. "Pax Productions: Complete Jazz Record Catalog," Pax Records Research File, Institute of Jazz Studies, Rutgers University at Newark (RUN-IJS).
96. "Art and the Dollar," *Record Changer*, November 1951, 7.
97. "Jolly Roger: Records for the Connoisseur," RUN-IJS.
98. For contrast with Pax records, see *Jelly Roll Morton Vol. 1* (Jolly Roger, 195-?), Sound Recordings Archive, Bowling Green State University (BGSU-SRA).

99. *Metropolitan v. Wagner-Nichols.*
100. "Recorders vs. Bootleggers," *Business Week*, February 9, 1952; "Platter Pilfering," *Newsweek*, February 11, 1952, 71.
101. William Livingstone, "Piracy in the Record Industry," *Stereo Review*, February 1970, 62.
102. "LP Jazz Reissues Squeeze Bootleg Diskers on Old Collector Items," *Variety*, May 9, 1951, 42.
103. "Platter Pilfering," 71.
104. "Bootlegging: The Battle Rages," *Record Changer*, December 1951, 3–4.
105. "Art and the Dollar," *Record Changer*, November 1951, 7.
106. "Our Position," *Record Changer*, December 1951, 5.
107. "2 Dealers Charged in Disk Bootlegging," *New York Times* June 11, 1960, 21; Robert E. Allison, Peter Korelich (a record presser), Larry F. Lee, Carl John Marts, Charles Richards, and William Thompson (a commercial artist) were also arrested.
108. "Fake Record Ring Broken; 7 Men Held," *Los Angeles Times*, October 3, 1950, 2; see also "New Jersey Bootlegging Crackdown Dramatizes ARMADA Convention," *The Cash Box*, June 18, 1960.
109. "Pirate Records," Brad McCuen Collection—Piracy 1969, 97–023, box 18, folder 9, Center for Popular Music, Middle Tennessee State University (MTSU-CPM).
110. "Swaggie Records Catalogue," Brad McCuen Collection—Piracy 1969, 97–023, box 18, folder 9, MTSU-CPM; Nevill L. Sherburn to W.T. Ed Kirkeby, May 13, 1966, Brad McCuen Collection—Piracy 1969, 97–023, box 18, folder 9, MTSU-CPM.
111. Ed Kirkeby to Stephen H. Sholes, May 9, 1966, Brad McCuen Collection—Piracy 1969, 97–023, box 18, folder 9, MTSU-CPM.
112. Peter Welding to Brad McCuen, February 5, 1964, Brad McCuen Collection—Piracy 1969, 97–023, box 18, folder 9, MTSU-CPM.
113. Brad McCuen to Stephen H. Sholes, April 6, 1966, Brad McCuen Collection—Piracy 1969, 97–023, box 18, folder 9, MTSU-CPM.
114. Yochai Benkler, *The Wealth of Networks: How Social Production Transforms Markets and Freedom* (New Haven, CT: Yale University Press, 2006), 31–2.
115. With the fragmentation and diversification of the industry that accompanied the boom of rock and roll music in the late 1950s, more independent labels and record-pressing factories emerged, but in the period of the Hot Record Society and Jolly Roger few options were available for people to press small runs of records; see Robert Burnett, *The Global Jukebox: The International Music Industry* (New York: Routledge, 1996), 106; and Pekka Gronow, "The Recording Industry: The Growth of a Mass Medium," *Popular Music: Producers and Markets* 3 (1983): 70.
116. James Boyle, *The Public Domain: Enclosing the Commons of the Mind* (New Haven, CT: Yale University Press, 2008), 224.

Chapter 3

1. *Touch of Evil*, DVD, directed by Orson Welles ([1958]; Los Angeles: Universal Studios, 2000).
2. John Corbett, "Vinyl Freak," *Down Beat*, November 2004, 18.
3. David L. Morton Jr., *Sound Recording: The Life Story of a Technology* (Baltimore, MD: Johns Hopkins University, 2006), 97.
4. John Corbett, "Vinyl Freak," *Down Beat*, November 2004, 18.
5. Interview with Dan Morgenstern, Institute of Jazz Studies, Newark, NJ, March 14, 2007; Will Friedwald, "Recording Jazz History as It Was Made," *Wall Street Journal*, December 4, 2010, A30.
6. David Suisman, "The Sound of Money: Music, Machines, and Markets" (PhD diss., Columbia University, 2002), 114.
7. Brian Winston, *Media Technology and Society: A History: From the Telegraph to the Internet* (London: Routledge, 1998), 4.
8. Jody Rosen, "Researchers Play Tune Recorded before Edison," *New York Times*, March 27, 2008, A1.

9. Winston, *Media Technology and Society*, 6.
10. William Lafferty, "The Blattnerphone: An Early Attempt to Introduce Magnetic Recording into the Film Industry," *Cinema Journal* 22 (1983): 19.
11. Oberlin Smith, "Some Possible Forms of Phonograph," *Electrical World*, September 8, 1888, 117.
12. Robert Angus, "History of Magnetic Recording," *Audio*, August 1984, 28.
13. Lafferty, "Blattnerphone," 19.
14. Ibid., 20.
15. Ibid., 27–8.
16. Ibid., 30.
17. On Vail and Alexander Graham Bell's vision of the telephone system, see Jeremy Bernstein, *Three Degrees Above Zero: Bell Labs in the Information Age* (New York: Charles Scribner's Sons, 1984), 1–2.
18. Mark Clark, "Suppressing Innovation: Bell Laboratories and Magnetic Recording," *Technology and Culture* 34 (1993): 535.
19. Clark, "Suppressing Innovation," 534.
20. Ibid., 535–6.
21. Millard, *America on Record*, 192.
22. S. J. Begun, *Magnetic Recording* (New York: Murray Hill Books, 1949), 9.
23. Millard, *America on Record*, 197.
24. Hillel Schwartz, *The Culture of the Copy: Striking Likenesses, Unreasonable Facsimiles* (New York: Zone Books, 1996), 234.
25. For an industrial example, see "Firms Use Tape Recorders to Cut Down Written Work," *Chemical Week*, April 25, 1964, 104.
26. Sam Dawson, "Revolution in Office Machinery," *Los Angeles Times*, February 24, 1953, 19.
27. R. H. Opperman, "Record Voice on a Hair-Like Wire," *Journal of the Franklin Institute* 237 (1944): 160.
28. Eric D. Daniel, C. Denis Mee, and Mark H. Clark, *Magnetic Recording: The First 100 Years* (New York: Wiley-IEEE Press, 1998), 87.
29. "New 'Soundmirror' Now Used at Hunter," *New York Times*, February 25, 1940, 49.
30. G. Schirmer, "Why Did More People Buy Their Soundmirror at Schirmer's Than at Any Other Store in the Country? (ad)," *New York Times*, November 30, 1947, 20.
31. Magnetic Recorders Company, "Now a Radio-Tape Recorder Combination (ad)," *Los Angeles Times*, March 28, 1948, E18.
32. David Sanjek and Russell Sanjek, *Pennies from Heaven: The American Popular Music Business in the Twentieth Century* (New York: Da Capo Press, 1996), viii.
33. David Morton, *Off the Record: The Technology and Culture of Sound Recording in America* (New Brunswick, NJ: Rutgers University Press, 2000), 11.
34. "How We Gave a Phonograph Party," *Phonoscope*, April 1899, 14.
35. Jonathan Sterne, *The Audible Past: Cultural Origins of Sound Recording* (Durham, NC: Duke University Press, 2003), 208–9.
36. For technical guides, see Begun, *Magnetic Recording*; and Michael Luxford Quartermaine, *Magnetic Recording: Wire and Tape* (London: N. Price, 1952); Begun was the vice president and chief engineer of the Brush Development Company, a pioneer in wire and tape recording that received contracts during World War II to adapt the technology for combat use.
37. Wallace S. Sharps, *Tape Recording for Pleasure* (London: Fountain Books, 1961), 7.
38. Sharps, *Tape Recording*, 74; see also Thurston Moore, *Mix Tape: The Art of Cassette Culture* (New York: Universe, 2005).
39. Rek-O-Kut Company, "Make Your Own High Fidelity Records (ad)," *High Fidelity Magazine* (hereafter, *HFM*), March 1955, 98.
40. Edward Tatnall Canby, "Make Your Own LP's," *Saturday Review*, August 25, 1951, 48.
41. Canby, "Make Your Own LP's," 48.
42. Ibid.
43. Morton, *Sound Recording*, 39.
44. Paul Affelder, "Berlioz—Beatrice et Benedict—Overture; Benvenuto Cellini—Overture (review)," *HFM*, March 1955, 53.

45. Radio Engineering Laboratories, "Connoisseur (ad)," *HFM*, March 1955, 101.
46. Duotone, "From a Tulip Comes New Scope for Your Listening (ad)," *HFM*, May 1955, 120.
47. "Scissors Dept.," *HFM*, April 1955, 9.
48. Radio Engineering Laboratories, "Connoisseur (ad)," *HFM*, March 1955, 101.
49. Louis Biancolli and Lester H. Bogen, *Understanding High Fidelity: A Guide to Hi-Fi Home Music Systems* (New York: David Bogen Company, 1953), 3.
50. Roy F. Allison, "An Audio Lexicon: Part II," *HFM*, March 1955, 83.
51. Nathan Broder, "The Battle of the Bach Bows," *HFM*, March 1955, 52; Fred Grunfeld, "When Mahlerites Meet: A Tournament of Titans," *HFM*, March 1955, 58.
52. Dana Andrews, "Living with Music," *HFM*, May 1955, 41; see also Sony Corporation, "How to Explain to Your Wife Why You Spent an Extra $400 for this Stereo Receiver (ad)," *Stereo Review*, January 1970, 30.
53. Elaine Tyler May, *Homeward Bound: American Families in the Cold War Era* (New York: Basic Books, 1999), 146.
54. Canby, "Make Your Own LP's," 48.
55. The Gould legend was spun by Joseph Mitchell in a 1942 *New Yorker* piece and later in his book *Joe Gould's Secret*, which was adapted for the screen in 2000; see Mitchell, "Professor Sea Gull," *New Yorker*, December 12, 1942, 28–42; Mitchell, *Joe Gould's Secret* (New York: Viking, 1965); and *Joe Gould's Secret*, DVD, directed by Stanley Tucci (New York: USA Home Entertainment, 2000).
56. James Goodfriend, "Piracy and Ethics," *Stereo Review*, February 1970, 43.
57. Ibid., 43.
58. Begun, *Magnetic Recording*, 220.
59. Russell Sanjek, *American Popular Music and Its Business: The First Four Hundred Years: Volume III From 1900 to 1984* (New York: Oxford University Press, 1988), 18, 199.
60. "The Vice Guide to Killing Your Parents," *Vice* 12, no. 8 (2005): 64.
61. Electronic distribution through the Internet has dramatically reduced the fixed costs of production and distribution in the early twenty-first century. Through its iTunes store, Apple can make available a much wider array of music in less-popular genres like classical and jazz than the typical record shop, which has limited shelf space and cannot cater to all niche markets. Sales of classical music have grown by leaps and bounds. See Barbara Jepson, "Classical, Now without the 300-Year Delay," *New York Times*, March 26, 2006, 23.
62. Goodfriend, "Piracy and Ethics," 43.
63. Ibid., 45.
64. Ibid., 43.
65. Ibid., 45.
66. Clinton Heylin, *Bootleg: The Secret History of the Other Recording Industry* (New York: St. Martin's Press, 1994), 28.
67. Philip L. Miller, "Mapleson Cylinders in the New York Public Library," *Notes* 13 (1942): 12–14.
68. Morton, *Sound Recording*, 92.
69. William Livingstone, "Piracy in the Record Industry," *Stereo Review*, February 1970, 62; for coverage of the original performance, see Henry Pleasants, "Miss Resnik Sings at Baireuth Fete," *New York Times*, July 27, 1953, 14.
70. Livingstone, "Piracy," 60.
71. Ibid., 64.
72. Ibid., 68.
73. Heylin, *Bootleg*, 35.
74. Livingstone, "Piracy," 65–6.
75. Boris Rose, "Roost Book," "The Sound of Hollywood," and "A World of Nostalgia Greats," Boris Rose Research File, Institute of Jazz Studies, Rutgers University at Newark.
76. Interview with Dan Morgenstern, Institute of Jazz Studies, Newark, NJ, March 14, 2007.
77. Telephone interview with Elaine Rose, August 22, 2011.
78. *Capitol Records v. Mercury Records*, 221 F.2d 657 (U.S. App. 1955).
79. John E. Mason Jr., "Performers' Rights and Copyright: The Protection of Sound Recording from Modern Pirates," *California Law Review* 59 (1971): 555; *Capitol*, 221 F2d at 663–4.

80. *Capitol,* 221 F2d at 661.
81. Ibid., at 663.
82. Mason, "Performers' Rights and Copyright," 556.
83. *Sears, Roebuck & Co. v. Stiffel Co.,* 376 U.S. 225 (1964); *Compco Corp. v. Day-Brite Lighting, Inc.,* 376 U.S. 234 (1964).
84. John Shepard Wiley Jr., "Bonito Boats: Uninformed but Mandatory Innovation Policy," *Supreme Court Review* (1989): 283–5.
85. Wiley Jr., "Bonito Boats," 284.
86. Michael Riordon and Lillian Hoddeson, *Crystal Fire: The Birth of the Information Age* (New York: Norton, 1997), 1.
87. Nick Lyons, *The Sony Vision* (New York: Crown, 1976), 39–43, 55.
88. David Hall, "Record-Industry Notes," *Notes,* 2nd ser. 25 (1968): 213.
89. "Listen as You Drive to Elvis—or Yourself—through Auto Stereo Tape Components," *Business Week,* October 9, 1965, 105; Peter Goldmark reflects on his quest for the ill-fated under-dash record player in the memoir *Maverick Inventor: My Turbulent Years at CBS* (New York: Saturday Review Press, 1973).
90. Abigail Lavine, "Earl Muntz, the 4-Track Madman," *8 Track Heaven,* http://www.8trackheaven.com/archive/muntz.html, accessed 11 August 2008.
91. Robert A. Pease, "Mad Man Muntz!" *Electronic Design,* July 23, 1992.
92. Bill Golden, "To Whomever," *8 Track Heaven,* February 1, 1996, http://www.8trackheaven.com/archive/golden.txt, accessed August 11, 2008.
93. Telephone interview with Bill Golden, December 2, 2007.
94. Ibid.
95. Richard Rashke, *Stormy Genius: The Life of Aviation's Maverick, Bill Lear* (Boston: Houghton Mifflin, 1985), 254.
96. "Lear Takes the Controls," *Business Week,* March 7, 1964, 111.
97. Rashke, *Stormy Genius,* 255.
98. Ibid., 256.
99. "Will Stereo Tapes Bring Music to Detroit Ears?" *Business Week,* November 6, 1965, 34.
100. "Music Maker for the Masses," *Business Week,* February 24, 1968, 108.
101. Golden, "To Whomever."
102. Rashke, *Stormy Genius,* 256.
103. "Will Stereo Tapes Bring Music to Detroit Ears?" 34.
104. "Listen as You Drive to Elvis—or Yourself—through Auto Stereo Tape Components," *Business Week,* October 9, 1965, 105.
105. Frances Rumsey and Tim McCormick, *Sound Recording: An Introduction* (St. Louis, MO: Focal Press, 2006), 178.
106. Ed Christman, "Vinyl Solution?" *Billboard,* April 28, 2007, 11; Morton, *Sound Recording,* 181.
107. Bob Thomas, "Earl Muntz: Hi-Fi(nance) Comes in 4 & 8 Tracks," *Los Angeles Times,* May 12, 1967, K11.
108. "Music Maker for the Masses," 109.
109. Bruce Weber, "Is Number up for 4-Track? Tape Executives Say Yes," *Billboard,* March 14, 1970, 11.
110. William T. Drummond, "Admitted Music 'Pirate' Tells How Bootleg Market Started," *Los Angeles Times,* July 20, 1971, B1.
111. "Music Maker for the Masses," 108.
112. William Burroughs, "The Invisible Generation," in *The Ticket That Exploded* (New York: Grove Press, 1967), 208–9.
113. Ibid., 208.
114. Paul N. Edwards, *The Closed World: Computers and the Politics of Discourse in Cold War America* (Cambridge, MA: MIT Press, 1997), 161.
115. One of the first references to a "content provider"—a person or organization that furnishes information—can be found in Seymour B. Sarason, *The Preparation of Teachers: An Unstudied Problem in Education* (New York: Wiley, 1962).
116. Lyons, *Sony Vision,* 28.

117. By the 1960s, talk of an "information revolution" became fashionable, especially among academics, computer firms, entertainment companies, and the makers of office equipment. RCA sponsored an exhibit on the subject in 1967; see "RCA Exhibit Is Tied to Information Revolution," *New York Times*, September 22, 1967, 77; Xerox Corporation, "Is Salesman a Dirty Word? (ad)," *New York Times*, January 9, 1966, 303; Harold M. Schmeck, Jr., "Oceanographer Urges Support For Research on Social Sciences," *New York Times*, January 27, 1966, 35.

Chapter 4

1. Mark Blackwell, Interview with Wim Wenders, *Ray Gun* 48 (August 1997), n.p.
2. Richard West, "Reds Like Rock and Roll—But Need Interpretation," *Los Angeles Times*, June 25, 1965, A1.
3. Artemy Troitsky, *Back in the USSR: The True Story of Rock in Russia* (London: Omnibus, 1987), 19.
4. Robert Burnett, *The Global Jukebox: The International Music Industry* (New York: Routledge, 1996), 106.
5. Edward Tatnall Canby, "Make Your Own LP's," *Saturday Review*, August 25, 1951, 48; Pekka Gronow, "The Recording Industry: The Growth of a Mass Medium," *Popular Music: Producers and Markets* 3 (1983): 70.
6. "The $100-Million Market in Bootleg Tapes," *Business Week*, May 15, 1971, 132.
7. Greil Marcus, "The Bootleg LP's," *Rolling Stone*, February 7, 1970, 36, 38.
8. "Bob Johnston Remembers," *Rolling Stone*, July 22, 1971, 19.
9. Charles Edward Smith, "Background to Bootlegging," *Record Changer*, January 1952, 3.
10. "Revolutionary War," *Time*, June 28, 1971, 72.
11. Bob Chorush, "Feds Are Leaning on Bootleggers," *Rolling Stone*, October 14, 1971, 10.
12. "Jimi Hendrix," *Inquisition*, vol. 2, no. 3, May 27, 1969, n.p.
13. Howard Sounes, *Down the Highway: The Life of Bob Dylan* (New York: Grove Press, 2001), 222–5.
14. R. Serge Denisoff, *Solid Gold: The Popular Record Industry* (New Brunswick, NJ: Transaction, 1975), 241–7; Clinton Heylin, *Bootleg: The Secret History of the Other Recording Industry* (New York: St. Martin's Press, 1994), 46.
15. Jerry Hopkins, "'New' Dylan Album Bootlegged in LA," *Rolling Stone*, September 20,1969, 5–6.
16. Hopkins, "'New' Dylan Album," 5.
17. Michael R. Frontani, *The Beatles: Image and the Media* (Jackson: University Press of Mississippi, 2007), 172.
18. "$100-Million Market in Bootleg Tapes," 46.
19. Heylin, *Bootleg*, 52–4.
20. "Disc Firm Sues over Dylan Bootleg Album," *Los Angeles Times*, November 29, 1969, A6.
21. Edd Taub, "Dylan: Bootleg Albums," *Protean Radish*, December 17, 1969, 16.
22. "Revolutionary War," 73.
23. Aubert Clark, *The Movement for International Copyright in Nineteenth Century America* (PhD diss., Catholic University, 1960), 35.
24. Heylin, *Bootleg*, 143; Deep Purple, *Purple for a Day* (Trade Mark of Quality, 1973?), Sound Recordings Archive, Bowling Green State University (BGSU-SRA).
25. "Bootlegs," *Hot Wacks* 7 (April 1979): 3; for an example of Ze Anonym Plattenspieler, see the Flamin Grovies [sic], *No Candy* (ZAP), BGSU-SRA.
26. Ed Ward, "The Bootleg Blues: The Rise and Fall of Rubber Dubber Records," *Harper's Weekly*, January 1974, 35; Marcus, "Bootleg LPs," 36.
27. Ward, "Bootleg Blues," 37.
28. Ibid., 36; Karl Marx and Friedrich Engels, *The German Ideology*, ed. C. J. Arthur (New York: International Publishers, 1970), 53.
29. "Revolutionary War," 73.
30. Lorana O. Sullivan, "Piracy on the High Cs: Classical Recordings Often Made Illegally," *Wall Street Journal*, December 3, 1969, 1.

31. Heylin, *Bootleg*, 45.
32. Ibid., 44.
33. "Revolutionary War," 73.
34. Ibid., 73.
35. Denisoff, *Solid Gold*, 368.
36. Heylin, *Bootleg*, 55.
37. The Beatles, *Sweet Apple Trax* (Newsound, 1970s), BGSU-SRA; The Beatles, *Let It Be* (Apple, 1970).
38. Charles Reinhart, *You Can't Do That!: Beatles Bootlegs and Novelty Records, 1963–1980* (Ann Arbor, MI: Pierian Press, 1981), 104–5.
39. The Beatles, *Let It Be* (Apple, 1970).
40. Reinhart, *You Can't Do That*, 160–1.
41. Patti Smith, *Teenage Perversity and Ships in the Night* (Ze Anonym Plattenspieler, ca. 1976); Patti Smith, *Horses* (Arista, 1975).
42. Lee Marshall, "The Effect of Piracy on the Music Industry: A Case Study of Bootlegging," *Media, Culture and Society* 26 (2004): 175.
43. Heylin, *Bootleg*, 108.
44. Charles H. McCaghy and R. Serge Denisoff, "Pirates and Politics: An Analysis of Interest Group Conflict," in *Deviance, Conflict and Criminality*, ed. McCaghy and Denisoff (Chicago: Rand McNally & Company, 1973), 303.
45. McCaghy and Denisoff, "Pirates and Politics," 302.
46. Ibid., 303.
47. Doug Rossinow, *The Politics of Authenticity: Liberalism, Christianity, and the New Left in America* (New York: Columbia University Press, 1998), 248.
48. Doug Rossinow, "'The Revolution Is about Our Lives': The New Left's Counterculture," in *Imagine Nation: The American Counterculture of the 1960s and '70s*, ed. Peter Braunstein and Michael William Doyle (New York: Routledge, 2002), 99.
49. Nadya Zimmerman, "Consuming Nature: The Grateful Dead's Performance of an Anti-Commercial Counterculture," *American Music* 24 (2006): 195.
50. Bruce Schulman, *The Seventies: The Great Shift in American Culture, Society and Politics* (Cambridge, MA: Da Capo Press, 2002), 87–90; Bruce Schulman, "Out of the Streets and into the Classroom? The New Left and Counterculture in United States History Textbooks," *Journal of American History* 85 (1999): 1530–1.
51. Rossinow, *Politics of Authenticity*, 248.
52. To the credit of Rossinow's thesis, some saw a live recording or unvarnished demo tape as more "authentic" than the official products released by record labels. Lee Marshall has also commented on the appeal of the authenticity of bootlegs in a genre of music—rock and roll—that often celebrated the rawness and rebelliousness of its performers; see Marshall, "Effect of Piracy," 175.
53. "Beatles Beat Socialisti Teakettles," *Los Angeles Free Press*, February 9, 1968, 16.
54 Ward, "Bootleg Blues," 37.
55. Chorush, "Feds Are Leaning on Bootleggers," 12.
56. William J. Drummond, "Admitted Music 'Pirate' Tells How Bootleg Market Started," *Los Angeles Times*, July 20, 1971, back page; Chorush, "Feds Are Leaning on Bootleggers," 10.
57. Patti Smith, *Free Music Store* (Brigand, ca. 1980s), BGSU-SRA.
58. Denisoff, *Solid Gold*, 172–201.
59. "Bootleggers Success Laid to Major 'Fantastic' Offers," *Billboard*, April 17, 1971, 12.
60. Taub, "Dylan: Bootleg Albums," 16.
61. Ibid., 16.
62. John Carpenter, "Bootleggers Hustle New Dylan Album," *Los Angeles Free Press*, December 19, 1969, 52.
63. "$100-Million Market in Bootleg Tapes," 44.
64. Incidentally, the label Gleason worked with in the 1970s, Fantasy, ran into legal trouble years earlier, when it sold 40,000 copies of an early Joan Baez tape without her permission. Ralph J. Gleason, "Perspectives: All the Quack Robin Hoods," *Rolling Stone*, October 14,

1971, 30; "Baez Wins Suit," *Billboard*, October 10, 1964, 6; *Baez v. Fantasy Records* 144 U.S.P.Q. 537 (Super. Ct. San Francisco County 1964).

65. "Piracy Hearing: Tape Piracy State of New York before Attorney General Louis J. Lefkowitz," *Performing Arts Review* 5 (1974): 40.
66. Interview with Francis Pinckney, Charlotte, NC, July 26, 2007.
67. Ibid.
68. Ibid.; House Committee on the Judiciary, *Prohibiting Piracy of Sound Recordings: Hearings before Subcommittee of the Committee on the Judiciary*, 92nd Cong., 1st sess., 9–10 June 1971, 92–108.
69. House Committee on the Judiciary, *Prohibiting Piracy of Sound Recordings*, 90.
70. Interview with Francis Pinckney, Charlotte, NC, July 26, 2007.
71. Robert A. Rosenblatt, "Tape Pirates: Industry Fights Bootleg Music," *Los Angeles Times*, February 28, 1970, 23.
72. "Revolutionary War," 73.
73. "Piracy Hearing," 40.
74. Ibid., 43–4.
75. Ibid., 46.
76. Heylin, *Bootleg*, 118.
77. Ibid., 179, 189.
78. Elvis Presley, *Elvis' Greatest Shit!!* (RCA Victim, 1982).
79. House Committee on the Judiciary, *Prohibiting Piracy of Sound Recordings*, 42.
80. "$100-Million Market in Bootleg Tapes," 45.
81. Ibid., 45.
82. Name withheld, e-mail message to author, New York, NY, September 27, 2007. (Tom Brown is a pseudonym.)
83. Ibid.
84. Elton John and Leon Russell, *Live at the Convention Center* (Rubber Dubber, 1971); Neil Young, *I'm Happy Y'all Came Down: Live at the Los Angeles Music Center, Dorothy Chandler Pavilion* (Rubber Dubber, 1971); James Taylor, *Live at the Anaheim Convention Center* (Rubber Dubber, 1971), BGSU-SRA.
85. Heylin, *Bootleg*, 80.
86. Ward, "Bootleg Blues," 36.
87. Name withheld, e-mail message to author, New York, NY, September 27, 2007.
88. Heylin, *Bootleg*, 83.
89. Ward, "Bootleg Blues," 37.
90. Name withheld, e-mail message to author, New York, NY, September 27, 2007.
91. "Bootlegs," *Hot Wacks* 7 (April 1979): 2.

Chapter 5

1. *Goldstein v. California* 412 U.S. 546 (1973).
2. Abraham L. Kaminstein, "Preface," in House Committee on the Judiciary, *Copyright Law Revision: Report of the Register of Copyrights on the General Revision of the U.S. Copyright Law*, 87th Cong., 1st sess., July 1961, x.
3. Glenn M. Reisman, "War Against Record Piracy: An Uneasy Rivalry between the Federal and State Governments," *Albany Law Review* 39 (1974–1975): 90.
4. W. M. Blaisdell, "Size of the Copyright Industries," in Senate Committee on the Judiciary, *Copyright Law Revision, Studies Prepared for the Subcommittee on Patents, Trademarks, and Copyrights of the Senate Committee on the Judiciary, Study No. 2*, 86th Cong., 1st sess., 1960, Committee Print, 1.
5. Kaminstein, "Preface," ix.
6. A parallel can be drawn to the hearings for the 1909 Copyright Act; early on, song publishers were preoccupied with stopping the illegal copying of their sheet music, and only when the prevalence of piano rolls and phonographs increased did they shift their attention to mechanical reproduction.

7. See Paul Goldstein, *Copyright's Highway: From Gutenberg to the Celestial Jukebox* (Stanford, CA: Stanford Law & Politics, 2003), 78–128, for an in-depth discussion of the "fair use" photocopying debate.

8. Kaminstein, "Preface," v.

9. Edward Samuels, *The Illustrated Story of Copyright* (New York: Thomas Dunne Books, 2000), 131, 136.

10. *The Oxford Companion to American Law*, ed. Kermit Hall (New York: Oxford University Press, 2002), 663.

11. Jisuk Woo, *Copyright and Computer Programs: The Role of Communication in Legal Structure* (New York: Garland Publishing, 2000), 3–4.

12. House Committee on the Judiciary, *Copyright Law Revision Part 2: Discussion and Comments on Report of the Register of Copyrights on the General Revision of the U.S. Copyright Law*, 88th Cong., 1st sess., 1963, Committee Print, 242.

13. Ibid., 381.

14. Ibid., 242.

15. Marci A. Hamilton, "Commissioned Works as Works Made for Hire under the 1976 Copyright Act: Misinterpretation and Injustice," *University of Pennsylvania Law Review* 135 (1987): 1284

16. House Committee on the Judiciary, *Copyright Law Revision Part 2*, 11–2.

17. Ibid., 13.

18. Ibid., 260.

19. House Committee on the Judiciary, *Copyright Law Revision: Report of the Register of Copyrights on the General Revision of the U.S. Copyright Law*, 87th Cong., 1st sess., July 1961, 18.

20. House Committee on the Judiciary, *Prohibiting Piracy of Sound Recordings: Hearings on S. 646 and H.R. 6927*, 92nd Cong., 1st sess., 1971, 16.

21. Alan Latman and James F. Lightstone, eds., *The Kaminstein Legislative History Project: A Compendium and Analytical Index of Materials Leading to the Copyright Act of 1976* (Littleton, CO: Fred B. Rothman & Co., 1981), xxxii.

22. House Committee on the Judiciary, *Prohibiting Piracy of Sound Recordings*, 21.

23. Melvin Garner, "The Future of Record Piracy," *Brooklyn Law Review* 38 (1971): 113

24. *Capitol Records Inc. v. Greatest Records Inc.*, 43 Misc. 2d 878, 880 (Sup. Ct., 1964).

25. Reisman, "War against Record Piracy," 102.

26. *Capitol Records v. Richard W. Erickson*, 2 Cal. App. 3d 526 (Cal. Dist. Ct. App. 1969).

27. *Capitol*, 2 Cal. App. 3d at 537.

28. Vaidhyanathan, *Copyrights and Copywrongs*, 19.

29. *Capitol*, 2 Cal. App. 3d, at 529.

30. Interview with Francis Pinckney, Charlotte, NC, 26 July 2007.

31. House Committee on the Judiciary, *Prohibiting Piracy of Sound Recordings*, 29.

32. New York State Legislature, *Laws of the State of New York, 1966* (Albany, NY: New York State Legislative Bill Drafting Commission, 1966), 3313.

33. "Piracy Hearing: Tape Piracy, State of New York before Attorney General Louis J. Lefkowitz," *Performing Arts Review* 5, nos. 1–2 (1974): 69–73.

34. "Record, Tape Pirating Bill Signed," *Nashville Banner*, May 11, 1971, n.p.

35. "Piracy Hearing," 72–3.

36. New York State Legislature, *Laws of the State of New York, 1966* (Albany: New York State Legislative Bill Drafting Commission, 1966), 3313.

37. Letter from Henry Brief, April 28, 1966, at 39, Bill Jacket, L. 1966, ch. 982, at Science, Industry and Business Library (SIBL) of New York Public Library, New York, NY.

38. Report by the Committee on Penal Law and Criminal Procedures, 1966, at 23, Bill Jacket, L. 1966, ch. 982, SIBL.

39. Letter from Henry Brief, April 28, 1966, at 39, Bill Jacket, L. 1966, ch. 982, SIBL.

40. Ibid. The text of the bill specified, "The word 'owner' shall mean the person who owns the master phonograph record, master disc, master tape, master film or other device used for reproducing recorded sounds on phonograph records, discs, tapes, films or other articles on which sound is recorded, and from which the transferred sounds are directly or indirectly derived." "An act to amend the penal law, in relation to the unauthorized copying

of phonograph records for sale or for use for gain or profit," February 14, 1966, at 2, Bill Jacket, L. 1966, ch. 982, SIBL.

41. Letter from Max L. Arons, April 29, 1966, at 50, Bill Jacket, L. 1966, ch. 982, SIBL.
42. Memorandum from Attorney General Louis J. Lefkowitz, February 8, 1966, at 16, Bill Jacket, L. 1966, ch. 982, SIBL.
43. Telegram from Thomas E. Ervin, April 22, 1966, at 1, Bill Jacket, L. 1966, ch. 982, SIBL.
44. Ibid., 4.
45. Clark had been obsessed with jazz ever since he strung up a long-range antenna from the roof of his parents' house in Rochester, New York, in 1938, in order to listen to live performances broadcast from Chicago, New York, and London. During a long life that included stints in banking and insurance on Wall Street, Clark amassed a large archive of live jazz recordings. See "Guide to the E. Payson Clark Papers, 1915–2004," *University of Chicago Library*, http://uncap.lib.uchicago.edu/view.php?eadid=ICU.SPCL.EPCLARK, accessed February 27, 2009.
46. Letter from Payson Clark, June 14, 1966, at 30, Bill Jacket, L. 1966, ch. 982, SIBL.
47. Ibid., 30.
48. Ibid.,
49. Letter from Harry V. Souchon, June 22, 1966, at 32, Bill Jacket, L. 1966, ch. 982, SIBL.
50. Letter from Payson Clark, at 25.
51. James Goodfriend, "Piracy and Ethics," *Stereo Review*, February 1970, 45.
52. James Boyle, *The Public Domain: Enclosing the Commons of the Mind* (New Haven, CT: Yale University Press, 2008), 9.
53. Letter from Henry Brief, June 28, 1966, at 45, Bill Jacket, L. 1966, ch. 982, SIBL.
54. Letter from Payson Clark, at 26.
55. Memorandum from Louis J. Lefkowitz, July 21, 1966, at 17, Bill Jacket, L. 1966, ch. 982, SIBL.
56. Walter J. Derenberg, "Copyright Law," *Annual Survey of American Law* (1968–1969): 431.
57. House Committee on the Judiciary, *Prohibiting Piracy of Sound Recordings*, 12.
58. Ibid., 18.
59. Ibid., 56.
60. Ibid., 46; see "The $100-Million Market in Bootleg Tapes," *Business Week*, May 15, 1971, 132.
61. "Piracy Hearing," 9–10, 54.
62. House Committee on the Judiciary, *Prohibiting Piracy of Sound Recordings*, 47.
63. Ibid., 6.
64. Ibid., 56.
65. Ibid., 25.
66. Ibid., 28.
67. Ibid., 4.
68. Ibid., 59.
69. R. Serge Denisoff, *Tarnished Gold: The Record Industry Revisited* (New Brunswick, NJ: Transaction, 1986), 58–9.
70. Christopher Knab and Bartley F. Day, *Music Is Your Business: A Musician's FourFront Strategy for Success* (Seattle: FourFront Media and Music, 2001), 108–10; Steve Albini, "The Problem with Music," in *Commodify Your Dissent: Salvos from the Baffler*, ed. Thomas Frank and Matt Weiland (New York: W.W. Norton, 1997), 164–76.
71. "Music Copyright Legislation Develops New Battle Fronts at Third of House Hearings," *Billboard*, June 14, 1947, 4; "Copyright Act Overhaul Move Seen in Offing," *Billboard*, January 31, 1948, 34; Mildred Hall, "AFM Charges Revision Gives Short Shrift to the Musicians," *Billboard*, July 10, 1965, 8.
72. House Committee on the Judiciary, *Prohibiting Piracy of Sound Recordings*, 53.
73. See first use of term in "Plug Payolas Perplexed," *Variety*, October 19, 1938, 41, and subsequent discussion in T. W. Adorno, "On Popular Music," *Studies in Philosophy and Social Science* 9, no. 1 (1941): 35–7; David Suisman, *Selling Sounds: The Commercial Revolution in American Music* (Cambridge, MA: Harvard University Press, 2009), 59; Kerry Segrave, *Payola in the Music Industry: A History, 1880–1991* (Jefferson, NC: McFarland & Co.,

1994), 221; Fredric Dannen, *Hit Men: Power Brokers and Fast Money inside the Music Business* (New York: Vintage Books, 1990), 52, 103.

74. Dannen, *Hit Men*, 3–17, 31–57; Denisoff, *Tarnished Gold*, 264–9.
75. House Committee on the Judiciary, *Prohibiting Piracy of Sound Recordings*, 69.
76. Ibid., 81.
77. House Committee on the Judiciary, *Prohibiting Piracy of Sound Recordings*, 57.
78. Joanna Demers, *Steal This Music: How Intellectual Property Law Affects Musical Creativity* (Athens: University of Georgia Press, 2006), 117, 142.
79. House Committee on the Judiciary, *Prohibiting Piracy of Sound Recordings*, 75; for more on Hart's career, see Michael O'Brien, *Philip Hart: The Conscience of the Senate* (East Lansing: Michigan State University Press, 1995).
80. House Committee on the Judiciary, *Prohibiting Piracy of Sound Recordings*, 75.
81. *Congressional Quarterly Almanac: 92nd Congress 1st Session 1971* (Washington, DC: Congressional Quarterly, 1972), 860.
82. The October 1971 act was titled "An Act to Amend Title 17 of the United States Code to Provide for the Creation of a Limited Copyright in Sound Recordings for the Purpose of Protecting against Unauthorized Duplication and Piracy of Sound Recording, and for Other Purposes"; see *Congressional Quarterly Almanac: 92nd Congress 1st Session, 1971*, 860; Sound Recording Act of 1971, 85 Stat. 391 (1971).
83. Celia Lury, *Branding: The Logos of the Cultural Economy* (New York: Routledge, 2004), 108–9.
84. For more on the Kovens' legal and managerial difficulties, see chapter 4; Linda Mathews, "U.S. High Court Upholds State's Tape Piracy Ban," *Los Angeles Times*, June 19, 1973, A3; William T. Drummond, "Admitted Music 'Pirate' Tells How Bootleg Market Started," *Los Angeles Times*, July 20, 1971, B1.
85. Interview with Francis Pinckney, Charlotte, NC, July 26, 2007.
86. Howard D. Abrams and Robert H. Abrams, "*Goldstein v. California*: Sound, Fury and Significance," *Supreme Court Review* (1975): 149.
87. *Goldstein*, 412 U.S. at 560.
88. Ibid., at 570.
89. Ibid., at 570.
90. *Brown v. Board of Education of Topeka*, 347 U.S. 483 (1954); *Griswold v. Connecticut*, 381 U.S. 479 (1965).
91. *Goldstein*, 412 U.S. at 574.
92. Mathews, "U.S. High Court," A3.
93. *Goldstein*, 412 U.S. at 571.
94. James Robison, "Record Industry's No. 1 Enemy—the Bootleggers," *Chicago Tribune*, 9 February 1975, 32.
95. "Piracy Hearing," 38.
96. Bill Anderson, "Tape Cassettes: Bootleggers' Boon," *Chicago Tribune*, May 22, 1973, 10.
97. On the prosecution of Sam Goody, see Jonathan Fenby, *Piracy and the Public: Forgery, Theft and Exploitation* (London: Frederick Muller Limited, 1983), 81.
98. "Piracy Hearing," 21.
99. *GAI Audio of New York, Inc. v. Columbia Broadcasting System*, 27 Md. App. 172, 340 A.2d 736 (Md. App. 1975).
100. Ibid., at 206.
101. Ibid., at 179–80.
102. Ibid., at 177–8.
103. "Suspect in 'Bootleg' Case Arraigned," *Los Angeles Times*, January 8, 1974, B3.
104. "Piracy Hearing," 16.
105. William Farr, "City to Crack Down on Phony Music Tapes," *Los Angeles Times*, December 16, 1973, B8.
106. "Piracy Hearing," 19.
107. On one day Schoenfeld visited "electronics stores, novelty stores, discount merchandise stores, record stores, and any other stores advertising or appearing likely to be selling inexpensive 8-track tapes" throughout New York City. Of fifteen scouted in Brooklyn, he found

five selling pirate tapes; one of five investigated were doing so in Flushing, Queens; six of ten in Jamaica, Queens; and six of fifteen in Times Square. In lower Manhattan he also found newspaper and tobacco shops selling eight-tracks for $2.79 apiece. "Piracy Hearing," 6–7.

108. "Piracy Hearing," 50.
109. Ibid., 51–2.
110. *National Broadcasting Co., Inc., and Columbia Broadcasting System, Inc. v. Donald Ray Nance, et al.*, 506 S.W.2d 483 (Mo. App. 1974); *A&M Records v. MVC Distributing Corporation*, 574 F.2d 312 (U.S. App. 1978).
111. George S. Grossman, ed., *Omnibus Copyright Revision Legislative History: Volume 15* (Buffalo, NY: Hein Law Book Publishers, 1977), 1244–6.
112. *A&M Records v. David L. Heilman*, 75 Cal. App. 3d 554 (Cal. App. 1977).
113. Mike Dembeck and David D. Porter, "City's Suspected Hub of Bogus Tape Industry," *Charlotte News*, December 7, 1978, 1A.
114. Dembeck and Porter, "City's Suspected Hub," 12A.
115. "2 Dealers Charged in Disk Bootlegging," *New York Times*, June 11, 1960, 21.
116. Bill Hazlett and Boris Yaro, "U.S. Jury to Probe Reports of Payola in L.A. Record Industry," *Los Angeles Times*, August 31, 1973, 3A.
117. Robison, "Record Industry's No. 1 Enemy," 32.
118. Charles H. McCaghy and R. Serge Denisoff, "Record Piracy," in *Crime in Society*, ed. Leonard D. Savitz and Norman Johnston (New York: John Wiley & Sons, 1978), 919.
119. Bill Anderson, "Tape Cassettes: Bootleggers' Boon," *Chicago Tribune*, May 22, 1973, 10.
120. McCaghy and Denisoff, "Record Piracy," 919.
121. "Record Piracy Act OKd," *Chicago Tribune*, September 26, 1974, 8.
122. Robison, "Record Industry's No. 1 Enemy," 32.
123. Maureen O'Neill, "Profit Wasn't Their Motive," *Newsday*, December 7, 1978.
124. Steve Wick, "FBI Sifting Bogus Recording Haul," *Newsday*, December 8, 1978.
125. Max H. Seigel, "F.B.I. Raiders Act to Smash Record Piracy," *New York Times*, December 7, 1978, C22.
126. Wick, "FBI Sifting Bogus Recording Haul."
127. "FBI Agents Seize Bootleg Albums in State Raids," *Charlotte Observer*, December 7, 1978.
128. Mike Dembeck, "Tapes Legitimate, Part-Owner of Raided Firm Says," *Charlotte News*, December 7, 1978, 1A.
129. Wick, "FBI Sifting Bogus Recording Haul."
130. O'Neill, "Profit Wasn't Their Motive."
131. Siva Vaidhyanathan, *Copyrights and Copywrongs: The Rise of Intellectual Property and How It Threatens Creativity* (New York: New York University Press, 2001), 36.
132. *Copyright Revision Act of 1976* (Chicago: Commerce Clearing House, 1976), 225.
133. Ibid., 225.
134. Ibid., 221.
135. Ibid., 222.
136. E. Fulton Brylawski and Abe Goldman, eds., *Legislative History of the 1909 Copyright Act, Volume 4* (South Hackensack, NJ: Fred B. Rothman & Co., 1976), 22.
137. Grossman, *Omnibus Copyright Revision Legislative History: Vol. 15*, 1301.
138. Ibid., 1301–4; Robert A. Gorman, "An Overview of the Copyright Act of 1976," *University of Pennsylvania Law Review* 126 (1978): 877.
139. Grossman, *Omnibus Copyright Revision Legislative History: Volume 15*, 1265.
140. Ibid., 1239.
141. Ibid.
142. House Committee on the Judiciary, *Prohibiting Piracy of Sound Recordings*, 57.
143. Pamela G. Hollie, "Piracy Costly Plague in Record Industry," *New York Times*, March 10, 1980, D1.
144. David and Russell Sanjek, *Pennies from Heaven: The American Popular Music Business in the Twentieth Century* (New York: Da Capo Press, 1996), 568.
145. United States Copyright Office, *General Guide to the Copyright Act of 1976* (Washington, DC: US Government Printing Office, 1977), 1:3.

146. "CQ Senate Votes 24–31," *Congressional Quarterly Weekly Report*, 34, no. 8 (February 21, 1976): 449.
147. Ibid., 449.
148. "House to Act on Copyright Law Revision," *Congressional Quarterly Weekly Report*, 34, no. 38 (September 18, 1976): 2551.
149. "Barbara Ringer," *United States Copyright Office*, http://www.copyright.gov/history/bios/ringer.pdf, accessed February 10, 2009.

Chapter 6

1. "Doobie or Not Doobie," *What's Happening!!* February 4, 1978.
2. For examples of the voluminous literature on the personal significance of sharing unique, personalized sequences of musical recordings, see James Sheffield, *Love Is a Mixtape: Life and Loss, One Song at a Time* (New York: Crown Publishing, 2007); Nick Hornby, *High Fidelity* (New York: Riverhead, 1995); Thurston Moore, *Mix Tape: The Art of Cassette Culture* (New York: Universe, 2005); and Jared Ball, "FreeMix Radio: The Original Mixtape Radio Show: A Case Study in Mixtape 'Radio' and Emancipatory Journalism," *Journal of Black Studies* 20 (2008): 1–21.
3. Alan O'Connor, *Punk Record Labels and the Struggle for Autonomy* (Lanham, MD: Lexington Books, 2008), 20, 49.
4. Louis M. Holscher, "I'll Trade You an Elvis Sun for a Beatles' Christmas Album," *San Diego Justice Journal* 1 (1993): 67.
5. Holscher, "I'll Trade You an Elvis Sun," 65.
6. Greg Shaw, "It Was Twenty Years Ago Today…" *Bomp*, http://www.bomp.com/x/?page_id=2, accessed September 14, 2008.
7. "Bootlegs," in *Hot Wacks* (Kitchener, Ontario: Blue Flake Productions, 1977), 2–3.
8. "Bootlegs," in *Hot Wacks Book Seven* (Kitchener, Ontario: Blue Flake Productions, 1979), 3.
9. Ibid., 3.
10. Jeffrey Ressner, "Bootlegs Go High-Tech," *Rolling Stone*, May 30, 1991, 16
11. Holscher, "I'll Trade You an Elvis Sun," 68; "Ban Bootlegs from Record Shows!" *Goldmine*, February 8, 1991, 6.
12. Lee Marshall, "For and against the Record Industry: An Introduction to Bootleg Collectors and Tape Traders," *Popular Music* 22 (2003): 58.
13. *Hot Wacks* (Kitchener, Ontario: Blue Flake Productions, 1977), 2.
14. *Hot Wacks Book Seven* (Kitchener, Ontario: Blue Flake Productions, 1979), 1.
15. Alireza Jay Naghavi and Günther G. Schulze, "Bootlegging in the Music Industry: A Note," *European Journal of Law and Economics* 12 (2001): 58.
16. Lee Marshall, "The Effects of Piracy upon the Music Industry: A Case Study of Bootlegging," *Media Culture Society* 26 (2004): 177.
17. "Record Hotline," *Hot Wacks Quarterly* 1 (winter 1979): 47.
18. Marshall, "Effects of Piracy," 176–7.
19. *Hot Wacks Book Seven*, 1.
20. "Record Hotline," 47.
21. Ressner, "Bootlegs Go High-Tech," 16.
22. Cason A. Moore, "Tapers in a Jam: Trouble Ahead or Trouble Behind," *Columbia Journal of Law and the Arts* 30 (2006–2007): 627.
23. Ibid., 626.
24. Ibid., 628.
25. Michael Getz, *The Deadhead's Taping Compendium: An In-depth Guide to the Music of the Grateful Dead on Tape* (New York: Henry Holt, 1998), 19.
26. John R. Dwork, introduction to Getz, *Taping Compendium*, xii.
27. Getz, *Taping Compendium*, 22.
28. Mike Tannehill, "Recording a Live Concert or, Hey Are You Recording This?" *Dead Relix*, November–December 1974, 16.

29. Charlie Rosen, "Wither the Poor Dead Freak," *Dead Relix*, November–December 1974, 7–8.
30. "Sound on Sound," *Dead Relix*, November–December 1974, 4.
31. Ibid., 4.
32. "Trade with the Hell's Honkies Tape Club," *Dead Relix*, November–December 1974, 18.
33. Melissa McCray Pattacini, "Deadheads Yesterday and Today: An Audience Study," *Popular Music and Society* 24, no.1 (2000): 7; "What Is a Tape Tree and How Does It Work?" *Stason. org*, http://stason.org/TULARC/music-bands/grateful-dead/6-What-is-a-Tape-Tree-and-how-does-it-work-Grateful-Dead.html, accessed July 24, 2012.
34. Pattacini, "Deadheads Yesterday and Today," 7.
35. *Dead Relix*, November–December 1974, back cover.
36. "Shit List," *Dead Relix*, November–December 1974, 5.
37. Ibid.
38. Peter Kollock, "The Production of Trust in Online Markets," http://www.connectedac-tion.net/wp-content/uploads/2009/05/1999-peter-kollock-the-production-of-trust-in-online-markets.htm, accessed October 24, 2008.
39. Mark F. Schultz, "Fear and Norms and Rock & Roll: What Jambands Can Teach Us about Persuading People to Obey Copyright Law," *Berkeley Technology Law Journal* 21 (2006): 695.
40. Dwork, introduction to Getz, *Taping Compendium*, xii.
41. Schultz, "Fear and Norms and Rock & Roll," 727; see also Yochai Benkler, "Coase's Penguin, or, Linux and the Nature of the Firm," *Yale Law Journal* 112 (2002): 369–446.
42. Moore, "Tapers in a Jam," 627.
43. Ibid., 628.
44. John Perry Barlow, "The Economy of Ideas," *Wired*, March 1993, 84–129.
45. John Markoff, *What the Dormouse Said: How the 60s Counterculture Shaped the Personal Computer Industry* (New York: Viking, 2005), xiv–xix, 96–7.
46. Fred Turner, *From Counterculture to Cyberculture: Stewart Brand, the Whole Earth Network, and the Rise of Digital Utopianism* (Chicago: University of Chicago Press, 2006), 207–9; Langdon Winner, "Cyberlibertarian Myths and the Prospects for Community," *Computers and Society* 27 (1997): 14–9.
47. Thomas Frank, "Why Johnny Can't Dissent," in *Commodify Your Dissent: Salvos from the Baffler*, ed. Thomas Frank and Matt Weiland (New York: W. W. Norton, 1997), 31; Lawrence Lessig, *Code and Other Laws of Cyberspace* (New York: Basic Books, 1999), 104–5; James Boyle, *The Public Domain: Enclosing the Commons of the Mind* (New Haven: Yale University Press, 2008), 180–1.
48. Yochai Benkler, *The Wealth of Networks: How Social Production Transforms Markets and Freedom* (New Haven: Yale University Press, 2006), 13.
49. Ressner, "Bootlegs Go High-Tech," 15.
50. Jim Walsh, "Singer Says 'Seinfeld' Tune Was Much Ado About…Nothing," *St. Paul Pioneer Press*, May 22, 1998; see also Stephen Thomas Erlewine, "The Shit Hits the Fans: Overview," *Allmusic*, http://allmusic.com/cg/amg.dll?p=amg&sql=10:0bftxqwgldfe, accessed September 15, 2008.
51. Ressner, "Bootlegs Go High-Tech," 15.
52. Robert Hilburn, "Dylan Songs out of the Basement," *Los Angeles Times*, July 26, 1975, B5. For a playful take on the claim that the *Black Album* was "*the* most bootlegged album in history!" see "People Who Own Bootleg Copies of Prince's 'Black' Album Given Offer of Amnesty," *Billboard*, November 26, 1994, 138.
53. Ressner, "Bootlegs Go High-Tech," 15.
54. David Gonzalez, "Pressed by Music Industry, New York Seizes Pirate Tapes," *New York Times*, December 9, 1990, 46.
55. Jeff Chang, *Can't Stop Won't Stop: A History of the Hip-Hop Generation* (New York: Picador, 2005): 127–8.
56. S. H. Fernando, *The New Beats: Exploring the Music, Culture, and Attitudes of Hip-Hop* (New York: Anchor Books, 1994), 12–3.

57. Matt Mason, *The Pirate's Dilemma: How Youth Culture Is Reinventing Capitalism* (New York: Free Press, 2008), 73.
58. Chang, *Can't Stop*, 30.
59. Ibid., 79.
60. Shaheem Reid, "Mixtape History," *MTV News*, http://www.mtv.com/bands/m/mixtape/news_feature_021003/index8.jhtml, accessed November 22, 2012.
61. Troy L. Smith, "The World Famous Brucie Bee of the Legendary Roof Top," *The Foundation*, Fall 2006, http://thafoundation.com/brucie.htm, accessed January 11, 2009, 7.
62. Fernando, *New Beats*, 6.
63. Steven Daly, "Hip-Hop Happens," *Vanity Fair*, November 2005, 250; Chang, *Can't Stop*, 129–30.
64. Chang, *Can't Stop*, 130.
65. Joanna Demers, *Steal This Music: How Intellectual Property Law Affects Musical Creativity* (Athens: University of Georgia Press, 2006), 91–2.
66. Fernando, *New Beats*, 225.
67. Ibid., 47.
68. Smith, "World Famous Brucie Bee," 13–4.
69. Frank Owen, "Street DJs Bring Live Flava Back to Hip Hop," *Village Voice*, October 25, 1994, 71.
70. Touré, "Biggie Smalls, Rap's Man of the Moment," *New York Times*, December 18, 1994, H42; Michael Marriot, "Long Before He Was B.I.G.," *New York Times*, March 17, 1997, B2.
71. DJ Kool Herc, introduction to Chang, *Can't Stop*, xi.
72. Joseph G. Schloss, *Making Beats: The Art of Sample-based Hip-Hop* (Wesleyan University Press, 2004), 27–8.
73. Ibid., 30.
74. Ibid., 29.
75. Owen, "Street DJs," 71.
76. Ibid., 71.
77. Reid, "Mixtape History," 1.
78. Smith, "World Famous Brucie Bee," 17–8.
79. Shaheem Reid, "Mixtapes: The *Other* Music Industry," *MTV News*, http://www.mtv.com/bands/m/mixtape/news_feature_021003/index5.jhtml, 5.
80. *Mixtape, Inc.*, DVD, directed by Walter Bell (New York: Pixel Propaganda, 2005).
81. Ibid.
82. Steven Stancell, "FOCUS ON: Funkmaster Flex and Goings On," *New York Beacon*, February 21, 1996, 28.
83. Funkmaster Flex, *The Mix Tape, Vol. 1: 60 Minutes of Funk* (Loud Records, 1995).
84. Charles E. Rogers, "DJ Clue Scores Big with New Album," *New York Amsterdam News*, December 30, 1998, 19; Reid, "Mixtape History," 1; Shams Tarek, "Jamaica's Own 'Bad Guy' Making Good in the Music Biz," *Queens Press*, May 16, 2003, http://www.queenspress.com/archives/features/2003/0516/feature.htm, accessed November 17, 2008, 1.
85. Steve Jones, "Money in the Mixtape," *USA Today*, April 20, 2006.
86. *Mixtape, Inc.*
87. Jared Ball, "FreeMix Radio: The Original Mixtape Radio Show: A Case Study in Mixtape 'Radio' and Emancipatory Journalism," *Journal of Black Studies* 20 (2008): 1.
88. Ibid., 11.
89. David Gates, "Decoding Rap Music," *Newsweek*, March 19, 1990, 60.
90. Owen, "Street DJs," 71.
91. Burnett, *Global Jukebox*, 61–2; for more on the relationship between independent and major labels, see Jon Pareles, "The Big Get Bigger," *New York Times*, March 19, 1990, 3.
92. Jones, "Money in the Mixtape," 1.
93. Fernando, *New Beats*, 242.
94. Vaidhyanathan, *Copyrights and Copywrongs*, 143.
95. For an example of DJs as careerists and tastemakers, see "TJ's DJs Tastemakers Only Conference/Ozone Magazine Awards Official Site," *TJ's DJs*, July 25, 2008, http://www.tjsdjs.com/toa/, accessed February 14, 2009.

96. John Yau, "Richard Prince: Spiritual America," *Brooklyn Rail*, November 2007, http://www.brooklynrail.org/2007/11/artseen/prince, accessed February 14, 2009.
97. Ian F. Svenonius, *The Psychic Soviet* (Chicago: Drag City, 2006), 218.
98. Ibid., 244.
99. Hillary Crosley, "DJ Drama Arrested in Mixtape Raid," *Billboard Biz*, January 17, 2007, http://www.allbusiness.com/retail-trade/miscellaneous-retail-retail-stores-not/4392944-1.html, accessed January 11, 2008.
100. *Mixtape, Inc.*
101. Tiziana Terranova, "Free Labor: Producing Culture for the Digital Economy," *Social Text* 18 (2000): 42; Franco Berardi Bifo, "Teaching Insurrection," *Through Europe*, March 17, 2011, http://th-rough.eu/writers/bifo-eng/teaching-insurrection-franco-berardi-bifo-brera-academy-milan, accessed June 21, 2011.
102. Statik Selektah, *Spell My Name Right: The Album* (Showoff Records/Brick Records, 2007).
103. David Suisman, *Selling Sounds: The Commercial Revolution in American Music* (Cambridge, MA: Harvard University Press, 2009), 59.

Chapter 7

1. *Diva*, DVD, directed by Jean-Jacques Beineix ([1981]; Troy, MI: Anchor Bay, 2002).
2. Peter Manuel, *Cassette Culture: Popular Music and Technology in North India* (Chicago: University of Chicago Press, 1993), 30.
3. "Pakistan to Pirate Books," *New York Times*, December 10, 1972, 5.
4. Michael Hardt and Antonio Negri, *Empire* (Cambridge, MA: Harvard University Press, 2000), 287; on domestic and foreign subcontracting, see J. Carlos Jarillo, "On Strategic Networks," *Strategic Management Journal* 9 (1988): 38; Cecilia Green, "The Asian Connection: The U.S.-Caribbean Apparel Circuit and a New Model of Industrial Relations," *Latin American Research Review* 33 (1998): 10–11; and David Harvey, *The Condition of Postmodernity: An Inquiry into the Origins of Cultural Change* (Oxford, UK: Blackwell, 1989) 150–7.
5. "Twelve Ways to Fight Piracy," *Journal of Commerce*, December 13, 1990, 14A.
6. B. Zorina Khan, "Copyright Piracy and Development: United States Evidence in the Nineteenth Century," *Revista de Economia* 10 (2008): 21–54.
7. "US Trade in Goods and Services—Balance of Payments (BOP) Basis," *US Census Bureau*, November 21, 2008, http://www.census.gov/foreign-trade/statistics/historical/gands.txt, accessed January 5, 2009.
8. Overall consumer prices increased by about 50% between 1972 and 1977, and by about 60% again between 1977 and 1982. For early 1970s figures, see *Historical Statistics of the United States* (Washington, DC: United States Government Printing Office, 1975). For later data, see *Statistical Abstract of the United States* published yearly by the US Census Bureau.
9. Laurence Kenneth Shore, "The Crossroads of Business and Music: A Study of the Music Industry in the United States and Internationally," (PhD diss., Stanford University, 1983), 143.
10. Gillian Davies, *Piracy of Phonograms* (Oxford, UK: ESC Publishing, 1981), 2.
11. Shore, "Crossroads of Business and Music," 152.
12. Shore, "Crossroads of Business and Music," 152; Paul Grein, "Unemployment Lines: L.A. Industry Personnel Face Major Challenges to Rebuild their Careers," *Billboard*, May 19, 1979, 3.
13. US Bureau of the Census, *1977 Census of Manufactures, Volume II: Industry Statistics, Part 3. SIC Major Groups 35–9* (Washington, DC: Department of Commerce, 1981), 36D–20; US Bureau of the Census, *1982 Census of Manufactures: Subject Series General Summary, Part 1. Industry, Product Class, and Geographic Area Statistics* (Washington, DC: Department of Commerce, 1986), 1–16, 1–17.
14. Shore, "Crossroads of Business and Music," 142–3.
15. Denis de Freitas, "Some Recent Developments in the United Kingdom in the Field of Copyright," *International Business Lawyer* 6 (1978): 508–9.

16. Pekka Gronow, "The Record Industry: The Growth of a Mass Medium," *Popular Music* 3 (1983): 72.

17. Mark Coleman, *Playback: From the Victrola to MP3, 100 Years of Music, Machines, and Money* (Cambridge, MA: Da Capo Press, 2003), xv.

18. Gordon McComb and John Cook, *Compact Disc Player: Maintenance and Repair* (Blue Ridge Summit, PA: Tab Books, 1987), viii, 2; Burnett, *Global Jukebox*, 18–9, 51–2; Coleman, *Playback*, 155 –6; Shore, "Crossroads of Business and Music," 215.

19. Burnett, *Global Jukebox*, 4; Jim Hollander, "International Markets: Labels Eye the New Frontier," *Los Angeles Times*, November 4, 1979, M6.

20. Hollander, "International Markets," M6; Markos Mamalakis, "The New International Economic Order: Centerpiece Venezuela," *Journal of Interamerican Studies and World Affairs* 20 (1978): 270; Ann Genova and Toyin Falola, "Oil in Nigeria: A Bibliographical Reconnaissance," *History in Africa* 30 (2003): 134; Brian Larkin, *Signal and Noise: Media, Infrastructure, and Urban Culture in Nigeria* (Durham, NC: Duke University Press, 2008), 222.

21. "40 Countries Meet on Piracy in Recording Industry," *New York Times*, April 5, 1981, 21.

22. United Kingdom Anti-Piracy Group, *International Piracy: The Threat to the British Copyright Industries* (London: Publishers Association and the International Federation of Phonogram and Videogram Producers, 1986), 29; Gladys and Oswald Ganley, *Global Political Fallout: The VCR's First Decade* (Cambridge, MA: Program on Information Resources Policy, 1987), 6.

23. Ganley and Ganley, *Global Political Fallout*, 9; Douglas A. Boyd, "Third World Pirating of U.S. Films and Television Programs from Satellites," *Journal of Broadcasting and Electronic Media* 32 (1988): 157.

24. Boyd, "Third World Pirating," 157.

25. Serge Schmemann, "Video's Forbidden Offerings Alarm Moscow," *New York Times*, October 22, 1983, 4.

26. Schmemann, "Video's Forbidden Offerings," 1.

27. Christopher S. Wren, "Off-Key or Off-Color, Tunes of West Worry China," *New York Times*, October 28, 1982, A2.

28. Jonathan Fenby, *Piracy and the Public: Forgery, Theft and Exploitation* (London: Frederick Muller Limited, 1983), 122.

29. Ibid., 127–8.

30. Ibid., 124.

31. Altaf Gauhar and Lee Kuan Yew, "North-South Dialogue," *Third World Quarterly* 1 (April 1979): 3.

32. UK Anti-Piracy Group, *International Piracy*, 9.

33. Ibid., 9–10.

34. Larkin, *Signal and Noise*, 223–4.

35. Ibid., 221.

36. Manuel Castells, *The Information Age: Economy, Society and Culture, Volume III: End of Millennium* (Oxford, UK: Blackwell, 1998), 72.

37. Larkin, *Signal and Noise*, 217.

38. David Edward Agnew, "Reform in the International Protection of Sound Recordings: Upsetting the Delicate Balance between Authors, Performers and Producers or Pragmatism in the Age of Digital Piracy," *Loyola of Los Angeles Entertainment Law Journal* 219 (1992): 227.

39. "Contracting Parties: Phonogram Convention," *World Intellectual Property Organization*, http://www.wipo.int/treaties/en/ShowResults.jsp?lang=en&treaty_id=18, accessed January 5, 2009.

40. Seth Faison, "Razors, Soap, Cornflakes: Pirating Spreads in China," *New York Times*, February 17, 1995, A; see also Shujen Wang and Jonathan Zhu, "Mapping Film Piracy in China," *Theory, Culture, and Society* 20 (2003): 97–125.

41. Davies, *Piracy of Phonograms*, 66–7.

42. Malcolm Anderson, *Policing the World: Interpol and the Politics of International Police Co-operation* (New York: Oxford University Press, 1989); Fenton S. Bresler, *Interpol* (London: Sinclair-Stevenson, 1992).

43. Lars Brandle, "Interpol Pledges Aid against Global Piracy," *Billboard*, November 18, 2000, 47.
44. Denis de Freitas, "Some Recent Developments in the United Kingdom in the Field of Copyright," *International Business Lawyer* 6 (1978): 508–9.
45. Davies, *Piracy of Phonograms*, 17.
46. De Freitas, "Some Recent Developments in the United Kingdom," 510.
47. Davies, *Piracy of Phonograms*, 125–7.
48. Ibid., 126.
49. Ibid.
50. Steven Erlanger, "Thailand Is the Capital of Pirated Tapes," *New York Times*, November 27, 1990, C15.
51. UK Anti-Piracy Group, *International Piracy*, 24–5.
52. Erlanger, "Thailand Is the Capital of Pirated Tapes," C15.
53. UK Anti-Piracy Group, *International Piracy*, 12.
54. Ibid., 32.
55. "Singapore Lays Down the Law," *Economist*, March 2, 1985, 66.
56. Eduardo Lachica, "U.S. Companies Curb Pirating of Some Items but by No Means All," *Wall Street Journal*, March 16, 1989, A1; "Run on Tapes in Indonesia," *New York Times*, May 31, 1988, D12.
57. Lachica, "U.S. Companies Curb Pirating," A8.
58. Ibid., A1–A8; Fenby, *Piracy and the Public*, 70, 116–9.
59. Lachica, "U.S. Companies Curb Pirating," A1.
60. International Intellectual Property Alliance, "IIPA Fact Sheet," September 2007, 1.
61. Charan Devereaux, Robert Z. Lawrence, and Michael D. Watkins, *Case Studies in US Trade Negotiation, Vol. 1: Making the Rules* (Washington, DC: Institute for International Economics, 2006), 73.
62. Devereaux, *Case Studies in US Trade Negotiation*, 47.
63. Autar Krishen Koul, *Guide to the WTO and GATT: Economics, Law, and Politics* (The Hague: Kluwer Law International, 2005), 21.
64. Lachica, "U.S. Companies Curb Pirating," A1.
65. John Parry, "5 Nations Block U.S. Move to Include Services in Talks," *Washington Post*, September 27, 1985, E8; Braga, "Trade-Related Intellectual Property Issues," 384, 405.
66. Devereaux, *Case Studies in US Trade Negotiation*, 37.
67. Koul, *Guide to the WTO and GATT*, 28.
68. "Whose Idea Is It Anyway?" *Economist*, November 12, 1988, 73; Duncan Matthews, *Globalising Intellectual Property Rights: The TRIPs Agreement* (New York: Routledge, 2002), 39; "'Dunkel Draft' Could Be Basis of New GATT Pact on Int'l Trade," *Manila Standard*, January 18, 1992, 17.
69. De Freitas, "Some Recent Developments in the United Kingdom," 510; Devereaux, *Case Studies in US Trade Negotiation*, 64–5.
70. Matthews, *Globalising Intellectual Property Rights*, 41.
71. Devereaux, *Case Studies in US Trade Negotiation*, 71.
72. Carlos A. Primo Braga, "Trade-Related Intellectual Property Issues: The Uruguay Round Agreement and Its Economic Implications," in *The Uruguay Round and the Developing Economies*, ed. Will Martin and L. Alan Winters (Washington, DC: The World Bank, 1995), 394.
73. Braga, "Trade-Related Intellectual Property Issues," 386–90; Edward Samuels, *The Illustrated Story of Copyright* (New York: Thomas Dunne Books, 2000), 48, 92.
74. I. Gopalakrishnan, "Delhi Playing for Time on GATT," *India Abroad*, January 24, 1992, 20.
75. Braga, "Trade-Related Intellectual Property Issues," 394–5.
76. Bernard Weinraub, "Clinton Spared Blame by Hollywood Officials," *New York Times*, December 16, 1993, D1.
77. William Safire, "Hold that GATT," *New York Times*, December 9, 1993, A31.
78. Devereaux, *Case Studies in US Trade Negotiation*, 73.
79. Telephone interview with George Stephanopolous, April 11, 2008.
80. Frederik Balfour, "Underground Music," *Far Eastern Economic Review*, May 6, 1993, 52.
81. Balfour, "Underground Music," 52.

82. "Skull and CD," *Economist*, December 23, 1995, 78.
83. Ibid.
84. International Intellectual Property Alliance, "2004 Special 301 Report: Pakistan," http://www.iipa.com/rbc/2004/2004SPEC301PAKISTAN.pdf, accessed August 3, 2005.
85. Jonas Baes, "Toward a Political Economy of the 'Real': Music Piracy and the Phillippine Cultural Imaginary," March 17, 2002, http://polyglot.lss.wisc.edu/mpi/conference/Baes.htm, accessed November 5, 2004.
86. David Gonzalez, "Pressed by Music Industry, New York Seizes Pirate Tapes," *New York Times*, December 9, 1990, 46.
87. Harvey, *Condition of Postmodernity*, 165–6.

Conclusion

1. James Plafke, "Limewire Is Being Sued for up to $75 Trillion Dollars, Judge Thinks It's 'Absurd,'" *Geekosystem*, March 23, 2011, http://www.geekosystem.com/limewire-sued-75-trillion/, accessed May 5, 2011; *Arista Records LLC v. Lime Group LLC*, 784 F. Supp. 2d 313 (2011).
2. *A&M Records, Inc. v. Napster, Inc.*, 239 F.3d 1004 (2001); *MGM Studios, Inc. v. Grokster, Ltd.* 545 U.S. 913 (2005); Victor Li, "Manhattan Federal Judge Kimba Wood Calls Record Companies' Request for $75 Trillion in Damages 'Absurd' in Lime Wire Copyright Case," *Law.com Corporate Counsel*, March 15, 2011, http://www.law.com/jsp/cc/PubArticleCC.jsp?id=1202486102650&Manhattan_Federal_Judge_Kimba_Wood_Calls_Record_Companies_Request_for__Trillion_in_Damages_Absurd_in_Lime_Wire_Copyright_Case, accessed March 25, 2011.
3. *Capitol Records, Inc. v. Naxos of America, Inc.*, 830 N.E. 2d 250 (NY 2005); Brendan Scott, "Some Notes on *Capitol Records, Inc. v. Naxos of America Inc.*," *Groklaw*, April 13, 2005, http://www.groklaw.net/articlebasic.php?story=20050412225604578, accessed November 24, 2012.
4. Michael Smith, "Gotta Fight for Your Right to Perform: Scope of New York Common Law Copyright for Pre-1972 Recordings Post-Naxos," *Loyola of Los Angeles Entertainment Law Review* 30 (2010): 590–4.
5. Ibid., 590; "The Sound of Silence," *Economist*, June 21, 2011, http://www.economist.com/blogs/babbage/2011/06/sound-recordings, accessed June 22, 2011; for the federal statute ending common law rights in 2067, see 17 USC § 301 (c).
6. Greg Kot, *Ripped: How the Wired Generation Revolutionized Music* (New York: Scribner, 2009), 28.
7. Dead Kennedys, *In God We Trust, Inc.* (Alternative Tentacles, 1981).
8. Edward Samuels, *The Illustrated Story of Copyright*. (New York: Thomas Dunne Books, 2000), 92.
9. *Sony Corp. of America v. Universal City Studios, Inc.*, 464 U.S. 417 (1984).
10. Steven Levy, "The Noisy War over Napster," *Newsweek*, July 5, 2000, 46–53; Spencer E. Ante, "Inside Napster," *Business Week*, August 14, 2000, 112–20.
11. Tiziana Terranova, "Free Labor: Producing Culture for the Digital Economy," *Social Text* 18 (2000): 48–9; Andreas M. Kaplan and Michael Haenlein, "Users of the World, Unite! The Challenges and Opportunities of Social Media," *Business Horizons* 53 (2010): 59–60.
12. Yochai Benkler, *The Wealth of Networks: How Social Production Transforms Markets and Freedom* (New Haven, CT: Yale University Press, 2006), 196–204, 369–71.
13. Lanier Saperstein, "Copyrights, Criminal Sanctions, and Economic Rents: Applying the Rent-Seeking Model to the Criminal Law Formulation Process," *Journal of Criminal Law and Criminology* 87 (1997): 1471–2.
14. *Congressional Record*, 105 Cong., 2nd sess., Oct. 7, 1998, 9952.
15. Doug Bedell, "Professor Says Disney, Other Firms Typify What's Wrong with Copyrights," *Dallas Morning News*, March 14, 2002, 3D; Jeet Heer, "Free Mickey!" *Boston Globe*, September 28, 2003, http://www.boston.com/news/globe/ideas/articles/2003/09/28/free_mickey/, accessed May 14, 2011.
16. Joanna Demers, *Steal This Music: How Intellectual Property Law Affects Musical Creativity* (Athens: University of Georgia Press, 2006); Lawrence Lessig, *The Future of Ideas: The*

Fate of the Commons in a Connected World (New York: Vintage, 2001); Siva Vaidhyanathan, *Copyrights and Copywrongs: The Rise of Intellectual Property and How It Threatens Creativity* (New York: New York University Press, 2001).

17. "Be HIP at the Movies," *Intellectual Property Office of Singapore*, July 27, 2004, http://www.ipos.gov.sg/topNav/news/pre/2004/Launch+of+anti+piracy+movie+trailer.htm, accessed June 2, 2011; Motion Picture Association of America, "Piracy—It's a Crime," http://www.youtube.com/watch?v=HmZm8vNHBSU, accessed June 2, 2011.

18. *International News Service v. Associated Press*, 248 U.S. 215 (1918), 250.

19. *Grand Upright Music, Ltd v. Warner Bros. Records Inc.*, 780 F.Supp. 182 (S.D.N.Y. 1991); *Campbell v. Acuff-Rose Music*, 510 U.S. 569 (1994).

20. "New Rap Song Samples 'Billie Jean' in Its Entirety, Adds Nothing," *Onion*, September 23, 1997, http://www.theonion.com/articles/new-rap-song-samples-billie-jean-in-its-entirety-a,4389/.

21. Lynne A. Greenberg, "The Art of Appropriation: Puppies, Piracy, and Post-Modernism," *Cardozo Arts and Entertainment Law Journal* 11 (1992): 14–16; C. Jill O'Bryan, *Carnal Art: Orlan's Refacing* (Minneapolis: University of Minnesota Press, 2005), 78; Kenneth Goldsmith, *Day* (New Barrington, MA: The Figures, 2003).

22. House Committee on the Judiciary, *Prohibiting Piracy of Sound Recordings: Hearings on S. 646 and H.R. 6927*, 92nd Cong., 1 sess., 1971, 28.

23. Harvey, *Condition of Postmodernity*, 155–6; Taiichi Ohno, *Toyota Production System* (New York: Productivity Press, 1988), 4.

24. Tim Quirk, "The Quiet Revolution," *Rhapsody: The Mix*, April 22, 2010, http://blog.rhapsody.com/2010/04/the-quiet-revolution.html, accessed May 6, 2011.

25. Chris Anderson, "The Long Tail," *Wired*, October 2004, 170–7; Eben Moglen, "Freeing the Mind: Free Software and the Death of Proprietary Culture," June 29, 2003, http://moglen.law.columbia.edu/publications/maine-speech.pdf, 3, accessed July 19, 2011.

26. Judith Stein, *Running Steel, Running America: Race, Economic Policy, and the Decline of Liberalism* (Chapel Hill: University of North Carolina Press, 1998), 277; James Boyle, *Shamans, Software and Spleens: Law and the Construction of the Information Society* (Cambridge, MA: Harvard University Press, 1997), 1.

27. "The Information Revolution," *New York Times*, May 23, 1965, section 11, 1; Greg Downey, "Commentary: The Place of Labor in the History of Information-Technology Revolutions," in *Uncovering Labour in Information Revolutions, 1750–2000*, ed. Aad Blok and Greg Downey (New York: Cambridge University Press, 2004), 228; Manuel Castells, *The Rise of the Network Society: The Information Age: Economy, Society, and Culture, Volume 1* (Oxford, UK: Blackwell, 1996), 21; Marc Uri Porat, *The Information Economy: Definition and Measurement* (Washington, DC: US Government Printing Office, 1977), 18.

28. Adam Arvidsson, *Brands: Meaning and Value in Media Culture* (New York: Routledge, 2006), 6.

29. Jonathan Fuerbringer, "Slow Unemployment Decline Foreseen by Job Experts," *New York Times*, October 17, 1982, CNE1.

30. House Committee on the Judiciary, *Copyright/Cable Television: Hearings on H.R. 1805, Part 2*, 97th Cong., 1st and 2nd sess., 1982, 1568.

31. Information Infrastrucure Task Force, *Intellectual Property and the National Information Infrastructure: The Report of the Working Group on Intellectual Property Rights* (Washington, DC: Information Infrastrucure Task Force, 1995), 10.

32. Kim Phillips-Fein has explored the sometimes uneasy alliance between the religious and corporate wings of the conservative movement in her *Invisible Hands: The Businessmen's Crusade against the New Deal* (New York: W. W. Norton, 2010), 231. Barlow's life illustrates that the conservative and countercultural visions were not totally separate; before founding the EFF, he was a committed libertarian and Republican activist, even working on Dick Cheney's congressional campaign in the late 1970s before eventually breaking with the GOP; see Bruce P. Montgomery, *Richard B. Cheney and the Rise of the Imperial Vice Presidency* (Westport, CT: Greenwood, 2009), 61–2; "John Perry Barlow: Biography," *European Graduate School*, July 19, 2011, http://www.egs.edu/faculty/john-perry-barlow/biography/, accessed on July 19, 2011.

33. On neoliberalism, see David Harvey, *A Brief History of Neoliberalism* (New York: Oxford University Press, 2005) and Downey, "Commentary," 230; for critiques of the paradigm, see Nick Gillespie, "Bush Was a Big-Government Disaster," *Reason*, January 26, 2009, and Daniel Ben-Ami, "The Malthusians who Masquerade as Marxists," *Spiked*, April 2011, http://www.spiked-online.com/index.php/site/reviewofbooks_article/10464, accessed September 1, 2011.

34. Noam Chomsky, "Rollback," *Z Magazine*, January–May 1995, http://www.chomsky.info/articles/199505-.htm, accessed September 1, 2011; Heather Ann Thompson, "Why Mass Incarceration Matters: Rethinking Crisis, Decline, and Transformation in Postwar American History," *Journal of American History* 97 (2010): 709.

35. David Garland, *The Culture of Control: Crime and Social Order in Contemporary Society* (Chicago: University of Chicago Press, 2001), 98; Eric Schlosser, *Reefer Madness: Sex, Drugs, and Cheap Labor in the American Black Market* (New York: Houghton Mifflin, 2003), 215; Thompson, "Why Mass Incarceration Matters," 703–4.

36. Thomas J. Lueck, "Police Name the Officer Who Killed African Man," *New York Times*, May 25, 2003; Barbara Ross, "Trial Stakes High for Widow, Cop," *New York Daily News*, February 6, 2005, 10.

37. Lawrence Lessig, *Remix: Making Art and Commerce Thrive in the Hybrid Economy* (London: Bloomsbury, 2008), xvii; available online at http://www.scribd.com/doc/47089238/Remix, accessed June 29, 2011.

38. Sarah N. Lynch, "An American Pastime: Smoking Pot," *Time*, July 11, 2008, http://www.time.com/time/health/article/0,8599,1821697,00.html, accessed July 1, 2011.

39. For a contemporary example, see Christopher Craig Latson, "Contemporary Pirates: An Examination of the Perspectives and Attitudes toward the Technology, Progression, and Battles That Surround Modern Day Music Piracy in Colleges and Universities" (MA thesis, University of North Texas, 2004): 26, 61–2.

40. Keith Roe, "Music and Identity among European Youth," in *Music, Culture and Society in Europe*, ed. Paul Rutten (Brussels: European Music Office, 1996), 85–97.

41. William Howland Kenney, *Recorded Music in American Life. The Phonograph and Popular Memory, 1890–1945* (New York: Oxford University Press, 1999), 3; see also Evan Eisenberg, *The Recording Angel: Music, Records, and Culture from Aristotle to Zappa* (New Haven, CT: Yale University Press, 2005).

42. "Arguments before the Committee on Patents, May 2, 1906," in *Legislative History of the 1909 Copyright Act, Volume 4*, ed. E. Fulton Brylawski and Abe Goldman (South Hackensack, NJ: Fred B. Rothman, 1976), 15.

43. David Suisman, *Selling Sounds: The Commercial Revolution in American Music* (Cambridge, MA: Harvard University Press, 2009), 59–75; Russell Sanjek, *American Popular Music and Its Business: The First Four Hundred Years, Volume III* (New York: Oxford University Press, 1988), 33.

44. Alex Veiga, "File-sharing Case Worries Indie Artists," *USA Today*, March 25, 2005, http://www.usatoday.com/tech/news/techpolicy/2005-03-25-indie-file-sharing_x.htm, accessed March 23, 2011; Jeff Leeds, "The Net Is a Boon for Indie Labels," *New York Times*, December 27, 2005, E1.

45. Sudip Bhattacharjee, Ram D. Gopal, Kaveepan Lertwachara, James R. Marsden, and Rahul Telang, "The Effect of Digital Sharing Technologies on Music Markets: A Survival Analysis of Albums on Ranking Charts," *Management Science* 53 (2007): 1359–74.

46. Ibid., 1372; see also Heather Green, "Kissing Off the Big Music Labels," *Business Week*, September 6, 2004, http://www.businessweek.com/magazine/content/04_36/b3898114_mz063.htm, accessed March 23, 2011; and Peter Spellman, *Indie Power: A Business-Building Guide for Record Labels, Music Production Houses, and Merchant Musicians* (Boston: MBS Business Media, 2006).

47. Bruce Fries and Marty Fries, *Digital Audio Essentials: A Comprehensive Guide to Creating, Recording, Editing, and Sharing Music and Other Audio* (Sebastopol, CA: O'Reilly Media, 2005), 72–3; "EAT'M Working with MP3.com," *CMJ New Music Report*, June 29, 1999, 29; on typical recording artist royalties, see Christopher Knab and Bartley F. Day, *Music Is Your Business: The Musician's FourFront Strategy for Success* (Seattle, WA: FourFront Media and Music, 2007), 108.

48. Glenn Peoples, "Spotify Is Finally Available in the US—Now What?" July 14, 2011, *Billboard.biz*, http://www.billboard.biz/bbbiz/industry/digital-and-mobile/spotify-is-finally-available-in-the-u-s-1005278192.story, accessed July 19, 2011; Casey Johnston, "Eager to Share, but Doesn't Quite Know How: Hands on with Spotify," *Ars Technica*, July 19, 2011, http://arstechnica.com/gadgets/reviews/2011/07/nothing-wrong-with-free-hands-on-with-spotify.ars, accessed July 19, 2011.

49. For a good overview of the service concept, see Stephen A. Herzenberg, John A. Alic, and Howard Wial, *New Rules for a New Economy: Employment and Opportunity in a Postindustrial America* (Ithaca, NY: Cornell University Press, 1998), 21–2; for the information economy, see Christopher May, *The Information Society: A Sceptical View* (Oxford, UK: Wiley-Blackwell, 2002), 3–18.

50. Benkler, *Wealth of Networks*, 55; Jeffrey Pepper Rodgers, *Rock Troubadours* (San Anselmo, CA: String Letter Publishing, 2000), 163–4.

51. Herbie Hancock, preface to John Alderman, *Sonic Boom: Napster, MP3 and the New Pioneers of Music* (Cambridge, MA: Perseus, 2001), xviii.

52. Ben Krakow, "Hail to the Thief: Music Blogs and the Propagation of New Music" (unpublished senior thesis, Vassar College, 2009).

53. Information Infrastrucure Task Force, *Intellectual Property and the National Information Infrastructure: The Report of the Working Group on Intellectual Property Rights* (Washington, DC: Information Infrastrucure Task Force, 1995), 10.

54. James Boyle, *The Public Domain: Enclosing the Commons of the Mind* (New Haven, CT: Yale University Press, 2008), 42.

55. Jack Temple Kirby, *The Countercultural South* (Athens: University of Georgia Press, 1995), 39–42.

56. Boyle, *Public Domain*, 35.

INDEX